EMBEDDED

EMBEDDED

THE MEDIA AT WAR IN IRAQ

Bill Katovsky   *Timothy Carlson*

THE LYONS PRESS
Guilford, Connecticut
An imprint of the Globe Pequot Press

The Lyons Press is an imprint of The Globe Pequot Press.

10 9 8 7 6 5 4 3 2 1

Printed in the United States of America

Designed by Claire Zoghb

Map by Stefanie Ward

ISBN 1-59228-265-2

Library of Congress Cataloging-in-Publication data is available on file.

For Edward Katovsky
And Katie and Amy Carlson

CONTENTS

INTRODUCTION

Let's start with one simple fact about the war in Iraq: Statistically, journalists were ten times more likely to die than the 250,000 in American or British soldiers.

Long before cruise missiles slammed into Saddam's suspected hideouts in late March, and long before convoys of Abrams tanks, fuel tankers, and Bradley fighting vehicles rumbled from Kuwait through holes bulldozed in Iraq's defensive berms, the Pentagon issued a Super Bowl's worth of media credentials—2,700 of them—to a worldwide army of reporters, photographers, and television and radio crews. "This will be the most covered war in history," observed Jim Wilkinson, the U.S. Central Command's director of strategic communications, prior to the fighting. His prediction hit the bullseye.

This journalistic invasion marked a significant turnaround from the first Gulf War, when a wary military, still trying to shake the Vietnam monkey off its back, micro-managed battlefield news by limiting press access. In the buildup to the new Iraqi campaign, war planners tossed aside any lingering doubts they had about the media by presenting a slick new public-relations concept known as "embedding."

Embedded reporters ate, lived, traveled, and slept with the troops. They choked on the same sandstorm grit, and carried the same mandatory gas mask and chem suits. They dined on the same MREs (Meals Ready to Eat), and bounced along the same rutted desert tracks. They faced the same enemy fire.

Not all embeds were created or treated equally. Ted Koppel, ABC's late-night institution, traveled with Major General Buford Blount III, division commander of the Third Infantry Battalion, while reporters from mid-size newspapers found themselves wedged into foul-smelling Humvees loaded with privates and specialists—kids actually, old enough to shoot, but not necessarily old enough to drink.

Embedding borrowed from earlier wars. General Dwight Eisenhower, Supreme Allied Commander in World War II, declared that "public opinion wins wars, and I have always considered as quasi-staff officers [the] correspondents accredited to my headquarters." Censorship was still the norm. Throughout the duration of the Vietnam war, the first television war, nearly 700 reporters rotated through the countryside, slogging through the jungles and rice paddies with U.S. troops. Given unfettered freedom, these war correspondents provided in-depth accounts, a blend of the good, bad and the ugly. But after the 1968 Tet Offensive, when CBS's Walter Cronkite told the nation that the war was unwinnable, the Pentagon started blaming the press for standing in the way of victory, while the press accused the Pentagon of lying about the war.

The next major military conflict showed just how deep this mistrust ran. When U.S. military forces stormed onto Grenada in 1983, navy gunboats kept the press away from the island. Six years later, the Panama invasion was hardly more accommodating to journalists, who were either left stranded on airport tarmacs in Miami and San Jose, Costa Rica, or sequestered in a Panama City warehouse throughout most of the fighting. On the eve of the first Gulf War, the media practically begged for access. Since Saudi Arabia only begrudgingly granted a limited number of journalistic visas under diplomatic pressure, the Pentagon was determined to call the shots, maintaining tight control over the flow of information through censorship, pool reporting, and press conferences bleached of meaningful content. This arrangement led to the reporting of false or misleading information such as the highly exaggerated success rate of Patriot missiles shooting down Scuds. At the time, then-Secretary of State Dick Cheney said, "I do not look on the press as an asset. Frankly, I looked on it as a problem to be managed." Only CNN, with live audio—and later, its fuzzy green video of the bombing of Baghdad—benefited from this war, placing Ted Turner's cable news station on the global map.

It took external market forces to break the Pentagon-press impasse. By the late 1990s, the explosive growth of the Internet, as well as cable and satellite television, influenced how information was disseminated. It had become technologically feasible to present battlefield news in real time. With satellite video phones, digital feed hardware, night vision goggles, and laptops, the media had a dazzling arsenal of audio-visual aids to describe events. Furthermore, Fox News and MSNBC were siphoning away viewers from CNN and the three major networks, while several independent and state-sponsored Middle Eastern stations, led by upstart Al Jazeera, began developing a new global constituency of viewers. A high-stakes media game unfolded prior to the start of the second Gulf War. Small armies of field producers, correspondents, and technicians converged on Doha and Kuwait City, turning the latter into a throbbing mediaopolis. CNN forces totaled 250, NBC's 200. Fox News was leaner with 150, and similar-size forces carried the broadcasting banner for ABC and BBC. The major networks laid out an average of $25 to $30 million for war coverage. And *Time's* war photo budget alone topped one million dollars.

But why should the Pentagon now embrace the media? After all, the press was initially prohibited from straying too close to combat zones in Afghanistan. What did the U.S. military hope to gain by opening themselves up to inquisitive reporters? Following the advice of Michael Corleone in *Godfather, Part Two,* who said, "Keep your friends close and your enemies closer," the Pentagon was preparing a surprise for the media. With Secretary of Defense Donald Rumsfeld's father-knows-best blessing, reporters were now going to have the coziest lovefest with the military since World War II.

The Weekly Standard described this remarkable transformation:

> On October 30, 2002 *Secretary of Defense Donald Rumsfeld wandered unexpectedly into a Pentagon meeting of Washington bureau chiefs of the major media outlets. This motley group had been meeting on and off since the war in Afghanistan. As journalists always do, we spent most of the sessions complaining. Our favorite complaint: lack of access. Secretary Rumsfeld, charming, impish, and in command had something to tell us: He was on board with the public relations strategy of embedding media with warriors. He wasn't kidding around. If there was a war with Iraq, journalists would be with the troops. In Afghanistan, he said, the Taliban and Al-Qaeda showed great skill in news management. The best way to combat that was to have accurate, professional journalists on the ground to see the truth of what was going on. He said he already had intelligence from Iraq that they were arranging things to mislead the press. "Having people who are honest and professional see these things and be aware of that is useful. So I consider it not just the right thing to do but also a helpful thing."*

Talk about shock and awe. As one UPI correspondent let slip after spending far too many dreary hours at Pentagon press briefings, where opaque, acronym-laced podium utterances ruled, "Reporters love troops. Put us with these eighteen-year-old kids and we just turn to jelly."

Unlike Afghanistan, where it was generally understood that it was time for serious 9/11 payback, Iraq promised to be dicier diplomatically, militarily, politically, and economically. New allies were desperately needed—anywhere. So the Fourth Estate was made an honorary member of this cobbled-together Coalition, even as skeptics questioned the underlying motives.

To embed or not to embed? Correspondents debated this question. There were inherent journalistic risks if they did, and inherent safety risks if they didn't. An accredited but non-embedded war reporter—an independent—whose movement was not theoretically restricted on the battlefield was dubbed a "unilateral," which meant exposure to greater dangers. Estimates placed the number of embeds at 600 and unilaterals at 2,100, with a great many of the latter working for the more freewheeling European press. The large news organizations combined embeds with independents for balanced coverage. Embedded and unilateral journalists covered the same war, but they experienced it in different ways. An embed's point of view was narrow and restricted. It depended on where the unit was camped and what it was doing. An enterprising unilateral might manage a broader perspective and talk to more sources, including Iraqis, but he or she often lacked the means and opportunity to get close to combat.

In the early days of the war, several unilateral journalists were killed by venturing too close to the fighting. Still, two of the most widely mourned media deaths in the U.S. were embeds. The first was *The Washington Post*'s and *Atlantic*'s Michael Kelly, who died in a Humvee crash. Kelly had made his name in the first Gulf War with his brilliantly nuanced reporting for *The New Republic*. Embedding was still more than a decade off, but Kelly was a classic pain in the butt with command HQ because he fearlessly made his way to the front lines. Scorning the easy path of "hotel warriors," he rented a car and drove toward the burning oil wells and past ghoulish miles of incinerated Republican Guard corpses. Since the ground assault had been so brief, the intrepid Kelly once found himself in a situation right out of a Monty Python skit when a group of surrendering Iraqi soldiers tumbled into his car.

The second high-profile embed death, NBC's popular David Bloom, was attributed to a fatal blood clot originating in his leg, a likely consequence of genetic predisposition aggravated by riding for fourteen hours a day in a severely cramped vehicle. His death left behind a grieving widow and two small children, while saddening colleagues and viewers. It dominated the twenty-four-hour cable news cycle for a day or so. The national media naturally began to question their own journalistic motives: What is the ultimate sacrifice for a war reporter?

Democracy always prevails in combat. A bullet or an RPG refuses to discriminate by name, rank, byline, or stand-up visibility on the evening news. The tally of fallen journalists rose as the war progressed. In Gulf War I, four journalists died. By the end of the third week of Gulf War II, the fatal count reached thirteen. (In thirteen years of U.S. involvement in Vietnam and Cambodia, the death toll was sixty-five journalists.) The U.S Army's shelling of Baghdad's Palestine Hotel, which served as the headquarters for the international media, emphasized the fragility of the journalists. In a speech at the Fairmont Hotel in San Francisco, Tom Wolfe quipped, "I can understand journalists getting fired, but not getting fired at."

It's an American tradition for the pen to ally itself with the sword. Jingoistic sentiments and national zeal were stoked during the Mexican-American War by horseback messengers and steamboats. While Matthew Brady lugged his heavy cameras around Civil War battlefields and created lasting art, 500 military war correspondents became unabashed propagandists for either the North or the South, sending reports by telegraph and turning the nation into obsessive newspaper readers. Instant war reporting had arrived. Newspaper mogul William Randolph Hearst treated the Spanish-American War as his own private crusade—and sales of his papers skyrocketed. The most famous World War II soldier-scribe was Ernie Pyle, whose newsroom cubicle was a foxhole before a Japanese sniper felled him on a Pacific Island. Decades before CNN's Peter Arnett provided an eye-witness account of American bombing raids over Baghdad during Desert Storm, CBS Radio's Edward R. Murrow broadcast from London rooftops during the 1940 German Blitz.

Since dead journalists make for lousy public relations, the Pentagon established strict criteria for embeds. While censorship was not tightly enforced, there were plenty of restrictions about what couldn't be reported — details of tactical deployments, precise location, specific numbers of troops, or identification of casualties before next-of-kin had been informed. These rules were amply detailed in a well-circulated document (see appendix) whose penultimate clause was evidence of the Pentagon's mastery of the new media: "Use of lipstick and helmet-mounted cameras on combat sorties is approved and encouraged to the greatest extent possible."

In this new era of embedded media, however, a tension existed between freedom of expression and following the rules. For embeds, the latter was a slack leash, but it was a leash nonetheless, leading critics to question the critical distinction between propaganda and journalism. Once embedded, ease of movement was drastically curtailed and unfettered mobility denied. The trade-off existed between generous access and narrow-aperture coverage. "Your radius of knowledge was basically about three hundred meters across," wrote Gordon Dillow of *The Orange County Register*, who traveled in an armored assault vehicle.

Objectivity was another large concern. How would the emerging friendships and emotional bonds between reporters and soldiers influence coverage? Could this fighting-hole fraternity alter news being digitally uplinked back home? How critical can the press be when these troops are also, as ABC News' John Donvan put it, "my protectors"? And by lusting for access and fresh story angles, perhaps with news editors back home stoking the competitive flames, at what point did embeds become a marketing tool for the military and less a countervailing force? To conflate Shakespeare with the Pentagon, "war makes strange (em)bed fellows." *New York Post* headline writers offered the juiciest appraisal yet: GOOD EMBED.

A properly trained soldier will heed these words in battle: Adapt. Improvise. Overcome. The smart embed practiced those traits as well. If stuck with a rear-echelon battalion or company, the quick-thinking journalist would hitchhike with passing military convoys to reach units closer to the fighting. Press-savvy commanders encouraged this unauthorized media migration. They wanted their stories told. It was win-win. Meanwhile, embedding produced blowback for those who played loose with reporting restrictions or ran afoul of literal-minded officers. About two dozen journalists were disembedded, forcibly ordered to leave Iraq by their own means or escorted with military assistance. In Geraldo Rivera's case, an U.S. Army helicopter airlifted him out of Iraq. His crime: outlining troop movements and locations in the sand.

Unilateral journalists also faced expulsion. The Iraqi secret police forcibly detained several reporters, threatened others, extorted money and supplies, and forced CNN's Baghdad correspondent Nic Robertson and the rest of the bureau to leave the country. Two journalists from Israel and two from Portugal—all accredited—were roughly arrested by U.S. forces in southern Iraq for two days, because their dark complexions raised suspicions they were Iraqi spies.

Since good war reporting demands a constant reshuffling of multiple narratives all jockeying for primacy and accuracy, there is much merit underlying the adage: "Truth is the first casualty in war." Perhaps, perception is the first casualty, and this has nothing to do with the buffoonery and outlandish statements from the former Iraqi minister of information. The U.S. and Arab media interpreted this war in stark contrasts. When Arab television trotted out a group of dazed, banged-up U.S. Army POWs, American television refused to air much of this disturbing and humiliating footage, citing self-censorship factors such as privacy, respect for the prisoners' families, and outright revulsion. Yet during the first few days of the war, American viewers witnessed a parade of emaciated, surrendering Iraqi army conscripts, their bony wrists held fast behind their backs with white plastic bands.

Just as American television shied away from explicit coverage, the Arab world concentrated on civilian casualties. Writing in the *Arab News*, Afnan Fatani, professor of stylistics at King Abdul Aziz University, asked troubling questions: "How can we forget missiles slamming into crowded apartment complexes, into family homes, market places, restaurants, roadside cafes and hospitals in Al-Mansour, Al-Shaab, Al-Nasr, and Al-Dora? How can we forget the grisly scenes in Hilla, 160 kilometers from Baghdad, where TV footage showed an angry father piling a burned and mangled infant onto a truckload of dismembered women and children?"

America refused to be yanked into two opposing camps once the war started. Hawks ate doves (and Dixie Chicks) for lunch. Large anti-war protest rallies faded from view. Just as this asymmetrical war turned into a lopsided victory, U.S. media coverage mirrored this disparity by asymmetrically focusing on feel-good American stories. There were laconic, Gary Cooper–sounding commanders, dirt-encrusted Marines from small towns, and weary supply clerks who were accountants and insurance agents back home. On the strategy and battle assessment homefront, a revolving cast of former generals and military analysts tirelessly debated this war on all the television and radio talk shows.

Television's intense wall-to-wall coverage was offset by its dizzy ephemerality. Complexity and substance were sacrificed for the searing images, a burning Iraqi tank or inspiring sound-bite from an exhausted Marine taking a breather from shoving another artillery round into a smoking howitzer. Television championed those feel-good scenes that reminded viewers of other popular wars: an American flag hoisted, happy Iraqi children waving to soldiers, an evil tyrant's statue being toppled. Footage of helicopters flying overhead seemed airlifted from *Apocalypse Now* and *Black Hawk Down*. What *New York Times* critic Michiko Kakutani referred to as "photogenic bombs" dropping on Baghdad was echoed by one veteran war correspondent as "an amazing sight, just like out of an action movie, but this is real." Saving Private (Jessica) Lynch out-Spielberged the master filmmaker himself. Despite lingering questions about what had really happened at the ambush site and hospital, the successful rescue mission led to a frenzied media rush to craft a movie about her ordeal. She became the real American Idol. Highest Q-ratings of the war.

The war helped cable television news. The viewing audience went from 2 million to 7.4 million during those first three weeks, while the three major networks held ratings ground. Internet traffic soared. Weblogs proliferated. Newspapers printed special war supplements. The public was granted front-row seats in this media multiplex, but all this instant, around-the-clock reporting led to greater confusion. A soldier's duty was to vanquish the enemy and stay alive. A reporter's duty was get the story. The public's duty was to make sense of all this sound and fury.

The U.S. Army's blitzkrieg to Baghdad lasted twenty-one days. Pre-war concerns of a long drawn-out siege and urban fighting vanished along with the remnants of the Republic Guard. The Pentagon, the public, the press, collectively breathed sighs of relief. In terms of media saturation, the Iraqi war campaign had reached its dramatic conclusion, though it wasn't until May 1 that President Bush officially declared an end to the major combat phase. But given the subsequent frequency of skirmishes and well-coordinated ambushes against U.S. forces, the White House declaration was hasty and premature. The protracted struggle to ensure peace and rebuild a nation will now occupy the attention of political and military elites. This process might take years. Will the American public monitor these developments as carefully and obsessively as it followed the war? By July 4, the number of reporters embedded with U.S. troops had dwindled to twenty-three.

Embedded is a book about the media at war in Iraq. Embedding also has a special meaning beyond a literal, limited definition of being placed with military units. Even independent correspondents faced the risk of being entrapped in the propaganda gears of a war machine. Many of the correspondents interviewed here explained why they subjected themselves to the dangers—and terrors—of combat by often repeating these truisms: "We wanted to be on the front lines of history. We wanted to write the first draft of history." Many first-time war reporters had no idea what the effect of live coverage might be, nor how physically challenging or perilous it might become. Nor its effect on the psyche to satisfy that primal curiosity.

As British author Philip Knightley masterfully recounts in *The First Casualty*, rarely if ever do armies or governments allow, much less encourage, objective, free, unbiased reporting on wars. Heavy censorship is the rule, with Vietnam being the curious exception. Those journalistic impulses to write the truth have almost always been warped and bent and twisted under the more powerful forces of national interest, force, propaganda, and ideology. From both the Pentagon and press's perspective, the embedding experiment was a gamble worth taking. On the surface, it was a demonstration of democratic values and freedom of speech in action, in contrast to the dark tyranny and disinformation of Saddam's government.

While many reporters went into this war fearing the loss of objectivity and took precautions, one lesson apparently learned from the first Gulf War was that network reputations became cemented by being up close when the firing started. Correspondents still found moments of truth and poignancy, even while failing to account for mounting civilian deaths or aggressively challenging the Bush Administration's pretext about taking out those elusive weapons of mass destruction. Some of the best reporting defied whatever spin the Pentagon tried to achieve when lethal mistakes were made on the battlefield, because an embedded journalist was there taking notes. Nor could the military muzzle its soldiers who spoke openly around embeds. Perhaps the most unforgettable quote of the war was overheard by *The New York Times'* Dexter Filkins who cited two Marine sharpshooters comparing notes about the difficulties they encountered trying to distinguish civilians from fighters: "We dropped a few civilians but what do you do? I'm sorry, but the chick was in the way."

A few of these correspondents quietly admitted that they became attracted to the adrenaline rush of battle. Others confessed that they continue to be haunted by what they saw and heard. Some reporters crossed the line of sacred objectivity and grabbed hand grenades, pointed out snipers, wore guns, or hired armed security. Still, it is impossible to fail to praise this talented throng of correspondents, employed by small local newspapers or reporting for the network giants. With few exceptions, they earned the critical distinction of delivering the journalistic goods under arduous and dangerous conditions. They were as fearless as the soldiers they covered. And as fearful.

Bill Katovsky
Northern California
September 2003

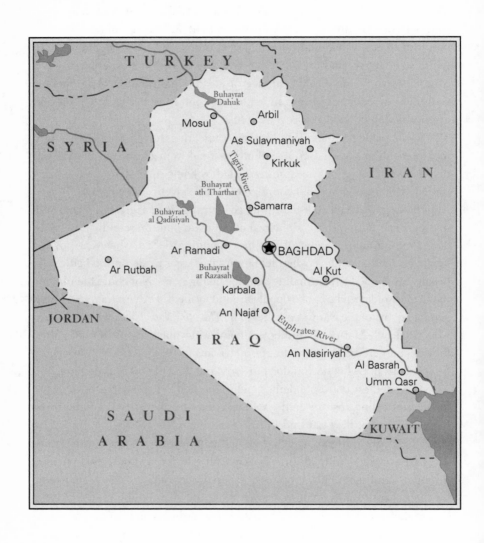

CHARGING INTO BAD-GUY COUNTRY WITH CUSTER

Detroit News Reporter John Bebow

> "I saw them without their skulls. I saw them disemboweled. I saw them shot up and raked by helicopter fire."

"It was the second day of trout season," recalls *Detroit News* reporter John Bebow. "Flies come out. Big trout begin to slurp." He recuperated from his forty days and nights in Kuwait and Iraq by heading up to northern Michigan for a much-deserved fly-fishing vacation. Just like some war-weary character in a Hemingway short story. Nothing was going to keep his fly rod from those feisty brown trout, not even a partially dislocated shoulder, courtesy of a roadside accident outside the slums of Saddam City. The mishap happened at night. The Humvee he was traveling in somehow veered into a dry irrigation ditch, and turtled, landing belly up. Had the eight-foot-deep canal been filled with water, he most likely would have drowned. "Religious persecution saved me," Bebow told readers in his newspaper war diary. "My ditch was dry. It was a Shiite ditch. Saddam Hussein often punished Shiite farmers by refusing to fill irrigation canals like this one."

"The accident wasn't my first close call," he explained. The thirty-six-year-old Ypsilanti, Michigan, resident decided he had tempted the newspaper deadline gods once too often. "It was time to disembed. Earlier, an Iraqi guided missile buzzed right over my head and exploded behind me. Explosions from Iraqi rockets—and American engineers destroying minefields—shook my tent quite often. Snipers occasionally fired at my convoys. I sensed I'd spent my last reserve of good fortune walking away from that Humvee. I started to feel the creep of dark shadows and wondered which passing Iraqi car would blow me up. The story was far from over, but my editors and I agreed it was time to leave."

■　■　■

I'm an enterprise reporter at the *Detroit News*. I'm supposed to do a few big-picture stories a month, ranging everywhere from charter schools to the problems with parole to suburban sprawl. This was my first time in a war zone. A colleague once said that war reporting is like cop reporting. It definitely had that feel. In Detroit, there are murders every day and it's to the point where much of the media don't even cover them anymore. But this was war, with people dying in conflict, and you can look at it through a different lens and then report it in a different way.

I didn't go through Pentagon embed training. Nor did I do much preparation other than run around and get supplies. I spent hundreds of dollars on stuff like backpacks and Kevlar body armor—things that you just never even conceived of trying on or buying. It really was more of a shock to get ready to go than it was to be there in Iraq. And it was much harder on my wife and my family than it was on me, being there. You don't have time to worry and obsess about the home front when you're over there, and a lot of Marines would say that too. "It's much harder on my girlfriend." "It's tough on my fiancé." You can see why so many military marriages don't turn out well, because the stress it places on the home front is tremendous, especially when you're watching the fear channels all day. If you're watching the fear channels, it's easy imagining that the war zone must be this hellish place filled with an unbelievable amount of gunfire, and that there's terror on every corner—it's just not like that. The public gets a warped view of just how zany things were over there. It was definitely zany, but it wasn't every-minute dangerous.

In the rear, it was pretty miserable. I'm sure there are a lot of embeds who didn't have a good experience. The Pentagon, I think, wanted us to all get the message out that the body of the spear is as important as the point of the spear. So they put people in these rear units and that was fine in the days leading up to the war, because we were able to tell that very important story. I forget the exact statistic, but in World War II, something like 90 percent of the veterans weren't on the front lines.

The Marines were really good. At first, when we all started rolling into the camps, they were a little distrustful. They wanted to know if we all worked for the Communist News Network, as they called CNN, or *The New York Times*, which they all thought was a Stalinist/Leninist rag. But when they got to know us a little bit, they enjoyed the discourse. They'd challenge you. They'd ask you about your opinions and if you didn't give one, they knew you were disingenuous. History is not lost on the Marines. They have a pretty good sense of their history and they had some questions about this whole world-policeman approach that we're trying here.

The prime motivating factor for the Marines was not, "We're going to obey our Commander-in-Chief"; instead, it was "This is what we gotta do to get home." I saw people motivated to cover their asses, to protect themselves, and to do their jobs. There was even a family motivation from people who were third- or fourth-generation military. I didn't get a sense of, "Yes, by God, this is a great mission." Actually, I take that back. There were a lot of people who had turned this into vengeance for 9/11, which remains a very warped perspective, but one that seems to be taking on greater significance. There was this conventional wisdom that said, "Well, Saddam's responsible for 9/11, so we're going to take him out. That's going to show the terrorists"—a rather simplistic view of what's been going on the last few years.

I was destined to see the war from a dusty airfield in south-central Iraq where nothing ever happened and captains watched my every move, until one day when I was out on a patrol with some MPs and I met this officer named Colonel J. J. Pomfret, from Pontiac, Michigan. We started talking. He said, "Oh, you're also from Michigan. Come on up with me and see the actual war." I'm thinking, "Okay, that'll be cool." So I did. I jumped on a convoy and caught up to him five days later.

Colonel Pomfret was like a lighter shade of Colonel Kilgore from *Apocalypse Now*. He wasn't the killer Kilgore; he was the "let's-go-have-wild-adventures" Kilgore, and he definitely felt that way. He was in his mid-fifties and thin as a rail. Tough as they come. Probably weighed 165 pounds, five foot ten; had a slight limp from an old injury. Just rock hard as a Marine is supposed to be. Had a real hunger for action. He was running a supply unit—a really smart logistics guy—but never wanted the infantry to be far in front of him. He wanted to be right there in the action, with this Custer-like, devil-may-care approach. It's almost as if he wants to die that way someday, just to get into the shit and get it over with.

For example, one day we're right near First Marine Division headquarters going up Highway 6, south of Baghdad. It's Saturday and he's running around as he always did, checking in with officers, checking who needs supplies. But sometimes that was an excuse for him to go off and have a good time and see what was going on. We got out in front of the First Marine Division headquarters and the tanks were rolling down the highway. We kept driving and we drove up in front of the tanks. I was in a truck right behind the Colonel. The only American presence were Cobra helicopters. We were beyond the front lines. We're just driving, checking things out. We're joking, "Oh, he probably wants to go over there and see what's burning," because there was a fire on the horizon from artillery. Then his major finally said, "No, we're going to turn around here." Our mini-convoy whipped back around and sure enough, I found out later that that area hadn't yet been secured. Later there was a little bit of fighting there. But Pomfret would just grin at that. He wanted to be near it and he wanted reporters around, but he was almost challenging you with this, "Okay, let's see if you're up for what you're in for here." He'd do that all the time when he saw reporters, and—as we got close to Baghdad—he served as a magnet for reporters.

Another time, ten cars full of British and French and Australian TV journalists pulled into camp and we all just traveled in one big convoy to Saddam City. It was not safe to have that many media vehicles. Oh, it was probably a circus train of—when you figure in camera crews and everybody else—probably fifteen or twenty journalists. I'd been riding around with the Colonel and his crew for ten days at this point, and I was in a Humvee with a 50-caliber machine gun on top. All of a sudden, we've got all these TV trucks right there with us. These guys traveled around with us all day, demanded the world, didn't quite get it, screwed up my reporting day.

Those other journalists just got in the way. It's really hard to get any sense of intimacy or stop at a camp long enough to talk to someone and get a real good story line when you've got all these people running around. Then at the end of the day, they just took off and looked for their next armed guard into Baghdad. That was the thing. The unilaterals—a lot of them lost their *cojones* when they got up there. They wanted to be unilateral; they wanted to run around and have the freedom of unilaterals until they got to Baghdad, and then they jumped in there. When it got zany and crazy, they tried to jump in with the units or the embeds.

Another day, we're back into Baghdad again, and two new TV crews are there—one was from France. We stopped in this soccer complex on the south side of Baghdad. We're doing some interviews, and the Colonel is ready to pull out. We get out to the street, and we've got to stop because one of the French TV vehicles got a flat. So we got to turn around and deal with this helpless French TV crew, and guess who fixes the flat tire? The civil affairs major, who that day really wanted to be over in Saddam City, making fresh drinking water for people. Instead he's serving as a AAA road crew for helpless

French reporters. It was maddening to me; it was maddening to the Marines. So that was the side of the Colonel that got a little out of hand when he never met a reporter he didn't like. Eventually he settled down.

The Colonel was a man of action, but he was not tight-lipped. He was a quote machine. It got to a point to where I just couldn't quote him any more in my stories because I'd used him so much. He would always give the best quote every day, but I just couldn't let this guy narrate the war for me. He'd quote Winston Churchill. It was either in the White House or somewhere in England, where Mr. and Mrs. Roosevelt had rolled up to his door and knocked. He opened and stood there bare naked, which caused a little bit of uncomfortableness. Winston Churchill supposedly said, "The Prime Minister of England has nothing to hide from the President of the United States."

Another war story the Colonel liked telling was to describe the battle scene at Gettysburg and to talk about the young assistant to Lee, who would say, "General Lee, you've just sent the same message to two of your subordinates, Yule and Longstreet." He basically did send the same message, but he gave Longstreet a paragraph and he gave Yule two pages. Lee would respond, "Well, that's because if I had given Longstreet two pages, he would have said, 'General, you don't trust me,' and if I'd given Yule two paragraphs, he would have said, 'Sir, I need further direction.'" The Colonel would use this as a way of explaining his "situational management" of his own people. He had a lawyer reservist who was in charge of his POWs, because it was a detail-oriented job, but he had this hyperactive warrant officer, who was off doing a million things every day because he couldn't sit still.

The Colonel was constantly saying, "I love each and every one of these Marines. They are magnificent." Another one of his favorite quotes, a classic military maxim, was "Go to the sound of the guns." I don't think there's any way that any American civilian journalist or military person in Iraq felt anywhere near what the Iraqis felt. I mean, the stuff we rained down on these people. The capacity that we have to kill is so chillingly efficient. We don't even begin to comprehend what those people felt. I saw them without their skulls. I saw them disemboweled. I saw them shot up and raked by helicopter fire.

One of the most memorable cinematic scenes I saw in Iraq—probably one of the best stories I did and one of the hardest to do—was west of Kut. We were on the move—it was only a few days from Baghdad. We're rolling along, and we saw this truck on the side of the road—a big Iraqi truck with a big bed to the back of it. Marines are constantly looking for more "bed space," which is room to put more supplies, more meals, more MREs, more water, more bullets, more ways to carry stuff. They never had enough of that. So they made camp about ten miles farther up the road and then real quick, the hyper warrant officer and the civil affairs guy rounded up a small crew to go back to try to get this truck going. They took with them their Iraqi freedom fighter named Arka. He was a translator from Dearborn, Michigan, so he made a perfect news story for me—going back to his homeland, hoping to get to his village. But in the meantime, he was serving the U.S. military as a translator. So, Arka gets in the truck, I get in the truck, a few other people get in the truck, and off we go back to get that other truck. We got back to the truck, which is still running. It's maybe twenty yards off the road. To get to the truck, the Marines basically step over three Iraqi bodies, without even a casual glance. They're like, "Oh, you know, those guys got fucked up," and then they go over and look at the truck. Well, Arka, the translator, gets down and handles the situation completely differently. He goes over, pulls back the jackets that are covering these guys' faces, looks at them, recoils from what he sees, and is really trying to come to grips with this reality: "These are my countrymen. They're dead and here are these cold-blooded Marines worrying about this truck." Well, the Marines are doing their job and Arka's doing what anybody in his shoes would do. It's just the way Arka and these Marines continued to handle this situation differently for thirty minutes. Somebody accidentally shuts the truck off so they had to get it going again. They find a bunch of tools. They're performing surgery on this truck, while Arka is over here wishing somebody would have performed surgery on these dead guys. Finally, they get the truck going, but the brakes lock up, they can't move it and we're going to leave in a few minutes. Arka goes down the road a little bit and sees a fourth body. I'm with him. I'm just kind of walking behind him; I'm not putting a microphone in his face or a notepad and saying, "How do you feel?" I'm just observing, you know. He sees a fourth body—guy's shot in both shins—just messed up. He goes across the road and there's a bunch of belongings. There's a little radio and some shirts and a yellow U.S. humanitarian aid package that says, "This meal is a gift from the American people to you." And he's looking at all this and getting very cynical. He's seeing these guys over there on this truck and he's looking down at their belongings and he says to the belongings—he's speaking to the belongings—"Why did you stay on the truck? Why didn't you run away? Why didn't you leave the army?" That put so much of the war into perspective for me, just through the eyes of this one Iraqi, because that's how complex the whole situation is over there. There's no black and white. There's no one view of what's going on, and that was just so evident in that late-morning scene, along a solitary road. Those are the moments I was constantly looking for over there, little moments that would turn into stories.

As a reporter I was trying to zig when everybody else zagged. I was just trying to write literally what was in front of my face every day and describe it in detail. That's what Ernie Pyle did in World War II. That's all he did; he took little existential scenes like that. I think Ernie Pyle's most famous column was about a captain who was brought down from a hill in Italy on the back of a donkey. In this day and age, that's about all a newspaper reporter like me can do. I mean, especially if I'm embedded, I can't give you this gigantic wide-ranging view of the war. I'm the only reporter there from my newspaper and I'm embedded in the middle of Iraq. I can't gather up six reports from six field correspondents the way The New York Times guy could in Kuwait City and write it all up and make sense out of it every day. All a guy like me can do is give really detailed, if possible, gut-wrenching snapshots of what's going on. That's what I was trying to do, and that's why I wrote about dead bodies quite often.

Those were the stories that really hit people. I got a lot of e-mail. Well, my wife was keeping an e-mail list and she would send out little notes to friends and that kind of grew, and the stuff that really left a lasting impression was the dead body scenes. It gave a sense of what the war was really about.

A very good friend of mine is an author named Jim Tobin. We used to be reporters together at The Detroit News in the early nineties, and he's always been a role model for me. He wrote the book Ernie Pyle's War that came out around 1997 and won a National Book Award. It was his first book. He worked on it for years. A lot of us were cheering him on and he made it out of the newsroom and is a famous author now. He's doing a book tour right now for his next book, which is about the Wright Brothers, called To Conquer the Air, a fascinating look at the race for flight at the turn of the last century. As soon as I knew I was going to the war, I got a Detroit News copy of Ernie Pyle's War out of our library and started carrying it with me everywhere. I took it over there with me and I read it on the plane to Kuwait. I'm no Ernie Pyle. None of us over there were, but it puts you in a frame of mind as a print reporter to capture scenes, to try to focus on the everyday grunts and their experiences.

I felt like I found some scenes that if Pyle were standing there, it'd be the kind of thing that he'd write about and do it a hell of a lot better than I did. I remember standing up near the border, before the war started, and it was the last time a PX truck was going to run up to this unit of grunts with one of the regimental combat teams. It was the last time these guys were going to see Pringles potato chips and RedMan chewing tobacco for weeks. I really wanted to capture that. I started hearing these Marines practicing Arabic phrases, such as, "Put down your guns." There were no other reporters around, and I remember thinking to myself, "Damn, I don't know where they are, but they just missed a great story."

There was another day I got up to take a pee. It was just before dawn and I went over to the ditch and took care of business. I looked over my shoulder and saw the guy who ran the POW camp. It was a slow day. I asked him, "Hey, tell me about your POW camp. How does this work? Do you have like three scraggly guys sitting there?" No news. Well, the next morning at first light, more than 100 people are sitting there who had come in the middle of the night, and they're starting to load them onto trucks. So I wander over and like always had my notepad in my pocket—I even slept with it there in case anything happened in the middle of the night. I walk over and it's another cinematic scene. It was like seeing the Jews loaded into trucks during the Holocaust. Obviously the Marines were treating these people with considerably more respect and they weren't on their way to a gas chamber. But just watching this scene of hopeless, lost souls, many of them barefoot many of them, with burlap bags over their heads, getting onto trucks to God knows where they thought they were going, and after all they'd probably been told about America, they very likely did think they were going to their own Holocaust. They were shivering. It was cold, but some of that shivering was due to fear. One of them walked by—he had one tennis shoe on and didn't have anything on the other foot. All I had to do was stand there and write down what was right in front of my face. I filed that story right before we pulled out, about 11:00 A.M., and everybody loved it. It appeared in USA Today.

I could have gutted it out as a reporter if I had a little rest. I came home and a couple of weeks later went fishing. How bad can it be? Well, I didn't have the reserve for adversity that I needed mentally. I wasn't getting any sleep. I was as grubby as I could be. I was hurt and I was probably a little too honest with editors about all that. I told them exactly what my state of mind was. I told them I was hurt and in today's corporate climate, how can editors take risks, leaving injured reporters in the field? It doesn't take too much to imagine some of the conversations they were probably having back in the newsroom. "Well, what if John gets killed now? We know he's hurt. We're really culpable." They can't let that happen.

I flew out of Baghdad on a CH46 helicopter with a few other journalists and some Marines going off to do some sort of mission. We landed once and dropped a couple of people off at a camp, then took off again. Remember the scenes from *Black Hawk Down*, where they're right over Mogadishu and they're seeing all the chaos below? It was just like that. It was really wild. I saw some of the neighborhoods I'd been in. I saw some of the mosques I'd been around. Then I saw some of these wealthy areas where you'd have some Mercedeses out front, but there's still trash on those streets. We flew back to this airfield. Then we caught a plane back to Kuwait.

I felt relief coming out of Iraq. I had too many close calls. One lucky bullet is all it takes. I never took off my Kevlar vest. (Right now, it's sitting at my desk in the newsroom. It has MRE juice running down the front of it. It's gross and disgusting, it smells bad, and I'm waiting for somebody to tell me to move it!) But I also felt something else, and it was, "God, I can't be leaving here, I'm not done yet. How can I be leaving here?" That last thought really lingered. It wasn't more than five minutes after I got back to the airport in Detroit when I'm telling my wife and some of my friends that I feel like I should still be there. I had the itch to return. It was especially hard for my wife to hear because I'd just gotten home.

The drain on my family was really hard and it might be too selfish for me to do it again. At the same time, somebody's got to do it, and there have always been drains on families. My wife's not a journalist. She doesn't have the journalist mindset that somebody's got to go do this. She's a musician. She's an opera singer and teaches voice out of a piano room in our house. She's not into that whole scene, but she still handled it wonderfully. I mean, her husband's in a war zone. She knew she was marrying a journalist, but as she said to me shortly before I left, "I didn't know I was in for this." I've always been a reporter in Michigan and do a lot of local news, so what would lead one to believe that I'm gonna end up doing international reporting? The gig—I'd love to do more of it.

If war broke out again and I had the opportunity to go, I'd have to think long and hard about it because it is an addictive experience. I'm not a warmonger and I hope we don't go to war with Syria or Korea or Iran or whoever the hell else we're thinking about going to war with, but we've always gone to war. America always has conflicts, and we've always needed really good journalists to be there for history and for the daily drama and news of it. I don't know when I'll be able to be in those kinds of scenes again—with my heart racing and just amazing things happening right in front of my face. Am I still reliving these experiences as flashbacks? No, I don't think so. Am I waking up in the middle of the night screaming? No. But I woke up the first morning I got home and looked over at this digital clock on my dresser and said to myself, "What's that digital clock doing in this Marine camp?"

COVERING WARS TAKES
HER FAR FROM HOME

San Francisco Chronicle Staff Writer
Anna Badkhen

> "Wars are bad, they are devastating, they are
> terrifying. There can be no good memories from
> a war."

Gaza. Afghanistan. Chechnya. West Bank. Kashmir. Tajikistan. Mosul. These are
some of the combat zones making up the recent travel itinerary of Russian-
based war correspondent Anna Badkhen, who is a staff reporter for the *San
Francisco Chronicle*. "My editors don't like sending me to fun places," dead-
pans the twenty-seven-year-old St. Petersburg native who lives in Moscow
with her five-year-old son, Fyodor, and husband, David Filipov, bureau chief of
The Boston Globe. With her shoulder-length brown hair, large blue eyes, and
indie-rocker good looks, she conveys a non-threatening, trusting presence that
is often a journalist's most valuable asset in precarious environments.

Badkhen has already earned several press awards for her literary-styled reporting, including two from Northern California media organizations. She writes
with a Chekovian flair for the telling detail. Once, to achieve an eyewitness perspective in Kabul, she spent a day walking, or rather tripping, inside a blue burqa:
"After I took my first few steps, I learned that the burqa is the most uncomfortable
piece of clothing known to womankind. The ribbon on the top was too tight. The
mesh, I discovered, was at the level of my eyebrows rather than my eyes, so I
couldn't see anything directly in front of me that wasn't level with my head or
higher. Loose threads from the embroidery on the inside of the burqa tickled my
nose and made me sneeze. Since I couldn't see my feet, I slipped in the mud. The
tail of my burqa got caught on the door handle as I was trying to climb into the
back seat of our car. Looking through the mesh hurt my eyes. I wanted to smoke,
but was afraid that I would set the flimsy nylon on fire."

We spoke with Badkhen shortly after her return from northern Iraq. She had just put Fyodor to bed. The previous time we talked was via satphone from Irbil and she was waiting for the ground war to commence outside Kirkuk, which was still under the control of Saddam's forces. "I am quite a fearful person," she confessed from her hotel room. CNN was playing in the background.

■   ■   ■

Usually, when I travel alone to places like the Middle East, I automatically become an honorary man. In southeastern Turkey, which is not much different from northern Iraq, hotel staff would inevitably call me "Mister" and "Sir," as in, "Good morning, sir!" I guess because talking to a strange woman is impolite, but failing to greet a patron is also impolite.

But when I travel with another male correspondent, I almost never get addressed at all, which, depending on my mood and tolerance at the moment, can range from frustrating to infuriating, especially when it concerns a translator that I, too, pay. In Afghanistan I worked with a translator for two months before realizing he didn't quite know my name. This type of sexism, however unpleasant, is not malevolent. It originates from local taboos that forbid men touching or addressing "someone else's" woman. Which is why if I and a fellow male correspondent are carrying heavy bags, a Middle Eastern helper would always grab my companion's bags, and not mine. It is up to my companion, then, to choose to help me or not to help me. But it doesn't make it less frustrating to spend weeks on end in a society that pretends so persistently not to notice my presence. I must say that whenever I asked a question, people translated it and gave me answers. It also helped that I could speak several words in Afghan Dari, which is very similar to Kurdish, and used those few words ("American planes are bombing enemy lines," "tomorrow," and "one coffee with a little sugar, please") whenever I could. People appreciated hearing me try so hard to communicate. I once made a mistake of mentioning that I am Russian to a teacher in Irbil. He wasn't hostile, but he was very disappointed. "The Russians let us down because they support Saddam Hussein," he told me. "Why?" I never mentioned that I was Russian again.

As for bonds, I always try to make friends with the team that I work with, because, in the end, my life depends on them. I've seen reporters yell at their translators and drivers in places like Afghanistan and Iraq, and although, thank goodness, I've never seen these reporters suffer later because of their failed relationships with their crew, it's a really bad idea. I've been very lucky and most of the people I've worked with in war zones have been great pals.

Also, these are the people with whom I spend days, and sometimes nights, in some of the most dangerous situations of our lives. We tell jokes and I try to learn the language. It's good to be a funny foreigner sometimes, and I'm not afraid to be funny and to allow having myself made fun of. Usually, a translator in a place like Afghanistan or Iraq is someone who is more educated, more experienced, more intelligent than me, but who has been forced to become a translator for a journalist because of the circumstances. I wrote a story about one of my Iraqi translators, who is a dissident and a writer who'd spent many months in Saddam's jails. He wasn't a very good translator, because he would space out a lot or forget where we were and start thinking about the book he was writing at the time, but he was infinitely intelligent and one of the nicest people I've met in my entire life. And his wife cooked delicious *dolma*.

For me personally, war reporting comes at a very high emotional cost. I don't know how many people wake up from nightmares with bullets in their foreheads, but it strikes me as a severe price to pay. I have these recurring dreams of being executed; I wake up right when whoever it is that's aiming at my forehead pulls the trigger. I have dreams of killing children. I have dreams of being tortured. I'm afraid the traumas of war must show, even at home. But I'm not a post-traumatic-stress-disorder-child-beater. I also feel very guilty about going away for long stretches of time. Leaving Fyodor behind is difficult, even though when I'm away he stays with my husband or a nanny. He has gotten used to the concept that I go away on long trips, but he'd rather have me by his side. I also know that he knows that I go off to wars, even though we don't discuss it in front of the kids and we try to prevent the kids from watching the news at home (my husband has a seven-year-old who often stays with us). Once, Fyodor called me while I was in Afghanistan and said, "Mama, be careful. I saw that there are tanks in Afghanistan." I can only imagine what actually goes through his head.

I try to never go on long trips, although the trip to Iraq was five weeks, preceded by a three-week trip to Turkey and northern Iraq, and use a nanny as little as possible whenever I'm home. The problem is, when I come home from a trip I'm usually too spent to be a very entertaining mom. By the time I recover, it's usually time to go away again. My parents are very proud of what I do, and I think by now they are pretty much used to the idea that I go to dangerous places. My father is a psychotherapist; my mother is a translator and a teacher of English. She has private students, all adults. They are extremely worried about me whenever I'm away, even if they are too considerate to show it. My dad recently confessed that when I go away for long stretches of time he reads books like *Harry Potter* and *Lord of the Rings*—magic books where the good always wins—to keep his thoughts away from my travels. I'm not sure what my mom does. I know they both definitely suffer more than they let on. I'm very close to my parents, who are both fifty. I know that all of my professional triumphs come at a very high cost for them. My husband is also a journalist, and he's a husband any war correspondent can only dream of. We have traveled together to some places, and he's the best travel buddy I've ever had, but when I go on an assignment alone and he stays home, he never lets me know how worried he is, although I know he's very worried. He makes going away so much easier for me, and I'm very grateful for that.

Still, there are certain things about war reporting that I find attractive. One is getting to go places and meet people I would never go and meet otherwise—and, of course, coming home with a lifetime's worth of stories and memories. Another is the purity of human reaction I get to see. Being under intense pressure—the kind one sees in a war zone—makes people act more earnestly. I get to see more grace, dignity, and generosity in a week on a front line than in a year in a "successful" place like Moscow. Finally, seeing my stories displayed prominently in the newspaper is an important part of the appeal. I'm not embarrassed to admit it.

I never started out thinking that someday "I want to become a war correspondent." It just happened. I got my first job as a reporter in July 1996 at the *St. Petersburg Times* [Russia], a small, biweekly English-language newspaper. In 2000 I moved to Moscow and worked at *The Moscow Times* for a year and freelanced for *The Boston Globe*, *Newsweek*, and *USA Today*. I became a stringer for the *San Francisco Chronicle* in 2001, then went to Afghanistan for the *Chronicle*, and by the end of that year, went on staff. Covering wars was just something they asked me to do, and I did it.

In March 2002 I went to Pankisi Gorge, Georgia, to cover the alleged Al-Qaeda presence there. In April 2002 I went to Israel/West Bank/Gaza. In June, as things were heating up between India and Pakistan, I went to Kashmir to cover the shelling and the separatist movement, and then to Gujarat, India, to cover the Muslim-Hindu clashes. In July I was in Chechnya. In September 2002 I went back to Afghanistan. In November I went back to Chechnya. Last

December I went to Jordan, hoping to get into Iraq, but Saddam's government denied me a visa on the basis that I have a Jewish last name. I went to northern Iraq through Turkey in February, returned in March, and a week later, went back into northern Iraq through Iran, for the duration of the war.

As I mentioned, I was in Iraq for five weeks, and yes, I was definitely ready to leave. I worked every day for about twenty hours under pressure and keeping up became very difficult toward the end. I was worried that it would affect the quality of my reporting, and, importantly, my sense of safety. Sometimes, the fear comes afterward. Looking into the barrel of a gun of an Afghan fighter (only later did I realize that he actually tried to rob me at gunpoint), revisiting the minefield I had to drive over ("Six hundred mines are planted there," someone later told me. "How on earth did you make it across?"), recalling how I had to lie facedown in a Gaza checkpoint as a Palestinian teenager tossed grenades at us, or how Israeli snipers shot at my feet to keep me from entering Jenin. Looking back I think, boy, that was really close.

But there is also a lot of fear present as I'm about to go into a war zone, or to a front line. It is the fear of the unknown, and it usually fades away as I get on a story—I guess reporting replaces fear. A few times I felt this fear when I was in a little town called Kalak, which for the last twelve years had been only 100 yards removed from the Iraqi front line. It was on the border of the so-called "no-fly" zone, which U.S. and British planes patrolled, a Kurdish-controlled enclave on the otherwise government-controlled left bank of the Zab-al-Kabir River. The Iraqi troops were perched on a ridge right above the town. They were so close I could see them lay mines on the slope and light cigarettes. Anyway, at one point, maybe a week or so into the war, the Iraqi soldiers decided they will shoot down into the town, basically at anything that moves. A lot of locals left the town, but some stayed behind. I went down to interview them, which was easy because everyone has very tall concrete or mud-brick fences. They wouldn't stop a bullet but they concealed us perfectly, so the soldiers didn't shoot. But to get to Kalak I needed to cross a bridge that was in full view of the soldiers, and certainly in their range of fire—and it was broken, so that no car could go faster than ten miles per hour. It was also narrow, wide enough for only one car to pass. If there was any oncoming traffic, our car would have to stop at a wide platform in the middle of the bridge to wait. That was eerie. But the creepiest day was when the Iraqi forces pulled west, maybe five miles or so, and began lobbing mortars and 105-mm shells into the town, aiming for the bridge. They nearly hit the bridge once, a few minutes before we were on it, trying to leave, and we drove past a smoldering crater. One of the mortars hit an empty kindergarten in a town on the other side of the river. Another killed a doctor.

There are no typical days covering a war. Sometimes I would make plans to go someplace the night before, but by the time I would wake up—usually between 6:00 and 8:00 A.M.—things would have changed. Usually I would wake up and check wires and CNN and BBC (yes, I had those in the hotel room in Irbil) to make sure there wasn't a "must do" story for the day ("U.S. Troops Capitulate Across Iraqi Plains, Saddam Announces All Western Journalists Will Be Hung from Toes").

Irbil is the largest city in northern Iraq, home to about one million people, mostly Kurds. It claims to be the oldest continuously populated city in the world, dating back to 7,000 B.C. It's a fairly neat town, run by the Kurdish Democratic Party, whose money, to the best of my knowledge, comes mainly from oil smuggling, Kurdish diaspora, and U.S. funding. There are lots of hotels and Internet cafes; I saw maybe a dozen of both. There is also a cell phone system that somehow works through London. Many people have cell phones, but a lot of people are dirt-poor and live in dreadful conditions in the ancient citadel. You can get pretty much anything from Levi's jeans to Johnson's Baby Shampoo to a Thuraya handheld satellite phone to a digital camera. It was quite a surprise, actually, because although I have seen pictures of northern Iraq on the Internet, I expected something more like Afghanistan— dilapidated mud-brick huts, people who've never seen a computer.

The Kurdish name for the city is Hawler, but the Arabic name is Irbil. The Arabs actually pronounce it *Arbil*, although I've also seen it spelled *Erbil*). I stayed for a few nights at the Arbil Tower Hotel which was okay but kind of shabby; I remember avoiding the bathroom. Then I upgraded to the DimDim Hotel, where the manager had lived in Canada and was a very nice and helpful guy. The room was better, but one night my bathroom flooded through a hole in the floor and I was overrun by cockroaches. So I moved to the Chwar Chra, the best hotel in town after a really small old hotel next door, which CNN had rented entirely for the duration of the war. The Chwar Chra had a magnificent lawn with a fountain out front, where patrons could eat lunch and dinner, and quite decent cuisine. I particularly liked the salad bar lunch, which I had to skip most of the time since it was only open between 12:30 and 4:00 P.M., during which time I was usually on the road.

I would usually go to the front line. There were many in northern Iraq, and sometimes I could go to more than one front line in one day. And there I would inevitably learn or see something that I would want to write about. One day, I went to the front line and saw that one of the peshmerga commanders brought his seven-year-old son to the battlefield ("I want him to grow up as brave as me," I believe is what the commander said.) There were mortars and 105-mm shells blowing up all around us, and the child was sucking his thumb amidst all this.

It was remarkably easy getting around northern Iraq. The roads were very decent. Most checkpoints were of the brake-and-wave variety, although in some checkpoints men looked into the car window, made sure I was what I said I was (*Sahafi Amriki*, an American journalist), smiled, and waved my car through.

I had a nice 4x4, a Hyundai. The driver was a bit hotheaded, a twenty-four-year-old man. He drove like a maniac. I had to keep reminding him that if no one is shooting at us when we're on a highway, it doesn't mean that we aren't interested in surviving. He also hit every single pothole on the road, laughing at the ones he would hit more than two days in a row. But we all lived. Another time, when the Marines entered Tikrit from the south, we tried to drive down from the north, and nearly drove into what U.S. Special Forces call a "killbox"—coordinates that are being targeted by U.S. warplanes. Meaning, I was in a car heading south and suddenly what apparently was a 2,000 pound bomb exploded about a mile ahead of me, on the road I was on. Then another one, and then another. That was also rather unpleasant. I thought, if I'd spent a bit less time chatting to peshmerga at a checkpoint outside Mosul, that would have been me. The pesh warned me that U.S. planes were bombing something somewhere down the road, but they didn't make it clear that the planes were bombing the road itself.

One of the more interesting peshmerga fighters I met was Jamal Star Ahmet. He was a star of one of my stories. I met him on a front line outside Kirkuk about two weeks before it fell. He was wearing a gold watch, white sneakers, a cummerbund with a wide knife tucked into it, and six hand grenades hanging from his leather belt. He had tattooed the word "homeland" on the knuckles of his left hand—to remind him, he said, of the free Kurdistan he and hundreds of thousands of other Kurds hope to have one day. He was standing on a hilltop that was a mass grave of victims of al Anfal, Saddam's campaign against the Kurds during which hundreds of thousands were killed or disappeared. The mound was under Iraqi government control just a day before, but the Iraqi army had pulled back, leaving behind heavily mined fields. Star Ahmet's family was among the Anfal victims, but he did not know if they were buried in the mound on which he stood. His home was twenty-five miles away, but he couldn't push south. He and his fellow peshmerga fighters were no match for Hussein's army, and they had to rely on U.S. air strikes to move toward Kirkuk. So he was standing on the mass grave, in a minefield overgrown with poppies and daisies, searching the sky for American planes.

I did have some interaction with U.S. Special Forces who were assisting the peshmerga. Well, they did save my life once. We were interviewing a group of Special Forces on a front line outside Mosul when Iraqi troops began to shell our hilltop with a 105-mm gun. The shells landed 100 yards away, then closer. The Special Forces guys were incredibly macho. They seemed to have come to northern Iraq straight from a Hollywood movie. They barely ducked as we reporters dropped face down on the ground. Their dialogue went like this: "That was a pretty good one," said one officer. "It's best when you can hear it," said another. "If you don't hear it, you're in trouble." "They got the range on that last one. Had they aimed 100 meters to the left, that would have been it. It'll be interesting up here when they get us bracketed." "The operational situation has changed and we gotta get out of here." Finally, it got too hot even for those guys, and they told us to hop into the back of their Land Rover pickup truck, saying, "It's getting hairy here. That's more story than you wanted." They drove us several hundred yards away from where the shells were exploding and gave us an interview, amazing me once again with their comebacks that seemed to have come straight from some very macho Hollywood flick. I think the interview part was actually payback—I had given two of them a ride to the base and a Pepsi when their car had broken down by the side of the road, and they remembered me. On the one hand, it seems natural that these soldiers did what they did; after all, it would have seemed strange if they had left us behind. Yet, protecting journalists was not part of their job since I was not traveling with the troops, and I suppose it made my assignment that much more difficult—and that much more independent. I had to rely entirely on my own sense of safety, but I also could go places where American soldiers were not welcome.

I think being embedded—which I was not—is a great idea and the process gives the public a dimension of the war we missed in, say, Afghanistan. However, I would prefer that it should not become the only way to cover a war. One of the risks, in my opinion, is that it is hard for a reporter, any reporter, to be critical of people he or she travels with and shares his or her daily meals. In a war zone, your travel companion becomes your closest friend; can we be totally unbiased when our friends have accidentally—or by mistake—shot a bunch of civilians in a bus and we have to cover the story? There always must be someone on the other side so that the reader or viewer has an idea of what the war is like from all sides.

Take Mosul in northern Iraq, for example, where two very different scenarios played themselves out. One day in Mosul, shortly after Saddam's regime fell, an Iraqi woman came up to us and asked to use a satellite phone. Phones had stopped working in Mosul when the war began, and she had no way of letting her relatives in Saudi Arabia know that she'd survived the war. We were three American journalists, and two of us had satphones. In a matter of minutes, there were dozens of people around us, each holding out a crumbled piece of paper with phone numbers in the U.K., U.S., Canada, Jordan, Kuwait, Syria, Lebanon, Germany, even Russia. These people were all professionals, residents of the most prestigious neighborhood in Mosul, reduced by war to begging American journalists for thirty seconds of satellite time. But they all spoke English. They formed orderly lines. Someone quoted William Blake. Someone else, an astrophysicist, explained to the crowd how a satellite phone works (I'm still not sure I know). An engineer came up to me and said that he didn't want to make a phone call; he wanted a job with the UN rebuilding the city. These people knew so much more than I ever will, and were so enthusiastic to rebuild their country.

But most Mosul residents had no time to celebrate the fall of the hated Saddam rule. The regime fell overnight, and by 10:00 A.M. the next day, anarchy filled the vacuum, dragging the city into a chaos of pillaging and destruction. Scores of young men dressed like Kurdish peshmerga fighters entered residential neighborhoods, looting and burning. By next morning, Arabs set up vigilante checkpoints on street corners. Kids no older than fourteen were looking at passing cars through the muzzles of their AK47s. There was shooting, but it was impossible to tell who fired at whom. I spent fifteen minutes in a hospital, and in these fifteen minutes I saw two wounded people brought in and two dead bodies—two brothers, both killed in a street fight—brought out. Someone fired at the hospital from a semi-automatic rifle. It was complete mayhem. As this was happening, the Kurds of northern Iraq were retaking land they claim to be their own, kicking out Arabs whom the Saddam regime had resettled into their old houses decades ago as he tried to ethnically cleanse the country. In one village, Kurds and Arabs agreed that they would shoot at anyone who crossed into each other's territory. In other villages, Kurds spray painted the word "taken" on houses they were going to reclaim. Scores of Arabs left their villages, fearing reprisals. Others took up weapons to protect houses in which many of them were born. When I left Iraq, the north was probably the most dangerous place in the country, and getting more so.

Do I have a "favorite" memory from Iraq? I don't believe I have favorite memories from any of the wars I've covered. Wars are bad, they are devastating, they are terrifying. There can be no good memories from a war.

THE RACE TO BAGHDAD

CBS Evening News Correspondent Jim Axelrod

"I do not come from a long line of brave people."

On the morning of September 11th, 2001, CBS network correspondent Jim Axelrod, 40, was enjoying a second cup of coffee with his wife in their Montclair, New Jersey, home. It was their eighth wedding anniversary and they wanted to spend some extra time together. The bus ride into New York City could wait. But the bus he grabbed never made it into the city. The Lincoln Tunnel had been shut down in the wake of the World Trade Center terrorist attacks, so the bus was forced to turn around. "This was the story of my career," recalls Axelrod, "and I was sitting three miles away on the other side of the Hudson River and I couldn't immediately get into the city. CBS was calling me on my cell phone. I'm thinking to myself, 'My career is in shreds right now because I had an extra cup of coffee with my wife, celebrating our anniversary.'" Although Axelrod finally made it to Ground Zero later that day—he drove his own car—the fact remains that the career trajectory of network correspondents is often measured by face time before the camera, and getting face time is an ongoing, high-stakes match involving producers, executives, colleagues, and of course, the breaking news story. "When the war in Afghanistan was about to start, I immediately volunteered to go over there," says Axelrod, who had spent three years as a schoolteacher in his twenties before changing professions. He landed his first television job at a Bangor, Maine, station, though it wasn't until his second posting, in Utica, New York, that he appeared before the camera. "Oh, I was so awful," he laughs.

Post-Afghanistan, Axelrod was battle-trained for Iraq's expected dangers and hardships. He got embedded with the infantry and became one of the first network correspondents to report from inside Iraq once the ground war had commenced. He even scored a journalistic coup by being the first to report live from the American-overrun Baghdad International Airport. For the war's duration, *CBS Evening News with Dan Rather* featured him almost every night. In Vegas that kind of hot streak is called running the table.

We caught up with Axelrod in New York City in mid-May. Our first interview was delayed because he was assigned to cover SARS. "I'm going survive the war and die of SARS in Toronto!" he joked. The second interview was postponed because he was wrapping up the final edit of an inspirational tribute to the Loyola College women's lacrosse team coach, Diane Geppi-Aikens, who was suffering from brain cancer. And our third interview was pushed back several hours because Middle Eastern terrorists had struck again: four well-coordinated car bombings destroyed three Western housing complexes in Riyadh, Saudi Arabia. Axelrod's broadcast duties were to cobble together a news segment, "Americans at Risk," which focused on a Virginia-based company named Vinnel, which trained the Saudi National Guard in firefighting and security procedures. Axelrod explains this down-to-the-wire process.

■　■　■

I was working on another project for the History Channel outside the building. I must have gotten back to the building about two in the afternoon. This was a real crunch time. These are high-wire acts without a net because you have to have something intelligent to say, something that people have not been hearing on the cable networks which have been covering the story all day. You want to have something fresh to say at 6:30, and you're playing beat-the-clock. At the same time, you want to bring new light to the situation. So days like this are incredibly challenging, in some ways more challenging than covering the war, where you have an all-you-can-eat buffet of video right in front of you. It may sound a little odd, but metaphorically speaking, when the broadcast center is getting a piece like this together, it sometimes feels a little more dangerous than being out in the war zone. While I was sitting on the set, somebody spoke to Dan Rather and he turned to me and said, "We got it confirmed. All seven American deaths are Vinnel employees. Work that into your tag." I had ten seconds to prepare. It was a *Broadcast News* moment. We were going down to the wire with this story. It doesn't happen very often, but in a professional sense, you live for that. That's what you're trained to do and hoping you can pull it off. It's an adrenaline rush.

Well, I always knew I was going to Iraq. I volunteered to go. I didn't know the exact date of departure. I didn't know who I would be assigned to be with. I was called by Senior Vice President for Hard News, Marcia McGuinness, on a Tuesday and she said, "Could you get on a plane Saturday?" This was something I had discussed with my wife, who was pregnant.

Covering the war was the great, pure, authentic experience of my career. I suspect it may be the purest thing I'll ever do. I was in the enchanted forest. CBS had purchased our Humvee and specially outfitted it with a satellite dish. We were able to pull over and within seven minutes have a signal established and be broadcasting to New York. It was amazing to be driving along in the middle of the desert and *Face the Nation* is on and they want to hear from us. So we pull over, and within seven minutes we're broadcasting the latest pictures of the desert.

For four or five weeks, I could call the CBS broadcast center and say, "I've got news! Put me on the air." Except for the days when we were in a blackout or we were in a convoy and couldn't stop—although I'd be reporting for radio at that point—I think I reported every day. And if visibility and appearances are the currency of a broadcast journalist, I felt like I was robbing the bank! The vault was wide open. While the media is a brutal and competitive business, with everybody always watching everybody else, I got the warmest congratulations from colleagues, however, about being the first to the Baghdad Airport and the first in Baghdad. But competition is the fuel that powers a lot of people's engines, and so what happened to me and my combat photographer Mario de Carvalho, was as much about dumb luck as anything else. We so happened to be assigned to a brigade of the Third Infantry that was first across the berms and were the tip of the spear.

You have to understand that we were living this sort of very narrow slice of the war, so I didn't have a great sense of the big picture. I still haven't seen a lick of video; I haven't seen a frame of what we produced. I knew that our coverage was going well based on feedback from New York, but I had no sense of how it was playing, how we were compared to NBC or ABC or CNN.

When we were still in Kuwait City, all the journalists who had been assigned to the Third Infantry were brought to the Hilton for a briefing. There must have been fifty or sixty journalists in this room, and I was with Mario. He was always the videographer that I partnered with. He's been with CBS for twenty-seven years. He's covered sixteen wars and conflicts and he is one of the best combat photographers in the world. I turned to him and said, "You know, odds are someone in this room isn't coming back." And it turned out that three people in the room weren't coming back.

On the morning we left from Kuwait City, David Bloom, who was friendly with several of my colleagues, took a nap in our suite. We woke him up and we walked down the stairs and laughed our way onto the buses that were taking us out to the military camps and shook hands goodbye. I certainly knew David in passing.

Michael Kelly was married to a former CBS staffer and the afternoon that we drove to the Baghdad airport—the last afternoon of his life—we were the only journalists, including Mario, myself, and our satellite technician Geof Thorpe-Willett, with the 369 Battalion. That was the lead battalion for the Third Infantry into the airport. So as we all lined up to make this final push to the Baghdad Airport, Michael drove ahead of us in his Humvee and he waved to us and we waved to him. He knew Mario very well. He was about a quarter mile ahead of us and his car took the RPG and they went into the river. We saw the ambulance going up and back, but we did not see what happened.

And the third was a Spanish journalist, Julio Parrado. I sat next to him on the bus on the way out to the desert and we talked for about an hour. So I knew or had personal interaction with all three of the journalists from the Third Infantry who died.

Ted Koppel was also with the Third Infantry. He had the run of the joint. The Third Infantry is divided into three combat brigades, so Koppel could sit at infantry headquarters and say, "Hey, you know, the Second Brigade seems to be taking on some good fighting for the next forty-eight hours. Let's go with them." And then he'd come back to the Third Brigade or the First Brigade, because he was with General Blount. I was stapled to the First Brigade combat team.

The day that David Bloom died, I'm sitting in the hangar at Baghdad International Airport, just stunned. Koppel walked over to me and I felt this arm around my shoulder and I heard, "Are you doing okay?" and I look up, and it's Koppel! He said, "Come on, I want to talk to you." We took a walk and he asked if I was okay. He gave me some perspective about how I have to concentrate on what I'm doing and there's plenty of time to mourn, but don't lose focus. You know, I had lost so much weight that four days before, my wedding band slipped off my finger. I lost my wedding ring in the Iraq desert! I was despondent. And Ted saw me frantically searching around the car, the Humvee, and then the desert, and he goes, "What did you lose?" I held up my hand and he said, 'Don't tell her until you get home. Don't tell her until you get home! She'll see it as a bad omen.'" He was very fatherly in the way he looked after not just me, but his team and a lot of people. He was very impressive. He's Class with a capital C. He doesn't have anything to prove to anyone. He knows who he is; he knows what he's done. He doesn't need to prove that in every interaction with people.

Being around him was like a Triple A ballplayer getting a chance to watch Babe Ruth up close and personal. I'd never met him before. I hadn't seen him work before. So it was such a thrill to watch one of the great broadcast journalists in the history of the business working, and be working in such close proximity. He's one of my heroes. If Dan Rather would have been there, it would have been the same story, but I watched Ted. He's a brilliant guy. He knows TV so well and he has, at this point in his career, such credibility and authority that he doesn't need to do a thing by way of cheap TV devices that help amp a story. He doesn't need to do anything other than very simply point a camera and share his observations of what's going on. It sounds a little quaint, doesn't it—a little old-fashioned—but he imbues it with such credibility and gravitas. It's also very simple stuff. Very simple. He's cool as could be; he's done this for forty years, and I'm a believer that there's no substitute for experience. He's not one of these young people trying to catch lightning in a bottle and have the right haircut and make sure that his chem suit is tailored just so. He's a giant in every way and he was such a mensch, a real decent human being.

Look, in the history of television news, anybody who's anybody has some sort of combat experience. You look at the giants, you look at a Rather, you look at a Peter Jennings, you look at Morley Safer, Ed Bradley—these are guys who all made their reputations covering war. Morley did some of the best reporting ever on television during Vietnam. It's clear to anybody who's trying to make a career for oneself what war can mean. But it's foolish to try to think of anything other than getting your story. Otherwise you're inviting trouble, because you're concentrating on something other than the immediate task at hand, which in a war zone can get you killed. It can contaminate your thinking, and that's not good. I looked at this war as a marathon and not a sprint. And I'm not a good sprinter. Long-term success is built on a long-term view and it's repetition; it's many years of offering people quality journalism as opposed to being flavor of the month. This gets back to guys like Koppel and Rather, who've offered the public levelheaded, rational reporting for forty years, which is a lot different from trying to parlay a leather jacket and a hit name into some kind of rocket success.

I had about three or four really frightening experiences in the war. I still haven't processed one of these incidents. When I tell the story, it might sound a little bit humorous, but I can only say how frightening it was to be in the middle of it. First, let me say up front, I do not come from a long line of brave people. When we got to the Euphrates it was my sense that the Iraqis knew the gig was up. They had heavily fortified a number of positions at the Euphrates. It was the fiercest fighting we had seen. There's lots of Iraqi mortar and artillery and it looks like something out of *Apocalypse Now*. Apache attack helicopters are coming through these palm trees. The area here looks so much different than the desert; it even looked like Vietnam. We're in so close, the Iraqi's mortars going over our heads. I'm asking my satellite technician Geof, "What are we going to do? What are we going to do?" And Geof is saying, "Well, I think we can get the dish up." He thought I was asking him how were we going to broadcast. I just wanted to bail out of there, to save our lives! So he pops up the dish and we do this live shot, which was incredible. It was live broadcasting from the front. Well, we pack up and we get in our Humvee and the military officer says, "Look, here's what you're going to do. You've got to go across this bridge and when you get close, you gun it and you'll get across. They're close, but their weapons aren't precise and they're not the best shots in the world. Keep moving, you'll be okay."

There were three of us in the Humvee. Our driver was Geof, Mario's in the passenger seat taking pictures, and I'm in the back. We get halfway over this bridge and the car dies. Battery quits. Nothing. Dead. The Humvee is now stalled exactly halfway across this bridge, while all of this fighting is going on. Artillery is flying over our heads. Mortars are flying over our heads. There are AK47 bullets flying over our heads and we're just sitting there. I'm thinking, "I don't know what my wife is going to tell my kids was so damn important that Daddy had to leave." Because, you know, that's it. We were under fire. We couldn't get out of the car. What we were we going to do? Our good friends at ABC saw what was happening and they drove right up behind us and pushed us across the bridge. So we're fond of saying that we were the first western television crew to cross the Euphrates with our competition right on our tail. But that's only because they were pushing us. We were never so happy to have ABC there behind us!

Getting to Baghdad International Airport was another nerve-wracking experience. We got there the night before and we couldn't get into the airport proper until early the next morning. There was a lot of artillery and mortar being exchanged. The "airport" is really a forty-square-mile area, so you're talking about a lot of terrain that is very hilly, muddy, lots of places for Iraqi soldiers to hide. As we neared the airport, a lot of active gun battles were going on. We saw many Iraqis surrendering. It was one of the first chances to see the state of the Iraqi army, but it wasn't like you could pull up to the tarmac and crack open a bottle of champagne. It took several hours to get the tarmac under control, and every time they'd open a hangar we didn't know if they were going to find a bunch of Iraqis. There was a point, however, in the morning when it became clear that the U.S. Army had taken about ninety, ninety-five percent of the airport, and the whole feel of the operation began to change. In the space of twelve hours, the airport had fallen, so it became clear that if this was a key, critical target that the Iraqis wanted to protect, they certainly were unable to muster a significant defense.

As part of the First Brigade combat team, I had an opportunity to document most of the killing, but most of the shelling was done long-distance by multiple-launch rocket systems. These guns could fire several miles and by the next morning, the combat brigade might be on the move, so it was not the kind of combat that was being done in close hand-to-hand situations. There was never any opportunity, or attempt to limit the pictures we took and fed to New York or to London. If we found bodies we would photograph them. But a lot of the killing was done out of camera's range. One exception, early on, was when we were taken to see a village while it was in the process of being cleared. Kiffl was a small village near Najaf, and there were some very intense gun battles. I saw maybe a dozen, fifteen bodies in the streets and on a bridge. I saw a couple of burned bodies, just a rib cage. I wrote the script, and referenced bodies in it, while highlighting an unusual find that I came across: a barber shop with a poster of New York City and the World Trade Center towers. Mario took many pictures of bodies and the barber shop and we fed those images to London, but I never saw the final report. I don't know what was cut and what wasn't.

We stayed at the Baghdad Airport for about a week. Then we went into the city to do a story about a particular company that lost two of its platoon sergeants within forty-eight hours. My brigade at that point was primarily responsible for airport security. After Baghdad fell, the focus of the story had shifted somewhat to the things that were going on in the city itself. We had other correspondents who were in better positions and, again, my assignment was to follow this one brigade, which was not as actively involved. We left Iraq with Koppel, who had gotten his crew on a C-17 U.S. Air Force transport plane. They knew we were trying to get out and he arranged to have us added to the manifest. Plus we were exhausted—just exhausted. The last week, Geof had left because his wife was having a baby. Mario and I were working around the clock. Mario was fixing a car, fixing a satellite dish, fixing video equipment. It was the most exhausting four or five days of my career—of my life, really. We were living in an Iraqi Airways luggage container. It's made of metal and it's about a four-foot-by-six-foot-by-five-foot semicircular piece of metal that they stuff full of suitcases, and then a forklift will pick the whole thing up and put it onto a plane. We were living in one of those in the middle of a parking lot at the Baghdad Airport. We hadn't eaten really well or slept well or bathed at all for the better part of a month. I just wanted to get to the hotel and sit in the tub.

DODGING DEATH

Voice of America's East Africa
Bureau Chief Alisha Ryu

"I played with GI Joe dolls when I was a kid."

Voice of America radio correspondent Alisha Ryu's regular foreign news beat is covering African wars. She's unfazed by mortars, AK47 rounds, the cordite-infused smell of battle, or life-threatening taunts by dictators like Khadaffi, who once accused her of being a CIA spy. Her VOA listeners represent a vast global polyglot of tongues and cultures, where fighting has been going on for years. "My audience is in China, Pakistan, Afghanistan, and Nigeria," says the unmarried forty-one-year-old reporter. "Very diverse. My audience doesn't care about the grunts and their stories. They care about the big picture. But we're not a propaganda wing for the U.S. and it really irks me when I hear that.

"Sixty some odd years ago, VOA was founded to counter Soviet propaganda. Today we are constantly battling State Department for more freedom and evenhanded coverage. VOA was the only organization that got an interview with Mullah Omar in Afghanistan. William Safire of *The New York Times* went bananas. He said, 'This is not Voice of the Taliban. This is Voice of America. How dare you use taxpayers' money to go do this?' We were not simply doing an interview with Mullah Omar. We were doing a broad-based piece about how the war in Afghanistan was going." That same unwavering conviction to be a stoic and impartial war observer brought Ryu to Kuwait and Iraq.

■ ■ ■

My father is Korean. My mother is Tahitian, but I don't know much about my mother actually. They split when I was quite young. I lived for the first seven years of my life in Seoul. My father was a businessman. He had a very interesting life. My grandfather was a Pentagon liaison for the Korean government. So I grew up among a lot of the U.S. military guys who used to come and visit us. My father was a huge WWII fan. I played with GI Joe dolls when I was a kid. I later grew up in Falls Church, Virginia. Then I moved out to Los Angeles for high school, and then went to UCLA, and USC for graduate work. I studied international relations. I've been doing international conflict news coverage since 1991 as a television reporter. I worked for NBC News, Reuters, CNBC Hong Kong, and contributed to reports for MSNBC.

As the East Africa Bureau Chief of *Voice of America*, I am based in Nairobi, Kenya. When I am not doing this I am covering civil wars in Africa. Nigeria is out of my jurisdiction. But I have Congo, Sudan, Somalia, Uganda, Burundi, Rwanda, Ethiopia, Eritrea, Djibouti.

I embedded with the Twelfth Aviation Brigade of Fifth Corps. These are the Black Hawk and the Chinook units. Originally I was embedded with the Second Brigade of the Third Infantry Division in Kuwait in December. I was out in the desert for a very long time. I was sleeping on top of M1 tanks every night. I was freezing. After that experience, I said to myself, I'm not quite sure if I want to do this again. I don't like the tanks. I get claustrophobic. Having to travel all the way to Baghdad in a tank just did not appeal to me, and it was cramped, really cramped. I was in an M1 all week doing live-fire exercises. They were firing all this ordnance. I was going deaf and I was incredibly un-comfortable. "I now know how they live," I said to myself. I wondered if there was an easier way to get up north. When the Twelfth Aviation Brigade slot opened up, I jumped at it.

The Twelfth Aviation Brigade, which also has Apaches, was attached to the Eleventh Aviation Regiment. Initially I thought that I would be hop-scotching across the battlefield and I would be able to see what was happen-ing on the ground from the air. What happened instead was the weather in Iraq just became terrible. The dust storms came in and visibility was awful. It grounded these aircraft for quite a long time. For a lot of the war, they weren't able to fly. The war began and I realized I just had to get up north. So, I went finally on the first mission the Chinooks had, to take some bridg-ing assets for the engineers up near Najaf. The crew had asked me, "What do you want to do?" I said, "I just need to get up north. Just drop me off any-where that you need to." So they said, "Well, okay," and they did. I was on the lead bird going up and we took small-arms fire. Sometimes it sounded like a pinging, sometimes like a popping—depending on what they were shooting. The outer shells of those choppers are not very thick. An RPG would have come through. They were missing us for the most part, but you could hear them whizzing past since we were slingloading, which meant the bird was open. I was sitting right next to the open hatch. I didn't have a helmet. I was sitting on my flak vest.

They literally dropped me off in the middle of the desert. And then the birds took off. They were going back to Kuwait to get more bridging material. I was alone. I wanted to say, "Hello. Is anybody here?" Then from a far off distance I saw a U.S. soldier walking toward me. He had his gun at the ready. He came up to me and said, "Do you know where you are?" And I said, "I hope this is Objective so-and-so." And he said. "Welcome to Iraq." I said, "Thanks." He had thought I was some general coming in on a Chinook for a surprise inspection. So they didn't know who it was coming in off the Chinook.

Anyway, my chopper that was going back to Kuwait got hit by an RPG round right where I was sitting. It took an RPG straight from the floor to the ceiling. Had I stayed on the chopper, I would have been killed. Nobody was injured, because the RPG went straight up the entryway. Those three choppers had to sit on the ground for three days, and they had to call in a Bradley company. That was the one that Brian Williams of NBC News was on the ground with.

This kind of thing always surprises me. In Afghanistan, I had a similar experience where I was coming back from a town called Faizabad to another town called Khujabaudhin. I was with my interpreter and my driver. We had driven up with a CNN crew to drop them off. They were going down to Pansheer Valley. I wanted to go to Faizabad because I wanted to see what the area looked like and talk to some of the people and observe the humanitarian aid that was coming in at the time. We were coming back. We were driving this little Russian Jeep on this narrow winding mountain road. Hairpin turns. Curvy roads with sheer cliffs on the bottom and ledges on the top. There was not enough road for my Jeep and this man and a donkey to pass, so I told my driver to stop and let the man and the donkey go first. So they passed by. They made the hairpin turn, and when a sufficient amount of time passed, I said, "Okay. Let's go." Just as we made the turn, there was this incredible explosion. Our front windshield went out. The donkey had stepped on a land mine. What happened was that a heavy rainfall the night before had dislodged an antitank mine and it had slipped down the slope. It was planted there in the eighties when the Soviets were there. When the donkey stepped on the mine, it got splattered all across the side of the wall and the old man was blown off the cliff. Had the donkey and the old man not been there, our Jeep would have run over it.

This has happened to me several times. I keep wondering: why is it some people who have everything going for them, their time is up? We lost a very good friend of ours, Michael Kelly, and yet, there's me, who should have been killed about nine lives ago, and I'm still alive. I don't understand it.

Maybe part of it is that I'm an extreme adrenaline junkie. You have to be a little bit in this business, unless you are so immersed in the military side that this is all you know. But I don't always do military. I cover low-level intensity conflicts such as urban guerrilla warfare. It's not all those big conventional wars that I cover. So if you are going to do this full-time, you really have to be an adrenaline junkie. You better love it or you're not gonna last. My father passed away in '96. I don't have a family, so it's actually very good for me, in this sense: I can do this without having a whole lot of people worried about me.

I am not existentialist by any stretch of the imagination, but what makes it fascinating for me is why people behave the way they do. In Africa I have watched hands being chopped off. I've watched a man being roasted alive, and his heart eaten. There is so much brutality that I saw that after a while I became numb to it. It is terrible to say. But it's true. I now have almost no re-action when I see dead bodies. It's really weird.

If you cover the wars in Africa, the genesis of these conflicts lies a hundred, two hundred, a thousand years in the past, and it is still continuing. There is an historic reason beyond everything. I really do sort of enjoy this history and the evolution of how people are now reacting to something that happened so long ago. Instinctively and intuitively, they behave exactly the same way that they did hundreds of years ago. They have learned absolutely nothing. History has such a huge grip on these people no matter how technological they become. They just can't shake it. I find that fascinating.

Democracy will fail when you don't have a base for it, or you don't have a culture for it, or when you don't have a tradition for it. It's not like you can have a tabula rasa and just say, "Okay, slate's clean. Everyone start over and be a democratic nation." No! Because they are bringing in hundreds of years of baggage with them. That's the problem. For this noble idea of democracy in Iraq to work, people will have to change their tribal instincts formed over centuries. Americans should take a serious look at what happened with Lebanon and its warring factions. Power has to be shared. It's the only way democracy can work and the only way they can enjoy peace. There are few examples of democratic governments. Shiites spend five minutes to say, "Thanks for getting rid of this Saddam monster. Now please get out!"

DOING GOOD DEEDS
WITH THE DEVIL DOCS

CNN and *Time* Medical
Correspondent Dr. Sanjay Gupta

> "You're wearing your Kevlar vest underneath
> your operating gown because you think you
> might get shot."

Neurosurgery is one of the most specialized fields in medicine. It requires superhuman nerves of steel to perform even the simplest of medical procedures. It's a career calling for the most demanding of doctors. Dr. Sanjay Gupta is a member of the staff of the neurosurgery department at Emory University's school of medicine in Atlanta. That's his day job. He's also CNN's medical correspondent. He went to Kuwait and Iraq to report on battlefield injuries for both CNN and *Time*, with his primary focus on the heroic exploits of a group of navy doctors known as Devil Docs.

As was often the case in this war, the individual sent on assignment to cover the conflict becomes a minor story himself. Gupta tried to save the life of a two-year-old child with a severe head injury. U.S. Marines at a checkpoint south of Baghdad had fired on a taxi when it didn't stop. One of the passengers was the child. Gupta performed emergency surgery on the child but it was too late. Another civilian casualty. Some media critics questioned Gupta's actions since a journalistic ethical divide has been breached between observer (reporter) and participant (physician). But in an interview with the *Detroit Free Press*—he grew up in Livonia, Michigan and nearby Novi, where his parents, both retired Ford engineers, live—Gupta batted away such criticism since he felt that he was "medically and morally obligated" to help. "They don't have any neurosurgeons, really," he said of the unit he was covering. "They'd talked to me before, sort of hypothetically: Would I help out?" Well, he did. The good doctor's medical expertise centers on the head, but his actions speak from the heart.

■ ■ ■

Devil Docs is a colloquial name for navy health care people and includes doctors, nurses, medics, and anybody associated with the medical care on the field. This navy group actually supports the Marines. Their name comes from the fact that the Marines were called the Devil's Dogs after a particularly fierce battle years ago. There are about a thousand Devil Docs in the battlefield.

Everyone always talks about $M^*A^*S^*H$—and who knows if there's ever going to be a television series about the Devil Docs—but I will tell you this. It is fascinating what they do. A lot of what we learn in medicine comes about as the result of wartime. People, resources, and techniques are pushed to the envelope, and that's why I think part of the reason that $M^*A^*S^*H$ was so interesting was what people could do in the middle of Korea. With Devil Docs we saw a lot of the same thing. But who knows if anything more entertainment-wise will come out of that?

We knew—from a medical standpoint—this was probably going to be a different sort of war. There was this imminent threat of chemical and biological weapons and as part of the medical care and triage, all these docs, nurses, and everybody had to be quite adept at recognizing chemical and biological symptoms, and then be able to treat it. The second thing was the mobile surgical unit. These mobile operating rooms are called Forward Resuscitative Surgical Systems (FRSS). There are forty-four members for each of these particular teams. Now, in addition to these units, there are three surgical companies: Alpha, Bravo, and Charlie. They're much larger surgical teams, with 259 members each. They also move, but they don't move nearly as quickly or efficiently as the FRSS's do. When I went out to Kuwait in early February, I said, "I want to see this thing in action, if it comes to that," since this was the first time that FRSS was going to be used in a conflict like this. At that time, obviously, we didn't know if the war was even going to take place, but that was one of the goals.

In this war, the operating room was totally mobile. When people think of operating rooms, they typically think of a pristine room in the middle of a hospital that's stationary, with all the resources they need close by. Here, the operating room was completely mobile. It could be broken down and then set back up all within two hours. Perhaps one day we'll see something like FRSS as part of medical care in the United States—to actually move mobile operating rooms to sites of disasters like Oklahoma City or Waco. From this war, we've learned that operating rooms can be mobile. We saw that work. We saw patients get good care and lives saved.

These mobile operating rooms can function in the austere conditions of Iraq, in the middle of this desert; sand blowing everywhere; dirt, grime; hot, up to 120 degrees some days; and yet they're still able to do surgical operations in the middle of the battlefield. It's an unpredictable situation and oftentimes you're wearing your Kevlar vest underneath your operating gown because you think you might get shot, or at least you worry about that as well.

I don't think anybody can really fully understand how bad these sandstorms are until you go through it. It's just interminable sand; it just gets everywhere—in your eyes, in your nose, in your ears—and it doesn't melt like snow might melt, it just stays there. It's not the nice granular sand that you might find at the beach, it's cutting, jagged, hurtful sand that cuts your face and dries your skin. Your goggles barely work because the sand is so fine that it gets even between the layer of the goggles and your skin.

The operating rooms were specifically designed to be able to tolerate this environment; there were zippered layers of tents so you'd walk in one layer, zip it behind you, and walk in the next layer, zip it up behind you, and that's how they kept stuff out. They had floors on the tent to try and keep the sand from rising up as well. The heat was very debilitating. One of the guys actually mentioned to me that he almost passed out once during the operation because it was so hot and he was getting so dehydrated.

The objective of a mobile surgical unit really was to take care of people who would otherwise die if they didn't get back to Kuwait City fast enough. The whole reason to move healthcare—in this case, operating rooms—forward was to try and provide a station that's very close to the front lines where people can get their operations very quickly—people who would have otherwise died. These docs weren't treating more common ailments of those who were too sick to be on the battlefield, but could travel to Kuwait, or even to Germany. We were seeing people who had very dramatic injuries. Closer to the end of the conflict, eighty percent were Iraqi soldiers. In the first Gulf War, the numbers were very similar in terms of eighty percent of the patients that were being treated at that point were Iraqis. The Devil Docs—and really the entire medical campaign—knew that the majority of the people they were going to be treating were going to be the enemy. These guys were totally prepared for it. They did not hesitate. They took certain precautions. Most of them did carry their sidearms. Sometimes if it was just logistically unfeasible for them to operate and carry their sidearm, they'd take it off and have it close by. These particular patient/prisoners—the Iraqis—were also stripped to make sure they didn't have any grenades on them or were concealing a weapon. After all that process took place, they were treated like anybody else.

The patients showed amazing gratitude. At first when they came in, they really didn't have a clear idea where they were being taken or why they were being taken there. Sometimes you could see by their expression or by their body language that they thought that maybe they were going to be treated as prisoners and tortured, but as soon as they figured out that the people who were there were doctors wanting to take care of them and they understood that, they oftentimes would kiss the surgeon's hands, they would say thank you the best they could. You could tell that they were very grateful for the care that they had received.

The people coming in were often very, very sick. Because it was a surgical unit dealing with battle wounds, it wasn't taking care of cholera and things like that. Sometimes if someone were so dramatically ill that they needed to get an IV just to get hydrated, they would receive that, but that was very rare.

There are two ways to think about triage here. Medical triage refers to the fact that patients who are most likely to benefit from an operation should go first. That doesn't mean that the sickest patients go first; it means the patient who is most likely to benefit. Someone could be a lot sicker, but the doctors have to make a judgment: "He's too far gone. We should expend our resources on this patient, who we could save, salvage, and possibly do some good." If there were an Iraqi and a Marine sitting there and the Marine just was going to die and there was nothing these docs could do for the Marine, but there was a chance to save the Iraqi, they would operate on the Iraqi. In reality there was no political triage. If Iraqis came in, they got the care just as quickly—except for the security precautions—and without hesitation as anybody else.

There were no neurosurgeons at the Forward Resuscitative Surgical Systems. These doctors knew that I was a neurosurgeon, and therefore they asked me to evaluate several patients and, in those cases, operate. I worked on five individuals. All of them were gunshot or had significant shrapnel wounds to the head. They were all in what's known as an expectant condition, meaning that they weren't expected to be able to survive a three-hour flight back to Kuwait City. That's why they were brought there to the FRSS. When you have a big blood clot within the brain because of shrapnel or a bullet wound, it exerts a lot of pressure on very vital areas of the brain. That pressure must be removed or the patient will die, so you have to basically remove the blood clot. Oftentimes, you remove the bullet or shrapnel in order to try and save the life.

We knew that four had survived at the time that I left Iraq. There were three Iraqis and two Marines. One Iraqi died. The two Marines I know are both living. I know that at the time I left Iraq, the two Iraqis were both still living, but I have not been able to follow up from here in the U.S on them. With head trauma, it takes a long time, up to eighteen months, to recover. I'm sure that both Marines are going to have some neurological deficits, but hopefully, they'll be relatively minor.

If you're presented with an opportunity—or are asked, in this case—to perform an operation that could potentially save somebody's life, then you put down your pen and paper, you put down your camera, and you do it. In this case, I had a unique skill set and happened to be in a particular location where that skill set was needed. But I think that most of the journalists and my colleagues here at CNN that I'd spoken with, if they came upon a burning building or a burning car and they had the chance—instead of taking pictures—to actually rescue somebody out of that, I think and I hope they would all do that. The people who I've talked to have. It's not even a question really. It's just common sense, and that's sort of how I felt about it. Yes, there was criticism. Yes, there was a question of journalistic integrity. Yes, there was a question that I crossed the line. My opinion was that crossing the line would have been *not* doing something.

The Devil Docs' job out there was medical triage, not political triage. If they asked me to take care of a human being who had been shot and they thought that I was the only person in the particular unit who could do it, then I would feel medically and morally that that would be the right thing to do. As far as how one of the members of the deck of cards or how Saddam Hussein himself would be taken care of or treated afterwards from a political, military, legal standpoint, is really up to people who aren't me.

My medical preparations were no different from anybody else. For my personal safety, I went through something called War Zone Training, which is something that CNN appropriately requires of its journalists when they go out into a war zone. The infectious disease department at my hospital here knew the particular diseases that are particularly prevalent—such as typhoid—in southern Iraq and Kuwait during that time of year, so I got my shots. I took along some medication for malaria, which I did not need to take. I also had some medications for anthrax, which I also did not need to take.

I wasn't that concerned about Gulf War Syndrome. It exists, and appears to have been something that was caused by an exposure in the Gulf War. It's one of the most studied, most heavily-funded research projects in the history of the military, but they haven't come up with anything. They can't pin this down on any particular thing. So I used common sense. I didn't do anything dumb. I didn't try to expose myself to anything unnecessarily. You can read lots of different studies about people swearing that an anthrax inoculation caused Gulf War Syndrome. Some people believe that all the depleted uranium sites caused that. Although, interestingly, there was a study that actually looked at Kuwaiti kids who climbed all over these uranium deposits; they didn't know what it was. Twelve years later now, they went back and looked at that population versus the population of people who did not expose themselves to uranium, and they really have found no difference, amazingly. It's just twelve years, but still that's a fairly long time.

We were concerned about chemical and biological weapons all the way up until the final day, because each step along the way we thought, "Okay, this is going to be Basra. It's for sure going to Nasiriyah, where they have the chemical and biological weapons." Then, when none of that panned out, we thought, "For sure, Baghdad. They're saving their chemical and biological weapons for Baghdad," but until we got the final all clear saying, "You can reduce your alert level," certainly everyone was concerned about it.

I was in Iraq and Kuwait for a total of six weeks. Two weeks the first time and then four weeks the second. I was remarkably healthy considering some of the conditions out there.

GROUNDHOG'S DAY AT CENTCOM'S MEDIA CENTER

New York Magazine
Media Critic Michael Wolff

> "If there was a lot of information, that would
> have been interesting to me. If there was no
> information, that was also interesting to me."

It was a verbal shot heard around the world. Squirming against the tedium of daily briefings at CENTCOM's media center in Doha, Qatar, *New York Magazine's* media critic and Grand Pontificator Michael Wolff posed a rapid-fire series of questions to the main attraction at the podium: General Vincent Brooks. "I mean no disrespect, but what is the value proposition? Why are we here? Why should we stay? What's the value of what we're learning at this million-dollar press center?" His queries stunned the otherwise unflappable Brooks with their simple out-of-the-box audacity. The telegenic one-star general—West Point's top-ranked graduate from the class of 1980—barked back "[You] are here on your volition and if [isn't] satisfactory to [you], then go home."

In a confessional aside to his readers, Wolff later admitted that his questions were the kind "to sour the dinner party," but he still believed they were warranted given the circumstances. "Other than the pretense of a news conference—the news conference as backdrop and dateline—what did we get for having come all this way? What information could we get here that we could not have gotten in Washington or New York, what access to what essential person was being proffered? And why was everything so bloodless?" As word of Wolff's questions in Qatar reached the talk-show bullhorns on the right, the reaction was swift and predictable since they smelled blood—liberal, anti-American blood! Rush Limbaugh branded Wolff a "potential traitor" for his CENTCOM contretemps. In that media nanosecond, Wolff conceded he had gone from being a reporter whose "job was not to cover the war but to cover the news conference about the war" to being the story himself. CNN interviewed him. Three thousand Rush-inspired "hate" e-mails clogged his in-box. And the weekly columnist's response to this newfound fame? "I was staying at the Marriott in Doha, but then switched to the Ritz because I was getting so much hate mail that I needed a faster Internet connection."

■ ■ ■

The profoundly interesting thing about Doha is that nothing happened. You would get up in the morning and head out to this place and you would repeat exactly the same motion from day to day to day. It was just kind of a weird existence because we were so far from the news. There was nothing there. I have never been in a situation where there were so many reporters so far from anything that was happening. We were trapped in these kinds of particular subsets. First, everybody there, at that point in time, was trapped in Qatar because we couldn't get visas to Kuwait, and we obviously couldn't get into Iraq at that point. So everybody's stuck inside of Qatar, then everybody is stuck inside the media center, which in turn is stuck inside of this very strange military base, which you can't get into either. Even the base itself is stuck inside of the desert. It's clearly placed somewhere where it will be as unobtrusive as possible. Then you're further stuck in your hotel of choice. There was an odd series of these almost existential challenges. Every place you went, you would say, "Why am I here? What am I doing here? Can I ever escape?" You would begin to have these conversations with yourself, and then you find out that everyone else is having exactly the same conversations, and so then you begin to have them with each other. That's actually the point at which this wildly insane, weird experience became a fun experience, even reassuring. Then this other thing happens in which you were not only talking to other reporters, but they were interviewing you, so the way we passed the time was that we interviewed each other. Then you would just complain, of course.

As for the answer to "Why am I here? What am I doing? Who am I?", it was because "I am a war reporter. That's why I'm here. That's why we're all here." But it would be impossible to be farther from this war. We didn't really feel we were among the soldiers. We were really cut off. There was this military base that was there and it was behind this fence and we assumed that a lot of soldiers were there, but I couldn't be certain. I certainly couldn't see them. Within the media center, there was a handful of press attaché officers and enlisted people wearing this odd camouflage gear. They didn't particularly seem like soldiers, they were just people walking around in these odd uniforms. So there was a real pretend feeling. I mean, they're carrying gas masks, but you know it was all pretend.

One of the interesting things is that we had all these reports of how much money the Pentagon had spent for this press center, and then we got to this place and it really didn't look like anyone had spent any money. There were four plasma screens. Originally there were seven, but somebody said it looks too much like *Who Wants To Be A Millionaire?*

The cameras were almost at all times focused on the briefer, and that's the message that was sent out to the morning shows in the U.S. The press center could have been in Florida, which is where CENTCOM is based, but I suppose from General Tommy Franks's point of view, it would have been unacceptable for him to be in Florida, although technically speaking, it would not have made a difference. Unlike Afghanistan, this was a significantly larger mission and there was also the inevitable comparison between this war and the first Gulf War. Obviously one of the things on their minds was the Schwarzkopf factor. Everybody in Doha was expecting that there was going to be a star here, and we assumed that that star would be Franks and that we would be as close to the guy running this theater as the reporters in the first Gulf War were close to Schwarzkopf, who was a star. He was great. He made great television. I'm sure he gave no more information than we got this time around, but the difference now—and it's an important difference—is that even when you're not getting information from the guy who has the information to give, you're still getting information by the very fact that he's not giving it to you. Brooks was obviously just a messenger; he was just saying what he was told to say, so there was no way you could measure the quality of that. He was not making the decision not to tell us something. There was no reading him and he was basically expressionless for a reason: He knew nothing. He's a junior general officer. In terms of being relatively unflappable, he did a pretty good job. Beyond that, he didn't do a very special job because there wasn't much of a job to do; he had been briefed as the briefer according to the daily script, then he went out and told the reporters that. The Bush Administration didn't want someone to upstage Rumsfeld, or to have another Schwarzkopf and become another power that had to be managed.

I had traveled to Doha without expectation because I had nothing to base my expectations upon. I was looking to get as close to the process of whatever information was being given out, if it was possible to get. I was in a win-win situation. If there was a lot of information, that would have been interesting to me; if there was no information, that was also interesting to me. I'm not particularly interested in the logistics of war. I'm not particularly interested in guns, and I'm not particularly interested in transportation, which is essentially what you're reporting on in that situation. To be interested in that, you really have to be functioning on a very granular level. To me, being an embed sounded like an incredibly claustrophobic thing. You're really trapped. Especially if you're inside a Bradley as some of these people were. Or the tanks—worse.

Obviously, to be able to cover the war from the ground in real time was new. The problem with that, of course, is that there was not any real information. The focus was almost an old-fashioned thing. It went back to the way the Second World War was covered, and it became very much about battles and the logistics and very divorced from any kind of political context. We went back to this Good War sensibility.

I had an unfair advantage in that I was not there in Doha covering the war. I had a certain amount of cover and my cover was uncovering the media. I was able to talk about things that were really not in the purview of so many other reporters to talk about. They couldn't talk about the process of reporting, the form of reality itself, and because they couldn't, they didn't. I was fortunate enough—and in this great position—to be able to do that. I was effectively saying, "It's not the news, it's the media. News is not the news; the media is the news." But the truth is that you go into the situation and you are really hamstrung. When your country goes to war—I'm not sure it's true in every country—you are obliged, at least in the initial phase, to shut up about it and get with the program. Now this can degrade, of course, when expectations are not met. When countries go to war, the stakes are very high and there's most often an enormous determination and a specific campaign to get people to see this the way you want them to see it, and that has an effect. But because these wars are so short, the idea that this is going to play out and that you're going to get the other side doesn't happen. All you get is this kind of initial rah-rah side. We begin with this sense of "We're all on the same side. We support our President in a time of war and there are American lives at stake." There is this built-in bias. Okay, let's just accept that. Then the issue becomes how to overcome that bias. So now there are two things that are going to reinforce that bias. Number one, if we win, if the news is at least from the military side, that's good news. Number two, if it's over very quickly, well then it becomes the story that's over. No one's interested anymore.

Let's look at the fundamentals of what people are really interested in. Let's look at this from a media point of view, which is bottom line—what holds the interest of your audience? What does your audience want to know? There's no evidence whatsoever that Americans are interested in things that happen outside of America. Quite the opposite. There's an enormous body of evidence that says we are not interested at all. We don't know anything about it; we don't have a background in it; we don't have a context for it; and we don't get anything out of it. It's just somewhere else, and on top of that, maybe there's good reason. This is an incredibly large, rich, exciting, overwhelming country and there's just only so many things that you can think about. We are the world, and in some ways that is quite literally—from a mind-share point of view—true. The suitcase is full. You can't force anything else into it.

Interest in the war itself was not that great, to be perfectly honest. There was a lot of media coverage, and in part that's obligatory coverage. Fox and CNN were speaking to very small audiences. Everybody does what they feel they have to do from an obligatory standpoint, but as soon as the interest goes, the networks, believe me, would just as soon not have anything to do on this. From an advertising and marketing standpoint, war doesn't make people want to buy stuff. Media buyers will tell you, "We're going to pull our schedule as soon as the bombs start to fall. We don't want to be around that stuff. Why would we?" Not only is war a downer, but people aren't really watching. The network guys know that war doesn't especially get great ratings.

In business terms, the CNN of this war turned out to be Al Jazeera. This was their great leap in credibility and in brand recognition. I assume that their audience has vastly expanded, and in many ways they became the real voice of this war, definitely. In the U.S. it was Fox News, yes. And I say this with some reservation. Fox did not become CNN through this war. Fox did not really increase its credibility during this war; actually, the opposite may have happened.

When Fox said I was a "traitor," did they really think I was a traitor? No, they don't really care. They're doing their thing. It's all about taking sides and in a sense, it's all about conflict, and we have fun in conflict. Good television is made out of conflict. The interesting Fox subtext is that you have two factors going on here—you have ideology and you have good television. They're playing the entertainment card. Even for Rush, it is fun and games. It's entertainment. That's what he understands. That's what Fox understands. I'm not sure any careers are ruined. I might argue the opposite, that in fact, careers are enhanced by this. That everybody is in this media loop together and it benefits everyone. In my own case, was this good or bad for me? Well, I can tell you that it's good for me. I'm all over the television. My magazine thinks it's wonderful press. My personal brand goes universal, goes international, though it's a little distressing to get all this e-mail and think, "Oh, my God, these people really don't like me." But in truth, it's money in the bank. I go to a restaurant called Michael's every day and yes, I'm a local hero!

"MY MARINES"

Orange County Register
Columnist Gordon Dillow

> "I finally got tired of carrying the hand
> grenade and I gave it back to him. I couldn't
> hold the thing and write at the same time."

A Marine and his rifle are inseparable. Like newlyweds. A Marine and his pack shovel are a marriage gone bad with regular alimony checks due. In Iraq, these lightweight, folding tools were used to dig fighting holes in the desert sand. But why were fighting holes necessary since America enjoyed such overwhelming firepower? For an answer, we turn to *Orange County Register* embedded reporter Gordon Dillow with Alpha Company, First Battalion, Fifth Marine Regiment, who explained the whole truth about these holes in his March 30 column called "Stolen Sleep."

> *"We're expecting an attack tonight, gents," Capt. Blair Sokol, thirty, of San Clemente, the commanding officer of Alpha Company, announces as the sun goes down. An enemy force has reportedly been spotted a little to the east, and a mortar or tank attack could be coming. So the men grab their folding shovels out of their packs and start burrowing into the soft, wet ground beside the highway that leads north. The quiet night is filled with the scraping of shovels and the tiny thuds of falling dirt.*
>
> *For the Marine infantrymen of Alpha Company, this is routine. They're used to living not just on the ground, but in it. They are experts at digging holes. They don't call them 'foxholes'—that, the Marines say dismissively, is an Army term, one that implies you're a frightened animal, hiding from the hounds. Instead, Marines call their holes "fighting holes" or "skirmish holes." Tonight, Alpha Company will dig skirmish holes.*

Fighting holes are deep, to shoulder height, and the standard measure is one M-16 rifle length by two M-16 lengths. Skirmish holes are simply depressions in the ground that protect Marines from horizontally flying shrapnel while they're sleeping or shooting. The recommended depth is just enough so that the prone body doesn't break the plane of the ground.

"Just make your hole shallow—grave depth," Lt. Nathan Shull, 25, of Minden, La., the executive officer of Alpha Company tells me and photographer Mark Avery—with morbid good humor—as we dig our own skirmish holes.

"The hole lets you sleep a little easier," says Navy Petty Officer 2nd Class Redor Rufo, 31, of San Diego, a battalion chaplain's assistant. "That's the thing you need most out here is sleep."

Like almost everyone else out here, the chaplain's assistant carries an M-16; in a firefight, his job is to be the chaplain's bodyguard. "He is protected by God," Rufo says. "But I'm just a little extra."

The holes dug, the Marines bed down inside them in their sleeping bags. The night is clear, with a billion stars overhead, and you can hear ducks in a nearby slough quacking. It is quiet, and for this little corner of the world, peaceful.

But the peace won't last long.

Dillow, fifty-two, is a newspaper wordsmith plucked from a bygone era when storytelling was appreciated as a much-neglected art form. During the Iraq War, Dillow churned out columns that whipped together the quotidian essence of Ernie Pyle (covering Marine grunts) with the black humor of Joseph Heller (wallowing in war's pleasurable absurdity). In the early '80s, Dillow worked the Central American civil-war beat for Hearst newspapers, and admits that he keeps finding himself gravitating towards writing about violent matters and crime. Dillow is also the co-author of a new book about Los Angeles bank robberies, *Where the Money Is*. (Now wouldn't that also be a splendid title for Saddam's memoir?)

■　　■　　■

I wrote the bank robbery book with a guy named Bill Rehder, who was an FBI Special Agent for thirty-three years. He was on the bank squad in L.A., until just a few years ago when he retired, and was involved to some degree or another with every bank robbery in L.A. during that time. He had a bunch of stories about strange bank robberies. We took a few of the best ones such as the North Hollywood robbery, and put them in a book. Your basic bank robber—it's sort of like a drug or a potato chip—can't just rob one. Once you rob one, even if you don't get caught, you're going to come back because it's pretty easy to do—to rob a bank once, twice, three times—eventually your luck runs out. Rehder became friends with one guy who was an interesting case. In the early eighties, he was an antiques dealer in West Hollywood, which is kind of a trendy area in L.A., who developed a heroin problem. He had a bunch of movie star clients and he led this secret life where he'd run the antiques store and then go out and rob banks to support his habit. His name was Eddie Dodson, known as The Yankee Bandit. He robbed more banks than anybody else in the history of the world. He robbed sixty-five before he got caught the first time. He goes away to prison, comes back, tries to go straight, and like I say, it's an addiction, got back on drugs again, and started robbing banks again.

The Gentleman Bandit—that's kind of a moniker—describes a number of different guys. It seems like anyone who's polite when they rob the bank, the FBI starts to call him The Gentleman Bandit. I don't know why that is. We had another from South Central who was a Fagan of bank robberies; he would get gang member wannabes—kids thirteen years old—to rob the banks for him. He had this whole network of kids robbing banks for him. Bank employees and managers are instructed to hand over the money. Since it's not your money, you cooperate. Actually, the companies that manufacture the dye packs pay a bonus to a teller. If a teller gets a dye pack in the stolen money, the company that makes the dye packs will pay three hundred bucks, four hundred bucks.

Even though my three-times-a-week *Register* column is strictly local, I can write about anything I want as long as the words "Orange" and "County" are somehow juxtaposed within the column. The process of my becoming an embedded reporter started last fall, when one of our editors at the paper got a call from the Marines saying, "We've got this new program to embed reporters. They would live, eat, sleep, travel, just be with a unit, and go wherever it went." So the editors put out the word, "Well, we're looking for somebody to do this." I thought, boy, I'd love to do it. I've written quite a bit about veterans' affairs and military stuff; guys who were in the service and that sort of thing. I didn't really cover Pendleton as a beat; I didn't have a connection with them, even though Pendleton is adjacent to Orange County. It's actually in San Diego County.

I was a U.S. Army sergeant in Vietnam in '71–'72, so the war was winding down; it was pretty much over. I was in an MP unit—Military Police. Mostly what we did was escort convoys up and down Highway 1. Vietnam was almost a mythical war to the grunts in Iraq. You've got to remember, these Marines, or most of them, are nineteen, twenty, twenty-one. They were born in the early years of the Reagan Administration. So for them Vietnam was something they heard about and everybody was aware of, but it didn't have much impact. For the Marines, Vietnam had the flavor of being the last—I hate to say "real war"—but the last kind of big war. It gets lumped together with Korea and World War II, and happened long before they were born. Some guys had been in the first Gulf War, and some had just missed it, but I don't think it had quite the impact on them that the stories of Vietnam or the stories of World War II had. They didn't seem to identify with it. The first Gulf War was a different kind of war. Plus, they didn't have the images that they're going to have out of this war because there was no media coverage.

The one movie that was mentioned to me time and time again—especially after we ran into something hot in Baghdad—was *Black Hawk Down*. Even though the movie was about the U.S. Army—and the Marines have a disparaging view about the Army—that's eternal, they've always been like that. It was the idea that, "Hey, this is like what we went through in this urban environment. Guys shooting RPGs at us, and this hostile population, and it was a close-in urban warfare kind of thing."

Marines pride themselves on being a much smaller service in terms of numbers. I think they total around 180,000, and they feel like they're the best. They're the elite. They have a different mission than the Army, which has a much bigger support base for logistics. While Marines look at some of the army elite units like the Rangers and the airborne guys with respect, there's a whole inter-service rivalry that says, "We're better than you are."

Marines call each other "Devil Dog." Sometimes it's just "Marine." If it's a guy they don't know, they'll say, "Hey, Marine." Same when they're wearing protective vests, which don't have a name on them and a lot of times you can't see the rank, either. So you'd see some guy and you know that he's an officer or at least a senior NCO, but you wouldn't know how to address him.

What Marines basically talk about is women. One problem with being a reporter for a newspaper is that you really can't capture what Marines are like.

I was a little concerned about this because I fell in love with these guys. I just really admired these young men; I thought they were tough and brave and just a great bunch of guys. But in a family newspaper, even when you're quoting them, you tend to make them sound more like choirboys than they really are. You're taking every "fuck" out and when you take out the word "fuck" from the Marine lexicon, you're reducing the words by like thirty percent. Every fucking word was fucking this or fucking that. It's the all-purpose modifier. It was things like "I wish I had a fucking shower." "I wish I had a fucking beer." "I wish I had a fucking MRE." That's just the way they talk—officers and men the same way. It's a construct that they use and in a way it gets poetical—the way they can string these "fucks" together. If some guy's saying, "I fucking told the fucking lieutenant that that fucking track was going to get caught in the fucking mud," it adds so much more emphasis and life than "I told the lieutenant that the track was going to get caught in the mud." But you can't put that in the family newspaper.

There were limits to what your editors were going to find sufficiently tasteful or acceptable for a newspaper-reading public. I refrained from describing dead Iraqis. It's the same way that TV news won't air certain images that are too graphic, even if there's a certain news value to them.

On the day after we crossed the border at about 9:00 A.M. on March 20th, our lieutenant got hit. I saw the guys that shot him get killed. Did it affect me? I gotta say, I was desperate to get a story. We were running up against deadlines. There's an eleven-hour time difference and this was in the morning, which meant it was getting late in the evening back home, and we wanted to get a story back and, in fact, in the first story I filed, I didn't even know that the lieutenant had been killed; I'd heard that there had been a medivac chopper called in, but it hadn't been announced that he was dead.

What happened is that after we went through the berm—actually it's two parallel berms that separate Kuwait and Iraq—we went to an oil-pumping station. We got there at about dawn on that first morning. There was supposed to be an Iraqi battalion that had been using it as a base, but most of them had apparently fled. The Marines were called in on an artillery strike on that position and killed quite a few Iraqis who were still there. We then rolled up in the tracks—amphibious assault vehicles. The way it works with Marine infantry is that they ride in these tracks and when they get to their objective, there's a ramp that goes down, and they pile out and deploy on foot. So they piled out of the tracks and started sweeping through this Iraqi position to check the bunkers and trenches and to see if there's anybody left. Most of the Iraqis they found just wanted to surrender, shouting, "We surrender. Don't shoot, don't shoot." A couple of them tried to get away. There was one guy who came roaring out of this underground bunker on a motorcycle—a motorcycle, of all things—and starts bouncing along the ground trying to get away, and the Marines opened up on him. They didn't kill him, but they wounded him and captured him. How much the Iraqis resisted was a little unclear. It was hard to tell who was shooting and how many shots were fired, but the strange thing was that Lieutenant Shane Childers was just standing by the side of a paved road when this civilian vehicle starts coming down the road. Nobody could figure out exactly what it was. "What's going here?" It was a white Toyota SUV and it pulls up next to the Marines and all of a sudden, a guy sticks an AK47 out and starts shooting and hits the Lieutenant in his stomach, just below his protective vest. He was alive for a few minutes. The corpsman came over and started working on him trying to save him, but all he said was, "I got shot in the gut," and then he died. As far as anybody knows, he was the first ground combat casualty of the war.

It was a shock to the Marines. They immediately lit up this vehicle with an unbelievable amount of firepower. The Marines' policy is—and I don't want this to sound worse than I intend it to be—if they take one round coming in, they're going to send a hundred rounds back. You totally overwhelm them. Somebody shoots at you, you just start sending rounds back, and that's what they did. They blew this vehicle apart. Amazingly, some of the guys in it survived, or at least they survived badly wounded. I don't know if they eventually made it through or not.

I wrote about how some of the guys seemed to revel in the combat adrenaline: "Hey, we're finally in this thing. We're doing what we're trained to do; we got some." The Marines have a phrase called "getting some," and it means getting some combat experience, but other guys were sobered by it. I remember talking to the young corpsman who tried to help Lieutenant Childers. I don't know if "traumatized" is the right word or not, but he was deeply affected by it. I mean, his job is to try to save people, and he couldn't save the Lieutenant, who he knew pretty well and was in his platoon. He told me later that he realized that he just hated war; he hated being in it; he hated everything about it.

On the day that Lieutenant Childers got killed, we were staying in the track and about fifty yards from us a Marine stepped on what they call a "toe popper"—a small mine—and it blew his boot off and seriously damaged his foot. Mark Abry took a picture of it and transmitted it to the *Register*. It was the first U.S. combat wounded in action photo that was shown. It wasn't that graphic as a photo, and yet it became controversial as to whether or not we should show Americans wounded, partly because he was recognizable. His family saw it and realized that their son had been wounded before they'd been officially notified. It was tough on readers. In World War II, as I recall from my reading, any photos of American dead were not allowed to be shown. As for the wounded Marine, his foot was damaged pretty bad. It took off a piece of it, but I saw him when my company came back to Camp Pendleton, and he was hobbling around on crutches and doing pretty good.

After I returned to America, I wrote a column saying, "I'm back," but I talked to some of the Marines who had come back and there was this feeling of missing the war. It was miserable and dirty and uncomfortable and painful and scary and yet there's the feeling that you're doing something that's important; that it's part of history and separate from whatever everybody else back home is experiencing. You're seeing something that very few people get to see or want to see or will ever have an opportunity to see. There's a rush to that. When you come back home and you try to resume the normal life, you miss it. When you're over there, you miss everything about home; you miss a Big Mac, you miss a cold beer, you miss a hot shower, you miss your wife or your girlfriend. But when you come back and you find out that, "Well, it's still a Big Mac and well, it's still just a beer," you start to glamorize and idealize it. You remember how close you were to these guys and the excitement of being over there and you think, "Wow, that was pretty cool. It was different." For me, at fifty-two, it's not like I really need career enhancement. It's the adventure of the thing. I know that it probably sounds cold that I'm trying to get adventure out of the misery and suffering of hundreds, thousands, tens of thousands of people, but think about it. Think what journalists do. We have a vested interest in chaos. We don't cover the plane that doesn't crash.

On the day that they hauled down Saddam's statue in downtown Baghdad, I talked to my wife on my cell phone and she said, "Oh, the war is over. They've torn down the statue." I thought, "Okay, well, we'll see." The next day Alpha Company—actually the First Battalion, Fifth Marine, of which Alpha Company was a part—got orders to go from the outskirts of Baghdad where we were and drive into the city and take one of the many palaces that Saddam had. On the way in we encountered just tremendous fire from the fedayeen. We had a couple wounded and Alpha Company's Gunnery Sergeant Jeff Bohr got killed when he caught a bullet in the head. We took the palace and then Alpha Company's assignment was to go north and capture this mosque where Saddam had apparently been seen the day before. So we start rolling out through the streets in these tracks and found ourselves going through a kind of *Black Hawk Down* situation. This was a very densely populated urban area, with very narrow streets. It was like a shantytown with barely enough room for the tracks to get through, when all of a sudden, we start getting hit by RPGs and AK47s. It was a tremendous amount of fire. As I said, when the Marines take fire, they start firing back. Tens of thousands of rounds were expended that day. Each individual track would carry boxes and boxes of ammo. The firefight lasted for about five or six hours. The Marines also called in an A-10 Warthog—the tank buster—to hit a building where we were taking fire from some fedayeen. They called in a couple of air strikes with one-thousand-pound bombs.

We had eleven tracks in the company—all Amphibious Assault Vehicles. Nine of them got hit by live RPGs. Ours got hit by a dud, but we got hit by AK47s, they clipped off some of our radio antennas. The bullets were flying.

The tracks have these rear hatches on top that you can open up and about five guys on each side can stand up on benches and look out and shoot or observe. So in our track we had the forward air controller, who was calling in air strikes, and we had the forward artillery observer, who was working on trying to get some artillery, though we didn't actually get any. Our company commander, Captain Blair Sokol, Naval Academy graduate, is six foot, seven inches tall—one of the biggest guys you've ever seen in your life—he's up there in the command turret of this track and he's firing his 9-mm at a guy that is poking an RPG over the wall of the mosque, and as he later said, "Hey, you know you're in trouble when the company commander is firing his nine." Several of the Marines were firing their M-16s. I was standing next to them and Mark Avery was standing next to me taking pictures. It was pretty intense. I started wondering if we were going to get out of there alive. A Marine next to me handed me a hand grenade; I would have rather had an M-16. After maybe ten or fifteen minutes, I finally got tired of carrying the grenade and I gave it back to him. I couldn't hold the thing and write at the same time.

A lot of people ask me if I was ever scared, and the answer, perhaps foolishly, is no, not really. Just as I started to get scared, I looked over at another Alpha Company track, one that had already been hit by an RPG, and I saw Marines in that track fighting for space in the hatches. There were more

Marines in the track than there was space in the hatches, and they were elbowing and pulling at each other to make room so they could get up and shoot—even though that exposes them to enemy fire. In the midst of all this, with enemy RPGs and rounds flying everywhere, I'm standing up in the hatch of our track, and the Alpha Company executive officer, Lieutenant Nate Shull, looks over at me, his face wreathed in smoke and soot, with this sort of wild warrior grin, and he shouts out, "Awesome!" And I decided then that if these guys aren't scared, then by God neither am I.

I don't know if I would have used the grenade. I don't know, I don't know. After things started to slack off a little bit, maybe not, but early on, yeah, I would have used it. I don't know whether I crossed the divide or not. I mean, what's your responsibility as a reporter? To be objective? Well, I couldn't look anybody in the eye and say, "Hey, I'm being completely objective," because I liked and respected these guys. I called them "my Marines." I lived with these guys. If I were to tell you, "Oh, I was completely objective," wouldn't you think I was bullshitting you? So, why not be honest about it? It always amuses me when reporters say, "Oh, you know, I have no feelings about an issue," or "I'm totally objective." I don't see how anybody can do it. That's what editors are for—to make sure that your copy comes out objective.

THE FIXER
Hasan Aweidah, aka PJ

"They didn't recognize that children were throwing nails under tires of their cars."

His reputation grew as journalists poured into Kuwait awaiting the start of the war. Hasan Aweidah, of Kuwaiti City, also known as PJ or "The Fixer" was the go-to guy for independent reporters desperate to gain entry into Iraq. If your car broke down or you needed help with sneaking across the border, this ultimate wheeler-dealer offered his services. He knew the person to talk to in dodgy places like Basra to measure the heat from the retreating fedayeen. He organized a campground for nervous unilaterals in the opening days of the war. He dispensed staying-alive wisdom to those who requested it. PJ is also a wealthy concert promoter, a capitalist with a philanthropist's generosity, who assisted in the evacuation of foreigners from Kuwait during the first Gulf War. His business card reads "Endless possibilities! Passion! Delight!"

■　■　■

I was born in Saudi Arabia. My mother is Lebanese, my father is from Jerusalem. I do events and shows with fireworks and pyrotechnics. Now I help the media people. When they arrived they didn't know the safety regulations. Ninety-nine percent of them were in the Middle East for the first time, and they were not embedding. Many of them were trying to secretly cross the border. I had to give them the clues how to get past the checkpoints: which way, what time. Then later on, some people got in trouble because things went crazy. A group of them got captured by Iraqis. Some of them were being shot at by the Iraqis. Other Iraqis had been putting some nails under their tires — all four tires. When they got out of their cars making interviews, walking here and there, they would come back, start the car. They drove little bit. The four tires were flat and they didn't know what to do. A crowd of Iraqis would come around us. These people said, "Okay, we will fix tires for you." They took tires, they were gone. They were not coming back. So what are the reporters gonna do? When they got stuck, they would call me by Thuraya satphone, "Please get us, PJ!"

I would call the Brits to come and help. In the beginning, the Brits said, "No, we cannot help these people. These people are not embedding. Forget it. Stay away from them." So we'd call another guy. He said, "Okay, you can help, but just help them for security. Temporarily." Soon we made a camp at Umm Qasr called Media Camp. We called it Ali's Happy Hotel. Every night we had between twenty-two to twenty-seven cars.

We provided information to drivers like how to avoid attacks by children when they start throwing stones at the cars. When you drive next to the children, you drive very slowly so they will not throw stones. The speed of the stone is less. Put cartons on the windows and cover them so the children will not throw. We instruct them about the nails under the tires. Before they get into their cars, they must look under their tires. This happens not only with us, but with the military. When the U.S. Army convoy stops, all the children come over and they are talking with the soldiers. They don't know. They are children. So they didn't recognize that they were throwing nails under tires.

I would help with directions, towns, locations of gas stations. There is a gas station in Umm Qasr. The owner used to fill up a car for one dollar. But his petrol supply was going down. He started filling cars for ten dollars. When no supply was coming, it went to fifteen dollars, then twenty. He is rich man now in Iraq.

Wherever I would go, media people would ask me, "PJ, what we have to do? What's going on here. What shall we do? How does it work? Can we go this way? How far is this city? How far is that? I have my car. My car is not working. I need help." One lady was a journalist with a TV crew. They were French. The guy with her was not helping at all, and she was like the man. You know what I mean? She is doing everything and he is not doing anything. They have a car, a GMC. After two days, the car won't run. The fuses for the lighter are gone. I have couple of them. I said, "Well, lemme check." I open the hood, check the fuses, change the fuses. I sit there. I ask, "You gonna go back to Kuwait?" She started crying. I asked, "Why you are crying?" She said, "I'm, gonna lose my job! Because I have a stupid guy that is not helping me at all." So I said, "Okay. Go inside the car. I will check the things." She couldn't believe it. Then she was happy. This guy, the stupid guy, also had these jerry cans. Instead of putting petrol in, he put water in them.

Many of these journalists came unprepared. Some of them, at the beginning, before the war started, they brought nothing! Like Fox News, NBC News, ABC News, Sky News. They came over with their machines: laptops, camera, and all these things. They said, "We want to rent cars." They start renting cars. No problems for them. They have the money, but they need some preparation. They are looking for diesel cars. "We want diesel! Let's get this!"—because they have this information from the U.S. Army that gave them some special specifications for cars. It should be diesel. It should be safe. So they have all the specifications, and they need to prepare them. In Kuwait, nothing is available. They want to go and buy a car. They cannot find one. They know me. "Come, PJ, help us."

They purchased their cars. A 1995 Hummer, they can buy for eight thousand dinars, which is $30,000. But there are no diesel cars in Kuwait. They never use diesel cars. It's not like in Saudi Arabia. So we start searching for used ones. We find three or four here, and that's it. Then the U.S. Army said, "Okay, you can go on petrol ones. No problem." Afterward, they said that nobody was allowed to bring their own cars. Everyone freaks out! Some of them had spent a hell of a lot of money for the gear and the cars—overhaul the engine, put on new tires, paint the car, everything. So the Army let some of them go with that. These were the top media people. As for the rest, they said, "Go on the tanks or the Humvees, okay?" Many had to leave behind their cars.

BEYOND GOOD AND EVIL
CNN Baghdad Bureau Chief Jane Arraf

> "I watched ordinary people take oil paintings
> of Saddam. One guy took this huge knife out
> of his shirt—a huge dagger—and stabbed
> Saddam in the eye."

When CNN chief news executive Eason Jordan revealed in an op-ed piece for *The New York Times* (April 11, 2003) that his network had failed to disclose what it knew about torture and killings in Saddam Hussein's regime, his confession rattled the media establishment and helped sabotage the brand equity CNN had built up as "the most trusted name in news." He admitted that there were "awful things that could not be reported, because doing so would have jeopardized the lives of Iraqis, particularly those on our Baghdad staff." Jordan wrote that in thirteen trips to Baghdad, he heard stories of electroshock torture, beatings, and brutal murders, including a Kuwaiti woman who had spoken with CNN. She was beaten daily for months in front of her father, then had her body torn limb from limb, the parts left in a bag on her family's doorstep.

Why this journalistic omerta? It was a result of the devil's handshake CNN made with Saddam's government to ensure that its permanent news bureau remain in Baghdad (and in the same building as the Information Ministry). About six months before Jordan's media culpa appeared, *The New Republic* singled out CNN's Bureau Chief Jane Arraf as "Saddam's stooge," who would "mimic the Ba'ath Party line" in a "go along to get along" strategy, and was serving no real newsgathering role except as an unwitting propagandist for this thugocracy. Yet Arraf's tenure in Baghdad was never a sure bet, and right around Christmas, she became the fourth CNN correspondent to be banned from Iraq in 2002; in August, Iraq expelled CNN's Christiane Amanpour, Wolf Blitzer, and Richard Roth. Arraf, who began her career as a Reuters correspondent in Montreal, remained in the Middle East, continued her reporting from Amman, Jordan, and covered the war in northern Iraq as a unilateral. She is now back at the Baghdad bureau.

■　　■　　■

There's nothing like a good driver since there's so much distance between stories — lot of road trips. Half of our time was spent in the vehicle. Our truck was a GMC. It was the vehicle of choice in northern Iraq, but not in Baghdad. People want to steal them in Baghdad, where the best is a beaten-up old jalopy no one else wants to steal. During the war, toward the front lines, we were always in a state of apprehension. Whenever we rounded the corner, our drivers had looks on their faces as if they were prepared for anything. I remember one scary moment. We had chosen a house up on a ridge near the town of Kalak on the front lines. It was close to Irbil — a place that was great for TV stand-up and was protected by a ridge — and from it we could see the bombing of Mosul. We could hear the blasts and we were shaken by the bombs. Perfect for live camera background shots. We manned it in twenty-four-hour shifts and placed our satellite dishes there. The house was more like a barn. There was no running water, no electricity. Animals were running around. Pigeons gathered in the main room. There were cats — no farm animals. But apparently we were a little too visible to the Iraqi troops and were within mortar range. At the end of one afternoon, the first mortar fell quite close. We had established a drill for that likelihood. We were to run for our vehicles. Amazingly, it went as choreographed, like a movie. As we got into the cars, two more mortar shells hit fifty feet away. We sped away. It was the fastest car ride I ever had. The next day we returned to see if everyone at the house was all right. A woman and her children laughed at us for running away. They were used to it.

Mosul used to be the second- or third-largest city in Iraq — about a million people — a potential democratic template for all of Iraq with a mix of ethnic and religious groups. Mosul is fascinating. Although it was under Iraqi government control, it was very far north and consisted of mostly Sunni Arabs, with a variety of Christians, Shia, Kurds, Sunni Kurds, and Azidis — mistakenly thought to be devil worshipers. The Azidis are so interesting. The brief version is they are an old religion which transformed itself over centuries. They believe they were the first man created. They believe in worshiping one god and yet are a mixture of several religions. They won't tell you they worship the devil. They worship the fallen angels. It contains elements of Zoroastrianism and fire worship. They number about 800,000 indigenous. Their homes were destroyed along with Kurdish places, but they had century-old caves under each house. I found one family with twelve kids. They named one of the children Dick Cheney. He had a very big impact on their lives in the Gulf War. They were so thankful.

Mosul was a template for what America hopes Iraq could be. It held the first democratic elections in Iraq for city council and first mayor. These were the first Iraqi democratic elections ever held. Just amazing. At the end of it all, they took a picture of the entire city council. All the ethnic groups were represented with seats on the city council. After covering Iraq for so long under Saddam Hussein and all that horror, it was just incredible. There was no violence in these May elections. Yes, it was pretty remarkable. Just two weeks before, the looting in Mosul was absolutely astounding; after the Iraqis withdrew, the special forces had not yet arrived. It was incredibly eerie. There was nobody in control. The Iraqi government police and army had all left. The Kurdish troops had not yet arrived. There were just a few peshmerga, and there was an absolute frenzy of looting. The Central Bank was on fire. Men rushed in and out with stacks of dinars, and they did not care at all about the fire. One guy was loading up a tractor-trailer truck from agricultural offices and said he was going to take it to a Kurdish town. Another said he was going to get married and had no furniture and was taking it back to his home. People on the street rushed by, carrying household appliances and yelling to me, "I am so happy! I have a refrigerator!" They felt they had been cheated. They got no oil money, and they wanted some things. We wanted to make reservations at the hotel until we realized it was being looted from top to bottom—mattresses, sheets, a piano, just everything. A whole city was being looted at the same time. They were looting the palace. It was extraordinary—this was one of the more tasteful palaces. Yes, this was one of Saddam's. He was said to go there once a year. It was on the banks of the Tigris. It was luxurious. I guess it is all relative. This one was not quite as obscene as the other ones.

It is really hard to put yourself in the place of Iraqis who have lived under the Iraqi regime for so many years. You have to have a bit of sympathy. To take a totalitarian regime and unleash it suddenly, you find things you never expected. During the first few days in Mosul and Kirkuk, I watched ordinary people take oil paintings of Saddam. One guy took this huge knife out of his shirt—a huge dagger—and stabbed Saddam in the eye. That image stays in my mind. That man was incredible. He was one of the tribal leaders. He said to me every single Iraqi could write a book about life under Saddam. This guy was very articulate in the way ordinary people often are. He told me under Saddam everything was a lie—until now. You could not use words freely, even the sense of apprehension was not gone. But he was so angry, and expressed it with his dagger upon the eye of Saddam.

The one thing I could never forgive or figure out was the looting of the hospital. It was inexplicable. Iraqis blamed everybody else. Arabs said Kurds were responsible; Kurds said Iraqis; Iraqis said Kuwaitis; no one could accept that their own group bore partial responsibility. It was always someone else who did it. It will take a while to recover from the utter shock of the rapid change. Many shops will stay closed because they are afraid they will be looted—not without reason. Right now there are not many re-recruited police back on duty in Mosul.

The U.S. military line is that things are a little better every day, but a lot of people are still afraid. In many places, there are not any police. Americans are doubling the number of military police, but it will be a long-term project to re-create the local police forces and the Iraqi army. This is the first time the U.S. has tried to establish democracy in a country with no government. It will be an immense challenge, and it will not happen as fast as people think.

Impatience is widespread in Iraq now. The impatience grows every day. It is a worrying thing. Talk to people and they are threatening a civil war. Take the simple thing like waiting in Mosul for cooking fuel. You don't think something so small could be so important, but this could ignite the city. If their men don't get bread, they will be desperate. If there is no gasoline, no fuel—people stand in line for hours. A woman said, "We wanted democracy. But we changed our minds. Now all we want is our fill of bread. Now we want Americans to go home." The thinking is turning. People now think that democracy is a nice idea, but it cannot replace electricity, the ability to cook food, and not feeling afraid. It is an interesting thing. People were really afraid before, under Saddam, for specific reasons. Now they are afraid in a more general sense, a fear of more shadowy things. Many are afraid that Saddam will pop out from underground. He haunts them to this day. This was a thing that was underestimated. Even today, May 10, the interim health minister has refused to denounce the Ba'ath party. He said he cannot denounce it. Not just for fear of Saddam, but because some of its principles were good.

Some of the U.S. generals have admitted to me that they were caught by surprise on a few levels. For one, they expected a humanitarian disaster that did not happen. It meant they were not prepared for the second stage. They did not get a wave of mass refugees, hungry people, and mass epidemics. Some other things handicapped them. Now they are working with far fewer troops. This creates severe complications for how safe people feel. They would like for the soldiers to leave, but they do not feel safe if they are not visible in the streets.

Fallujah continues to have an impact on the people, but right now, because there is no central source of information, it will be more felt on a local level. The world may know of it, but many Iraqis not in the area are unaware of it. So far it is not a national issue, except in the sense that it is perhaps a metaphor for resentment felt, and a perception that the Americans did not handle this very well. These people have been colonized over and over by more than one country. They say the Brits have done this so much better. They share a rapport with the Iraqis. They speak to them. They are not as trigger-happy, and not as aggressive, and do not make impressions that have violent intentions like the Americans are making. Americans walk around with helmets, and full body armor, and thus are not winning the hearts and minds.

To go over the factual part of the reasons CNN was kicked out of Baghdad, let me begin by saying that since 1991, we have maintained a bureau here. I stayed three very long years. Then I went off to Istanbul to open a small bureau there. When things heated up in Iraq, I agreed to come back as bureau chief. In November Saddam issued his pardons and opened up Abu Ghraib prison, and three days later people showed up at the ministry of information in Baghdad. Older Shia women demonstrated. I was doing live shots. I reported what was right in front of my face. It was not always a question just of personal integrity. You can view it with regard to journalistic ethics, but people faced different consequences. The ministry of information made it clear that if anyone broadcast that, they would be shut down.

The relations between media and the ministry of information were always elastic. In February 2002 they had a referendum on Saddam trying to re-create the vote he had achieved eight years earlier in which he received ninety-nine point nine percent of the vote. The people were required to go out and answer: Do you want Saddam Hussein as your leader? Obviously, it was not an election and obviously there were consequences for people who did not approve him. I reported on those circumstances. When we first started, they felt CNN was the only channel they had to the West. By the time we left, they said we were an arm of the U.S. State Department.

I can't believe you can cover Iraq outside Iraq. Of course, it is nice not to have restrictions on your broadcasts, but we were in the center of a whole furor in which *The New Republic* called me the stooge of Saddam. Bottom line, they said we should have left Iraq and relied upon opposition coverage. I think that showed a complete misunderstanding of how a journalist works in a totalitarian regime. Also, there is the issue of protecting people you work with. There was never any doubt whatsoever that people were tortured and jailed in Iraq. Yet there was no way in the world we could have reported on any specific person. To do so was difficult and challenging. In no case could we report on a person still living in Iraq who had been tortured. No matter how carefully we reported it, and who it was sourced to. People who criticized us did not understand the circumstances of reporting under a totalitarian regime like Iraq. I did not hear anyone come up and tell me what and how I could have done things differently. Which is not to say that I did not do a lot of soul searching. Every day I asked, "God, am I doing the right thing? Could I say more? Should I even be here?" Of course, I felt I should have been here.

Now, I cannot believe this country has changed. That Saddam has gone. That you can walk down the street and see all the people I knew who so carefully had to hide their feelings and thoughts. Now they are alive and have a hope for the future.

O BROTHER, WHERE ART THOU?

Washington Times
Chief Photographer Joe Eddins

> "It seemed that all these generals were calling
> from the Pentagon demanding to know what
> the heck is going on?"

Joe Eddins is the first to admit that he wasn't *The Washington Times'* top photo draft pick to cover the war. "One of our staff photographers took a job with the Associated Press the day before he was supposed to get on a plane to Kuwait," Eddins explains. Another photographer went through media boot camp before realizing, in Eddins' words, that "it was not her brand of vodka."

■ ■ ■

Looking back in hindsight, a lot of the fear we experienced seems silly and overreactive. There were quite a few Marines who were absolutely positive that we were going to get slimed at some point.

I had been embedded with the Marine Expeditionary Force (MEF) Forward Services Support Group (FSSG). This was the forward element of the command structure of the entire supply operation for the MEF. All the combat service support groups were basically under that command element. It was not a real sexy place to be if you were a photographer.

We spent the first night of the war in a bunker, which is basically just a hole dug in the sand. This was at Near Breach Point West, watching the Army Multiple Launch Rocket System (MLRS) go off to the west, the artillery peppering the battlefield, and everyone is oohing and aaahing like it's the Fourth of July. As we are sitting in this bunker, someone looks straight up over our head, and someone says, "What's that?" It became very apparent to everyone there that it was a Scud because it was heading from the north going south. You could see the light going right over the top of our heads.

That was a sobering experience. At the same time, it was comical, because here were a bunch of guys with a possibility of getting killed, and all of a sudden we heard this muffled guy at the end of the bunker start channeling *O Brother, Where Art Thou?* Only half of us got the reference, but I certainly got it. We heard one guy say, "Man it's a Scud going to Kuwait!" Then there is silence. Then some time goes by and you hear somebody else behind his gas mask say, "Damn, boy! We're in a tight spot!" In *O Brother, Where Art Thou?* there is this scene where they are stuck up in this hayloft with the sheriff chasing them, and they light the barn on fire, while George Clooney keeps repeating, "Damn, boys, we're in a tight spot!" The bunker just started riffing on the movie. There is another scene where this guy called Delmer keeps offering Clooney fire-roasted gopher, "Care for some gopher, Everett?" So we are watching Scuds going over and another guy would be saying, "Boy, when I get out of here, I'm gonna have a gopher MRE!"

I made some fantastic pictures the second day of the war of the first Scud alert of the day—we had about five or six of them. There was serious fear on some of these Marines' faces because they knew damn well this hole dug in the middle of the ground wasn't going to protect them from a Scud landing. I also have pictures taken three hours later of the fifth Scud drill. Then everyone's just kinda lollygagging, walking to the bunker, sitting on top of the ridge, smoking a cigarette. People just got kind of accustomed to it.

I decided to stay as an embed with FSSG for a while at least. We were then at Camp Viper, southeast of Nasiriyah. I would then hook up with Combat Service Support Group Eleven, where a reporter named John Bebow from the *Detroit News* and I had struck a deal with our foreign news desks. Because he did not have a photographer there, and I did not have a writer, we were going to trade pictures for stories, which made both of our desks very happy. During the four or five days, there was this lull in the fighting as the convoy lines tried to catch up. I had decided to let Bebow travel ahead of me and planned to join him in a few days once the offensive got rolling again, because I still felt that an important story was going on in the rear. The supply lines, especially for the Marines, had been stretched so thin and was so lightly defended that worries about ambush and counterattacks were very real. This was the first time in history that the Marines were called on to stretch their logistics train for such a lengthy distance. Marines usually establish a beachhead, then push inland twenty to thirty kilometers, and then hand things over to the Army. Now they were being asked to push inland over three hundred kilometers, and maintain supply, and logistics, and the security for those supply routes—a daunting task for a light mobile force with a lot of outdated equipment. They moved a good bit of equipment with civilian tractor-trailers bought or rented in Kuwait, which were broken down all over the place. Meanwhile, Soviet doctrine that Iraqis followed dictated: Bypass the tip of the spear and attack the supply line. I felt like I was still in the right place, especially seeing as Nasiriyah was still pretty hot, and the Army convoy had been ambushed after taking a wrong turn, where Jessica Lynch was taken hostage, and all that.

I sometimes went out on vehicle checkpoints. There was still a big concern about fedayeen disguised as civilians transporting weapons back and forth between Basra and Nasiriyah. They were also getting good intelligence from civilians who were being stopped on the roads, but the one thing that became very evident through talking with the lance corporals and whatnot is that there is a huge difference between the Marines who work on the supply side and the grunts who do the fighting. Essentially what happens is that the various job descriptions are filled within the supply side with the highest rated people to do a certain job. So they filled the electrician slots with the best electricians that they had available. They filled the construction slots with the best construction people that they had. Then everyone who is left over, they say, "Congratulations, you are now the security company."

A lot of these kids have not had a lot of intensive combat training since boot camp. It was painfully evident when I went out on patrol in a Humvee with some of the Marines. After fifteen minutes they were bored. Their heads were inside the truck. They were talking about this, that, and the other thing, and not paying attention to the fact that, frankly, they could be killed at any second. I am not trying to criticize them as Marines. It's just the fact that that is not their job.

Late one night, my point of contact, Captain Kevin Coughlin, asked me if I wanted to go with them to the Saddam Hussein Canal where the Sixth ESB (Engineer Service Battalion) were setting up water purifiers. The commanding officer wanted to have a look at the situation.

I said, "Sure. Yeah. I'd like to get out of the camp and take a ride." On the way up, there was a lot of radio traffic about what sounded like two Marines who had gone behind a berm and not come back. Everyone was a little antsy already because civilians were wandering through the dunes and wadis, so there were some very tense few minutes. Everybody had their guns drawn, and they got out of their Humvees, and set up a perimeter and monitored civilians.

Once they found a secure way to get to the Saddam Hussein Canal, I got out of my Humvee and started taking pictures. Maybe about five minutes into it, Captain Coughlin came to me and said, "You gotta get back in the Humvee." I said "Well, what's going on?" He said, "I really can't explain it to you right now. You just have to get back in the Humvee." I had assumed that there was an attack coming or we were getting ready to move out. I had no idea.

The Sixth ESB were setting up these water purifiers on a rise of land which dropped maybe five meters down to the water. Then on the opposite bank were small sand dunes, maybe about twenty meters high, that you could not see over even sitting on top of the Humvee. It was about seventy-five yards to the other side. The Marines had control on the south side of the canal where they were setting up the water purification units. They had nobody on the other side, so obviously there was a security issue, because it was hard to see over the dunes on the other side of the bank. An opposing force could come rolling right on top of them, and be all over them before they could do anything about it. Well, when they put me in the Humvee, I noticed that there were a bunch of guys actually swimming in the canal. At this point I began hearing a couple of enlisted Marines outside the Humvee talking very angrily, and it started to dawn on me what had happened. The major in charge of that unit was worried about security and had sent four Marines into the water in their full uniform—with their Kevlar flak vests and weapons—to swim across to the other side to set up a perimeter security. Now, if you talk to Marines, they will tell you they are trained to a certain extent to be able to swim with their gear, but it would seem to me that you would have to exercise a little common sense in this situation. There was no enemy on top of them. They could have taken some precautions, but this major didn't. He sent these four Marines into the water without any kind of flotation and without any safety line. Two of them drowned.

Because I got there about ten to fifteen minutes after the incident occurred, they were in the water looking for them. The two Marines who made it were trying to provide security on the other side of the canal. I started taking pictures from the Humvee and asked the Captain, "Can I get out?" He said, "No, you have to stay in the Humvee." I'm not going to make excuses for the guy. He is a lawyer by trade. There was no public affairs office (PAO) with my unit whatsoever. There were no other media with my unit. Now, he and I had talked early on about the fact that I understood the rules as far as releasing photographs of injured Marines and that kind of thing. I said to him, "You and

I need to come to an understanding that there are going to be things I am going to shoot for the sake of history. I will respect the rules of seventy-two hours for injured or killed Marines so the parents can be notified and that kind of thing. But I have a duty to document this for history." And he seemed to be quite understanding of that.

Then suddenly we are in a situation where Marines have been killed. While they weren't shot or had stepped on a land mine, it was certainly a combat situation. He wanted me in the Humvee and not outside taking pictures. He would not let me speak to anyone who was there. He didn't give me a chance to get anyone to speak on the record. When I got back to the camp I reported what I had seen to my newspaper. Told them that I had pictures. Our Pentagon reporter Bill Gertz began to make phone calls to the Pentagon concerning this situation.

Well, the next morning I am greeted by the Captain asking, "What the hell is going on?" It seemed that all these generals were calling from the Pentagon demanding to know what the heck was going on. They wanted to know why this *Washington Times* reporter was asking all these questions about these Marines who had drowned.

Of course, I explained what had happened. I also said that I would respect the Marines' rules that until these kids' families were notified we should sit on the story. No one else had it. In any case, we eventually went with the story. Unfortunately I was quoted by our reporter. The morning after it came out, I was greeted by the Captain who had printed the story out from the Internet. He held it to my face as I was trying to shave. He said "Well, here's your story. I just want you to know that a lot of the officers in the COC (Command Operations Center) are telling me not to talk to you. To steer clear of you, not to help you out, that kind of thing. I'll do what I can for you." I had to make a snap judgment. Was this really worth ruining any chance of my covering larger aspects of the war later by getting into a big confrontation with this guy? He had already caught wind of the fact that there were quite a few Marines who were very upset at the fact that those Marines were sent into the water without a safety line. They were very upset with the major who was in command there.

Basically, from that point on, any understandings about photographing certain things fell by the wayside. Every request that I made to go with them on convoys was answered, "Well, nothing's really going on today," and a polite smile. Then, a sergeant who was riding security would come back at the end of the day and say, "Oh man! We went up to the Euphrates River and there were Cobra attack helicopters and helicopters strafing all sorts of stuff. It was really great. You should have been there." So it became pretty evident that with a smile on their faces, that I was being blackballed.

They established rules and I was willing to follow them, but the troubling thing was that they weren't willing to follow my rules. I was here to do a job. My one saving grace was when the Brits rolled into town and I actually had a couple of days with the Brits from Sixteenth Air Assault and Third Parachute Regiment. These guys were all Northern Ireland vets. They knew how to take down a car on the highway. They knew how to secure a perimeter around a stopped vehicle and to safely interview some of those people and get some intelligence. When the Brits invited me to go along, I said, "Hey, I'd love to go out with you guys." They said, "Sure! Hop in!" And off we went.

My favorite photograph taken during this time was of an individual by a stopped bus. The bus probably had twelve men on it. They were all middle-aged or older men. The bus was filled with tomatoes and onions. They were coming from the Basra area toward Nasiriyah. There was one individual who was very upset, and according to the translator, he wanted to know why they blew up his house. "Why did you drop a shell on my house?" It made for some tense moments and some interesting pictures. The guy was very animated and had a lot to say about how these conflicts go.

The Brits had also set up their rules for me. The counter-intelligence guys said, "Look, you can't take a picture of our faces, or of the interpreters' faces, because these guys are Iraqi or Kuwaiti and you really could put them and their families in danger. We'd appreciate it if you just didn't do that." So I didn't. The Brits were fine with me taking their pictures. Any pictures of them taking people out of the car was fair game.

After the drowning story ran, there was a lot of foot dragging about letting me leave the unit. "Well, we are not sure if we can get you on a convoy." Eventually, I managed to get on a convoy that was headed to an airfield they had set up there in southeast Baghdad. The ride was probably about two hours. That was great. I got to ride in the turret of a Light Armoured Reconnaissance Vehicle (LAR) and take pictures the entire way. I stayed with CSSG Eleven for a couple of days. The day that Baghdad fell, I was at the Republican Guard training facility southeast of the city. It was spookily empty. I later hooked up with a caravan with guys from *Sky News* in Britain. Then I actually ran into a friend of mine, Andy Nelson, who was working for the *Christian Science Monitor*. He had driven into Iraq by himself, and been adopted by another

Marine outfit. We all caravanned together into Baghdad the next morning. It was like rolling up to the Ramada in Des Moines, Iowa. There was no one on the street. We rolled right into downtown. Showed our ID cards to the Marines on top of their M1 tanks. They let us through and we just pulled into the Palestine Hotel and started taking pictures.

When I was with my original embed, I was very detached from the war. Three days after this canal incident happened, they took away my Thuraya satphone. Of course, I immediately thought, "They are really upset with me now. They are taking away all my means of communication." But it turns out that all the journalists had their Thuraya satphones confiscated. There was some kind of intelligence that someone in Dubai, which is where the company is located had sold all of the codes for the journalists' phones to Baghdad. There was a fear that people sending pictures and stories could be triangulated on that signal for artillery strikes. But the interesting thing about this—and which made a whole new set of obstacles—was trying to figure out a way to piggyback on some Marine's e-mail and get my pictures into the paper, which I managed to do. On the other side, it was an awakening experience. Being a member of the media and being plugged into so many different perspectives and inputs all the time, I suddenly found myself really being in the same situation as the average Marine, which is: All you know is what's right in front of you. I don't have enough fingers and toes to count how many times a day the first question that a Marine would ask me is, "So, what's happening in the war? Do you know what's going on?" The rumor mill was amazing.

MEDIA GATEKEEPER AND TROUBLESHOOTER
U.S. Army Colonel Guy Shields,
Public Affairs Officer

"A lot of people went across the border sooner
than they wanted to. And then they were calling
us to bail them out."

Colonel Guy Shields was the U.S. Army's point man at the Kuwait Hilton, in charge of media credentialing, embed training, and processing. Very often, he was also the troubleshooter unilaterals called for help in the field. A calm, self-assured man, he represented a self-confident American military that had rediscovered its belief and optimism in its own character—unafraid of the media and once again eager to share its story. Career U.S. Army Public Affair Officers (PAOs) like Colonel Shields realized that a rigid group of security-first, Vietnam-paranoid Army PAOs forfeited a golden pro-military opportunity in the 1991 Gulf War by keeping the press at bay. Now, buoyed by the apparent success of the embedded journalist program, Shields felt comfortable offering unguarded, shoot-from-the-lip opinions.

"We registered over 2,700 media," he boasted from his Kuwait office in late April. "And they are still coming in. Half of them were from the U.S. A lot of news organizations had support staff. CNN probably had 150 to 200 support staff. The other networks did too. So these were not all practicing journalists. They were all involved. But that might include soundmen and cameramen, drivers, translators." The responsibility to monitor the media accreditation process resided with Shields and his small hard-working staff. His office handled embeds and unilaterals. He dealt with high-profile television personalities like Geraldo Rivera, who broke the rules, and backpacking solo journalists, also known as sojos. He treated everyone in the media fairly, equally, without prejudice.

■ ■ ■

I got my undergraduate degree in education at the University of Minnesota, and I received a degree in national security in 1992 from the Naval War College. I wrote my thesis on Eisenhower and combat correspondents.

There were no more than two hundred journalists at any one time in Vietnam. Given what it took for TV, they were still using film that needed to be shipped back to the States to be developed. It would take forty-eight hours at best. No instantaneous coverage. You had the Five O'clock Follies in Vietnam, but journalists basically had free rein. They could get on or off any helicopter, in any unit, and just go travel the countryside, but they rarely stayed with a unit more than a few days.

The next war after Vietnam would be Grenada. That is where they kept the media on a different island way away from the military action. That probably is not one of the stellar performances. After that comes Panama. Similar thing, where they tried the pool reporting system and the pool failed miserably. There were already a few hundred journalists down in Panama. With all those journalists there, why do you need a pool? But anyway, they did it that way.

I was a public affairs officer (PAO) at Fort Ord, and later, a battalion operations officer in Panama. Whenever the media would show up at my unit in a bus, it meant that I had to pull a minimum of a platoon off what they were doing to provide security. So I got to see both sides. Yes, there was some backlash from Vietnam; the pool concept was a way to try to manage the media and to provide some semblance to handle the logistics of it. During the first Gulf War, logistically, just a small number of media went forward, because at that time the media had to find a way to get the news back to their audience. A huge contributing factor to embedding working was that technology took away this major logistical hurdle.

It also created a heckuva challenge, too. With the news being instantaneous—live coverage from the front—you would see the good, the bad, and the ugly. It was real time. We'd watched something on TV live and five minutes later the phones in the press center would light up saying, "Can you verify this?" We'd say, "Well, we're watching it on TV so it's probably happening." But officially we hadn't gotten the confirmation through the reporting system yet. It created some embarrassing situations because the normal reporting system, even if everything is going well, takes a half hour to an hour to get reported. For example, there was a firefight going on outside of Basra, and we were watching it on TV. The media called, "Can you verify that this is happening?" I said, "We are watching it just like you are."

One of my concerns was that higher headquarters—the Department of Defense (DOD)—would be beating us up wanting to know more information. It is very hard on a commander to learn about stuff for the first time by watching it on TV, but higher headquarters understood exactly what was going on, and accepted it.

Because of instantaneous reporting from the battlefield, the media were inside our decision cycle. There was absolutely no way to place any spin control. The media were right there. They were reporting. So don't even think about trying to BS them. You could not put spin on what the embeds were putting out. That was very beneficial. You had 600 pieces of the battle coming out with no spin. If you put together all those 600 individual pieces, you can get a pretty good overall picture.

Some journalists insinuated that we were trying to kill journalists. I actually had a major correspondent tell me that. This was after the Palestine Hotel in Baghdad was shelled. I said, "We don't target journalists." She replied, "Well, you knew journalists were in that hotel." I said, "I can't say for a fact that the young gunner in that tank knew there were journalists in that hotel. All he knew was that he was taking fire from that hotel." She then had the gall to say, "Well, at least the Iraqis aren't killing journalists." I said, "Well, how about the rocket attack yesterday where it killed two?" She said, "That's different." I replied, "What is different?" Well, maybe the journalists who were staying in the Palestine decided to embed on the wrong side. They were knowingly living and working with the Iraqi military in Baghdad. All those media had uniformed minders until Saddam's statue came down.

If it weren't for the training, discipline, and control of the Coalition soldiers, a lot more journalists would have been killed in this war, because the journalists were driving the same vehicles that the bad guys were. I took her comment very personally. If we were targeting journalists, there'd be a lot more deaths, but that would be implying that the military doesn't like media, and that is just flat out not true—that the soldiers don't like the journalists. I would propose to you the exact opposite. Soldiers like to have their story told. Bonding may have taken place. There will probably be some journalists that become godparents to some of the soldiers' kids. When you go through combat together, a bond is formed, but those journalists were still more than capable of reporting fairly and objectively. A lot of folks have said that because of the embedding process, the media won't be able to report objectively. That's a pile of crap. That's like saying that if you're a soldier trained to kill, you can't be a peacekeeper. Trained, disciplined soldiers can do anything professionally. Journalists can bond with somebody and still do their jobs professionally. The only people who have said that journalists could not report objectively because they were being co-opted were people who had no concept of what embedding was all about. They were just letting their biases speak out.

Embedded journalists caught some pretty significant events going on. In Karbala, for example, the Western media covered the good and the bad. Western media showed both sides. They did a pretty good job of telling the story of how we went to great lengths to minimize collateral damage.

In mobile warfare, which this war was, you don't have time to stop and count casualties. If your objective was to kill as many people as you could, then you'd want to know, but that was not our objective. In fact, it was the opposite. We did all we could and were probably pretty successful. If you look up the number of Iraqi formations where they just walked away and left their rifles and equipment behind, that was a good thing. Body counts? No utility to it. Takes too much time. They aren't a measure of success. Whenever you're moving through a town and bypassing enemy, you suppress the enemy as quickly as you can and move on to the next objective, and that is the way it worked.

Before the war started, many nonembeds or unilaterals would ask me, "How do you get across the border?" I replied, "I got two thousand of you. I can't do a special deal for anybody." A lot of them found their way across the border. They got into some great locations. They got some great stuff early on. Probably better than most folks, and did well. Having said that, experienced British war correspondent, Terry Lloyd, didn't have that same kind of luck. A lot of people went across the border too soon, and then they were calling us to bail them out.

The unilaterals were frustrating. There was huge pressure from their editors to go across the border. There was one young rookie photographer. I don't even remember his name. This was early on. But he was having dinner in the restaurant where everybody ate. As I was walking by, he asked, "Sir, can I talk to you? My editors have ordered me across the border tomorrow. What do I do?" I said, "Shit, don't go!" He said, "It's my job. I got to go." I answered, "Okay. But the safest thing you can do is only travel during the day. Find yourself a military unit and stick with them ninety percent of the time. The unit is not going to kick you out at night. Most military units actually want to have journalists around, though they won't say that." That was my advice to that kid. But unilaterals were under pressure because the embedded folks were getting such great stuff. It wasn't safe.

The first two nights of the ground war were hectic because we had a number of unilaterals who rushed the border. They got across, then got in firefights, and they were calling us, "Help us! Help us!" Those first two nights were the toughest two nights I had here. The first few nights it was bandit country. They were shooting all over the place. It was crazy: fedayeen, Republican Guards, suicide missions. The journalists had no sense of the real danger. They would ask, "Where do we go?" I said, "Well, I know we have strong points of Coalition Forces to the south, but by telling you to go there, I could be signing your death warrant. I could be sending you into an ambush." Lieutenant Colonel Hovatter and myself were spending time on the phone teaching individual survival techniques: "Make sure you stay low. Get down low. Get in the ditch."

We did a press briefing for the media that first night when Terry Lloyd was killed. We got the word out. We had two to three journalists killed. But the first time anything goes wrong they call us and say, "Come save me." And we get some of them back. Then the second night—the same damn thing—and some of the same damn people! "Come help us," they begged. I said, "I just talked to you last night!" They would go, "We-uh, we thought it would be safer today." I responded, "Are you people crazy? No story is worth dying for!" After that second night, I said no more.

Surprisingly, very few of the embedded journalists actually went through media boot-camp training. Now most of the Western journalists understood what they were getting themselves into—basically a month or so of no showers and really rough conditions. I had a female journalist come into our press headquarters. She was based somewhere in Asia. She was being embedded with one of the U.S. divisions. We had briefings beforehand here. After the briefing she asked me, "Well, I understood it. But how am I going to get back and forth to the hotel?" I said, "You won't. Let me explain what this is all about. You are going to be living in the field. You are going to be eating MREs. You are going to be living with the unit. They don't have showers. There will be mud and dust. You will be digging a hole for the rest room probably." She was just appalled. She unembedded herself before the fighting began.

The most notable disembed or suspension of embedding was Geraldo Rivera. I spent an hour here going over ground rules with him before he re-embedded. When I explained to him what he did was a violation and how it could have been used by the bad guys, he said, "Okay, now I understand."

We bent over backwards for all the regional media, including Al Jazeera. The decision to embed Al Jazeera was made at a much higher level than mine. We bent over backwards for them and Abu Dhabi television. We bent over backwards. We did monkey flips for these folks. We gave them extra chances. I don't read Arabic, and I don't speak Arabic, but after watching Al Jazeera and Abu Dhabi on TV, which we got—I had Kuwaiti-based translators—though we gave them the opportunity to be responsible journalists, they failed miserably.

I'll give you a prime example of Al Jazeera's idea of responsible journalism. They covered the daily briefings at CENTCOM. They had Vince Brooks on one half of the screen, then on the other half they would show wounded children—split screen. When the Iraqi information minister was putting out his bullshit, he had the full screen. Al Jazeera was putting out whatever the Iraqis said. Their reporting was totally anti-American.

With that said, we used to watch the Iraqi information minister every day. This guy was great! In the United States, he would have been a millionaire. We loved the guy. I kept hoping and expecting that he'd be doing a briefing that last day, when the tanks arrived, and he was going to say, "I'm out of here! I'm going to Disneyland!"

WAR-GAMING WITH LIEUTENANT GENERAL WILLIAM WALLACE

USA *Today* Reporter Steve Komarow

> "The General had orders come down from on top to shut up. It was a real problem for me covering a guy who was told to shut up."

"The enemy we're fighting is different from the one we'd war-gamed against." That was the frank assessment to reporters at Army Fifth Corps headquarters by Lieutenant General William Wallace, the U.S. Army's ground commander in Iraq midway into week two. A litany of setbacks including suicide bombing missions, hit-and-run ambushing, tenacious fighting by Ba'ath Party militia and Saddam fedayeen, and overextended supply lines had dampened the general's enthusiasm for swift victory. Wallace was old-school Pentagon, a Vietnam-era commander who believed in massive, sustained troop buildup before committing to ground combat, a martial philosophy at complete odds with Secretary of Defense Rumsfeld and his lean-and-mean rapid-deployment strategy.

The press pounced on Wallace's comments. "War-gamed" gained immediate cachet as the latest in Pentagonese, and was usually paired with that shopworn standby from Vietnam: quagmire. Just how long was this war going to last became topic A on Sunday television talkfests. Nor had the White House war-gamed the prospect of its ground commander publicly airing his battlefield concerns. Rumsfeld's dismissive retort to Wallace was: "I suppose everyone can have their own view." USA *Today* staff writer Steve Komarow, who covered conflicts in Kosovo, Panama, and Afghanistan, was embedded with the General's command staff. Wallace may have lost this particular political battle with the White House, but he helped win the war.

■ ■ ■

His name is the same as Braveheart's, though General William Wallace goes by Scott—his middle name. He's not a micromanager. He's a rather unpretentious fellow. He didn't get any more showers than the other guys. We flew around constantly between command posts in Black Hawk helicopters. Because the Fifth Corps, which he commands, is based in Europe, and the two main divisions under him, and the third one, the 82nd, were not units that were habitually under the Fifth Corps, and, I think, as a result he felt he had to personally go visit all the time. This is his nature anyway. He is an old cavalryman who likes to go out and smell the whatever. Visiting with the division commanders, brigade commanders, even down to company level occasionally. As a journalist, it was enlightening. I probably had the best big-picture view of the army ground war that any reporter could possibly have. On the other hand, it was frustrating, if you are trying to develop a story. You want to spend a few hours in a place and really talk to people, and we were just constantly hopping around. I had a lot of overview but not a lot of depth sometimes.

It appeared that Wallace was running out of military chess pieces to use. First of all, they were hoping the southern forces would just capitulate and they could run up to Baghdad and not worry about all these cities that were in between — Nasiriyah, Najaf, Karbala — all these places in the middle. What happened instead is that the army had to go in and really clean them out so their supply lines in back weren't vulnerable. They had to protect the rear and go fast. They had to constantly rotate and juggle forces so that the Third Infantry and 101st Airborne would go in behind them or they'd leapfrog ahead. It must have driven the soldiers mad. In fact, I have talked to a couple company commander-level guys and they just couldn't believe it. Every time they thought they had a mission — it's stuff that they trained for — then vroom! They are somewhere else!

One incident stuck in my mind. At one point, they had to secure a cross-roads at Karbala. This wasn't the most critical mission of the war, but the General was absolutely out of forces. He had nothing left, and he knew it. Because he is a three-star general, he had this big phalanx of Bradley fighting vehicles protecting his command post. There were probably sixteen vehicles. He took about twelve of them and gave them to the 101st Airborne. Arguably he didn't need all of them anyway because he wasn't on the front lines, but it just showed that he was absolutely out of forces to commit. He made a very funny gesture that I couldn't put in the newspapers. It was a little too colorful. He reached his hand to his rear end, yanked it out, and made a Bronx cheer kind of sound. To be blunt, it was like he was pulling it out of his butt at this point, and he is not a very flamboyant or colorful guy.

We experienced gunfire a couple times. One mortar landed about forty yards from us. The mortar rounds had been coming in all day and they were getting closer to the command post. I took note of it personally. No one else there seemed to even care. It seems the soil in Iraq is like quicksand. The mortar would hit, WHUMP! and it kicked up a bunch of sand, but it sank in the ground before it exploded, so the impact was relatively minor. Nobody was hurt. I was pretty safe. They don't take a three-star general anywhere without a whole lot of protection around him.

Wallace had three command vehicles known as C2Vs. It was what he called an Assault Command Post. These things were wired to the nth degree. What they are is an armored Winnebago mounted on an MLRS chassis—Multiple Launch Rockets System. It was bristling with antennas and dishes. Just like a Bradley fighting vehicle, it is sealed for germ and chemical warfare. It is over-pressurized, so when you close the door, your ears hurt. You feel it. You had to get used to it, but it was really annoying because people would come in and out all the time.

The other command post for Fifth Corps was the rear command post. It basically sat in Kuwait the whole time. Then there was what was called the TAC, for Tactical Assault Command. It's meant to be knocked down and put up in a couple of hours. The Command has representatives from all the different fighting elements, everyone from the Special Forces guys to the artillery to the lawyers—everybody. They called in strikes from there, and they had projection screens and everyone worked off a laptop.

When we were in the army command post, or even in the General's command vehicle, we could watch live video feeds from what's called a hunter. The Corps controlled the hunters, so they would have the hunter feed in the command post. We'd watch as Iraqi artillery or something moved along a road. We'd hear them calling in the fires to take them out. We'd hear, "OK F-18 on the way. F-16 on the way." Then the screen would go black and white with a flash. We'd just see the smoke. It was like a Tom Clancy movie. It sounds horrible, but we didn't see the people who were killed. It was more striking when we'd come to a spot and there were just bodies rotting in the sun. The smell of human bodies rotting is an awful thing. It just hits you. I soon stopped looking. That is very un-journalistic. I'd take a glance if I had to. Some people really stare at the bodies. I would just not look. By the Baghdad airport, for example, some engineers were cleaning up the vehicles that had been hit. The engineers were sent to get all these wrecked vehicles off the road so that army and Marines and higher command would have better access. They were picking up these vehicles and clearly there were human remains infused in these wreckages. You couldn't say there were bodies. They were just pieces of humans. It was just something you really don't want to see or smell. The soldiers were holding rags to their faces to try to hide the smell. I heard a captain phone in on his radio telling the people at the graveyard to dig an extra big hole because they couldn't separate the remains from the vehicles. They just took the whole vehicles and plopped them in the ground.

The General rarely minded my presence. There were a couple of occasions his aide would tell me not to come in. For example, in his meeting with Task Force 20, which was the Special Forces Task Force, I didn't sit in on those meetings. There were other times when I'd get waved off. It was just something where the other side wouldn't have been comfortable. I should mention though, about a week into the war, he made some comments to colleagues. We were at a spot at the command post of the 101st Airborne and I wanted to talk to General Petreus, who is the 101st commander. There were colleagues from *The Washington Post* and *The New York Times* who grabbed General Wallace for a few comments on how the war was going. He actually said what he'd been saying all along. That it was a tougher fight than they thought. The *Post* and *Times* both made it into front-page stories highlighting the fact that his assessment didn't exactly synch with the Pentagon's assessment.

Certainly the Pentagon propaganda machine was displeased with his comments because they didn't jibe with what they were saying. He had orders come down from on top to shut up. It was a real problem for me covering a guy who was told to shut up. I couldn't quote him. Now, being with the command post, I still had great sources of information. He was told to just lay low for a while. He really didn't mind that much because I don't think he enjoyed the media coverage. He was happy to be out of the spotlight. He is one of the last of the Vietnam-era generals.

He wasn't criticizing the war plan. What he was saying was already reported by everybody anyway. It became an inside-the-Beltway game. I am a veteran correspondent at the Pentagon. I know how that is played, but I was unaware that it was anything special because I hadn't been tuned into the Beltway thing. While he was in Iraq our paper had already had him saying basically the same things that ran in the *Post* and *Times*. We just hadn't had him doing it as a setup versus Rumsfeld. That was the difference. It's the policy discussion.

There are many people in the military with a strong feeling that the public and the military are too separate, that if the general public loses its connection with the military, it will eventually stop supporting it, so embedding is a good democratic instinct. To put it in a more cynical light, I think that the military would rather know where the media is instead of having media racing all over the battlefield getting killed and captured. The fact is, Iraq was a place where it was possible to sneak into and cover.

Let's put a note of caution about being an embed. Reporters didn't see everything. There was very little coverage as far as I could tell of Special Ops. I know of some reporters whom the military actually planned to put with Special Ops and the plan fell apart. There were probably things that went on that we didn't know about and will be reported later. I'm not saying good or bad, but I am saying that we should not assume with embedding that everything was covered, and everything was sanitized.

I was in Panama as part of the Department of Defense [DOD] media pool, which is probably a good contrast to Iraq. After Grenada, where basically all the press was banned from covering the invasion, the Pentagon came up with the idea for these little flash operations to have a pool of reporters. I was working for Associated Press, which put me in the pool. When Panama ramped up they called out a pool, but it was really sort of an afterthought, and there was no real plan to integrate any coverage. After the operation started, we were called out to Washington and then sent down to Panama. They didn't know what to do with us down there once we got there. We were taken to the Army headquarters at Quarry Heights. We were kept basically locked in a room at Army headquarters, while they allegedly were trying to get us a helicopter to watch the fight. By the time we could do anything, it was all over except for catching Noriega. We were shuttled around to a few aftermath scenes and some show-and-tell stuff, but there was no real coverage of the war itself. I was frustrated and exhausted. When you are in the DOD media pool, you feel like you're trying to serve every reader in the country, and we couldn't do very much. I'll never forget all the struggling we were doing and then Sam Donaldson shows up with his own helicopter, a case of wine, a crew and all this stuff. He apparently was friends with the general. We were like, "This is too surreal to believe."

On the other hand, let me say embedding is not entirely new. The military after Panama certainly tried to accommodate the press more. In Kosovo

I was "embedded," also with a command level by coincidence. General Craddock is now a three-star general and assistant to Rumsfeld. I went in with them right at the beginning and shadowed him and his guys. It was a much smaller operation and it was peacekeeping. It wasn't a war. But they were now more open to coverage by the media.

DEATH IN THE AFTERNOON

El Correo and Telecinco
Correspondent Mercedes Gallego

"I didn't really have friendships with the
Marines. I thought they were very intolerant."

Mercedes Gallego, journalist for *El Correo* and correspondent for Telecinco, was born in Barcelona and raised in Cadiz in the south of Spain, where her family is from. Her father is a farmer and mother a housewife. As a young child, she says, "I always was crazy for reading. I wanted to be a writer or a journalist. My family, they don't read at all. When I was little, my father thought that buying books was a waste of money because after you read them you don't touch them anymore. He thought that only the books he bought for school were worth it because you used them for the whole year."

After graduating from Madrid University with a degree in journalism, Gallego, thirty-one, became the Mexico City–based correspondent for *El Pais*, Spain's largest newspaper, for five years before moving to New York City. Her apartment is a few blocks away from the World Trade Center. She experienced 9/11 in a personal way—as a reporter and local resident. In this small emigre media community, she made new friends—fellow reporters from Spanish papers like *El Mundo* and *El Perodico*. She was especially close to Julio Parrado, the twenty-eight-year-old correspondent who was killed when an Iraqi artillery shell landed near an army command post outside Baghdad.

■ ■ ■

I covered important government things in Mexico and Central America. I used to travel and cover elections in Guatemala, elections in Nicaragua. I traveled frequently to Cuba because of business between Cuba and Spain, for good or for bad. Then *El Pais* offered me New York City and I took it because Mexico was very interesting professionally, but I was very tired in a personal way. It's something that you can do for a while, and I did it for five years. I thought it was enough and it was time to move on. The violence was very high. It's dangerous in Mexico City. My apartment was robbed, and every week I had a friend who was assaulted. One of my friends was raped, and they took her car, and left her far away. Another friend was taken out of his car with a gun. Another friend was beaten up for his watch and he needed plastic surgery. Everywhere in Mexico City was like that. The police are normally getting paid by the people who are the criminals, so there's no point. Sometimes you go to the police station and they rob you again.

I have a visa for working as a correspondent for my newspaper. I certainly feel like a foreigner in this country. I think New York is different because New York is a place where everybody can be a New Yorker, since the first moment they get here, but in general, in the country, I feel like a foreigner. I've been based in New York for four years. Julio was one of the first people I met in New York. We became very good friends. We also went to the Quantico media boot camp together. We traveled together to Kuwait. We were there for a week before we embedded. We were very close. Since we were embedded with different units—I was with the First Marine Division, Headquarters Battalion, First Regimental Combat Team, and he was with the Third Infantry Division—we spoke only a few times. After they took our satphones out, I couldn't talk to him anymore.

On the day he was killed, several people told me about it. His death was confirmed by the television. It was around 7:00 P.M. I spent the night crying until I fell asleep. I was inside an armored vehicle and we were going into Baghdad that night. It was very scary. People were very nervous. They were expecting the worst on the entry to Baghdad, so not many other people were paying attention to me. For women, this was a tough place anyway. A navy medic traveling with us was very supportive, but the rest of the people were into other things.

In the morning, we went into Baghdad. We set up the camp again and I wrote my story—or polemic—about my last experience with Julio and the few weeks we had spent together. Julio was in very bad condition; he didn't have a contract with his paper, El Mundo, and he had been working for them for six years. He was worried that he would get fired if he didn't cover the war, and so he asked me something personal. He asked me to say, in case he died, that he didn't want the paper's editor to go to his funeral. Then also that same day, my other colleague, Jose Couso, from Telecinco—that's the same Basque-region television station I work for—was killed at the Palestine Hotel. I didn't have time to deal with all this. We were just getting into Baghdad the next day, it was crazy. There was shooting all over; it was coming from the buildings. I was going around all day trying to get my story and to find a secure place. So, you hold the pain for later.

Everybody thought I could be next. I discovered that my friends, my relatives, my boyfriend were calling me, telling me to get out of there. He's a cameraman based in Miami, but he lives with me in New York most of the time. He was working at that time for NBC in Kuwait. He was panicked. Personally, I was always more worried about losing a leg or something like that than being killed.

I didn't see a lot of fighting. I wasn't really in the front. Normally, the fighting I saw was because they attacked the unit, but I didn't see the Marines advancing, opening fire. Most of the time, there was an infantry unit ahead of us, shooting artillery and advancing, and we moved behind them. There were times, however, when incoming artillery would wake us up in the middle of the night and we jumped into a trench. We were scared, certainly.

When you're moving, you have to sleep in the truck. If the truck stops long enough, you take your sleeping bag outside and you sleep on the ground. When you're on the ground, then it's okay. You get used to that. It actually feels pretty good, though it's very tough because you're not in a hotel.

You are also scared when the convoy is moving. They drive at night and then part of the convoy gets lost because it's very difficult to see. The night vision goggles don't always work great. So anytime that you knew your vehicle was in the back of the convoy, you got scared and you spent a few hours lying down on the bottom of the seven-ton truck—filled with sandbags to protect you from mines—to avoid the snipers.

I was embedded for a month. In the beginning, I had a laptop that I connected to my fax phone. Later, I used satphones from the military, but it was very hard to dictate anything on those phones because they don't have a wire to connect to your computer. Then, because I couldn't use my phone anymore, I left my computer behind. I now had to write on paper. My notebook was the only thing that I had to dictate for the phone. At the end, I ran out of pages in my notebook and I had to search for another one. I was quite concerned when I was running out of paper.

Spain had the largest antiwar sentiment of any country in Europe—ninety-one percent of the population was against this war—and so it did affect my coverage. You've got to be careful what you say or write. You can't be too much on the side of the Marines, because they will question your objectivity as a journalist and because people were very sensitive to it. They were very antiwar and very anti-American. On the other side, you cannot tell the Marines what you feel about the war because then they start calling you a "liberal" journalist and they would blacklist you. You had to keep your thoughts to yourself.

I didn't really have friendships with the Marines. I wasn't very happy with the friendships. I thought they were very intolerant and I couldn't express my own opinions without getting into a difficult position with them. I remember the day when they kicked out a photographer because he had taken a picture where you can see a map, and that was forbidden. These guys were pissed off. I was trying to convince them that they shouldn't blame all of us for that. We didn't even know that guy—he was in a different division. I was telling them that if you take 700 reporters, not all of them are going to play by the rules; some of them are going to go wrong. If you also pick 700 Marines, not all of them are going to be totally honest. They said, "Oh, that's true. If you pick seven hundred Marines, you're going to find some gays and some liars." I was thinking, "Wow, is that the sense of honesty you have? A gay person is not an honest person for you?" But, of course, I didn't say a word because I had seen before how they would react when you're telling something that they consider liberal. That was the key word for them. A liberal was like a demon. They were anything but flexible or tolerant, but I didn't write about any of this in my articles. I was a reporter. I was saying what I was watching. I didn't express my feelings.

To be honest, I was against this war and against what they were doing. It was tricky to always be hiding my feelings. I never saw the need to make war and never believed the weapons of mass destruction. I never understood why they had to go and take over another country when there are so many dictators in the world that are, in fact, allies with the United States. I've covered Guatemala. I've covered Nicaragua. I thought that this was another way of intervention, of doing over here what they were doing in Central America—of customizing the government. I'm not surprised that Rumsfeld is the guy who cut a deal with Saddam Hussein in the eighties. It was like watching old dinosaurs.

HELLO TO ALL THAT

U.K.'s *News of the World*
Reporter Chris Bucktin

> "I think we are more fierce in the press than
> the Americans are. If the jugular is presented,
> we will go for it."

News of the World in the U.K. is the world's largest English language newspaper, with a circulation of just over four million. With that kind of readership, one would suspect that the British military would do everything in its power to accommodate the paper's embed. Wrong. Scandal-mongering and sensationalism are time-honored crafts practiced by British tabs—which made the military especially uneasy having a rogue reporter snooping around its ranks. Despite winning a bushel full of national press awards, including one for his investigative stories about a big-time drug dealer that led to fourteen convictions, Chris Bucktin, of East Yorkshire, discovered that war reporting presented many new challenges, the foremost being stiff upper-lip resistance from officers. "In the next war," Bucktin reflects, "I think I'd be an unilateral, because you can access a lot more information. I was too cocooned. And all you can do is put out information about what you know."

■　■　■

I was embedded with engineer regiments whose primary role was with the Sixteenth Air Assault Brigade, which included the parachute regiments. They fixed blown-up bridges or cleared away mines. I was with them for about two weeks. We breached the border so everybody else could follow through. It was a four-meter sand wall, then a four-meter sand ditch. There was one lad on a bulldozer going through. You didn't know what the hell was on the other side. There could have been a whole army. The adrenaline was incredible.

When I was with the engineers, editorial was a major factor with them. Because there was an undercurrent of antiwar feeling, the British army wanted the support of the public and would do anything to get that support. It was just frustrating. Everyone else was getting some good stuff. I couldn't move anywhere. The paper had another photographer flown out to work with me, but they wouldn't let him join me. There was a transmission ban by the British during the first four days of the war. The annoying thing was some journalists who were supposedly embedded were getting stuff back.

The British are generally more reserved. America has a much more liberal access to information. In some quarters of the British Army they're fearful of the press, especially the tabloids, which are very powerful organizations. It's the Fourth Estate, as it were. It's different in America, because you don't have such a national press like we do and because of the size of your country. Your press is a lot more fragmented. I think we are more fierce in the press than the Americans are. If the jugular is presented, we will go for it. But when you're embedded, you can't really piss 'em off. You piss 'em off, you're out of there.

Papers such as ourselves can speak to the entire nation very quickly. *The Times*, *News of the World*, and the *Sunday Times* are all part of the same group. We are a prowar paper. That doesn't mean we approve of war. That means we are in support of the war the government has chosen as its path. We support the troops as well. *The News of the World* is traditionally a soldier's paper. We speak their language. Blue collar and strong. Always has been and always will be. A big contingent of soldiers buy the *News of the World*, including officers as well. A lot of army recruitment comes from our paper. The officers would rather see their stories in our paper than something like *The Times*, because it's good for the recruitment. They want to see stories about the Desert Rats — the kids who are going to be driving these tanks. Readers will say, "I want to be a Desert Rat."

As an embed you were very much restricted in the stories you could look for. You didn't have a free role. You basically reported what you saw, and what you were privy to. On the whole, I was able to produce stories that I wanted to do, such as when some British soldiers were killed by friendly fire by the Americans, but I felt quite restricted at times about what I could and couldn't report. For instance, in the British press, you couldn't write that soldiers were wearing gas masks, or what guns they were carrying, or where the soldiers were. I often had to check my stories with the censors before I sent them.

I just wanted to stay alive. To be honest, I kept my hopes low and my ambitions low. I always kept my mind's eye open. I didn't know what to expect. I don't think anyone does, no matter how many wars you have done. I don't think you can be prepared for what the next war's going to bring. The only thing I had ever seen on this scale was the Bradford riots in Yorkshire, and that was a helluva riot in 2001. It was caused by racial tension between Asians and the police. There had been an arrest made of an Asian man. It just inflamed the whole situation, and was probably worse than the L.A. riots. Yet I always felt safe in that instance, because it wasn't me they were attacking. Whereas in Kuwait, there was a Scud alert. I felt genuine fear like never before. I've had guns and knives pulled on me. I've had death threats. But I felt genuine fear, because there is nothing you can do. You don't know where the Scud is going to land or if your number's up. So it woke me up. It brought the reality home. It really did. Before I came out here, people asked, "Are you nervous? Are you afraid?" and I wasn't. The Scud landed about three kilometers from our position.

What surprised me was the pace of war. Always on the go. Always moving forward. Then, a helluva lot of waiting around. The men would sit around for days. If they sat around too long, there was danger it could affect morale.

The military sensed that tabloids were only looking for scandals, for example if an officer started shagging around. Obviously that is what they were worried about. I have a classic example. This was back home. I was at this Yorkshire night club talking to this girl who asked, "What do you do for a living?" I said, "I tell ya what. I'll give you six jobs and you tell me which one of the jobs it is you think I do." I give her six jobs and one of them was the job I did. "The last one is it," she says. Then she runs off. I said to one of the lads, "There you go. That's why I don't tell people." She came back, and she had about thirty lads with her. They wanted to kick the hell out of me because three weeks before, our sister paper, the *Sun*, had done a story on all these junior officers getting pregnant by the soldiers from Dover, and they thought it was a story about them.

IT'S DÉJÀ VU ALL OVER AGAIN

GLOBE TV Executive Producer and
ABC News and *Nightline* Correspondent Mike Cerre

**"These young Marines had turned from
boys into men in the space of an afternoon."**

San Francisco broadcast journalist veteran Mike Cerre tapped into the global-village zeitgeist years before the Internet made it fashionable. As the founder and executive producer of GLOBE TV, Cerre transformed his former job skills as news anchorman and reporter at the NBC affiliate in San Francisco into creating an international magazine series that focused on documentaries like the 1994 World Cup and the forty-year anniversary of the Cuban Missile Crisis. He enhanced his stature as a global storyteller by licensing the worldwide television rights to *GEO Magazine,* which aired on the Arts & Entertainment Network and on foreign networks in thirty countries. Cerre was also the editorial director and executive producer of the *One Digital Day* book and CNN television special.

Yet with all his broadcasting bona-fides and four Emmys, when he showed up in Kuwait as an early-bird embed with Marines' Fox Company 2/5—several months before the ground war began—he was flying solo, a fifty-six-year-old freelancer schlepping all his gear and camcorders inside his expedition-size backpack. He moved about as a proverbial one-man media band until his cameraman showed up several weeks later. The further irony is that for the war's duration, Cerre received nearly as much television air time—primarily on ABC News and ABC's *Nightline*—as any of the cable and network top dogs who toured the battlefields in Humvees and were often supported by rear-echelon battalions of field producers, technicians, cameramen, and go-fers.

Cerre's life contains other delicious ironies. He saw combat action in Vietnam but lives in Marin County—one of the most liberal antiwar enclaves in the country. His youngest daughter was head of the Peace and Justice Coalition at her private high school. "My family couldn't understand why I was going to be so involved in this war," said Cerre, "having been in a war before and not anxious to see another one. And I was very much against war. We as a family with some friends went to a January peace march in San Francisco to demonstrate our concern about the foreign policy. I then ended up going to Kuwait the very next week. My eighteen-year-old daughter was very much torn between Marin activists, who are against everything that the government stands for and her father, who is involved with a military unit. My wife was upset that someone at my age and professional stature would get back into the grind of a being a war correspondent again. They were totally befuddled by my decision to do this."

■ ■ ■

When I was in Vietnam, I was a lieutenant with First Marine Division. I was a forward aerial observer. I saw friends die. I even met Ed Bradley from CBS there. I was also responsible for spreading a rumor. We had this new kind of bomb under the plane, and I told a reporter it was a mini-nuke, so we soon had all these other reporters crawling all over us trying to find out if it was true. I was later wounded and air medivaced out with what's known as a million-dollar wound.

Before I had gone over to Kuwait to cover the buildup to the Iraq war, I asked myself if I was trying to relive my youth, to redo something I had done thirty-three years ago—to be in a war situation. I was worried that long-buried fears and apprehensions would resurface—things I had never thought of in three decades. I was concerned about how I would react. Once in Kuwait, the Marines would ask me what it was like being shot at. They wanted to hear about my personal experiences of fear. Others would ask me for advice. They were as green as I was when I was in Vietnam. A lot of the junior officers came up to me and shared their apprehensions, concerns, and reflections going into combat. All I could do was assure them that it was very natural and normal, and that what they were feeling was probably no different than any other junior lieutenant going into combat for the first time. They had concerns like, "Will I be able to make the right decisions? Will I be able to get all my men out safely and accomplish the mission?" A lot of times I'd be talking to the enlisted men and noncommissioned officers (NCOs) and they'd be gung-ho and excited about the prospects of seeing combat. At some point I would tell them that it's not all peaches and cream, especially when you start seeing some of your friends get wounded or killed or civilians getting hurt. I told them not to be too anxious for it, because it's not all that good.

The war really began and ended on April 4th for our whole unit. That was the day we were engaged in a five-hour firefight going the last forty miles into the greater Baghdad area. The combat was rather intense. We had our first fatality in the loss of First Sergeant Ed Smith when an Iraqi ammo dump blew up. This was a really devastating blow to the psyche of the whole company. It was then followed that evening by a civilian tragedy in which eight people were killed at one of our checkpoints.

Smith was a twenty-year Marine veteran, with eighteen of those years as a Recon Marine, which is a kind of special operations for the Marines. He also worked for the Anaheim, California, police department. He had put in his retirement papers before the war, but they were frozen because of the troop buildup. He was physically a very imposing man, probably had to be six-foot-two, 230 pounds—a real hulk of a man; a very softspoken, senior NCO whom the troops absolutely feared, revered, and respected. When the notification came down that he was the man who was down, it was a real mortality check for the rest of the unit. They were in absolute shock hearing that of all the people that went down, he was the first one. These young Marines had turned from boys into men in the space of an afternoon. They all suddenly had this thousand-yard stare. Their grief set in about two days later, when the official notification came that he did succumb to his wounds. When they last saw him, he was mortally wounded but still alive, and so it took about two days before the official notification came down that he had died.

On that same day the ammo dump blew, I was involved in probably the worst nightmare for the Department of Defense concerning the embed process because I was right there when this civilian tragedy happened. The incident started when a civilian vehicle tried to come through the checkpoint and ignored the warning shots. The Marines opened fire to try to disable the vehicle—which they did. Two people were killed in that vehicle and in the backseat were women and children who were wounded. We were treating their injuries as we heard Marine snipers sending warning shots off to other vehicles that were coming down the road. They began sending off more shots because the drivers were ignoring the warning. I looked up and saw the headlights of a truck. I could hear it accelerating. The Marines opened fire on it and disabled the driver. The truck careened, hit a dirt mound on the side of the road, flipped up over on its side, and went right over our heads. It crashed maybe fifty feet beyond us. It was a dump truck that was beige with military painting and had military colored stripes on the radiator. The driver had an AK47 and a set of uniforms in a duffle bag in the back of the truck. But following right behind was an agricultural truck and a minibus filled with civilians. The Marines opened fire on all the vehicles as they came through the checkpoint. They killed three children and two women on the bus. Because I had such an open relationship with the unit, they knew I was going to have to make this report. We were all in shock as we set up the videophone. It was a horrible scene but I couldn't hold back. I couldn't pull any punches. I had to say exactly what I saw and how bad it was. As it turned out, I think the full disclosure worked to the benefit of everyone. There was no need for other reporters to find out what really happened because I was there as an eyewitness. While I was giving the live report, the executive officer of the company and two of the platoon sergeants were standing on the other side of the camera watching me. After I finished the report, the executive officer walked up to me and said, "You were fair."

Later, on May 8, I was at a reception with Rumsfeld and Tommy Franks in Washington, D.C. and I discussed this incident with Pentagon spokeswoman Victoria Clarke. Her reaction was that, yes, she remembered it, and we were both amazed that this was where, in the embed process you do get very close to these units. These people had become friends of mine and protected me through some terrible combat, and here I was now reporting on something which I thought was probably going to end the careers of the officers involved, or certainly taint their whole experience and mission over there with some kind of controversy.

The problem for reporters is not to cross the line in a story. It's even more difficult when you're in the middle of a story and that story happens to be a five-hour firefight. At one point during that battle, I found myself flashing back to my old days as a lieutenant in Vietnam and began using the instincts and some of the logic that I had to use then in combat. I didn't have a weapon, so I wasn't and couldn't be involved in combat, but I felt I had a responsibility to help the unit. I thought the best thing that I could do was to try to look ahead up the road and spot the oncoming civilians and point them out to the gunners so that they wouldn't wield the guns around and shoot them inadvertently. I was calling out the positions of the civilians because the gunners who were shooting out of the sides of the vehicle were not really looking forward. I wanted to give them a heads-up that they would be seeing something coming up via truck or in a ditch or near a building or something of that nature.

When you're a young man and you go into combat, you go into it quite naive and you come out of it a little bit wiser. You hope you never have to do it again. So here's this thirty-three-year time gap and I was doing it again and knowing what the consequences would be. I was quite apprehensive of how I would react, how I would feel. As it turned out, it felt like it was just yesterday. Everything came back rather quickly—all the training, all the instincts, the vernacular. I was surprised at some of the expressions that I was using. I'd be calling out the positions, "Eleven o'clock no joy, no joy"—which means you can't see or can't hear. If someone said, "You see the red truck," I'd say, "No joy, no joy" until I spotted it. Most of the time I was calling out by clock signal directions—"Eleven o'clock civilians in a ditch," "civilians eleven o'clock to one o'clock". It brought me right back to Vietnam.

The unit I was with, Fox Company 2/5—Second Battalion, Fifth Marines—has been the most decorated battalion in the Marine Corps. It goes back all the way to World War I and was one of the companies that was in the battle to re-take Hue during the Tet Offensive of 1968. They lost seventy percent of the company then. It took them a week to go a block. Members of that unit, Fox 2/5, Class '68, were regularly corresponding with this current class of Fox 2/5. They gave them encouragement and support and sent them things—just trying to share their professional experiences as best they could and to help prepare them for what they might have to encounter in Baghdad.

Before embeds were official, I joined my unit on the eighth of January. It was an arrangement I had with the commanding general of the First Marine Division even before the official embed process came down. He agreed to allow me to stay with one unit; he'd seen a story in the *Saturday Evening Post* profiling a Marine rifle squad through their whole evolution in Korea and was always fascinated by that—and was fascinated by the prospects of being able to do it here. So even before embeds were authorized by the Department of Defense, I was embedded with this unit. I went down to Camp Pendleton and accompanied the company to an old abandoned Air Force base in Victorville, California, which was designed to simulate urban street fighting. As part of the combat training exercise, everyone wore these vests with sensors, so when a sniper or an enemy shot at them, they would record a hit and the instructors would say, "You're down." "You're wounded." "You're killed," or whatever. It was quite realistic, and they were incurring seventy to eighty percent casualties the first few days they were going through the training, which was quite humbling—and terrifying—to them because it gave them a much greater appreciation for what they might have to encounter in Baghdad.

My cameraman, Mike Elwell, was with me at Camp Pendleton, but he didn't fly over with me to Kuwait. For the first three weeks in Kuwait I did the shooting on my own; then he joined me and we went back out to the desert of Kuwait for about two more weeks. After that he was with me all the way like a rock. We were two old guys; in fact, it was funny. I'm fifty-six and Mike is only about four months younger than me. The Marines were concerned that we both had the same name, and that in the heat of combat they'd yell out "Mike" and there'd be some confusion. So they said, "We're going to have to give one of you a nickname. Mike Elwell's got a gray goatee and beard and very gray hair, so we'll call him 'Junior.'" He loved that. That's the only thing that made his day—when through all the depravity they'd say, "Hey, Junior!"

The other thing that was kind of fun was that we'd see these wannabe network Scud Studs arrive in Kuwait, who must have been wondering what these two old farts were doing here, just being freelancers. I will tell you that Ted Koppel absolutely saved ABC's coverage. If it had not been for Ted Koppel and Richard Engels in Baghdad, who was also a freelancer, and myself, I don't know what ABC would have had. Well, what happened was the war kicked off early and our unit went across, so we had about a six-hour lead on all the other ABC colleagues as well as all the other networks. We were the first unit in. Koppel and the Third Infantry Division didn't go in for at least twenty hours after we went in—almost a whole day behind us, so we were doing most of the reporting from the first six hours of the invasion. Then the next day Koppel's unit started on the move and at that point, Koppel, I think, really dominated the coverage all the way through and did a phenomenal job of adding real context to the whole thing. A lot of stuff while I was there came across very breathless because of the invasion and because we were moving. Whereas Koppel's view of the battlefield was much broader than where I was on a company level. He had a much better sense of the big picture. He had more access to helicopters and vehicles to move around and see things. He could report on the grand scheme of things.

For those first six hours, we used a satellite phone. I was able to get the satellite phone working up on top of this armored assault vehicle as we went through the berms. We were embargoed from the time we left the staging area to the time we got up to the position on the line of departure. We left the staging area on March 17 when Bush made the speech, and there was a forty-eight-hour deadline. We were up on the line of departure on the eighteenth about a mile from the border, and we weren't supposed to go in until that

Saturday, the twenty-sixth. Then they started firing missiles into Kuwait and started moving tanks up along the border where we were going to cross over, so the decision was made almost instantaneously—to go right away and it was like an old cowboy movie—everybody just jumped on the horses and roared. So we went across, but I couldn't make any reports until we got into Iraq.

Our company had even done a dress rehearsal on how we were going to breach the border. We did it at night. They had set up some fake berms south of the border for us to practice going through. The engineers would go ahead with bulldozers to cut a hole to blast an opening through the berm, fence, and concertina wire. They were going to use these camping glow sticks to set a path, so that as we came racing across the desert at night we'd find the opening in the berm where we were going to go across and then the lane that they had cleared for mines. It was like a runway they had set up with these chem lights. I knew that when we went from blue chem lights to make the breach and then green chem lights to get through the minefield, we were into Iraq. You could hear me on the radio say, "I see the lights; I see the blue; we're green; we're through the berm; we're in." So we broadcasted going right in across the border.

We drove all night and got about forty miles inside Iraq, due west of Basra, and at daylight, when the sun came up, we stopped to refuel. At that point, a lot of people didn't even know the war had started—certainly the Iraqis didn't—and I was able to talk live by videophone with Peter Jennings. I think that was the first report inside Iraq—when the sun came up and there was still some firing going on and all kinds of vehicles were coming down the highway, having no idea the invasion had started. We later had 2,500 Iraqi troops surrender to our units.

The worst part was the sandstorms. We were on a foot patrol when one sandstorm hit us in Iraq. We immediately went to ground and to find each other, we had to put our arms or rifles out so that we could feel them. That's how bad the visibility was. We crawled back to our lines, and I imagine it took us a good hour to get maybe 400 yards. I've been out on the oceans in hurricanes, snowstorms, monsoons in jungles, but I've never been in a natural event that has been as disorienting as these sandstorms were. All you could hope to do was try to lie down, and cup your hands over your mouth to breathe.

We didn't have a vehicle. Mike Elwell and I carried everything in these huge expedition packs. I had one change of clothes, about ten to fifteen pounds of Handi-Wipes, a knit cap, and for washing, I used an old trick—a sponge in a Tupperware container—because I knew there wouldn't be enough water for bathing. I would give myself a sponge bath as best I could inside my chemical suit, which I never took off for twenty-two days. It gets pretty foul inside those chemical suits, which have a charcoal lining that's supposed to be absorbing the chemicals. I also had scarves for the sandstorms, one extra set of clothes, which I never used, and socks.

The most indispensable piece of gear I had was a little shortwave transistor radio, which I would dial into the BBC, which was the only way I knew what was going on and to find the whole big picture. I had those camping towels that roll up very small. I had one pair of Gore-Tex hiking boots, which became a big problem because Gore-Tex is water resistant and water repellent. With the chemical suit on and with the chemical boots—which are like rubber galoshes—over them, you sweat profusely. In fact, most of the Marines gave themselves trench foot because their feet were so wet from being inside the chemical boots. The same way with me. My feet were just frying all the time with the heat. Since we were pretty much on the move, there weren't many nights when we could take our boots off. During many nights we stayed inside the assault vehicles and slept sitting or leaning up. When you've got thirty guys in a vehicle, there's no room to take your boots off, not to mention the fact that the smell would be pretty bad. Yeah, it was just terrible, miserable conditions.

We brought four cameras with us, one fairly professional camcorder, a Sony 150, which is a $3,000 camera, and three other consumer-type camcorders, most of which were destroyed by the sand. On the first night of the invasion, I had trashed my main camera. I had a little shotgun microphone on it and as we were rolling across the desert at night we hit a ditch. I ended up in the gunner's hatch, literally did a somersault, and came down inside the assault vehicle right on top of the camera. It ripped off the whole top of the camera. I got some duct tape and sealed it up as best I could, but everything was destroyed.

By the end of my trip, my camping watch was broken. I probably started out with twenty pens, and all of them were gone or broken. I started out with four pairs of reading glasses—all four were smashed. Everything I had was broken. I don't think there's anything I had that wasn't broken. Just everything got destroyed.

When I finally came home—or finally got out of Baghdad—instead of coming straight home after I got finished in New York doing *Good Morning America* and a couple of shows—I flew back to Camp Pendleton for the funeral of First Sergeant Smith. My family joined me down there for the funeral, as did

Mike Elwell's wife. We were joined by other families from the unit. Since the mail had been very poor going to Kuwait, they realized that the only way to connect with the troops was through me, because they kept seeing my reports on ABC News or *Nightline* every week. That was the only way they could find out how their guys were doing. They set up an e-mail chain letter and my family was included. Whenever I was able to connect by satellite or had access to e-mail, they would send over this huge e-mail letter that I would then parcel out to all the troops, who would then make a big e-mail on my computer. When I could I'd send it back. My family would help with the Marines' wives to distribute it to all the individual families. As my family started to read some of this correspondence and see how emotional these families were and how thoughtful the Marines were, my wife and my daughter took on a whole different understanding of what this war was all about. They became very much involved in the whole process. We're still in constant communications with those families while their husbands and sons and brothers are still over there. I went back two weeks ago to Kuwait to do some final interviewing with some of the Marines for an *ABC Primetime* special. They were brought down from Iraq so they could be interviewed. I was able to catch up with them and get them cleaned up; get them showered; get them some good food and a twenty-four-hour Cinderella liberty. So we are still very, very close.

Meanwhile, my daughter made it a point to make sure that magnificent Marin County would feel this war as best she could possibly make it by keeping not only her dissent going with her Peace and Justice Coalition, but sharing some of the letters and my reports with her classmates. When I gave my first speech at her school on April 25th, the place was packed. I talked to them in the context that these Marines were their age who, right or wrong, had made a commitment to do something, were doing something, and were making great sacrifices, and that if they wanted to oppose the war, fine, but they have to make sacrifices equal to these guys who are involved in it, or else they just didn't count as far as I was concerned. They had to be as committed as these Marines were committed. I think they were impressed by the selflessness of these Marines—their maturity and their sense of commitment—and which is sometimes hard to find in kids this age. They understood that they were living through a part of history, and this was not a time to be sitting on the sidelines; if they were for or against it, they ought to be involved because it was an important part of history. Whatever else they had going in their lives, it could not be as important as what these guys were experiencing and what the country was going through. My daughter's still very much opposed to the war and the reason behind it and the decision to do it, but she also has the ultimate respect for the troops, which is something that was different during the Vietnam era.

CAPTURING THE WAR'S MOST MEMORABLE IMAGE

Time Magazine Photographer Yuri Kozyrev

> "I don't use body armor because I must move. It's also better to be exposed so they can trust you."

Time magazine's director of photography, Michele Stephenson, speaks fondly of her supremely talented stable of photographers sent to cover the Iraq War, including legendary James Nachtwey. Yet one soft-spoken Russian with sad eyes, Yuri Kozyrev, came up with perhaps the war's most indelible image: the badly wounded twelve-year-old boy named Ali Ismail Abbas who lost both his arms in an American missile attack that killed his mother, brother, sisters, and stepfather. Instead of being intrusive and shoving his camera lens in the boy's face, as competitors did a few days later, Kozyrev quietly stood back in the fading twilight of the room and carefully squeezed a frame showing Ali's aunt putting her comforting hand on her nephew's head.

"Yuri went to the hospital and was the first photographer to find the boy," Stephenson explained. "He shot it in a respectful way and rendered it in a powerful painterly composition. When we received the picture, I thought it was *the* picture of the war. We talked to many people on the staff and asked, 'How would you feel if it was your child? Would this be an invasion of the boy's privacy?' Ultimately, we decided it was a transcendent picture. It will last forever as an icon that says more about this war in terms of civilian casualties. It was so painful to look at such a beautiful child injured in such a horrible way. Yuri caught it in a elegant and powerful way." Within days, Kozyrev's photograph inspired donations from around the world that paid for Ali's transfer to a Kuwait hospital that saved him from certain death by blood poisoning.

■　■　■

I am Russian. Born in Moscow. I have been a photographer many years. I was lucky with the teaching I got from Moscow University. I studied all the great photographers, people like Henri Cartier-Bresson, Josef Koudelka, W. Eugene Smith, Robert Capa, and James Nachtwey. I was lucky to work with James here. We were both on assignment for *Time*. We shared the hotel room. I saw how he worked.

Last year was very good. I wanted to go to Afghanistan from the beginning. The rule of the assignment was to use digital. I went there for *New York Times* and *Los Angeles Times*. It was hard, but it was a great experience. I spent six months there. Same with Iraq, but I only worked for *Time*. First time I came was in September. I was supposed to spend only two weeks. But I was lucky. I extended my visa to two months.

To shoot then was hard because there were always minders. They were trained by the KGB. Sometimes they could not understand what I really wanted. I would want to stay for a while and wait for a picture. It's only pictures for them. The second trip was more easy. They knew me. It was in November, when inspectors came. So I covered them. It was boring—waiting, waiting, waiting. At the same time, I found that there were some interesting opportunities. For the first time when the minders didn't follow us, we'd go to some place and we were free to cover the story. My third trip was at the beginning of this year. In January I was sure the war would happen. This time it is great. The best. I have a long assignment. So living is good.

I knew this war would be different than other wars I covered. I spent a lot of time in Chechnya. At the beginning of the second Chechnya war, I started with Russians and after two months, I left them and found a great fixer who helped me to join the rebels. Before the Iraq war, we were by ourselves. We were caught between the Iraqi side and the American side. We were in the middle— between the two powers. It was something new. We didn't know how it would break. Of course, there were many rumors about Iraqis. Who knows? They could arrest you. They could kidnap you. You get used to it. Maybe they will use us as a pawn. All of us who stayed here didn't know exactly how it would be.

When the war started I was in Baghdad. I took pictures of the bombings from the roof of the Palestine Hotel. We had opportunity to cover the bombing only twice. We saw what was happening on the other side of the river, but it was more important to be on the ground, to get to the right places, which were destroyed. I was anxious to get to the hospital. Try to cover military stuff. It was really hard. I was lucky. I met some members of the Ba'ath Party, and they were angry because of the bombing—with Americans, with foreigners. Sometimes they allowed me to stay for awhile, and I could take some pictures of them. It was on and off.

I found the young boy Ali by chance at Yarmuk Hospital. It was not far from my hotel. I went to the hospital many times, and I found him.

At the hospital, Ali was on the bed covered with this material. A woman was behind him. The doctor allowed me in for a short time. Ali was dying; I was not sure that he would survive. They allowed me to be in the room for a few minutes. A light came in from the window. It was very dark. I used a long exposure, so it was only natural light. With digital you can push up speed of the film. I could only stay for a short time—a few frames. With Ali it was clear I couldn't come closer to him. He was suffering.

Then the doctor told me the story about his relatives, and I left the hospital for the village the same day. It was really hard. I went with a driver. We got to the village and there was only one person I talked to. When we drove back we were stopped by a group of village men with AK47s. They were really angry and they made us sit on the ground. It was very scary.

Sometimes it works that I am Russian. At that moment, it worked, but they were really angry, because the day before they lost seventeen people from a U.S. bomb—Ali's family, among them. But that photograph of Ali was useful. He got help. People donated money. Medical help. Of course, there were many boys who needed help, but I am glad I could help one.

I don't think about danger. What's more important to me is I can see the most extreme forms of life and death. I always prefer to be with the weak side. See what's happening.

I used a digital Canon and sent by satellite phone and laptop. I don't use body armor because I must move. I had a bad experience with armor in Chechnya. It's also better to be exposed so they can trust you. But we missed a lot of stuff in this war. We could not join the Iraqi side, so we didn't know what happened in their military camps.

Why do I do this? It is very simple. I am a news photographer. I recently had an odd conversation with another photographer. He told me that an old French lady asked him, "Are you with peace? You a member of peace team?" And his answer was very simple. "I am a war photographer." It was before the war, but it's true. I think it is the same with me. I am here because I knew that the war would happen. Before the war I tried to show how the people were living, and to cover all different sides of the war. I don't care about secrets.

BACK TO BAGHDAD
CNN International Correspondent Nic Robertson

> "The Ministry of Information didn't like anything
> that looked like they weren't in control or looked
> like we had any sort of power."

CNN's Nic Robertson was trained in engineering at Aston University in Birmingham, England, and Dundee College of Technology. For a cable network news correspondent whose job in Iraq was to cover missiles crashing into Baghdad, there is a touch of irony regarding Robertson's first job offer—working at a missile production factory—which he declined. Instead, his career trajectory followed a different arc when he became a satellite broadcast engineer working on TV transmitters. Within two years, he was setting up CNN satellite dishes in Baghdad for the likes of Peter Arnett and Bernard Shaw, the megastars of the first Gulf War. While Arnett, the 1966 Pulitzer Prize–winning veteran international correspondent stumbled into a career sinkhole as the narrator of a discredited 1998 CNN documentary claiming the U.S. military used nerve gas on its own soldiers in Vietnam, then ambushed his own comeback by granting an obsequious interview to state-run Iraqi television, the telegenic Robertson has become CNN's latest Scud Stud. We spoke with the forty-year-old Robertson near an empty swimming pool at the Palestine, next to CNN's post-Saddam headquarters in Baghdad.

■ ■ ■

When the Iraqi government kicked me out of the country, I was disappointed on a number of levels—competitively and professionally. You've put so much energy and effort in just being able to be there. You had the minders very close by. I suppose it would have been like being embedded and reporting that the morale in the military was bad. You would have quickly found yourself not very close to the front line. It was important to give our audience access to a story in the same way that audiences of other organizations have. It was disappointing because you're putting the effort into trying to cover the situation, and then you know when you leave there are other journalists who will cover it. When you commit yourself to covering a story like this war, you have a belief there is a value in covering it. Yes, there are inherent risks, but once you've taken that step of personal faith, that it is valuable to do it, so when you're kicked out, all that is thrown away.

It had been clear to me because of what happened in 1991, in talking to Iraqi officials, that they wanted journalists to tell their side of the story. They were going to highlight the humanitarian and civilian tragedy. I believed they would let people stay and do their work after a fashion. I believed it was going to be possible to do it.

Iraqi officials had made it clear to us that they believed they made CNN because they gave us all that access in the first Gulf War. They believed that we owed them a return favor. But they had become increasingly angry that that wasn't happening over the last four or five years. They banned a number of CNN people. They banned our bureau chief. We were only allowed four international people to work here. BBC had ten.

There wasn't a particular story that made them decide to boot us. Just that we weren't being professional. That we were creating rumors. So they put the major squeeze on us. They really didn't like the fact that CNN carried influence with other journalists, rightly or wrongly. People would come to us and say, "I work for a small newspaper and my editor said just do what CNN does." When we decided to move to the Palestine Hotel, we told the ministry of information this is what we would do, because were aware of the impact and knew it would potentially mean a lot of other people would move there, too. We did our best to play that down. The ministry of information didn't like anything that looked like they weren't in control or looked like we had any sort of power. It was like dealing with a union. We were a threat to their power. That is how they react to things. It was incredible.

The Iraqis looked to Peter Arnett to be the voice of western journalists, and he knew a lot of the minders really well. There was probably a lot of pressure on him to do something for them, but to do an interview with Iraqi TV, one has to know what one is getting into. I was with him in 1991 as an engineer. I learned a huge amount from Peter and have a huge amount of respect for him. One of the things I learned from Peter was to focus on what you believe in. Particularly when it comes to staying on a story. If other people are going to leave, fine. Let them leave, but if you think you can do the story, then stay. I think he came back here this time because he felt really connected with the story, and as a journalist, he'd been frustrated by the fact he hadn't been able to work for a while. This was a good opportunity to start again as a correspondent for MSNBC and *National Geographic Explorer*, but a lot of people found it offensive that he should say that journalists were welcomed and were being treated well when there were journalists at that time being picked up and placed in jail. Only he can answer why he decided to make those remarks.

In retrospect, it was valuable to be on the outside where we were freer than we would have been had we been in Baghdad. I was now reporting from the Jordanian-Iraqi border, so I was able to draw on all my experiences, and there were things I may not have been able to report from Baghdad that I was able to report from outside. The coverage we provided from Baghdad was difficult under the circumstances because of the restrictions the government put in place. It was difficult to get a free and accurate account because people were inhibited from talking to you.

After Saddam's statue fell, we returned the next day. I had just left Jordan for Kuwait. I was able to sit on the set with one of our anchors and just spend about three or four hours talking about what was happening.

The hardest part for me was coming back to Baghdad. I didn't expect that. Leaving, I felt we had done a good job. We'd tried everything to stay. We'd been forced out. So I felt good professionally because I had done everything I could. When I came back, that is when I felt a sense of loss. I felt disappointment when I saw my colleagues who were here because I knew what I hadn't been able to cover, but you have to be philosophical about this. It was a bad break, but I've had really good breaks throughout my career.

My first job overseas was with NBC at the Berlin Wall. The Berlin Wall was coming down. They needed an engineer. The Berlin Wall seemed to be a much more joyous event than Saddam's statue coming down. There was a lot more caution around this, and there still is. It is like after taking down the Berlin Wall, people really thought that Communism was about to come back, but once they pulled down the wall, capitalism took over eastern Germany. Here, people are very, very guarded and cautious. The people certainly aren't rushing into the streets to celebrate this newfound freedom.

ONCE A MARINE, ALWAYS A MARINE

San Francisco Chronicle Reporter John Koopman

"You wanted to send a message that Third
Battalion, Fourth Marines was not to be trifled
with. That was the philosophy behind violent
supremacy."

Marines are a proud, stubborn, insular bunch. They will "semper fi" each other
long after the last shots are fired. They believe in tradition. They believe in broth-
erhood. Their martial bonds last a lifetime. Which made embedment all that
much easier for *San Francisco Chronicle* reporter John Koopman, who served in
the Corps from 1976 through 1980 as a sergeant specializing in radio communications. Now it was time to reenlist as an embedded reporter. In early February,
2003, he joined up with the Third Battalion, Fourth Marine Regiment, which was
conducting training exercises in the Kuwaiti desert. "Unlike other embeds," recalls Koopman, "I didn't wait for the Pentagon to assign me a slot with a unit of
their choosing. I understood the best place to see action." And that would be
with the Marines, whose time-honored point-of-the-spear way reaches back to
the Halls of Montezuma and was now pointed toward the Gates of Baghdad.

Twenty-seven years ago, Koopman was all of seventeen, from a small
Nebraskan town when he arrived at Parris Island for boot camp. Now, middle-aged,
with a wife and eight-year-old boy, he returned to kinder, gentler drill instruction:
media boot camp at Fort Dix, New Jersey. "It was a bit like summer camp," wrote
Koopman in one of his *Chronicle* war dispatches. "After hours, we joked and had a
good time and ate Philly cheesesteaks at off-base dive bars. And some started talking like soldiers. Richard Leiby, *The Washington Post* writer, reminded people to
keep their heads on a swivel (look around for booby traps and enemy soldiers). In
the barracks we talked about getting a 'sitrep' (situation report) on whether there
would be morning 'pt' (physical training). Nick Kulish of *The Wall Street Journal* got
some 'good intel' on a Korean barbecue place. And we all agreed that Leatherman
tools are real 'high speed' (Air Force for first-rate, or really cool)."

■ ■ ■

I went to boot camp in 1976, right out of high school. I had nothing to do and no place to go, and my parents didn't really have money to send me to college. I grew up in a real small town in Nebraska. It's called Howells and is about an hour-and-a-half drive northwest from Omaha. I went to Parris Island. It had heat, humidity, and sand fleas. It was at a time when drill instructors could still swear, but it was just after the time that they banned actual outright physical violence against people. In those days, they could use the words "fuck," "shit," anything you wanted, and at that time you were a "fuckin' maggot!'" There was no sugar coating. Those guys were all Vietnam vets. They all had a whole ton of combat ribbons. It was tough, it was brutal. They really were there to weed out anybody who was even remotely weak. It wasn't so much the physical part of it. I had played football and wrestled in high school, so physically, I was up to the challenge, but mentally, some of the stuff that they put us through was just harsh. It was meant to test your will.

Not long after I got there, one of the other recruits tried to commit suicide by jumping off the third-floor barracks. He survived, but he broke a leg in the process. The senior drill instructor called the platoon together in the barracks and he said, "You know, I just never realized that boot camp was so tough that somebody would actually try to commit suicide, so if it's all that harsh, I don't want anybody here who doesn't want to be here. Any of you who want to leave now, just come on up to the front here, stand here at attention. Just come on up, and we'll take your names and we'll process you out, because I don't want anybody to have to go through that." So, of course, five or six guys go running up to the front of the squad bay, and the rest of us are standing at attention. I'm thinking, "What idiots!" Sure enough, the drill instructor just launches into this screaming match. He said, "You think I was going to let you out of the Marine Corps. You're nuts! In fact, now that I know what a bunch of pussies you are, I'm going to make it doubly hard on you! I'm going to work on you until you crack!" He took all their names down and then he sent them back and he said, "I want to be looking out for you and I'm going to make everything just doubly tough on you!"

My worst day in boot camp was the Bicentennial of the United States of America, July Fourth, 1976. Everybody had the day off except us. The drill instructor that day decided that since he was miserable, he would make our lives miserable. We spent the entire day doing punishment calisthenics. This was called bends and thrusts: You're standing at attention, then you would drop down to your hands on the pavement, shoot your legs out behind you into a push-up position, then reverse it and bring your legs back up and stand up. He then made us go back inside the squad bay to clean everything up, and if he didn't like it, we would have to take our footlockers and dump them out in the middle of the floor and take all of the bedding off of our racks and dump it. Then we had to run outside and do some more bends and thrusts. This went on all day long. By the end of it, we were just whipped. We absolutely, physically, just couldn't move another inch. I remember, we were on our backs doing leg lifts—punishment leg lifts—and I was near tears, thinking, "This is just insane. I can't put up with this a minute longer!" By that time, even he had wrung himself out, so eventually things sort of got better, but that was the worst day—Bicentennial. I'll never forget that.

By comparison, media boot camp was not even remotely as difficult or as mentally challenging as even an hour of Marine Corps boot camp. There were mainly three days of a lot of classroom work. We learned about terrorism and infantry tactics and chemical, biological, nuclear devices. Then, finally, we got out into the field and we'd learn things like how to take cover if the truck convoy was ambushed. For a lot of the guys who hadn't ever been in the military, media boot camp was eye-opening, especially the technical challenge of being in the military. They had this sense of "Well, if you're a soldier or a Marine, you're just dumb, and basically you just carry a rifle and a pack around and somebody tells you where to set up and you set up." But, I mean, the more you know about it, the military requires a whole bunch of skill sets such as land navigation—how do you get from point A to point B out in the middle of nowhere when you don't have a street map to guide you, or how do you defend against a chemical attack?

In my session, there were around sixty reporters and photographers. We broke down into squads, and the squads were about ten each. They never let us shoot a weapon. We went out one time to a live-fire exercise, where there was a squad of soldiers in foxholes who were carrying the various weapons that a standard infantry squad would carry—a 50-caliber machine gun and the other one was the Mark 19, which is like an automatic grenade-launching device. In the distance, there were a bunch of old, messed up vehicles that they used for target practice. So everybody fired off those weapons just to familiarize the reporters and photographers with the sound, the smell, the sight of the weapons going off. How does an M-16 sound when it's firing on fully automatic? Actually, the M-16s these days go off in three-round bursts, unless you carry this squad automatic weapon. Of course, when I was in the Marines, I fired all these weapons except for the Mark 19, which we didn't have at that time. They never put a gun in our hands at media boot camp, and, of course, the U.S. government forbade reporters from carrying firearms during the war in Iraq.

At Fort Dix we had physical training in the mornings and they put us through a wringer. I work out pretty regularly myself. We would do forty minutes or an hour of real strenuous calisthenics and running. I tell you, it was pretty tough, and a lot of the reporters were really sucking wind.

We spent classroom time talking about various wounds and how to deal with them when we were out in the field. They would put us on these deuce-and-a-half trucks as if in a convoy, and we would drive along and all of a sudden, we would come upon a bunch of soldiers who were play acting that they had been ambushed by enemy forces. They used a lot of actors' special effects things to simulate various wounds. The woman I ended up tending to had a stick impaled in her eye. Other people had to deal with sucking chest wounds. Basically you find a piece of plastic, like an ID card, and cover the wound and tape it in place so that you prevent air from getting inside and you can re-inflate the lungs. For the most part though, the idea is to stop the bleeding, help them breathe, and find a medic.

I arrived in Kuwait on February 18. I went early because obviously there was no start date for the war. I also wanted to be able to spend some time with the Marines, so I was comfortable with them, they were comfortable with me, and it would be a seamless transition. The unit I was assigned was Third Battalion, Fourth Marines, which is part of the Seventh Marine Regiment of the First Marine Division—and I had met them earlier in December of last year. What I didn't want to do was arrive one day and have the war start two days later.

There were quite a few embeds in Kuwait when I got there. I don't know how many because there was a combination of embedded and unembedded or unilateral types, and for a long time, it was a little bit difficult to separate one from the other. It was kind of an odd and difficult time when I first got there, because the military would set up in these tent cities way to the north, near the Iraqi border, and we were into Kuwait City, so you couldn't just drive out there and say, "Hey, I want to interview some guys; I want to do the story." You had to work through the military public affairs system and you had to get escorts.

Because I had been in the Marines, I had to spend less time getting people to trust me. I could go in and ask the question right off the top, or I could preface a question by saying, "Look, without revealing operational security details, tell me about your job or what makes your job different from your buddy's job." They understood that I knew what they couldn't say, as opposed to what I wanted them to say. Sometimes a reporter would come in and ask, "Well, why is your weapon on the top of this vehicle?" They felt like I understood them better, or I didn't have to ask as many questions. Once a Marine, always a Marine.

Marines are a different group, especially compared to, say, the U.S. Army or the U.S. Air Force. There's a natural cockiness about them and a sort of desire to be noticed. They like attention. They're like high school football players. They will say, "Oh, reporters. Yeah, I'm tough, I'm bad, I'm a Marine. Let me tell you how tough I am." In the army and the air force, you get a lot more of a bureaucratic sense of "What's my job?", "What's my mission?"

When I got to the Third Battalion, Fourth Marines, commanding officer Colonel Bryan McCoy's philosophy was once he knew me and trusted me, he just opened up. "Go wherever you want, ask whatever you want, and you understand what the security issues are. As long as you know that and I know that you're not going to abuse that trust, do whatever you want; talk to whoever you want; write whatever story you want." It was completely open and unfettered that way. Colonel McCoy was such a character. You could go to McCoy and ask him anything. He would respond with something that was quotable, interesting, sometimes controversial, at any time of the day or night. He liked the attention. He was supremely confident in his abilities and he loved being a Marine, so with the media, he just liked to be able to convey that.

He's an army brat. I think his father did a couple of tours in Vietnam. He went to the University of Oklahoma, then commissioned in the Marines, and spent basically most of the time with the infantry. He's been a platoon commander, a company commander. He took a company to Iraq in the first Gulf War, although the action that he saw was rather limited. Throughout that time, as most officers do, he bounced around between having an active command and going to various schools. He worked as an aide to the Chief of Naval Operations in Washington, so he got some pretty good contacts with the Pentagon sources, and then just found himself in charge of a battalion for this war, which is a great place to be. In talking to him, he pretty much said the same thing. If there's a fighting war going on, what you want to be is a company commander or a battalion commander, because those are the only two positions where you're really engaged in the fight at the same time as having command of men. He had about eleven hundred men under his command, no women. Combat battalions don't have any women by law. Women can get into various combat support units to get near the fighting, but they cannot be assigned to a fighting combat battalion.

His men liked him a lot. I say this objectively because I have talked to a lot of them and I have watched the Colonel from a distance. He liked to mingle with his Marines; he liked to talk to them and find out what their problems were, and they liked him. He was not a desk jockey kind of a guy. Even during combat, he would get up close. He would drive right up to where the fighting was going on. I asked him about this one time, and he said, "Well, you know the way it works is command and control—I command, the rest of my staff controls." So he could be out in his Humvee chasing around, checking things out, and he had, of course, a radio. The rest of the battalion staff people were back in that central location with all sorts of radios at their disposal, and he could call back and he could say, "Well, I'm with Kilo company and we need artillery support at grid coordinate XYZ." They would call in artillery on that site or he would let them know what he saw. I'll just say one more thing about McCoy that I think is very telling. He would go out and fight himself at times with his M-16. He would do that because he wanted to make his men understand that he was the kind of leader who wouldn't ask them to do anything that he wouldn't do himself.

There's a fine balance between putting yourself foolishly at risk and joining the battle so that your troops know that you're with them. To give you an example of that, here's something that I witnessed McCoy do near Basra. We were driving along a road behind a company of American tanks that was firing at a bunch of Iraqi armor. I think mostly it was abandoned stuff. It was near an Iraqi army barracks. So we're driving along in the tanks, and all of a sudden, somebody looks over to our right, which is behind the area where the tanks are firing, and thirty yards from us is an Iraqi tank buried in the dirt with its turret exposed. This is something that they would do a lot, especially a tank that was maybe not in good working order. They would just bury it and use it as an artillery piece. Not only was the Iraqi tank turret sticking up out of the mud, there was a machine gun on top of it. Nobody was visible, but there it was, and if somebody was in that tank, all they had to do was to traverse the turret a few degrees and they would be aiming right at us and they could just blow us away. So, McCoy and his radio man jump out of the vehicle, run over to where the tank is, and they start checking it out. Well, the top hatch is what they call battle-locked from inside, meaning that somebody inside has locked it into place. So he goes running back over to the Humvee and he starts shooting at the tank trying to get whoever's inside to open up or start firing back. Everybody in the Humvee is firing at this tank, but nothing is happening, so McCoy runs over, picks a grenade out of his pouch and tosses the grenade at the tank. A grenade doesn't necessarily do anything to the tank except rattle the cage of whoever's inside — you're trying to get somebody out. Nothing happens. We end up driving back down the road and just have another one of the tanks shoot it, but the word of McCoy fragging a tank spread like wildfire among Marines in other battalions: "Hey, man, we heard your CO was tossing grenades at tanks!"

The Third Battalion saw as much combat action as anybody. They were engaged in a minimum of six significant fights, which doesn't sound like a lot, but that goes basically from Basra all the way up to Baghdad, and those were actual significant, severe, stand-up, face-to-face, toe-to-toe kind of battles. There weren't too many other units that had many more than that.

McCoy liked to use the term "good kill" a lot. I understood that meant that a good kill is just that; you're out there killing the enemy, and that's good. If you can do that, that's a good thing. You certainly never heard the term "bad kill." He would use "good kills" due to the difficulty of engaging the enemy, because there were lots of times that we would see an Iraqi APC in the distance and shoot it to make sure it couldn't be used again. Well, you don't know necessarily if somebody is inside there or not. Or if you saw a bunker, you might fire a mortar at it. It's not that that was a bad kill, but if there was an Iraqi standing there firing an AK47 at you and you shot him and killed him, that's a good kill; you know you've killed an enemy soldier. It's not about good or bad, a good kill is just that you're out there killing the enemy.

As we moved northwest toward Baghdad, we started hearing all these accounts of things that went bad, especially around Nasiriyah. We heard about the army supply convoy that got ambushed and the people killed and taken prisoner, and then there was another ambush where a whole bunch of Marines got killed due to a fake surrender. Some Iraqis had a white flag, the Marines went out there to take them prisoner, and then the Iraqis opened fire with RPGs and AK47s and killed a bunch of them. So far, there was not that much enemy activity on our march column, but the Marines decided they did not want to have a replay of Nasiriyah. If there were intelligence reports of a lot of militia and guerrilla activity in these small towns along the way, they would go in there with what they called "going in heavy," which was not taking in any soft-skinned Humvees or any kind of light-skinned vehicles, but only going in with armor and fully loaded Marines. They would go into these places and if they saw anybody carrying a rifle or with any kind of hostile intent, they'd kill them. They wouldn't just shoot up the place just for the sake of doing it. If they saw civilians, they would treat them nicely or whatever, but the idea was that you went in and you used "violent supremacy." It was kind of like being the big bad-ass kid on the block. If somebody wanted to pick a fight, you would just squash them with artillery, mortars, rocket fire, heavy machine-gun fire. The idea was to not only kill as many Iraqis with hostile intent that you could, but also to send the message that there would be no replay of Nasiriyah. If somebody wanted to surrender, then they better come to you. If they didn't come to you and if they showed any kind of hostile intent, you'd just lay waste to them. You wanted to send a message that Third Battalion, Fourth Marines was not to be trifled with. That was the philosophy behind violent supremacy.

The concept of violent supremacy, certainly from an independent viewpoint, could be argued as good or bad. I didn't feel either way, to be honest. To me, it was always about observing, watching them do what they did, and then simply reporting on it after the fact. I had to believe that there were times when the locals probably thought they were being too harsh. These Marines would go into houses—they would bust down doors, get up on roofs, and basically assert themselves. You had to wonder, "Well, did people think they were just like animals and brutes?" There was no real way to find out. The embedded process was such that you had to stay with your unit, and this was one of the drawbacks of embedding.

While I rode with the Colonel near Basra, I had switched over to ride in the Humvees with David Howell, the sergeant-major of the battalion. He was the senior enlisted man for the battalion and his job was to maintain and enforce order and discipline. During battle, he would go to wherever the fighting was, kind of like the Colonel, but in a more detailed way. If they needed reinforcements or supplies, or if he thought that their order and discipline was breaking down, he would do whatever it took to keep it going. We got really close in on some stuff in that. In the battle outside the city of Kut, the driver of that Humvee was shot about ten feet from where I was, and later died.

I was shocked really, but it's really hard to describe. I was standing next to him as he was firing a grenade launcher at a bunker and I didn't feel, necessarily, that there was a raving firefight going on about thirty yards from where we were standing, which was on the backside of an armored vehicle. I felt relatively safe. I left his side to get a different vantage point and take a look at the battle and when I got back, he was down on the ground and the Sergeant-Major and a U.S. Navy medical corpsman were working on him. His name was Mark Evnin. At first, I didn't even recognize him. I thought it was somebody else, and I walked over a little bit closer and I saw that he was lying there and I thought, "Damn, how did that happen?" He had a couple of bullet holes in his lower abdomen. They were working on him. They called up a Humvee to evacuate him back to the battalion aid station and I saw them loading him on the stretcher. When I saw him, he was alert, he was fine, and so, I guess, my feeling was, "It's too bad that Mark got shot; it's unfortunate, but at least he's alive. At least he's going to be okay," because in my experience, as a reporter, anytime you get somebody who is stable and alert, and you pack them on an ambulance or whatever, they usually make it. Later on, we stopped by the battalion aid station and found out that they had put him on a helicopter to evacuate him and we were all joking, "Good for Mark. He's out of this. He's going to be going back, he's going to be in a hospital, he's going to be getting sponge baths from pretty nurses. Good for him." It was only later that night, right around dusk, the Sergeant-Major called me aside and he said, "Look, Evnin didn't make it." At that time, we really didn't have any details of why he didn't make it. A couple of weeks later, I happened to meet the doctor who worked on him. With a lower abdomen wound, you never know what that is. I was thinking that maybe it was some kind of peritonitis or toxic shock. He said, "No, it was hemorrhage." He must have gotten hit in an artery or something in there and it wasn't external bleeding; he was bleeding internally and they couldn't stem it in time and he died.

I had another close call. It was right outside of Baghdad. At a bridge over the Dyala Canal, and the battalion was trying to take the bridge. The Iraqis were on the other side putting up some pretty fierce resistance. The Marines spent all of one day firing across the bridge, and then the next morning, the idea was the Marines were going to fire a bunch of artillery and mortars onto the other side and then rush. They couldn't drive anything across the bridge, but they could run and walk across, so the idea was they would soften up the other side and then run across it. While we were waiting there on the south side of the bridge, an artillery shell hit and it landed right on top of a Marine armored personnel carrier. It hit so close that I got sprayed with hot engine oil all over the back of my vest. The hatches were closed. The crew chief and the driver were inside the vehicle at the time the shell hit. If the shell hadn't hit that vehicle or if it had landed three meters short, it probably would have killed twenty guys because that's where they were staging and getting ready to run across this bridge. The vehicle itself absorbed the blast. I was close enough to feel the blast, the wind hit me from the rear, but fortunately, there was no shrapnel coming with it, so I was all right. When I got down on the other side of the wall where it had hit, it was just this nightmare scene. There was blood and oil all over the vehicle. Two died and four were wounded.

After the artillery shell landed, all the unilateral photographers who were with us just swarmed on the scene. I watched five photographers taking picture after picture of the wounded, of the guys treating the wounded and, well, of the dead, too. They shot every inch of that scene. What made me feel queasy was not that they were there taking the pictures, but, if you've ever been at the scene of a story, especially where there are dead and wounded, photographers look physically like vultures, you know? Like in this case, sometimes there'd be three or four guys, and they would get together in a huddle almost and they'd be there snapping all these pictures and sort of moving around—as the Marines were moving—to get the best shot. They physically look like a group of vultures picking over dead meat. It's only afterward that they determine which photograph to use. They edit the photos and it all looks very professionally done and nobody really has a beef with it. Even some of the Marines I talked to said the same thing, "Look at those guys. They look horrible." I would say, "Well, you know, this is why I like being a reporter, because I don't have to do that. I can stay twenty yards back and I can observe and I can take notes, but I don't look like a vulture."

The immediate effect on the unit was just incredible shock. Nobody really could believe that it happened. At first, it was thought to be an American round, because the Marine artillery had been pounding the shore of this canal all morning and the Iraqi response came at the end of an American barrage. I don't know that it really mattered in the final analysis. People were walking around just dazed and shocked. Some of these guys had to deal with the wounded; some of these guys had to deal with the dead. They had to scrape them up, put them into their bivy burial sacks, and remove the bodies. It was horrific and it delayed the taking of the bridge. McCoy had to reassert control. He sent the word down, "All right. We lost two dead, we lost some wounded, but the mission goes on. Now we have to get back and get ready to go."

After seeing their buddies killed that way, it's really a tribute to their own training and discipline that they were able to regroup and say, "Okay, we've got to put this behind us. We still have a mission to do. You can't just spend the rest of the day mourning and moping for your dead comrades. It's time to get on with the mission." But that was the last major battle of the war.

Overall, I'm a real fan of the embedding process. It's the way wars should always have been covered, and probably it's the wave of the future. The Pentagon stuck with it through the end, even though they did a few things that were not exactly conducive to the media. For example, they assigned single slots as embedding assignments, but a newspaper needs to have a reporter-photographer team working together.

People talk about embedding's limitations and how they felt restricted or too close to the unit, and I found the arguments ridiculous. The bottom line is if the military's going to be open enough to say, "Look, you can come with us. We will let you see everything you want to see and cover the war from this close-up seat," of course, it's not a perfect environment; of course, you can say, "Well, gee, you know, we would like to do this; we would like to do that; we would like to have more access; we would like to be able to talk to the enemy soldiers." Well, you know what? That's fine, but that's unrealistic. Not since World War II have you really been able to have reporters sitting in and watching the battle as it unfolds. Even in World War II there was censorship. There might have been a few cases of problems like that in some units, but in my case, there was not a single bit of censorship. I remember one day, it wasn't until we were in Baghdad and we had a little time on our hands and I was sitting there talking to McCoy one night and he said, "You know, I never have read any of your stories." I said, "Well, here," I had my laptop and I had the unedited versions that were still there. I just opened them up on the computer and said, "Go ahead. Knock yourself out. Read the stories."

People asked me before I went, "Why would you want to do such a thing?'" especially family members or friends. All I could tell them was, "That's the story. That's what you do as a reporter. You want the biggest story around and certainly you can't get any bigger than war." I had never witnessed war before, and as a reporter you get to experience different things in a way that most people don't ever get to. So to me it was, "Whoa, war. I've never seen a war. How would that be? How would I comport myself? How would I deal with this? How could I handle this?" I had covered local or national disasters before. I've seen a lot of dead people. I've covered airplane crashes. I covered the Soviet war in Afghanistan to a limited extent in the border areas of Afghanistan and Pakistan. I spent three days in a Pakistani jail for trying to cross the border. I've seen ugliness, I've seen bad things, but I had never seen a firefight up close. I'd never seen people shooting at each other. Until this war, I had never seen a man die. And I saw a man die; I saw several men die at the moment that they died. I don't think it's changed me. I guess I've done this job long enough that I'm pretty good about compartmentalizing things. I can see something as it happens, horrific as it is, and it just functions in that part of my brain that says, "Well, that's important for the story. How am I going to portray that?" As opposed to, "Oh, my God! I just saw somebody die!" When I became a reporter after I served in the Marines, the first times I would have to cover an accident or a murder, I was squeamish. You can talk about shooting and killing the enemy all you want while being in the Marines in peacetime, but until you see a dead body, it doesn't mean anything.

TRUTH VS. BEAUTY

Montreal Freelance Photographer
Robert J. Galbraith

"People must think I am completely whacked
out. But it's my balance."

It is mid-afternoon in downtown Kuwait City, and freelance photographer
Robert J. Galbraith, of Montreal, whose images are published in the *Dallas
Morning News, Houston Chronicle, The New York Times*, and the Associated
Press is stalking a baby bird down a broad sidewalk as he's looking for an address to a camera store. "It's limping," he says. "You see the yellow beak? It is
juvenile. The wings have not fully developed. It's called a brancher. It's a
European house sparrow. The mother will come down and feed it. It's just left
the nest and in the next three days its wings will grow out fully. But it's very
vulnerable to cats. I want to photograph it because of its innocence. This is exactly what I do. And when you tie in nature with misery, you get a great reaction."

The native-born Scotsman and birdwatcher is also limping—metaphorically.
He had spent the previous month in Iraq photographing scenes of nature and
war like some saint devoted to recording the wretched in beautiful composi-
tions. But the pressure of trying to achieve this pictorial juxtaposition was caus-
ing him to mentally unravel. His nerves were exposed and seemed damaged
like an opened roll of film. Galbraith's photos from both Gulf Wars have found a
home in a book called *Iraq: Images of War*. In 1990, he put together another
book, *The Oka Crisis—This Land is Our Land*, about an uprising by the Mohawk
Indians trying to stop a golf course being built over their ancestral graveyard.

■ ■ ■

I left Baghdad because I could tell it was time to retreat. You can only work
on little sleep for so long. I was under danger and stress. I was starting to lose
my judgment. I wasn't thinking right, and that can get you killed. I knew it. I

needed to come to Kuwait City and spend $250 a night to recover and replenish myself through rest and recuperation. It's just the cost of doing business. In Baghdad I was shooting the looting. There is a lot of risk in getting the transition of a nation uprooted, but it is where I feel compelled to be. To record people on the edge, a nation in misery.

Things got really bad my last week in Baghdad. They were looting the national library of Iraq, and the looters had set up a shop in front of the goddamn place and were selling the most important documentation of our world history for pennies! These books needed a humidifier—just like a Cuban cigar, and they were just selling them. Many of them probably dried up and blew away as dust. The scene reminded me of the grand library of ancient Alexandria, Egypt, which was torched. At the time, it was the most important museum in the world.

I'm an amateur archaeologist in Canada. I work for the University of Montreal. I'm an expert at finding Indian sites. There's this saying in our archeological field: "If you don't know your history, you will never find the future." This is what's happening in Iraq. I believe that external forces are coming in and annihilating the history of a people, and that history is the soul of the people.

Ninety-nine percent of the Iraqi people I talked to were very kind. They would give anything—tea, whatever they had. They were very thankful for the Coalition being there. The first thing they'd tell me is that they don't want to be run by religious zealots: "We want our freedom and we will choose our religion." There is a small minority, maybe people from Syria or Iran, in there to stir the pot and show hatred toward the Western civilization. Iraqis want freedom.

I was told by the curator of the Museum of Civilization that Saddam Hussein was a huge backer of the history of Iraq—the one good thing. I thought he wouldn't give funding to archaeological digs or the Babylon site, but he did and was very supportive. He put more money into the archaeology and the preservation of Iraqi history than he did his people. In the ancient city of Babylon, there are beautiful ruins and the beautiful reconstruction of the walls of the fortress. On top of the highest hill in the background, there is a big beautiful palace built by Saddam. Everywhere you try to take a panoramic photograph, Saddam is there. That was his idea, to be tied in with the beginning of civilization like some kind of a god. While it's a beautiful palace, if I had anything to say or do about it, I would erase the palace from that region because of his memory. It is the same as building mosques under false pretense. You can't buy your way into God's heart. You can't buy your way into the heart of a nation or the history of a nation. This is what he was doing—building these mosques to influence and gain favor with religious zealots throughout the world. Some of the mosques he built in Baghdad look like nuclear power plants. They are massive. It was as if he were writing a check to get to God. As we know, God was not on his side. Saddam had killed millions of his people. He is a bastard like Pol Pot. He used gas, and what kind of coward uses gas in a war?

When I am working in an extreme zone like Iraq, the realization of how nature works is an escape mechanism for me. One minute I can be photographing looters and misery. The next moment I am looking at a butterfly on a flower and photographing it. Rather than just being a one-dimensional photographer, this is all part of what I want to show. Take yesterday, for example, when I was stopped at a roadblock. I had a look at this little nearby stream. I saw some water lilies and a toad. I will come back and photograph the toad. People must think I am completely whacked out, but it's my balance. If there were more whacked-out people like me, maybe the world would be a better place some day? We are all one in nature. Even though there are savage things happening in nature, there are even more savage things happening with humanity.

Unlike most of the embedded photographers who are staff journalists, I'm a freelance journalist, which means I have to go closer to the danger. If I don't get the photos, I don't get paid. I am a turtle. I carry everything on my back. Wherever I go. So I can move out of an area fast. Lots of people bring vests, and jackets, and helmets. I can't function that way. So I roll the dice every time I go out on the street. Throughout my life I have become very streetwise and I can read a person. I can usually see a situation before my journalistic colleagues are able to see it. This is a talent I adapted from being a professional bird-watcher. I have great peripheral vision. I see things other people won't. What also happens is that I shoot my best when I'm fatigued and burned out, because I don't think. I just shoot what comes automatically in my mind. It's not something predestined. I don't go looking for something. It is automatic.

But lately, I've had nightmares. Not the usual ones. Worse, far worse. I dreamt that bombs and rockets were blasting into my home in Montreal. I heard my children screaming. They were being shot at and I couldn't move. I knew it was time to get out and take a breather because I will be going to Kurdistan shortly. I want to show the plight of the Kurds.

WHERE THE BOYS ARE

Leaf-Chronicle (Clarksville, Tennessee)
Military Reporter Chantal Escoto

"Some guys got shrapnel wounds, but they pretty much kicked butt."

It was day twenty-two of her embedded assignment with the First Battalion, 327th Infantry Regiment of 101st Airborne and *Leaf-Chronicle* (Clarksville, Tennessee) military reporter Chantal Escoto was looking forward to her convoy's road trip that would finally take her unit into Iraq. But the journey turned into an endless slog. Here's an excerpt from her reporter's journal, dated March 28th, and which originally appeared in the Gannett-owned *Leaf-Chronicle*:

It was a road trip I'll never forget—and neither will my butt or legs. The marathon military convoy from Camp Pennsylvania, Kuwait, to Iraq was supposed to take only fifteen hours, and the route was predicted to be smooth sailing on a paved road. It took three days. As I watched the huge convoy line up at the camp, I was amazed at all the firepower. Avenger anti-aircraft missiles, TOW anti-tank missiles, MK19 grenade launchers, 50-caliber machine guns and all the individual weapons, such as assault rifles. I had to laugh because any friend of Saddam was definitely not going to get past this bunch without a little one-on-one contact.

It seemed like it was taking forever to get going, and when we finally did start to roll out, the storm moved in. It started out innocently enough with a light sprinkle and mild wind. It was actually kind of nice because I knew the rain would keep down the dust. With more than 400 vehicles, we were barely out of the gate when people started having problems with their vehicles—flat tires, little or no power, leaking fuel and brake lines. This, of course, slowed things down, so we were able to watch the terrific lightning storm. I was one of the lucky ones because I was in a covered Humvee, but a lot of guys had to travel in open trucks. Then the wind started to blow incredibly hard, with hail at times. It hurt.

Oh, and did I mention all the doors were taken off the Humvees, including the one I was in? The officer who had ordered the doors off for tactical reasons—the open doors make it easier to get in and out when someone's shooting at you—called back over the radio after he was getting blasted with freezing rain and said, jokingly, "Who's the idiot who took these doors off?"

Good thing we were wearing our new chemical protective suits. We found out how waterproof they were. The storm lasted all day and all night. I was cold, even with a sleeping bag and poncho liner. The guys in the trucks had it much worse. My poncho liner eventually flew out the open door, never to be seen again.

Drivers were falling asleep, along with their assistant drivers. People were losing contact with the vehicles in front of them and turning onto the wrong roads. When we finally set up camp after the third night, I thought it was so wonderful to sleep in a horizontal position.

Five days before the convoy left, Camp Pennsylvania witnessed one of those war scenes that shakes the very essence of trust that bonds soldiers together in a common cause. The First Brigade's command tent was attacked with grenades and small-arms fire, resulting in the deaths of two soldiers and injuries to thirteen others. The assailant was a sergeant in the 101st who had converted to Islam. Escoto's tent was only two hundred yards away from the command tent. "The first thing I did after I heard that first grenade was put on my Kevlar helmet and vest and get my notepad," she recalled, "and run out to find out what was going on."

■　■　■

I grew up in southern California. I was in the army for five years. My first duty station was in Germany from 1988 to 1990. I was in a general supply company. We would go pick up warehouse supplies and tactical gear from other warehouses and store them in our warehouses in Stuttgart, Germany, which is about forty miles north of Frankfurt. I drove a big truck. I was there when the Berlin Wall came down. That was my first big look at democracy and freedom.

It had an effect on me. I'd be on the autobahn driving my truck and I'd see all these guys in their little matchbox cars coming from Hungary, because that was right before the wall had come down and they were just all streaming into western Germany. They kept asking American soldiers for cigarettes. They were happy to see Americans.

From 1990 through 1992, I was stationed in Fort Ord, California, also doing supply. I was with the forward support unit, which does support for infantry, taking in their engines and transmissions and making sure the mechanics fix them. I was doing shop-office type of work. I got out of the army and moved to Fort Worth, Washington, to be with my second husband, who is retired military. In 1995 we moved to Clarksville, Tennessee. A friend sold real estate out here, and so we packed up the truck and moved to Tennessee. Both of us had never been here before, but we were told that it was a good place to live. That is how we ended up near the Fort Campbell Army Base.

I used the Army College Fund after I got out of the army. I went to journalism school at Austin Peay State University and in my senior year, started working for the Leaf-Chronicle as an unpaid intern. I wanted to work for a real newspaper rather than a college newspaper. After I graduated they hired me as their crime and safety reporter. I did that probably for about a year and a half and then I took over as Fort Campbell's reporter. I covered change-of-command ceremonies and training exercises. I went to Kosovo for about a month to cover the Second Brigade of the 101st because they were sent as part of a peacekeeping mission. I had to really push to get that assignment. I worked with a public affairs officer and she pulled strings with the Department of Defense. I pulled strings with my editor. It was a really great deal because it was pretty exclusive. No other local media were going. I was the only one.

In Kosovo, I'd go out on missions with different military intelligence companies. It was a great experience. You'd go through the villages and the children would come out every time they saw American trucks and start running and waving at us. That was a good first start as far as being embedded, though they didn't use that term then. It was more like a "report on the troops." And there was still a public affairs person trying to control me, but half the time he couldn't. A lot of times the intelligence guys would say, "Come with us," so I would just go and not tell the public affairs person, and he'd then get all upset.

About three months after the September 11 terrorist attacks I went over to Afghanistan with the Third Brigade of the 101st. This time, fourteen reporters from other media outlets went with me. I knew that it would be a little bit tougher to get exclusive access, but then again, we were going into a more dangerous situation and we didn't know what was going on in Afghanistan. We stayed at the Kandahar base.

When I heard about the possibility of being an embed in Iraq, I made sure to be the first one on the list. Then it turned out there were sixty reporters or media outlets who were going to be embedded with the 101st going into Iraq. Because they had a good success in Afghanistan by letting reporters come in, they figured they were just going to go all out with Iraq. Post 9/11, they knew they were going to get good coverage.

While I was at Camp Pennsylvania in Kuwait, my editors kept wanting these war stories, but we were still preparing for war, not going anywhere. Then, on March 23, I had just finished filing my stories for the day around 1:00 A.M. local time when there was a grenade attack. First one grenade, and then another, then small-arms fire. I had no idea what was going on. I put on my gear and went outside. I saw soldiers wearing their shorts and their battle-rattle — you know, their gear and their weapons. I heard sergeants yelling, "Get over here, you need to get over here!" I thought, "Wow, this is my first experience of war, this is the true rubber-meets-the-road experience." I was listening to the brigade radio, hearing things as they were unfolding. At first they thought it was a couple of Kuwaiti interpreters. They found these guys, put them in handcuffs, with their faces on the ground. It was pretty sad, and they ended up leaving the camp after they were released. Then we heard about an unaccounted guy, Sergeant Akbar, who was with the 325th Engineers. Part of his guard duty was to watch over the grenades. They found out that four or five grenades were missing. That is when they figured out what happened. In the meantime, I had my satellite phone and told the commander, "Look, I need to call this in now." He said, "Well, we shouldn't." I replied, "What is the meaning of me being an embed?" So I called it in. Apparently the attack had already made the news because when the grenade attack had happened, guys from *Time* magazine and CBS News were on their satellite phones and calling into their office, too. It was kind of scary. Scud alarms were going off, which means you had to put your mask on and go in the bunker. Well, that's the worst thing you can do if somebody is shooting small-arms fire, because you can't see and you're running out into the open. So it was pretty chaotic for about five minutes, but after that everything got under in control.

Once we left Camp Pennsylvania and entered Iraq, I was the only woman among 700 guys. You don't want to seem like what they are expecting to find in the typical woman, you know, to be whiny and complaining. I would do what I have to do, especially like personal hygiene stuff. If I had to go to the bathroom, they would be respectful of that. I'd get my poncho liner and go off somewhere. That got tough because there aren't too many trees in the desert.

They didn't treat me any different, but in a way I wish that they did. One thing that bothered me was when they would start talking about nasty things or pornography. They'd be watching pornography on DVDs or looking at pictures, and I'd say, "If you guys are going to watch this, just let me know beforehand so I can leave."

I'm a little bit older than these guys. I'm forty years old. Some of them would call me mom. So, I became a mother figure to some. I'd go up to them and ask, "Are you eating enough, dear?" Trying to play up the mom thing. Some of them even confided in me because they felt that with guys in the infantry, it's hard to talk about if you are scared. So some guys would come see me and talk about their wives or talk about all the little sweet things that they'd do for their wives. If they said that in front of their peers they would be called wimps. But as far as them trying to make passes, no, there was nothing like that. My husband was worried about that, but there was nothing going on like that.

We saw a lot of fighting. We had taken over an agricultural complex where a huge weapons cache was stored. Then there was a military compound where some heavy fighting took place. Miraculously, my battalion didn't take any casualties. Some guys got shrapnel wounds, but they pretty much kicked butt. I was pretty close to the fighting when they took over the agricultural complex. We arrived on the back of a Humvee. One of the tanks had blown a hole, or what they call breach, to the compound, but it was near where the cache was stored. There were all these AK47 and mortar rounds going off. We thought that people were shooting at us. We were totally sitting ducks.

There was another time when we had just left the city of Amarah. The people were still in the streets cheering when we got ambushed. Two soldiers from other companies in our convoy got shot, one in the arm and another one in the leg. They weren't fatal wounds. During this time we were in a street with tall buildings. We could hear the U.S. troops fighting back. You could hear the 50-caliber. Everybody took out their M-16s but they didn't know where the enemy firing was coming from. There was no safe place for me to go. I stood in the back of the Humvee, just praying to God that nothing hit me. I'd look out and see chunks taken out of a building from the 50-cals. It was scary. I was a noncombatant but I told them I'd be ready to pick up a gun if I had to. Earlier in the war,

I got these guys to show me how the big weapons work, "Just tell me where the safety is." They're pretty easy to use. It's point and shoot.

After Baghdad fell, the brigade's mission was pretty much involved with only peacekeeping, and there was really nothing going on where we were, but because my passport was messed up, I didn't actually get back to the States until April 27.

When I came back I didn't want to talk about the war. I was more reserved. I didn't want to be around people. I just wanted to be a recluse and just stay in and not talk to anybody. I wasn't hurt physically, but I was going through something psychologically, or emotionally, or mentally, or whatever. I wanted to go back to work but I missed my family. Some people said it was post-traumatic stress disorder. I still get jumpy around loud noises. I didn't want to read or see stuff about Iraq. There were things that I had seen at that agricultural compound which really affected me. All these dead Iraqi guys just laying around the compound. They didn't move the bodies. There were flies all over them, and then the flies got on you. That freaked me out. Then I saw children who were half burned by bombs.

I am now going through counseling, which I'd never done before, but I figure I don't need to try to win this war on my own. I also have been talking to the soldiers' wives, telling them, "Look, you know, your men have probably seen a lot more than I have, and I was affected by all this." I am not sorry I went through this experience in Iraq. It's just that I didn't expect to have the emotional damage that it did. I thought I could handle it. It messed me up. I started smoking again when I was over there in Iraq. I hadn't smoked for over ten years, but it was the only thing that would keep away the flies. Then I came back and it was harder for me to quit than I thought it would be. That was one of the things my husband didn't like — my smoking — and he didn't realize that I needed to have time to transition. My stress was magnified because he didn't understand what I had been through and I didn't want to talk about it. It put a real strain on our marriage. As for my fourteen-year old son, he probably just wanted his mom back. We're going to California for a couple of weeks and hang out with family and stuff, so it's getting better.

THE BIRDS AND THE BEES AND A PEST NAMED GERALDO

KSTP-TV (Minneapolis–St. Paul)
Reporter Dean Staley

> "The soldiers were making jokes that they
> should have tied Geraldo Rivera to a Humvee
> and driven him back through the desert."

The Minnesota-based ABC affiliate, KSTP-TV, has scored several impressive firsts in its broadcasting history. Owned by Hubbard Broadcasting, which operates stations in New Mexico, New York, and Minnesota, KSTP was the first full-color television station in the United States and the first to inaugurate regularly scheduled seven-day newscasts. So it should come as little surprise that the progressively minded Twin Cities station was one of the few regional stations in the nation to have embedded reporters—telegenic duo Joe Caffrey and Dean Staley—cover the war.

We talked with Staley just after he returned from Iraq. Before enduring Minnesotan winters, he had been a correspondent for ABC News and worked out of the Atlanta Bureau, where he followed high-profile stories such as the Columbine High School shootings, John F. Kennedy, Jr.'s fatal plane accident, and the Elian Gonzales case. "With Elian, several hundred journalists camped out by his relatives' house," recalls Staley. "I had a camera guy. I'd stand in front of the camera and do live reports and then we would also put together a minute-and-a half report that was the news of the day. Then I'd go back to the motel, sleep, come back, then, basically do reports in front of his house for another eight to ten hours. This went on for about a month."

■ ■ ■

I was a Peace Corps volunteer when I got out of Boston University. I taught beekeeping and soil conservation for two years in Paraguay. It was very primitive working conditions. In many ways, it was not much different than being an embed, in terms of sleeping on a cot, no electricity, no running water, that sort of thing. We worked with Africanized bees down in Paraguay, and so getting stung thirty or forty times in an afternoon was not a big deal, sort of par for the course. Africanized are just like regular bees. They are no more toxic than regular bees; they are just really aggressive and tend to all get excited at once. So you end up getting stung a lot of times. Beekeepers are used to getting stung and build up a resistance. It's just like getting pinpricks. They are very painful at first but then it doesn't bother you much after that.

Bees have been around for many million of years and are highly organized, and though I think bees are probably more efficient than the military, I was still awed by the army's ability to move as many people as they did and keep them all watered, fed, and from bumping into each other, more than they did.

I was embedded with the Fifth Battalion of the 159th Aviation Brigade of the 101st Airborne. It was a battalion of thirty Black Hawk helicopters and their job was essentially picking up troops at a designated area, sometimes in the middle of the night, in the dark, moving them onto choppers and moving them into the fight. That could be either a hot landing zone or an area near the fight, close enough so the soldiers could hike to the site.

Flying in a Black Hawk was exciting and thrilling. My first experience was flying fourteen feet off the deck at 110 knots. It's a powerful aircraft, and when it's not loaded down it's nimble. We didn't have any hot landings. In fact, one of the interesting parts of this entire war was that the 101st Airborne's air assault specialty was not needed. They had expectations that they would be flying certain missions, and those missions got cancelled because the Third Infantry Division was rolling forward north so quickly. Black Hawks are fairly fragile; they're fairly vulnerable to small-arms fire. They have typically what is called a blast blanket on the bottom that they use for combat operations; it's about a half an inch thick and is supposed to stop some small-arms fire and shrapnel. But otherwise it's not an armored aircraft, and that aspect actually informed its missions. One example: We had a mission to fly into Baghdad International Airport to take that airport, and the air-assault portion was an important part of our mission. They got intelligence that there were so many people lying in wait with small arms and anti-aircraft weapons that instead of flying in the infantry, they trucked them in because they were afraid they'd get Black Hawks shot down. There was also the political element of the war. There was a higher priority on not losing American lives, so they were much more conservative about air assault.

The pilots call the Black Hawks birds. They are some of the best pilots in the world at what they do. You really had to be impressed with these guys. There are hardly any other people in the world who have had as many hours as they've had in the cockpit of a Black Hawk, and certainly not flying with night vision goggles or in foul weather conditions. They have over 4,000 hours in a Black Hawk, which for helicopter time is incredible. They've been doing it their whole lives. While they don't seem to have that sex appeal that Tom Cruise and his guys had in *Top Gun*, they did have that army aviator mentality, which is being a maverick. You wear your mustache a little bit bigger than what the regs say, and you get in trouble now and then because you're goofing off. For example, they got bored because there wasn't much going on in our camp, particularly after Baghdad fell, so one day, they said, "Let's go see what's in those bunkers." We jumped in a Humvee and drove over to these bunkers and started digging through them. They were filled with munitions from just about everywhere in the world—explosives, rockets, mortars, and blasting caps. They got in minor trouble on another occasion. A one-star general with the 101st Airborne was driving by their tent and his Humvee kicked up a lot of dust from the desert. So they yelled at him, "Slow the fuck down." The Humvee stops and guess who gets out but the general. The next day they were all marching in full battle-rattle as well as digging survival ditches.

I never heard them compare themselves with navy pilots. They were just proud of the aircraft they flew. Even the guys who flew Chinook helicopters, those big cargo helicopters with the dual rotors, were proud of being army aviators. They liked to brag about what they could do with Chinooks. It was a kind of a rivalry between the Black Hawk guys and the Chinook guys, because the Chinook guys looked at the Black Hawk guys as, "You get all the sexy publicity such as the movie *Black Hawk Down*, but we do air assault, too. We just fly these big clumsy-looking aircraft."

The Black Hawks have amazing killing power. Their M-60 guns go all the way back to the Hueys in Vietnam and they haven't really changed. An M-60 fires a 762 round and is a much bigger round than say an M-16 fires. The M-60s are big chain-fed, automatic guns. They use two door gunners. But one of the interesting secrets is, you know, those things aren't particularly accurate because with the prop wash coming down off the rotor, when a round comes out of a chain and out of a barrel, it gets pushed down and to the side, depending on which side of the aircraft they're firing from. A lot of times they'd say, "This is really just to get people to duck, just a big thumper, so we open up with this and hope people get out of our way because they're not particularly accurate." In fact, we were flying some missions when we heard the pilot on the intercom telling those guys, "Now look, keep your eyes out, if you see somebody, don't shoot at them, because some of the special forces guys are carrying AK47s. If you see someone with an AK, don't shoot them, they may be one of ours, and if they're shooting at us, we may not even take the time to fire back." The Black Hawk is not the kind of aircraft that if someone is shooting at you, you stay and engage them. It's the kind of aircraft where you're safer if you keep it moving.

I was never particularly scared flying in those Black Hawks. They fly very fast and very low to the ground, which means that if you're a bad guy you better know they're coming or by the time you see them, they're gone, they're over you. It's like being in a small town: There's a big bank building in the center of town, and from the building's fifteenth floor you can see just about everywhere in town, but you can't see the first floor. You got to be up close to see the first floor, and that's kind of the philosophy with the Black Hawks since these guys are flying so low and are below radar. We flew thirteen feet off the ground when we were going into Iraq the first day. The land was flat and featureless.

Our battalion did not lose any Black Hawks. The Fourth Battalion did. They had two bad dust situations: one where they took off with a heavy load and the other one was a brownout landing where they just lost the ground. When you lose the ground in a Black Hawk, in any helicopter, you're in big trouble. A brownout is terrifying. You're coming down to land, you see the ground, and all of a sudden small swirls of sand and dust are moving around. As you get lower, the helicopter moves forward, staying ahead of the dust that it is kicking up. It's always moving into clean air. But as it slows down for a landing that dust begins to catch up to it, and it begins to be engulfed. So there's this dust cloud that starts to form at the tail of the aircraft, and moves forward toward the cockpit. As it moves past your window when you're in the back, you can't see anything outside. You can't see two inches out the window. All you see is dust. You know in a second and a half, that's all the pilot is going to see. So they have to get really good at understanding the timing of that and being close enough to the ground when they finally lose total visual in the cockpit. With an absolute brownout, you don't know if it's fifteen feet down or five feet down or 500 feet down. And at any time, anyone in the crew can call "go around," which means climb back up out of the dust and let's try this again.

I think we did a good job of telling the story of dust landings because that was one of the first things pilots had to do. Once they got their aircraft off the ship and put the props back on them and had one test flight, they started to get everyone qualified in dust landings. Which meant you had to go out for a certain period of time and do a certain number of dust landings until the pilot in command felt that you were qualified to be out there flying in dust. When they do dust landings they do this training back in Fort Campbell, but it doesn't compare to the conditions they had in Kuwait. The sand is so fine it's almost like a powder. It's like talcum powder.

Before I left, people'd say be careful over there. I'd just shrug my shoulders and said that my biggest fear is that these Black Hawks are going to bump into each other. That turned out to be fairly true. Early on we lost a CH46 that had four American crew and eight British troops in the back. There were two Black Hawks that ran into each other over the Bay of Kuwait.

Virtually every day we sent back to our station a two-minute piece, which in itself would take five or six hours to feed back because of the portable satellite equipment we had. We shot it in Sony, using very small professional DV cams. We moved the video into laptop computer on a firewire, did all the editing on that laptop, and then fed out of the laptop through a satellite phone back to Minneapolis. We had a phone bill one month that was $40,000.

During the sandstorms you couldn't go outside. I doubt we could have gotten a signal through all that sand. We had a flat satellite panel that had to stand on the ground; it would have just blown away. Those storms lasted several days. We, in fact, were stuck for five days in Iraq on our first mission. It was supposed to be just a day trip, so we didn't take any of our satellite equipment. We were just stuck on the ground in the middle of the Iraqi desert, holding security all night because it wasn't a secured area. The concern was that Iraqi soldiers would try to sneak up and blow up the helicopters in the middle of the night. Well, during the day, we really got to know the people we were with: a couple of pilots and two crew chiefs. There were six of us aboard that particular Black Hawk. We didn't have a tent. We'd either sleep out in the sand, or a couple of nights, me or my photographer went over to one of the Chinooks. Its insides are huge — they drive Humvees up in the Chinooks. It was like the Chinook Hilton, and the crew would be playing cards at a little table that they made out of MRE boxes, so it was much more comfortable than a Black Hawk.

We even did a couple of stories about sandstorms that aired on the Weather Channel. One story was about this lost patrol. Three guys coming back from a night patrol, and they got lost in the sandstorm. They were only about a half-mile from the camp and they couldn't find it, because the wind was blowing and howling, like being in a blizzard. I went out with the patrol that was sent to find them, and they had radios and GPSs and were trying to contact these guys. It just became a story about this incredible storm.

We had absolute control over what we covered. It wasn't possible to relate the whole experience to the station and have them get into a discussion about what is the story of the day. It was left to Joe and me in terms of what was happening. Those things were fairly obvious. We had a Scud attack one day, or one night we had what we thought was a terrorist attack in our camp. It turned out to be a Kuwaiti soldier who was driving through the desert along this road and ran flat, straight, seventy-five miles an hour into the big dirt berm that was built up around our camp. Not only did he survive the car accident, but the soldiers opened up on him with one of those M-60s and they only managed to shoot him in the hand. He was really lucky that they didn't kill him.

During one mission our battalion flew infantry guys into the fight near Karbala and dropped them off. Joe and I decided to get off with these guys. Before, we'd done those missions and stayed on the helicopter. This time we jumped off with the infantry and hiked into the city with them and took fire. That was probably the most eventful day in terms of being right next to the fight. We got shot at when we got on the outskirts of town. We were taking heavy fire all day long and they actually ended up killing about sixty-five Iraqis.

We were a block away from the fighting. All day long it was boom-boom-boom-boom, da-da-da-da, boom-boom-boom. I heard the whizzing of the bullets go by, whether a foot, or two feet, or ten feet, I couldn't tell. Joe and I realized that we were stuck with these guys, and from then on it was just doing what you could to protect yourself: staying down, keeping your eyes open for someone coming from the flank, or from behind, or from someplace you might not expect. That was a real wake-up for us. We had worked to get there, I mean, it wasn't easy to convince the leader of our battalion to let us go off with the infantry for a couple of days. I never felt like I was going to die. I don't know if it was because we were so busy working, but there wasn't time for that kind of reflection. It wasn't until afterward when Joe and I got to talk about it that we thought, "Wow, that was a close one." Joe got hours of tape from being on the ground there in Karbala. We aired the whole piece, which was about two minutes long, and told the firefight from beginning to end.

We never saw any dead Americans, but we did see—in our camp outside Baghdad—a truckload of seven freshly taken prisoners with cloth sacks tied over their heads, their hands zip-tied behind them, and two dead bodies and one wounded. The bodies were wrapped in dirty clear plastic. They took the bodies from the truck and moved them into body bags, and then moved the wounded to a hospital. What had happened is that soldiers from 101st were out on patrol when they got attacked by these guys and essentially shot them up, and killed two of them, and wounded one, and took the rest prisoners. We showed thirty or forty seconds of video of their unloading the bodies and maybe a sound bite from one of the soldiers who arrived just after the fighting. We did not do overly graphic super close-ups, but we didn't hide the fact that they were bodies, and that they were laying there, and that there was death. We didn't try to sanitize it. There wasn't backlash from viewers, but neither was there praise. It was some of the first real ugliness that we had been able to show our viewers back in Minneapolis. It was edited and shot so that it didn't disturb anyone overtly, but neither did we shy away from the fact that there were Iraqi victims.

We went over there with a clear understanding that our mission was not to try to cover the war, but to cover the Fifth Battalion of this brigade and bring home real personal stories from within that battalion. It turned out that part of our world became, almost by default, a sort of Bob Hope or Red Cross role where people knew we were covering the 101st. Our station would get an e-mail saying, "My husband is in the 101st, he's with this battalion, would you please pass along this message," and for the most part that was impossible because we really only had contact with a relatively small portion of the 101st. But we did pass along messages to people who were in our immediate battalion and they were the pipeline for a few other people in the brigade.

There was another role that I had not anticipated. Our station does promotions with the Minnesota Twins, so they asked us to interview soldiers from Minnesota during the game and have them throw out the first pitch via satellite. They would appear on the jumbo screen between innings throughout the game. So throughout the game people got to see Minnesota faces up on the screen from Iraq, saying hello to their families.

Just by blind luck, we ran into Geraldo Rivera. Our battalion had orders to fly him out of Iraq, making sure that he got to Kuwait. The soldiers were making jokes that they should have tied Geraldo to a Humvee and driven him back through the desert. The soldiers were outraged. They took it personally that he had been drawing maps and giving away battle plans. But there were also people among our battalion who wanted their picture taken with him, who shook his hand. These were guys who had been in the desert for weeks now, and he was the first celebrity who's come through. It was a little bit of a diversion for them. Joe and I were sitting under a tarp out of the sun editing our piece, and we looked up and this Humvee pulled up and Geraldo got out. He was wearing a big black hat, almost like a bush hat, but he had one side folded up sort of in the Australian style. He had an entourage around him, one of whom was his brother who works as a producer for him and a couple of camera guys. And then they had a ton of equipment, equipment that probably took up a Black Hawk all by itself. We interviewed him and asked him about what he was doing and where he was going. He downplayed the fact that he was being kicked out. He said, "It was just a misunderstanding. I suspect I'll go back to Kuwait City, I'll get a shower and get some rest, and I'll be back in a couple of weeks." Which turned out, I think, not to be too far from the truth. One of the soldiers came up to us and said, "We stink-palmed Geraldo." Apparently one of these guys stuck his hand down the back of his pants and rubbed it around before he went to shake hands with Geraldo. This was the army way of getting even with him. The soldiers showed Joe and me pictures. They had it on digital camera: a picture of this guy with his hand down the back of his pants, then a picture of him shaking Geraldo's hand with that very hand. Joe and I just shook our heads. This sort of army justice was new to us.

SORRY, NO ROOM SERVICE AT
SADDAM'S PRESIDENTIAL PALACE
Los Angeles Times Staff Writer David Zucchino

> "It was a very surreal experience, especially at
> night, when it took fifteen minutes to walk from
> one room to the other, going down these halls
> with your footsteps echoing and all these spooky
> shadows around. It was like *The Shining.*"

Los Angeles Times writer and Pulitzer Prize winner David Zucchino is a veteran
war correspondent with over two decades of experience covering conflicts in
the Third World. Previously, at the *Philadelphia Inquirer*, he was reporter, foreign
correspondent, foreign editor, and the project editor for Mark Bowden's twenty-
nine-part serial on U.S. troops in Somalia, "Black Hawk Down," which became
a bestselling book and popular movie. During most of 2002, he lived and traveled with U.S. troops in Afghanistan, because "it's important to be with the
people who are fighting a war," and thus decided to view the next war in Iraq
as an embed. In his May 2, 2003, post-Iraq summary for the *L.A. Times*, the
fifty-one-year-old Zucchino described his experience:

> *During seven weeks spent with half a dozen units, I slept in fight-
> ing holes and armored vehicles, on a rooftop, a garage floor and in
> lumbering troop trucks. For days at a time, I didn't sleep. I ate with
> the troops, choking down processed meals of "meat, chunked and
> formed" that came out of brown plastic bags. I rode with them in
> loud, claustrophobic, and disorienting Bradley fighting vehicles. I
> complained with them about the choking dust, the lack of water,
> our foul-smelling bodies and our scaly, rotting feet. I saw what the
> soldiers saw. And, like most of them, I emerged filthy, exhausted,
> and aware of what Winston Churchill meant when he said that
> "nothing in life" is so exhilarating as to be shot at without effect."*

Most important, I wrote stories I could not have produced had I not been embedded—on the pivotal battle for Baghdad; the performance of U.S. soldiers in combat; the crass opulence of Hussein's palaces; U.S. airstrikes on an office tower in central Baghdad; souvenir-hunting by soldiers and reporters; and the discovery of more than $750 million in cash in a neighborhood that had been the preserve of top Iraqi officials. Yet that same access could be suffocating and blinding. Often I was too close or confined to comprehend the war's broad sweep. I could not interview survivors of Iraqi civilians killed by U.S. soldiers or speak to Iraqi fighters trying to kill Americans. I was not present when Americans died at the hands of fellow soldiers in what the military calls "frat," for fratricide. I had no idea what ordinary Iraqis were experiencing. I was ignorant of Iraqi government decisions and U.S. command strategy.

■ ■ ■

I'm based in Philadelphia for the *L.A. Times*. I cover national and foreign news. I've been with the paper since September 12, 2001. I had taken a job with them in the summer of 2001 and wanted to take some time off before I started, so I was going to start in November or December and was just relaxing. Then September 11 hit and I was in Philadelphia and the paper was desperate to get as many people as possible to New York because the planes weren't flying. Early the next morning, I took an Amtrak to New York and started work the following day.

I was at the *Philadelphia Inquirer* for twenty-one years. I covered wars—Bosnia, Chechnya, Ethiopia, Libya, Angola, Mozambique, Uganda—for them during this time. I started in Lebanon in the early eighties, covering the civil war and the Israeli invasion and then the Marine peacekeeping force. When the Marines barracks were blown up, I only lived three or four miles from the airport. The explosion was enormous. It blew me out of bed. It was at 6:21 A.M. I immediately wondered what was going on. My driver/translator showed up at my apartment and said he heard on the militia radio that there'd been a huge explosion at the airport, so we headed to the airport. They hadn't set up a perimeter. There were just pieces of guys laying everywhere. Guys still alive, trapped, trying to get out. The whole building at the airport where they'd been staying just fell down on top of them. It had an atrium lobby. The truck had gone right into the lobby and dumped the whole building down. It was pretty awful. There were 241 casualties.

I would mention the Beirut bombing to some of these young guys in the Iraq war, and they only had the vaguest idea that something had happened in Lebanon and that some guys got blown up, but they didn't know if they were Marines or they didn't know why or who did it. I don't know about the rest of the country, but people have either forgotten it or never even realized that it happened, which was strange because that was really the beginning of the suicide attacks against American interests.

In Beirut I had a lot of close calls with snipers and car bombs. In Iraq it was RPGs. Several of them went right behind the Bradley vehicle that I was in and exploded against nearby walls. I had gone in a raid into Baghdad in a Bradley. All these guys assured me, "Oh, you'll be safe. A Bradley's one of the safest places to be in." Then, once I got inside with the Bradley crew and we're going up on this gun run into Baghdad, I said, "Wow, this is pretty safe in here," and they then said, "You crazy? We've lost several Bradleys. RPG hits here and it goes right through." They gave me several examples. I don't think they had anybody killed, but they had some guys seriously wounded and they had some Bradleys disabled—not destroyed, but disabled.

Riding around in a Bradley is very claustrophobic and confusing. Any sound from the outside is amplified and sounds a lot worse than it is. On April 9, when they were making the raid into Baghdad, it was incredibly loud, hot, stifling; there's just no air inside and your only view is through these little glass vision blocks that are maybe three inches high and six, seven, eight inches wide. It's a prison in there. It's hard to see what's going on with all the smoke and the craziness and the speed. It's very disorienting. You're in the middle of a battle, but you really can't see what's going on other than that little narrow view you have out of that vision block and, of course, you listen on the radio—there are five different radio nets going on—so you're just picking up pieces of information.

When I first talked to soldiers they said that they hoped they didn't have to kill anybody. They hoped they didn't get any resistance and that they would roll right into Baghdad. But once the battle started, it was very much a strong sense of self-preservation. Anything that looked like a threat and anything that moved, they just shot at. There was a lot of tension; a lot of fear; a lot of anxiety in the Bradley. You are pretty exposed roaring down the middle of the street with guys in bunkers on either side and guys shooting down from buildings and these vehicles coming out of alleyways. During the battle, there's not any thought or any talk about whether you should be firing. It's just blasting away, and all the rest of the vehicles were blasting away too. You could see things blowing up; you could see things burning. As we sat and talked about it later, I didn't get any sense that they were crowing or were euphoric about how many guys they killed. I didn't hear anybody saying, "I got this many guys." They were glad it was over and they were glad to be alive.

I started out with 101st Airborne, but because they were not in the thick of the fight—or as they put it, they were "guarding the gas station"—they were getting frustrated. A lot of these guys kept saying that they didn't really want to be there, but as long as they were in Iraq, they wanted to do what they were trained for, and that was to do air assaults against an enemy. They'd be moping and complaining about sitting there in the middle of the desert getting fried every day. They ran out of suntan lotion and were short of water. They spent their days training, and practicing, and digging their holes, and trying to stay out of the sun. The officers told me that they were having a hard time keeping the guys motivated, and keeping their edge, because they really weren't doing anything. Then they would get excited when a new mission would come in and they would start training for it, walking through the rehearsals, and the commanders would have them all pumped up. Then they'd have to come in and say, "Didn't happen. We'll get a different mission." They were just up and down; up and down and living in very difficult conditions where they're sleeping in the dirt.

The 101st unit I was originally with stayed in Kuwait, so I had to leave those guys and traveled with an infantry unit called the Rakasans, which means "unfolding umbrella" or "opening umbrella" in Japanese. I asked the soldiers the story and they said that postwar occupation forces in Japan were doing training exercises, and the paratroopers came down in their parachutes, and apparently the Japanese called them Rakasan with their unfolding or opening umbrellas.

Originally, they were going to air assault right into the airport, and my understanding was that they decided it was too risky to have the helicopters go up around the airport because they weren't sure they had taken out all the anti-aircraft artillery around the airport. That's why they decided to go by ground to get to the airport. These guys were complaining, and very upset, and frustrated because it was going to take a day and a half of just driving through the desert, bumping on these trucks. Because they didn't have enough trucks, these guys were piled in on top of each other. It was extremely uncomfortable, and we had gone all night until about 5:30 the following morning. There had been nothing to see in the desert. It's just flat landscape. Suddenly they hit a canal. There was no road. They were just driving through the desert, and for some reason the vehicle in front of the one I was on veered to the left and then veered back onto this causeway. There was dust everywhere and it was dark. They had night vision goggles and the lights were out for security reasons, so that made it all the more difficult. It was very confusing and our driver followed the truck that had gone to the left, and instead of getting back on the road, the truck drove straight into the canal. All of us in the back were dumped into the water. I was at the very rear of the truck so I just popped right back out of the water, but some of the guys in the front, including the two guys in the cab, were trapped underneath, because all these boxes fell down on them, and they had all their heavy gear on. Some of them had to be cut out with knives. Two of the guys were vomiting up water and they were revived with mouth-to-mouth resuscitation. Everybody survived, though they lost a lot of gear and, of course, the truck. I lost most of my gear — two satphones, computer, tape recorder, and notebooks. Journalistically speaking, I was now combat-ineffective. Luckily, there was this great guy named Gregg Zoroya from USA Today who let me use his satphone.

Since I was there to cover the war, I wanted to get where it was happening, and obviously Baghdad was where it was going to happen, so Gregg and I decided to talk to some of the Third Infantry guys we had seen on the airport tarmac. As we approached them, all these tanks and Bradleys came roaring in, smoking and smeared with oil and shot up full of holes and with really exhausted, sweaty-looking guys. We started talking to them and realized they had done the very first run through Baghdad that morning and were just coming back in. It was a three-hour gun run. They lost one tank, which they destroyed to keep it out of the Iraqis' hands. They also lost a staff sergeant commander on a tank. He was hit, I believe, by an RPG.

Their assault on Baghdad lasted three, four days, and I got to the presidential palace on the tenth of April. This was the main presidential palace and it had been completely emptied. A lot of the doors had been taken off. They were these nice mahogany inlaid doors. The palace had been cleaned out of most furniture and furnishings; it still had the curtains and the chandeliers, and some office furniture and beds left, but everything else had pretty much been cleared out. It was obvious that whoever had been there had anticipated the attack and gotten the hell out of there. All kinds of bunkers had been dug in around the palace grounds. The Republican Guard had either been killed or had fled and left their uniforms. There were helmets, and boots, and uniforms, and berets spread all around the palace grounds in addition to a lot of bodies among the rose bushes, and in the gardens, and palm trees.

There was one dead Iraqi guy who had been run over by tanks. He had fallen in the road and had just been repeatedly run over. His body was just flattened like a cartoon character. It just turns paper thin and there's not much left. It's upsetting because, as I wrote the story, the guys were joking and making all kinds of comments and laughing at it. They called these guys "crunchies" because they get crunched underneath the tanks.

The palace itself was beautiful, with marble and thinly tiled doors, gardens, and courtyards, and high-ceiling rooms with chandeliers, and nice silk curtains. It was gorgeous, a nice place to stay, so I just laid my sleeping bag on the floor. I had my choice of hundreds of rooms. I found a chair and then I had a little table. There was no electricity, but this was luxury. I kept calling for room service but they never showed! Before, I had been writing on scraps of paper and at one point, I got stuck in the Bradley and had to write on the MRE box. I now had a computer that Geoff Mohan of the *L.A. Times* had given me. I tried to write during the daytime and then at night I would turn on my flashlight. I was in good shape by this point.

Some command people with the Third Infantry Division had taken one of the offices as their command post and they were sleeping in a few of the rooms, but otherwise the palace was just completely empty and deserted. It was interesting just to wander to room after room and see what was there. I expected somebody to jump out from one of the rooms. But no one was around other than the few American soldiers. There was no food so we just ate our MREs. There were kitchens and inside the refrigerators the food had rotted. The cabinets had eggs and cheese and stuff that had gone bad. There was lots of beautiful chinaware, silverware, and tablecloths. There was no running water, so the officers gave the orders that the soldiers could use the toilets because there were just dozens of them, but the rule was that they had to go outside and get a bucket of water and flush it. They didn't want to turn this place into a sewer.

You're in this gorgeous multimillion dollar palace with marble floors and chandeliers, but you have no electricity and no running water, so it's like camping out. You can't really use all these beautiful tile and marble bathrooms because there's no water. The sinks are incredible and there's little bars of Lux soap set up everywhere and little boxes of tissues. At night it was pitch black and you had to carry around flashlights or candles. It was a very surreal experience, especially at night when it took fifteen minutes to walk from one room to the other, going down these halls with your footsteps echoing and all these spooky shadows around. It was like *The Shining*. I felt like I had broken into somebody's house. In the afternoon, I'd go up to one of these beautiful bedrooms with balconies overlooking the rose garden and take a little nap.

Behind this particular presidential palace was a zoo—a big enclosure that had lions, cheetahs, a bear. They were emaciated and obviously hadn't been cared for or fed for a while. Some scouts from the Third Infantry Division were posted there. Nearby was a pen full of live sheep, which I assumed had been the food source for these animals, so they grabbed this poor bleating and struggling sheep the first day and dropped it into the pen. The cheetahs tried to jump on it and attack it but they were too weak; they couldn't kill it and they just bloodied it a little. Then the lions rumbled over and drove the cheetahs off and the lions were able to kill it, but they were pretty weak, too. So the lions sat and had a feast and the cheetahs kept running up trying to grab a piece and would get chased off by the lions. The bear, evidently, had been given a piece of the sheep earlier and it was dragging some entrails around and dining on it.

This was all so strange. I wasn't prepared for this. I had no idea what Baghdad or the palace complex was like. The soldiers had the same reaction. It was overwhelming after coming up through the desert and seeing nothing. I'd spent a couple of nights before riding through neighborhoods by some of the government's ministries where there were people living in slums, so it was a shock just to see this opulence and this concentration of wealth.

I reported that soldiers found more than $700 million inside different locations. As I explained in my stories, this was money that was stored very neatly in stacks in galvanized aluminum boxes that were sealed with metal rivets and had an actual seal with Bank of Jordan green plastic tags and serial numbers. Basically, the first load of this money was found by two engineers who were attached to this battalion I was with. They were told one day to go out and find a saw and cut down some of the overhanging branches in this beautiful palace neighborhood where the tree limbs were banging against the trucks and the Humvees. They had seen these two small cottages that were sealed over with cinderblocks and cement. They thought this was odd, so they got a couple of tools from their truck and got inside where these boxes were stored. They opened one up and it was full of U.S. hundred dollar bills, sequentially brand new and uncirculated.

An L.A. *Times* photographer named Rick Loomis and I heard about this find and got over there while the guys who had found the money were still around. And then a sergeant who had been through the neighborhood said he had remembered seeing another cottage also sealed up the same way. He took a squad of guys and went over to the next cottage and breaking in, found roughly the same amount of money inside. We ran over there with these guys and they were all joking about, "Wow, it'd be great to take some of this money." They talked about that movie, *The Three Kings*, with George Clooney. They kept saying, "Well, nobody's going to miss a little." Later that night, a driver on the truck, who was supposed to take the money to the headquarters at the airport, stuck $300,000 in a cooler; another guy, an engineer, had taken a duffle bag and tossed $600,000 up into a tree; a couple of other guys had taken three boxes—and there was four million in each box— and stuck them in the canal. That next morning the officers, who were responsible for making sure all this money got where it was supposed to go, realized that some of the boxes were short once they were opened up. They went looking in the canal, and because the water wasn't even deep enough, they could see the top of the boxes. Then they saw the money in the tree. When I left Baghdad, they were still deciding whether they were going to charge these guys. It was a complicated situation; they had offered them amnesty and said if everybody came forward, they wouldn't be punished nearly as harshly. But they had been confined to quarters and were being investigated by the CID—the Criminal Investigative Division. The investigators explained that the charges could lead to a full court martial and actual prison time at Leavenworth, depending on how it played out and how cooperative these guys were.

The soldiers were so excited when the money was found. That's all anybody was talking about. Guys were running through the woods the next day looking for more cottages. They were swarming everywhere, and finally the commander had to stop them. It was like a treasure hunt. The colonel in charge of the unit said, "The treasure hunt's over!" He ordered these guys, "I don't want to see anybody wandering through the woods," because these guys would say, "Oh, I'm going out on patrol," and they'd go wandering looking for places where the money had been hidden. It was insane.

One day I was with the scouts from the battalion when we had come across a bank robbery in progress in Baghdad. They recovered four and one-half million dollars in cash. They arrested a bunch of guys. They had to save them from a mob. They had evidently been inside this bank for several days. They had tunneled their way in. They had a small amount of explosives and had tried to blow the safe. Then they had tried to drill through it, and they just finally got into it when the scouts happened to come by and noticed the door in the back.

With things definitely winding down and the fighting long over, I decided to leave Baghdad. I'd been away for two months and I just wanted to get back home. I'd been away from my family the entire time. I have a wife and three daughters who are twenty, seventeen, and fifteen. They're used to me going off by now. They worry about me and they're always delighted to have me come home. They're always interested in what it was like. They were definitely all opposed to the war, and very confused as to why the war had to be fought, and very interested in what it was like on the ground. They also know that it's my job, that this was an opportunity to be really part of the story—to get inside it. So they understood that.

For more than a week after I got back to Philadelphia, I kept waking up in the middle of the night not knowing where I was. It wasn't really a nightmare. It wasn't terrifying, but I kept waking up and wondering, "Was I at the palace? Was I in the desert? Was I in a tent?" I just didn't know where I was. It would take a minute or so for me to figure it out. This was just disorienting because during this war I was moving from one place to another every night, sleeping in trucks, and sleeping on the ground. So I kept waking up and thinking that I was in a room full of soldiers or out in the desert. I was really confused as to where I was. I'd have to get out of bed. I would stumble around my own house because I didn't remember what room I was in.

AMBUSHED ON THE HIGHWAY

Philippines TV (ABS-CBN) Correspondents
Eric Tulfo and Maxie Santiago

"This incident didn't cause me to think about
my mortality. I am a war correspondent. If I were
counting, this is probably my fifth life."

We interviewed this pair of intrepid television reporters in Kuwait City's
Sheraton. They had just returned from Baghdad and were fortunate to make it
back alive. ABS-CBN is a global television station based in The Philippines. It
launched its Filipino Channel in 1992.

■ ■ ■

Eric Tulfo

We are based in Kuwait because our stationary satellite transmitter is here. We
left here around Monday morning very early—around 4:00 A.M.—with our
two cameramen. We needed to travel to Baghdad to interview the task force
commander Colonel Eric Schwartz. He gave me some background and the
latest update with the situation in Baghdad. Afterwards, we decided to leave,
though some U.S. soldiers said it was dangerous to go back. But we still did
because I have to do my live report at 1:00 A.M local time here in Kuwait because I can't file from Baghdad. So we left Baghdad around 5:00 in the afternoon in a rented Pajero.

We should have stayed. By 8:00 P.M, we were just outside Al-Kut, between
Baghdad and Basra, when this guy just appeared from nowhere on the road.
His face was covered with a kaffiyeh and he was wearing a cap. He was holding an AK47. Then he started shooting. I heard four or five rounds. Boom,
boom, boom, boom, boom.

I said, "Oh my God." That was all I was able to say before ducking. Sure
enough, the first round was intended for me. It hit the windshield right in
front of me—where my head was—but I was able to seek cover behind the

dashboard. It left behind a neat little hole. That first round evidently hit my correspondent Maxie Santiago. It grazed her right shoulder.

The next round was intended for our tires. He was a good shooter. He hit our front right tire. So we already had a flat but I still had to drive out of the ambush area. I drove twenty more kilometers, then the tire just gave up. We were able to replace our tire. We drove sixty more kilometers. We found this little town called Al Kumaiti near Al Amara. We were looking for help — British forces, American forces. What we saw instead were people standing there with AK47s. "Oh shit, we are in trouble." We pretended that we were looking for a doctor instead of Coalition Forces. We didn't want to offend these villagers. But we could not leave because about twenty to thirty guys surrounded our vehicle. They keep on pointing to a building, saying, "Doctor!" I said, "No, I changed my mind. I want to go to Basra." They replied, "No! Doctor, doctor." So we followed them. Fortunately we got to a doctor and his wife, who was also a doctor. They treated Maxie's arm and my cameraman, who got a bullet graze on his head. As they were treating us, the mob didn't leave. They kept asking money from the doctors, saying, "Hey, could you give us a commission? I am sure they are going to pay you in dollars. Could you give us at least twenty to twenty-five percent commission?" I told them we didn't have money. They allowed us to stay in his clinic, but around 5:00 A.M, we left the place because they said that they would be coming back.

Maxie Santiago

My head still hurts, especially when it's cold. Everything happened so fast; we were driving and we just saw this man. He came from nowhere. I just heard shots. I didn't feel nervous. I just felt my arm going numb. Then I kept quiet. I could feel blood oozing from my right arm.

This was my first experience like this. I used to work in radio so I didn't go out much in the field. This was my first time really to go out in the field since the war started. Some of the Arab reporters didn't want to go into Iraq. So, it is just like shooting two birds with one stone because I also work for ABS-CBN and I speak a little Arabic, enough to communicate with some of them, enough to get out of trouble.

Eric made the right decision by continuing to drive even when we had a flat. If not for him we would have all been dead. Our lives depended on him during that time, because if we stopped — all dead.

We wanted to be a part of history as it unfolds. Because if you are there, you can see what is really happening. It is not enough to see everything on TV, or hear it over the radio. You have to be there. As a journalist, it's your instinct. So in your own perspective you can see what's really happening there. When you get in there, they might say "humanitarian aid," but people are starving. The reality is, they are starving, and they need more aid, but in press releases they say, "Oh, they are getting all the aid. Everything is okay." This is propaganda mileage. But if you are there, you can really see what's happening. So you can tell the whole world the whole truth. It's your responsibility as a journalist to tell the truth. Now that I came close to dying, I guess it's made me more courageous. It made me braver. This is my second life. I consider God gave me this second act because I have a mission to do. So there are still a lot of things to do as a journalist. This was a good experience for me. Not only as a journalist, but for my whole life.

Eric Tulfo

As for the second cameraman whose head got grazed, he started to talk about God. He got religion. He seemed like he was going through a nervous breakdown. He didn't want to do this any more. So he went home.

This incident didn't cause me to think about my mortality. I am a war correspondent. If I were counting, this is probably my fifth life. I have been to Mindanao, in The Philippines, where they have the MILF rebels who ambushed the military convoy I was following.

Actually, the situation in Iraq is very similar to the Philippines during the time of Marcos. Suppression of freedom. Dictatorship. All this military. They are a rich country. So it was of interest to our viewers. We show them video feeds of people living in mud houses, and their leaders stealing all their money and living in palaces. Their reaction, "Oh this guy is just like our former dictator here." They can relate. This is why we do our jobs. We weren't ordered to go to Baghdad. I was supposed to just cover the southern portion of Iraq, Basra and Umm Qasr, but we decided to go beyond our area. We had a reporter assigned to Baghdad but he left.

I have dual citizenship. I used to be with the U.S. Army from 1988 until 1994. I was with the 82nd Airborne. I was based in Germany and then I was attached to the Third Infantry Division. That's my unit. I was here in Desert Storm. I was with an anti-aircraft tanker. I was able to talk to some of my buddies still with the Third ID. "What the heck are we doing here, man? This is another Vietnam." The older guys said, "This is not our war, man. This is not the United States. This is Iraq."

My job is deliver the news as it happens. It's my responsibility. I have a commitment to tell the world this is what's happening in this other part of the world. Plain and simple. I used to write for a newspaper before I joined the army. When I joined the army I was looking for a way that I could still write, so I also contributed to an army paper called *Army Journal*. When I got out, I became a stringer for AP.

Now I must leave the Middle East and return to Asia to cover the SARS outbreak. Everybody else was scared to go to the places where the outbreak started. Not me.

THE MORAL COMPASS OF IRAQ

New York Times
Baghdad Bureau Chief John Burns

"Every lie tells you a truth."

He refused to be bullied by Iraqi Ministry of Information minders who monitored his every word in *The New York Times*, threatening expulsion or worse. "Before the war," John Burns wrote in an April 20 wrap-up, BAGHDAD DIARY: LAST DESPERATE DAYS OF A BRUTAL REIGN, "this reporter was already on a blacklist Iraqi officials maintained for journalists considered hostile to Iraq, mainly because of articles about the system of terror that sustained the power of Mr. Hussein." Burns and *Times* colleague, Thomas Friedman, are the only two individuals to have won two Pulitzer Prizes for international reporting. Burns won for his work in Bosnia in 1993 and in Sarajevo in 1997.

Burns' fearless brand of reporting elicits dramatic responses by repressive governments. In 1986, the Chinese government tried to silence him with a six-day day incarceration. In Iraq, he flummoxed his Mukhabarat minders by detailing the horrors of Saddam's notorious Abu Ghraib prison, a catacomb of execution and torture chambers, following a staged release of prisoners which led to a riot in October 2002. They retaliated by refusing to renew his visa—which only temporarily sidelined him. At fifty-eight and with remarkable vigor and commitment, Burns returned to Baghdad under a temporary visa to cover peace activists and stayed through the war. With his leonine beard and thick, curly hair, he projects an Old Testament quality that is tempered by his Shakespearean eloquence. Burns appeared regularly on PBS's *News Hour* and on ABC News, his photo in the upper left hand of the television screen. The following interview with Burns took place on May 1, 2003, in *The Times'* bureau headquarters in Room 1620 of Baghdad's Palestine Hotel.

■　■　■

From the point of view of my being in Baghdad, I have more authority than anybody else. Without contest, I was the most closely watched and unfavored of all the correspondents there because of what I wrote about terror whilst Saddam Hussein was still in power. I have very strong feelings about this. My pieces were written over several years. But particularly from October 2002 through to the war, I described how Saddam had turned this country into a slaughterhouse. Where he might have been responsible for the deaths of as much as a million people. Where this place is to be compared to nowhere on earth that I know of—and I spent decades as a foreign correspondent mostly in nasty places. I did eight years in China. I did the Soviet Union. I did Afghanistan. I covered apartheid in South Africa. I was in Bosnia. So terror, totalitarian states, and their ways are nothing new to me, but I felt from the start that this was in a category by itself, with the possible exception in the present world of North Korea. I felt that that was the central truth that has to be told about this place. It was also the essential truth that was untold by the vast majority of correspondents here. Why? Because they judged that the only way they could keep themselves in play here was to pretend that it was okay.

There were correspondents who thought it appropriate to seek the approbation of the people who governed their lives. This was the ministry of information, and particularly the director of the ministry. By taking him out for long candlelit dinners, plying him with sweet cakes, plying him with mobile phones at $600 each for members of his family, and giving bribes of thousands of dollars. Senior members of the information ministry took hundreds of thousands of dollars of bribes from these television correspondents who then behaved as if they were in Belgium. They never mentioned the function of minders. Never mentioned terror. In one case, a correspondent actually went to the Internet Center at the Al-Rashid Hotel and printed out copies of his and other people's stories—mine included—specifically in order to be able to show the difference between himself and the others. He wanted to show what a good boy he was compared to this enemy of the state. He was with a major American newspaper. Yeah, it was an absolutely disgraceful performance. CNN's Eason Jordan's op-ed piece in *The New York Times* missed that point completely. The point is not whether we protect the people who work for us by not disclosing the terrible things they tell us. Of course we do. But the people who work for us are only one thousandth of one percent of the people of Iraq. So why not tell the story of the other people of Iraq? It doesn't preclude you from telling about terror. Of murder on a mass scale just because you won't talk about how your driver's brother was murdered.

There was one major media organization—the BBC—that didn't even go to Abu Ghraib prison on the afternoon of October the 20th last year. Imagine being in the Soviet Union, and you had a chance to be admitted to the heart of darkness at the time of the Great Terror. That is what Abu Ghraib was all about. You had the BBC thinking it was inappropriate to go there because it means that it causes trouble. I couldn't find among my colleagues a single one who had read the human rights reports about Abu Ghraib. When Abu Ghraib came down, most didn't even know where Abu Ghraib was.

We were summoned on that Sunday morning to form a motorcade outside the information ministry. They didn't tell us where we were going. It turned out to be Saddam's first tactical response to Bush. That he was declaring an amnesty. It was supposed to be a limited amnesty, but it turned out to be an unlimited amnesty because they couldn't control it. The crowds that gathered in hope of finding their lost ones broke the gates down. Then you had the people of the Iraq sovereign for hours. There were a quarter of a million people inside that prison. Surging back and forth looking, trying to liberate. The prison went on hanging people during all of this. The crowds had to break into certain cell blocks to stop it.

So this was a mammoth event. But as we headed west on the motorway, anybody who'd read the human rights reports knew where we were going. The problem was even when we arrived outside it, ninety-eight percent of them had never heard of Abu Ghraib. Had no idea of what it was. These were people who came from Amman by a road which goes right past the prison. You can't miss it. It's a ghastly place.

I found myself in the execution chamber—Special Judgment Division—where twenty or thirty butcher's hooks hanging from the ceiling rusty and red, soiled trousers were thrown about the room. It was horrid. Protests started in the days that followed. Sweeping across this prison floor were mostly women. Looking for sons, husbands, brothers, who had disappeared years before; wailing and throwing themselves on the ground and appealing to Allah. You couldn't miss this. They then formed themselves into groups and went to protest outside intelligence ministry buildings, which is phenomenal. They never protest. Some of my colleagues chose not to cover that. Saying it would only get you into trouble.

The whole performance was woeful. I knew that I was walking a very fine line. The question was not so much could I get a new visa, because I was sure the time would come I couldn't even buy a visa. The question was, would I end up in Abu Ghraib myself?

In February I was denied a visa. Then I found there were visas available. I was in Amman. Some of my rivals who had omitted to notice that Iraq was a terror state were busy here sucking up. They were very pleased with themselves. These were people who'd argued that it was essential to be in Iraq for the war. I got a visa of dubious quality; it was a visa which allowed me to come in and cover the peace movement. I assumed I would be thrown out immediately. I arrived only two weeks before the war.

I went to the ministry of information director, General Uday Al-Tayyib. I said to him, "We'll never agree about the nature of this society. But you're about to go to war with the United States. I think that you need America's principal newspaper here." He said, "You've written a great deal about killing here in Iraq, Mr. Fisher," as they called me, which is my middle name. "This is good. This is a shame for the Iraqi people. But now the Americans will be killing Iraqis. Will you write about that?" I said, "Whether it's an Iraqi government that is killing Iraqis, or an American government that is killing Iraqis, it's the same to me; I will write about both."

They accredited me. But I was immediately warned by friends in the ministry that it was a ruse; I would not be given a minder. They took my passport away and held it for five days until a man who is said to be a deputy director of the Mukhabarat showed up one day—a certain Mr. Sa'ad Mutana. He was assigned to be my minder. He was an extremely unpleasant man. At this point a dozen people from the information ministry came to me and said, "Get out!" He was certainly the senior official. He introduced himself as a former general. The reason they kept me here is that when the war starts, I could become a hostage. Well, I stayed. On the night of April 1, they came to my room at this hotel and said, "You're under arrest. We've known all along you're a CIA agent. You will now collaborate with us or we will take you to a place from which you will not return." They stole all my equipment. They stole all my money. Then they left. The hotel had no electrical power at the time. They said, "You stay in your room." I assumed they left somebody outside. I went out into the darkened corridor. There was nobody there, so I slipped into the stairway. To tell you the truth, I didn't know what to do. As it happened, a friend of mine, an Italian television correspondent, happened to be coming up the stairwell. She asked, "What are you doing?" I replied, "I really don't know. I'm at wit's end." She said, "You come to my room. They won't attack my room." She is a former Italian communist who had not challenged them. So there's a strange inversion. I found my safety at a critical moment with an old friend who had not challenged them.

I then arranged a meeting with Al-Tayyib through my Italian friend. "Director," I said to him, "if something happens to me now, the facts are all well known to my newspaper and well known to people in Washington, and you will be held directly responsible. If something happens to me, you will go before an American military tribunal and I wouldn't be surprised if you were shot. So you better do something to stop it." He seemed frightened. He was a bully boy—a former head of the Mukhabarat in western Europe. He had been *persona non grata'd* out of France in the 1990s for espionage and intelligence activities, including assassination.

The director said, "I'll see what I can do." Then I arranged another meeting with him. The second time he started shouting at me. This shows just how loathsome these people are. A week earlier I had been apprised by *The Times* that the ministry of information building was to be destroyed in twenty-four hours. We had a general notification that the ministry of information and the Al Rashid Hotel were not excluded from the target lists. But as long as we were all in those buildings, they wouldn't attack.

So we had moved to the Palestine Hotel, but the TV networks were still filing from the information ministry because they were not allowed to file from anywhere else. Which is why CNN got expelled. They refused to go on filing from there; they used a videophone to file their stories on the first heavy night of bombing on March 21. They were caught with a videophone and they were expelled by dawn.

So in the three or four days that followed, I got a call from *The Times* saying that they had certain indications from the Pentagon that in twenty-four hours the information ministry would be gone. So I got up at 2:00 A.M., and I said to people downstairs, "Get Mr. Al-Tayyib here." He arrived at 5:00 A.M and I said to him, "Listen to me and listen carefully. I'm not going to cause a panic among journalists. I remember what you did to CNN the last time. I don't want to be accused of spreading alarm and despondency, but you've got to close that ministry down, because anybody who's in that building tomorrow night will be killed. We have friends in Washington. People who are concerned about my welfare and that of other American correspondents. That's how we know it."

For twenty-four hours he said he'd see what he could do. They did nothing. That night at 8:00 P.M, I went to every floor of the ministry. I told everybody. "Get off! Get off this building. It's going to be attacked this night."

When I got back to my hotel room I got another call from New York saying it's been put off twenty-four hours because of weather. It was after my second meeting with Al-Tayyib that they raided my room. He shouted at me. He said, "We know you're a CIA agent because they attacked the ministry." I said, "You lying son of a bitch. I told you that because I come from a newspaper and a country who cares about people. We were told this on the basis of human decency. Not just for ourselves but also for Iraqis. They didn't want to kill innocent Iraqis. You failed to do anything at all about it." I went there two nights running to get people out. As a result, there was only one person injured. A secretary to the minister. Which is pretty amazing considering they hit the building with seven or eight cruise missiles. I said, "You're a son of a bitch. You know exactly what the truth of this was. I told you as a matter of decency and you did nothing at all. Now you invert this to say I'm a CIA agent." The end of the story was that on the night of April 8, he stole $200,000.

Now this son of a bitch sits in his home about three miles from here, saying he expects to be reappointed director general of information. He has been meeting with director generals of ministries and is using a vetting process where they will disqualify only senior Ba'ath Party officials. I think this guy will be disqualified because he was a Mukhabarat official, but he is now saying to visiting correspondents, "Well, of course, we all knew it was time for a change in Iraq." This was a man who is incapable of telling the truth, who attempted at every opportunity to seduce Western women correspondents. He was screwing people in his office. He had photographs of himself and Saddam Hussein and a box of Viagra. This was a loathsome character altogether.

Now left with the residue of all of this, I would say there are serious lessons to be learned. Editors of great newspapers, and small newspapers, and editors of great television networks should exact from their correspondents the obligation of telling the truth about these places. It's not impossible to tell the truth. I have a conviction about closed societies, that they're actually much easier to report on than they seem, because the act of closure is itself revealing. Every lie tells you a truth. If you just leave your eyes and ears open, it's extremely revealing. We now know that this place was a lot more terrible than even people like me had thought. There is such a thing as absolute evil. I think people just simply didn't recognize it. They rationalized it away. I cannot tell you with what fury I listened to people tell me throughout the autumn that I must be on a kamikaze mission. They said it with a great deal of glee, over the years, that this was not a place like the others.

I did a piece on Uday Hussein and his use of the National Olympic Committee headquarters as a torture site. It's not just journalists who turned a blind eye. Juan Antonio Samaranch of the International Olympic Committee could not have been unaware that western human rights reports for years had been reporting the National Olympic Committee building had been used as a torture center. I went through its file cabinets and got letter after letter from Juan Antonio Samaranch to Uday Saddam Hussein: "The universal spirit of sport," "My esteemed colleague." The world chose in the main to ignore this. For some reason or another, Mr. Bush chose to make his principal case on weapons of mass destruction, which is still an open case. This war could have been justified any time on the basis of human rights, alone. This was a grotesque charnel house, and also a genuine threat to us. We had the power to end it and we did end it. At a cost of 130 American lives and thirty or forty British lives. So we could say that if you add in several thousand Iraqis—let's overestimate this and say 5,000 Iraqis—probably fewer people died in the six weeks since this war began than would have died if Saddam Hussein's killing machine had gone about its daily business. So to my mind, it was always on that basis that the war should have been justified, but you'd have never have known it by reading most of the coverage of the war by those correspondents. Dante Alighieri said, "The hottest place in hell is reserved for those who remain mute in the time of moral crisis."

In this profession, we are not paid to be neutral. We are paid to be fair, and they are completely different things. For example, in Bosnia it was perfectly clear from very early on who were the principal villains of that war. Yes, the Muslims and the Croats got off some mayhem. But who started the war? Who did the overwhelming majority of the killing? The Serbs did. I worked for an editor at the time who wanted me to iron out of my stories any implication that there was one principal offender. He would have been happy with a story that said, "They are all as bad as one another. This has been going on in the Balkans since the beginning of time." This attitude comes from a complete misapprehension as to what our business is. Yes, we should be absolutely ruthless as to fact. We should not approach a story with some sort of ideological template that we impose on it. We should let the facts lead us to conclusions, but if the conclusions seem clear, then we should not avoid those on the basis of an idea we are supposed to be neutral. Because if that were the case, they might as well hire a stenographer, and a stenographer would be a lot cheaper than I am.

As far as I am concerned, when they hire me, they hire somebody who has a conscience and who has a passion about these things. I think I was a little bit advantaged in this, because I am fifty-eight years old.

Look, I don't believe in the journalist as hero, because I think that wherever we go, and whatever degree of resolve that may be required of us, there are always much, much braver people than us. I travel in a suit of armor. I work for *The New York Times*. That means that I have the renown of the paper, plus the power of the United States government. Let's be honest. Should anything untoward come to me, I have a flak jacket. I have a wallet full with dollars. I'm here by choice. I have the incentive of being on the front page of *The New York Times*, and being nominated for major newspaper prizes.

The people who we write about have none of these advantages. They are stuck here with no food and no money. I don't want to be pious about this, but for a journalist to present himself as a hero in this situation is completely and totally bogus. I remember my father telling me toward the end of the Second World War—he was a senior officer in fire command in the Royal Air Force—the word came out that Churchill wanted to award a VC—Victoria Cross—to a fighter command and that nominees should be put forward. He put forward people who had flown throughout the war in conditions of enormous hazard. In the end, they gave the VC to someone who had done one spectacular thing in a moment. My father said, "The real courageous thing to do was to go out every single day without the lure of the spectacular." We have the lure of a spectacular reward. That draws us on. I got a Pulitzer Prize in Sarajevo, which was awarded for "bravery" or something somewhere in the citation. I said, and I absolutely meant it, "I assume that we are talking here about chronicling the bravery of the people of a city that was being murdered. That was where bravery came into this. Then there were no rewards save the possibility of surviving." So I don't want to present myself here as anything like that. No, I don't. As a matter of fact, I think this vainglorious ambition is part of the same problem really. It is the pursuit of power. Renown. Fame.

I am being very indiscreet here, but by the time I joined the profession, it wasn't in pursuit of power, or money, or fame. My salary was $19 a week or something. First thing my first city editor said to me was after I was irritated because I had been shut out of a city council education committee and went back to the small paper and complained, "In this business, where the carpet begins, you halt." I've never forgotten that. It has something to do with how you configure yourself in the landscape in which you operate. You are paid money to go out and bring something back. That you are not the story. That your renown and your success are a subsidiary to all of this.

Early in my career I made big mistakes. My first assignment to a totalitarian society was China in 1971, when I allowed myself to be seduced by the siren voices of the great sinologists of America. They told me before I went, "Well, you are basically a stupid young American boy. You should have been a British boy. The Chinese are vestigial. This is a great society. Don't judge China by your own standards. Judge it by *its* standards. There is a great and noble human experiment under way in China called the Cultural Revolution." Well, the first night I was there, there were bodies floating down the Po River in Canton. I said to my interpreter, "What happened to these people?" Some of them had been bludgeoned. He said, "Perhaps some of them fell in the river. Right?"

It took me about a year and a half to get the courage to realize that I was living in a place where I was absolutely incarcerated by lies. That virtually everything that the government said was a lie. That virtually everything I learned from Chinese people in the presence of other Chinese people was a lie. That I was extremely restricted to twenty-five kilometers from the center of Peking. Wherever I went I was followed by state security people, but all the same, I had two eyes and two ears and it took very little time, beginning with the thirty bodies in the Po River in Canton, to begin to realize that the truth was about 180 degrees from the official truth. Once I came to the realization I was working for a paper called *The Globe and Mail* in Canada, *The Times* was syndicating what I was writing because they had no correspondent there. Then I wrote a story about "A Thousand and One Ways to Lie in China." Abe Rosenthal was then the editor of *The New York Times* and he asked me to go see him and he offered me a job, saying that *The Times* had had a number of people who had gone to China, but wrote without much critical insight. Abe said this is where I'd gotten a job. Well, I had learned. I am not saying these things are natural. They don't necessarily come naturally to somebody who has lived his life in a free society, but I learned my lesson, because I behaved for the first year like a useful idiot. Then I decided however little it is that I can acquire with my own eyes and my own ears is of much greater weight than this lying mendacious murdering state will tell me. The way I like to think of it is if you have a jigsaw, with perhaps 2,000 pieces, and you ought to be able to accumulate twenty or thirty of those pieces, but what do you see on the jigsaw? You'd see some forms of yellow and black. You'd see a tail. Right? Pretty soon you begin to get the idea you've got a tiger. It's not so difficult.

There is corruption in our business. We need to get back to basics. This war should be studied and talked about. In the run up to this war, to my mind, there was a gross abdication of responsibility. You have to be ready to listen to whispers.

BOYS IN THE BRADLEY

San Francisco Chronicle Reporter Carl Nolte

> "God likes the side with the most weapons,
> I noticed."

Carl Nolte was back in Iraq. The first time, during Day Two of Desert Storm's 100-hour ground war, the veteran *San Francisco Chronicle* reporter toured the southeastern region of the country from a U.S. Army Apache helicopter. Together with NBC's anchorman John Chancellor, they had hitched a ride with Lieutenant General William Pagonis, who surveyed the battleground with military pride. "We were flying along over the desert," Nolte wrote, "across the invisible border with Iraq and into a sort of high plateau that seemed to be swarming with American armor—tanks, Bradley fighting vehicles, long trains of supply trucks all driving deep into Iraq. We got past the leading edge, and Pagonis got on the intercom. 'You see anything in front of us?' He meant to the north, where the Iraqi army was supposed to be. 'No,' we said, 'nothing.' 'That's right,' he said, 'There's nobody there, nobody. We fooled 'em, we pulled it off.' He said what we were seeing was a vast flanking maneuver, a sweep to the left, with two U.S. Army corps that would cut off the Iraqi army and win the war very quickly."

Twelve years later, Nolte, sixty-nine, returned to Kuwait and Iraq, though he swapped air for ground: The former U.S. Army sergeant wanted to witness this war squeezed inside a clanking Bradley fighting vehicle as part of U.S. Army's Charlie Company, Third Battalion, Seventh Regiment—which was also his old unit. He also earned the "gray-heart" distinction of being one of the oldest reporters to be embedded with combat troops. (The "oldest reporter" honor went to George Wilson of the *National Journal*.) The regiment's next oldest guy was fifty-one. His name, oddly enough, was Sergeant York.

■　■　■

Ernie Pyle always referred to the army as "our army" and used "us" and "we." Always. On page 214 of *This Is Your War*, which is a collection of his WWII dispatches, he wrote, "Last, and most important of all, was the feeling of vitality, of being at the heart of everything; being part of it. No mere onlooker, but as a member of the team. I'll have to admit, there's an exhilaration in war, an inner excitement that builds up to an intenseness seldom achieved in peace time. The Army accepted us correspondents as part of the family."

If I were part of the family, I was like the poor relation, I'll tell you! We were draftees in the late '50s. We hated it. We hated every minute of it. We hated every second. We promised ourselves we'd never be nostalgic about it. I was on active duty for two years and with the reserves unit in the Ninety-first Regiment at the Presidio Army Base for three years. I had to do the third year because I needed the money. I ended up a staff sergeant. I was a wonderful writer of orders at headquarters. The orders were administrative orders such as somebody's released or assigned and transferred to somewhere else. They weren't orders to go and fight somebody or rescue Slim Pickens. At that time, the Bay Area was ringed with seven or eight military bases. The Presidio was built originally by the Spanish in 1776 for purposes of defense and never fired a shot in anger at anybody over its long history.

I pursued a career in dodging. After the reserves I planned to go to law school and instead I got a job working for the University of San Francisco in sports public relations. I had been the sports editor of the campus paper when Bill Russell played. Then, I began my newspaper career, and here I am.

In the first Gulf War I was a unilateral for about six weeks. I then realized that the ground war was about to start. I had a big, white, brand new Chevy Caprice that I was not going to drive through a minefield by myself, so I went back and got into a press pool. Since I hadn't been campaigning for a pool, I was given a shitty one. It was central command supply. Actually it was kind of interesting, but everybody had written about it already.

I had a notebook and I had a laptop, but I didn't have a printer, and they wouldn't let me use the laptop because when you're with a pool, you were subject to military review or censorship. They'd say, "No, no, you're liable to change it, so we can't do that." So I had to bring a typewriter, for Christ's sake, in addition to my laptop. It was this big stupid-ass typewriter, which I still have. I don't know what to do with it. I mean, typewriters are like Model T Fords or something. It's an Olympia.

It was while I was in that army helicopter that I was being censored. Prior to that, I was in the rear! I mean, goddamn it, here's a hundred-hour war and I was in the rear, but we saw that missile go over—the last one that hit the people in Saudi Arabia. It killed about forty-four. I'm glad it wasn't us; it was that strange feeling. We saw it fly over at night. And then later, I talked them into letting me go into Kuwait in the back of the truck.

The television networks made that first Gulf War look like highlights for the eleven o'clock news or a baseball game. Every single swing is a home run—WHAM! Missiles never missed. Coming back to the Gulf, I talked to a guy on an airplane about that. He had given me his business card. He was involved with the missile program. He said that the Patriots were not designed to shoot down missiles in the air like bullets shooting at a boat. You wanted to knock the warhead or engine off, so the warhead goes off on its own self. Now, he said, they're really pretty good.

I didn't see a lot of Iraqi casualties in the first war. I did see a lot of Iraqi prisoners of war. With casualties, the Muslims believe the person should be buried on the day of his death. They make a big effort to get rid of casualties. I went to the Highway of Death and all the dead people had been removed, but it sure smelled like it. I used to have recurring nightmares about that. The nightmares were that I was not lucky enough to be born in this wonderful, happy country; I could have been born in Iraq. In a different time, I could've been drafted into their goddamn army, not this army, but in their army. The roles were reversed. I wasn't a lucky American in an F18, I was a poor Iraqi fuckhead. Then the Iraqi high command says, "Okay, we're going to go invade Kuwait." So we invade Kuwait like we're supposed to. And the next thing you know, they all become panic-stricken and say, "The Americans are coming! They're going to kill us all. You better get out of here!" So I jump in a car, I'm driving up the highway, which looked exactly like the Waldo Grade [just north of the Golden Gate Bridge], and there's this huge traffic jam. Everybody stops. The Americans jump us with their aircraft and I'm trapped. No defense, right, because we're boxed in. All we have to protect ourselves are our AK47s. We have no command. We have nothing. So it was pretty scary. God likes the side with the most weapons, I noticed.

It always seemed to me that there was unfinished business from the first war. I talked to the guy in charge of the Marine Memorial Club in San Francisco. He's the president and CEO—General Mike Mayet. He was the commander of the First Marine Division in the Persian Gulf War. He thought that the U.S. had won the war, but lost the peace of the war. He thought we did not go far enough at getting rid of Saddam Hussein. We had to go back and do it again. We were almost to Basra and we pulled back. We should have not pulled back and leave the Shiites to get done in. Saddam Hussein used helicopters on them.

It was strange being back in Kuwait. I remember standing in front of the Sheraton Hotel in 1991. It was a wreck. I said, "I'll never come back to this place again." Now it's all been rebuilt. It has a doorman with a top hat. All these rich folks were coming in and having $30 buffet lunches—much more than I'm used to paying for lunch! I went around and looked at the city. It had all been totally rebuilt, except that the Sheraton had a museum of Iraqi outrages and in another hotel, they had a similar exhibit. The main Kuwait museum had been looted by the Iraqis, so the locals burned it down. It had contained the finest collection of Arabic art in the world.

I saw this second war from inside a Bradley fighting vehicle. It was like riding with a cavalry and you're inside the horse. It was very noisy. You couldn't talk. It's a track vehicle, so there's a clattering sound and it's rough riding, especially over terrain. It could run over berms and ditches and stuff, but inside the thing, you're bouncing all around; you have to hang on. It can hold seven. We didn't have seven, we had five—myself and four soldiers.

It was extremely unpleasant, because you're all entwined with each other. Some other guy's feet are in your face; your feet are in his face. There's not much room to sit because all this equipment is in there, too. We had to go to sleep when it was dark, because you couldn't show lights at night. So we'd be lined up like logs on the ground, sleeping alongside the vehicle, out of the wind, if possible, hoping not to get run over by somebody.

We had personal hygiene every morning—that's the army's euphemism for washing your teeth and using baby wipes. It wasn't too good. We didn't have any bathrooms. We just dug a hole in the ground.

The soldiers thought I was their mascot. They always introduced me to others as their reporter. Other soldiers would ask, "Who's this guy?" They'd respond, "He's a reporter." Then they'd say, "You got a reporter?" "Yeah, look at this. He's an old guy, too!"

One morning, the lieutenant was getting all jumpy saying, "Come with me, Carl." I thought, "He's never talked like that before. It must be some big cheese coming here." He didn't want me wandering around. I asked, "Who the hell is he?" because I didn't realize at first it was Ted Koppel. He looked like an actor to me! He was wearing a war correspondent outfit right out of the movies. He was surrounded by technicians and people were taking his picture. I thought we were props in his show. He looked right through me. After

I saw Koppel, I had to take a crap in a ditch and I wondered if he did that as well. I don't think so.

Once in a while, I'd see a colonel and I'd say, "How's the war going, colonel?" He'd say, "It's going good." He'd ask me how I was doing and I'd ask him stuff: "What are we going to do?" He'd give me a vague idea. Some people rode with colonels all day. I rode with the sergeants. Most of the war correspondents practice a kind of "gotcha" journalism. "Oh, man, they shot three civilians at a fucking roadblock" or something. I actually talked to a soldier who did that. Two weeks had already passed. I mean this guy's not exactly Ernest Hemingway. He's not very eloquent, but you could see in his face that he really felt bad about it. It was at a roadblock near Karbala. He said the driver of a Nissan pickup truck came at him at a roadblock. He yelled, then fired a warning shot, but I guess he didn't wait long enough between the warning shots. He then opened fire with his .25 caliber machine gun. It fires 200 rounds a minute. Afterwards, he said, "Oh, Christ, they were fucking farmers on the way to the market! I don't know what they were thinking about!" He felt genuine regret that this had happened.

In our regiment, we had fourteen Bradleys and none of them were knocked out. By way of comparison, in the first Gulf War, 2,000 Iraqi tanks were knocked out while the U.S. lost only three. But according to the Powell Doctrine, we were undermanned, because Powell wanted 500,000 troops. Here it was only 200,000. Still, the equipment makes all the difference. It's like the San Francisco 49ers playing the Galileo High School in football. The executive officer of the Third Battalion thought that we had far superior firepower, that since the 1991 Gulf War, our American weapons had gotten better and the Iraqis' had been degraded. When I asked him carefully, "In your professional opinion, what do you think is going to happen?" he said, "Well, we're obviously far superior to them in every way." They had no air cover—you could run convoys fifteen miles long up the highway without getting hit. Remember in World War II, German and Japanese planes streaking the shit out of everything. It ain't like that.

After we went across the Euphrates River, we got shelled pretty good one night. I was inside the Bradley hoping to hell it wouldn't hit me. The shells were landing three hundred yards, four hundred yards—not that close. I wasn't terrified or anything. Yeah, they were firing at us. They were trying to hit the Bradley and I was inside of it. One sergeant said, "A lot of people think these things are steel coffins, but they'll survive anything but a direct hit from artillery." I forgot to ask him how big the artillery he meant.

In our unit, only one guy was wounded in the war. He got shrapnel in the eye. They thought he might lose his vision, but he came out okay. I hurt my finger by banging it on a football. We were playing football one day and I said, "Throw the football to me." He threw it to me and I couldn't catch it right. Shit!

I liked being an embed with these guys. I got the opportunity to see the war in a way soldiers see it, the compromising they have to do. In other words, you first have to get them to trust you, so you can see what it is they see. You have to maintain your own professionalism to keep the reporting impartial. I'd joke, "If you guys fuck up, I'm gonna report it." They'd say, "Yeah, yeah." Then I'd answer, "Okay, don't fuck up. If you fuck up, don't let me find out, because I'm gonna report it." I was very impressed with the American soldier. They were pretty good; they were professional; they didn't swear too much; they even burned their garbage all up—the Sierra Club would have liked them. So you have two things going on here: You want to see the war real closely and you want to try to distance yourself at the same time—that's pretty hard to do. It's like that song from *Gigi*: "Gigi, am I up too close, or back too far?"

REPORTING FROM THE TRENCHES

CBS White House Correspondent and Weekend Anchor John Roberts

> "For journalists, the world's most comfortable maximum security prison is the White House, where they believe that the less information you have, the better off you are. Whereas with the military, the more information we had, the better off we were."

Go where the story is. That's been John Roberts' motto for years. *The CBS Evening News* veteran could have easily opted to cover the war from the banks of the Potomac but he preferred the Tigris and Euphrates. He chose Baghdad over the Beltway. Roberts has been the anchor for the Sunday edition of the *CBS Evening News* since March 1995. He is also its Senior White House Correspondent. His journalistic beat embraces a wide, eclectic range of topics, from medical and health issues to politics to natural disasters like fires, hurricanes, and earthquakes. He joined CBS News in June 1992 as co-anchor of the *CBS Morning News*. Prior to that, he had been co-anchor of *Canada A.M.*

■ ■ ■

I was with the Second Light Armored Recognizance (LAR) Battalion out of Camp Lejeune in North Carolina. It's officially part of the Second Marine Division, but for this conflict, they were attached to the First Marine Division, which is housed at Camp Pendleton, California. We crossed the line of departure, quite a bit west of where the Fifth Regimental Combat Team and the Seventh Regimental Combat Team went in, which was at Highway 80 right there at the border. They went up through Umm Qasr and Basra. We crossed through the desert. We first came upon civilization, if you will, near this fairly large chemical weapons storage facility from the first Gulf War. We hooked up with the main highway there and went north in through Nasiriyah. It was our unit that went into Nasiriyah, following the 507th and the First Battalion of the Second Marines, who had all the ambush trouble there, and it was our unit that actually punched through to the other side and broke the back of the Iraqi resistance.

We were typically traveling with the headquarters support battalion because our commander, Lieutenant Colonel Eddie Ray, was very concerned for our safety and, I guess, rightly so. He was obsessed about safety, and it's to his credit, because every person in his unit who was in active combat came back. They only had a couple of light casualties. There was one member of the second LAR who was killed. He was from Charlie Company, but it was actually attached to another unit and he was accidentally electrocuted by a low-hanging wire as he was riding in the 50-caliber defensive position of the seven-ton truck.

Our Hummer was decked out with what looked like pretty sophisticated communications equipment; it had antennas and satellite domes and a satellite dish, and we rode all the way through the war thinking, "Well, if you were an Iraqi and you were looking for a vehicle to target, you'd want to target: a) a soft vehicle; and b), a command vehicle." Of all of the vehicles that there were in our column, ours looked the most like a command vehicle. The commander thought that as well and that's why he tended to keep our vehicle back from the front a little bit, but allowed us to ride up front in a 50-caliber, hard-shell Humvee.

Our communications equipment was, to a large degree, more sophisticated than the Marines', particularly on the move. They have VHF radios with strong encryption, so they're guaranteed secure communications. Our communications weren't secure, so from that standpoint, they weren't as sophisticated as the military's. But we had videophones that allowed us to transmit video going sixty miles per hour. We didn't have to stop. The only time we needed to stop was if we were re-aligning the antennas, but once we had aligned the antennas, they were good to go regardless of how quickly we were moving.

Our videophones were directional. At the very beginning of the war, we had to promise that we wouldn't actually start broadcasting until we left the line of departure and had actually started moving. But in terms of operational security, because the videophones that we were using had pinpoint beams and were highly directional, they thought that those couldn't be DF'd, or located via direction finding. There was a point during the war where we had to stop using our Thuraya satellite phones because they're more omnidirectional and there was some concern that the Iraqis might have been able to direction-find those, so there were a couple days where we had to stop using that, but we were always good to go with the videophones and with our satellite.

We did receive enemy fire on several occasions. One time we were just south of Nasiriyah when a couple of mortars came in. The Saddam fedayeen used a tactic where they would let the armored columns come through, then they would try to attack some of the soft targets in hit-and-run attacks. There were a couple of mortars that came in very close to our vehicle. There was another time when we were just south of Al-Kut, where a couple of artillery shells came in as well, but typically what would happen is if an artillery shell came in, all that did was tell the Americans where the Iraqis were firing from. They would just open up with a barrage of their own artillery and suppress that. So any time the Iraqis tried to open fire on us with any kind of large-caliber weapon—like an artillery gun—they would immediately get pounded. The real danger seemed to come from those guys who would sneak up late in the day as the sun was going down or at night and lob a few shells into a forward position. That was the biggest danger that we really faced on the road.

In terms of what kind of images we could air, there are certain pictures that you just can't show on television. We saw plenty of those, so you had to sanitize your coverage to some degree. I couldn't walk up to a bus that had been hit by 25-mm cannon fire and see all the dead Iraqis lying around, blown into bits and pieces, headless bodies or whatever—I can report on that—but I certainly can't show those pictures on television. You have to sanitize your coverage somewhat for American sensibilities, but really it's just the pictures that were sanitized. It certainly wasn't the words.

I remember that as I was walking up to the bus I just mentioned, I was wondering how I was going to react because, though I'd seen dead people, obviously, in the past, I'd never seen that scope of carnage before. Twenty-five dead Iraqis just scattered about on the sides of this bus, in front of the bus. As I was walking out, I started talking to myself, "Okay, you just have to be calm, keep breathing; let's see how you react when you get there." It was pretty horrible to see all those guys lying around. There was this one guy whose feet were facing me; he's lying out of the back, his feet were facing me, he was sort of spread-eagled on the ground. As I walked up, his body was in perfect shape, but when I got right up on top of him, his head was missing, like it had been removed. Then there was another guy whose head was blown into three pieces and part of his body had been ripped off by a shell. I was actually quite surprised that I didn't have the visceral physical reaction that I thought that I was going to have. I thought that

I'd probably fall to my knees and start heaving, but I didn't. I did have an emotional reaction. I said to myself, "Gosh, this is tragic. These poor people," regardless of the fact that they're enemy soldiers. You have to have some sort of human pity for them.

A couple of hours afterwards I filed my report, but certainly those images keep coming up in my brain. Even today, just recalling it, I can feel the sensations that I had when I was there. To some degree, the longer you sit with it, the more it sets in your mind and the worse you feel about it. But the one guy who I really felt sorry for was a prisoner of war—the Marines had been using high explosive rounds against Iraqi vehicles—and the whole left side of this poor fellow's face was completely burned. It was ash, and I just know the agony that he must have been in as he was kneeling on the ground with the plastic flexicuffs on this hands and waiting to be taken away to the camp where they were keeping the POWs. I had a sense of how much pain he must have been in, and I felt very bad for that guy.

Certainly, after the Marines were killed in Nasiriyah, the soldiers kicked it up a notch and there was a certain sense of, "Let's go in there and show them how the Marines do it," as opposed to "We've got a job to do." They're professional soldiers, and while I think emotion does tend to get the better of them on occasion, that certainly wasn't the way that they were all the time.

When we moved past Nasiriyah, we started getting reports that there was going to be a thirty-day pause in the war. These were not reports that were coming from stateside. These were reports that were coming from within the units that we were traveling with. They were going to wait to bring in the Fourth Infantry Division; that they were going to beef up the 101st Airborne; and that we were just going to sit there in the desert for thirty days and then we were going to push forward. Then, within twenty-four hours or forty-eight hours, the delay was reduced to fifteen days, and then after we'd been sitting in this one area, moving back on the same road for four days, we heard, "We're leaving in two hours." We were going to go on to Al-Kut, and our unit was tasked with pinning down the Baghdad division of the Iraqi Republican Guard.

There was certainly a lot of talk that they hadn't come with enough guys, that everything was getting bogged; the logistics trains were tied up beyond belief. At one point, the regimental combat team that we were attached to was down to one MRE a day, was almost out of ammunition, and only had three hundred gallons of fuel in reserve. During this time the logistics guys were going out of their minds. They were trying to figure out how they were going to make this whole thing roll forward. If there were more stiff enemy opposition, they would have been in a lot of trouble. If they had had some sort of division that could have counter-attacked, I wouldn't want to think what would have happened. But the air power was so effective dissolving a lot of the opposition that a lot of the Marines would say, "Where are these guys?" Perhaps it was the air power that pinned them down or weakened them to the point where they were no longer an effective fighting force. But if they had decided to launch a major counter-attack, our greatest worry was during one hellacious sandstorm. There were erroneous reports that elements of a division were moving south and we thought, "Shit, you can't see anything with this sandstorm." Real-time satellite observation is nonexistent because it can't see through the sandstorm. If these guys decide to come now, there's going to be some real trouble. As it turned out, all the reports were false. They just kind of evaporated into the desert.

CBS was very concerned about us, particularly after journalists started dying. Dan Rather would call my wife on occasion and just say, "Things were going along all right, don't worry. Everything will be all right." I've got a son who's seventeen and a daughter who's eleven. They were all very concerned before I left, and I guess kids kind of put it out of their minds, but my wife was very concerned. Particularly after Mike Kelly and David Bloom died, but it was the next day when two journalists were killed in a rear position to the Third Infantry Division that I called her up and said, "You haven't heard about this yet, but I want you to know this happened, so that you know it wasn't me." She just lost it. She was on the phone crying, saying, "Come home, come home, come home." "Look," I said, "everything's going to be all right. I'll stay in touch with you. I'll get through this."

While it is a great honor to be one of the CBS anchors and to fill in for Dan on the evening news, there's no other sensation like being out there in the field, particularly in a story like this. That is the place to be. To have the opportunity to cover it from the front lines as opposed to way back in the rear at some joint information bureau, as many of the journalists had to do during the Gulf War, there's no substitute for that, either. You're right up there, riding the tiger with the rest of the guys. You're in as much danger as they are, which is a little uncomfortable, but you figure they're weathering the storm and so you should be able to as well. It's interesting that you find you're a little bit more resilient than you thought you might have been. I recall that the first few days that we spent out in the field in the main camps in Kuwait, I was trying to meticulously keep our tent clean, and try to keep up my own personal hygiene as well. By the time that we left the line of departure, I basically said, "Screw it. I'm not going to stay clean!"

Any time that you have television with a unit, it tends to be a little bit bigger deal. All the guys want to get on TV because they know that the folks back home can see them. There were still some skeptics even after we left the line of departure; we had been living with these guys out in their camps in Kuwait for a couple of weeks. But it was interesting that when they got their first delivery of mail and found that everybody back home was staying in touch with their unit by watching our reports suddenly all of that skepticism evaporated and we became a welcome part of their unit.

We slept in tents prior to the start of the war, but after the start of the war, there was no time to set up a tent or take it down. Typically, what we would do was follow the standard regulation that you sleep on the left side of your vehicles so that anybody who drives through would know that if they go to the left side of the vehicle, there could be some people sleeping there. So every night we would dig what's called a slog trench, which is about six-feet long so you could lay down, and a couple of feet wide, a couple of feet deep. It would take several hours to dig. That's to protect against artillery, so that if artillery comes in and hits the ground and sprays shrapnel, if your head is below the ground, there's a good chance that the shrapnel will go over you. It protects you from almost anything except for a direct hit. So every afternoon you'd grab your entrenching tool and dig a trench, and you'd put your sleeping gear in there, and you'd spend every night sleeping in a hole. I shoveled my own dirt. There's nobody else to do it for you. They were all busy digging their own.

I don't think there were any other White House television correspondents who were embedded. There were a couple of print guys and photographers, but as far as I know, I was the only correspondent who's attached to the White House. For me, the real difference between covering the war and covering the White House is the flow of information. For journalists, the world's most comfortable maximum security prison is the White House, where they believe that the less information you have, the better off you are. Whereas with the military, the more information we had the better off we were.

We knew the entire first few days of the American battle plan two weeks before we left. During the late afternoon of the day that we left to start the ground war, we were at our dispersal area. They had the camouflage netting covering everything, and there were probably twelve or fifteen journalists who were there. The commander brought out this roll-down map and he walked us through the first five days of the war with arrows, and charts, and graphs, and placements, and all that, and we literally knew every move that was going to be made in the next five days. To have that degree of information flow — of course, it was all given to us on the basis that we wouldn't say anything until after we had reached these certain objectives — but every day you'd be able to report on what you had done or what you were doing. You couldn't report on what was about to happen, but it gave you a sense of where you were going so you had an overall perspective of the war that you could relate the individual events to. If you know the game plan, you know you can tell where all the players are, and you know how the game is going.

Covering this war was a tremendous journalistic experience. It was a life-changing experience. I came out of this with a different perspective on who I am and what's important to me. You do a lot of soul searching while you're there and it opens up your mind to some concepts that perhaps you had rejected in the past. You think that you might not come back from this war, and that so many things that you used to think were so important really are so trivial in comparison, that it does reset your priorities a little bit. You cherish the moments that you have just a little bit more than you did in the past. You want to slow down the blurring passage of time that your life has become and enjoy a few more of the moments, because you know that it could end at any time. When you go, what is it that you want to take with you? What are the things that you want to be able to say that you've done in your life when your time eventually comes? You're looking at your own mortality.

I've been to shit holes the world over. I've seen death and destruction. I've seen pain and suffering, but it's always been in some other place. But here, I was actually living it day to day. It wasn't like when I was in Turkey after the earthquake. I could just pick up and half a day later be in a five-star hotel in Istanbul. In this war, you were there living with these guys every day; you were in every bit as much danger as they were; anything that happened to them affected you and anything that happened in the country affected you as well. When you live it from that perspective and you're so immersed in it, then it's a different experience. It's not the sort of thing that you go out, you take a look around, and that night you're back in your hotel room saying, "Well, that was quite a scene, wasn't it?" If you're under fire, that night you're going to be under fire. The next day, you're going to be under fire. If you're living under the threat of artillery attacks, you go to bed every night worrying about that, and say, "Please, God, don't let it happen tonight, or tomorrow, or the next day."

TRAPPED IN THE MEDIA CROSSFIRE

Al Jazeera Correspondent Amr El-Kakhy

> "I couldn't get the American commander to
> make any response available."

Before he became a television reporter for Qatar-based Al Jazeera, Amr El-Kakhy worked in BBC's Baghdad office for five years. Born in Cairo and educated at Cairo University with a degree in English literature, the thirty-seven-year old is married and has two children. Despite criticism that Al Jazeera is a mouthpiece for intransigent anti-U.S. viewpoints, El-Kakhy admits to being "proud of working for Al Jazeera. It is the only independent, in the literal sense, station in the Arab worlds. It is not a state-run media. The Qatari government does not control us. Does not tell us what to do here. All choices are made absolutely on merit. I am sitting there producing on the desk whatever I think of. I just do it and nobody interferes with me. We just discuss it like any other news desk."

While reports cite a struggle between a conservative, Islamic faction and a secular group of free speech advocates within Al Jazeera, El-Kakhy cites another reason Al Jazeera has a bad-boy rep within the Arab market, which it dominates with 40 million viewers. "The main problem Al Jazeera has with the Arab governments is that Al Jazeera has no taboos whatsoever," said El-Kakhy from a cafeteria at Al Jazeera's modern broadcast facilities in Qatar in mid-April. "That is what makes them really anxious, always monitoring Al Jazeera, always complaining about our reports of such things."

■ ■ ■

Nobody likes what we did. The Iraqi government criticized us. Even my colleague who had spent five months in our Baghdad newsroom, and was the longest-serving member there, came back and said, "The authorities were not happy about you being embedded with the Americans."

There was supposed to be four teams from Al Jazeera embedded with the U.S. military, but I and my cameraman were the only ones to make it through due to problems getting visas to Kuwait, and then getting proper media accreditations. The Kuwaiti government did not want to give me accreditation. Al Jazeera had its offices closed in Kuwait. We were reporting about American forces coming. Even using in-house reports from AP or Reuters. It was all a bit sensitive. So due to delays, we couldn't begin reporting from the beginning.

The day we arrived, we were supposed to be embedded with the Fifteenth Marine Expeditionary Forces [MEF] at a camp in northern Kuwait. Camp Commando was the headquarters of the Marine Expeditionary Forces. We were treated very well. The people were happy that we finally joined them. They were disappointed that we couldn't join at the first place. For us, the purpose of being embedded was to make a balanced reporting on the war. When you have been in the field, you know there are always claims and counterclaims. It is very difficult to check and verify what's going on. We explained that we want to do all that, both the military side and the humanitarian side, because that is the truth of the total. We say, for example, "There were two lost in the battle in return for twenty dead Iraqis."

We stayed at Camp Commando for two nights. Waiting for the officer of the Fifteenth MEF unit to pick me and my cameraman up. Part of the embedding ground rules said that we were not allowed to use our own transportation. So that put restriction on us as to what equipment we could use. We had to use a satellite videophone and that made it difficult to get through most of the time. Of course, a lot of people were using these channels, which was technically a pain in the neck. It takes a long time. Ideally we use two satphones, but with all frequencies in constant use, we had to go with one phone ninety percent of the time. We also use an antenna we have to put on the ground and direct it to the proper direction.

We arrived at the Umm Qasr port on March 22. The next morning we actually went into the northern part of the port. We were not taken to the south port—the old port. I was listening to the top Iraqi information minister claiming, "No, the fact is, the port did not fall." Actually, Mohammed Saeed al-Sahaf Saraf was a star during the war. A star in the sense that people loved the way he spoke, the way he expressed the position of the Iraqi government. His vocabulary was superb. He said that the port was still being embattled by both forces, but I was inside the port. The commander of the Fifteenth knew I was there. He was establishing a command post, which means we were theoretically safe. So I reported that I was inside the northern port. I toured that northern port. I was there. I saw it for myself. I went through the warehouses of the new port. To the pier. Everything. I could explain that. I said "We did not go to the south port. Yet. American troops told me there are a few warehouses in the south which are still under fire, and are not 100 percent secure."

The Iraqi authorities then accused me of being pro-American. I was accused of promoting their claims without verification. My editors asked, "Are you sure you are there?" I said, "I can't talk about the city." They asked me, "What is the situation exactly?" I could explain it. "Are you under restriction? Are you under any sort of pressure whatsoever?" They were cross-checking because they needed to know. They are concerned about their reputation for objectivity and for my safety as well. So we have to be able to say, "Absolutely, that's what's happening."

I had not yet been taken to the southern port. I don't know anything about the city inside there. I couldn't verify what's being said. But on the very next day, there was an ambush by the Republican Guard. They had acted as if they were surrendering. They waved white flags. The Americans did not take the usual measures. They were supposed to make them get out of their cars, and lay down without any sort of weapons, and come over to them to surrender. Then they were under fire. So they turned and maneuvered back to the port. At the same time, when the first bullet was fired, we couldn't talk about future operations. We could know, but we were not supposed to speak. That is for information only, not for broadcast.

I asked to go on one of the operations to the front lines. "Take me and my camera. Do the filming. Go and come back. We would not know beforehand." That never happened. I asked for reasons. Actually there were misconceptions about Al Jazeera from different commands. I was told a lot of the troops said: "Why should we have Al Jazeera? They are the enemy. It is the potential enemy's channel. How do the people of the Arab world view this military campaign? I actually spent a lot of time explaining if we had Bin Laden five or six times on air, we had loads of interviews with Secretary Powell, Condoleezza Rice, Donald Rumsfeld, the officials, ambassadors, briefings, press conferences, live on air. Even in this case, the balance is in the American favor.

We had never been to the front line. It only happened during this ambush, and we happened to be there. Sky News had just arrived with their vehicle and satellite news broadcasting equipment. We started broadcasting on the satellite phone straightaway. The battlefield was an open place. It was a plain with no place to hide behind a building. Then went up to this wall; my cameraman was just before me. We could not broadcast it live because I needed a one-kilometer cable to broadcast live, and I needed a satellite channel to get through. We did live interviews with the American forces with their M-16s who were up there on the wall firing shots. So that was the only day I saw for myself a battle. It was not because I was taken to the front line.

During this time, I experienced a lot of arguments about the flow of information. I'd ask questions. I'd ask for interviews. I'd get rejection of these interviews. Then came the day when Thuraya satellite phones were banned after two French reporters were escorted out from being embedded. They had made a phone call that can trace the satellite signal through the GPS used. There was no explanation by the Americans. I asked them to comment on banning the Thuraya phones. It's handheld. Big, like a brick. With an antenna. I had a satellite phone. Unfortunately, the Thuraya phone was very handy. Longer battery. Clearer than the others. It could do everything. It is heaven compared to the alternatives. I asked the media officer, a captain with the Fifteenth MEF, who was with me, "Okay, can you comment about this ban on camera?" He said, no, he couldn't even mention that. He only said according to the ground rules, we cannot talk about the enemy's capabilities of electronic warfare.

I always felt there were a lot of misconceptions, which resulted in keeping information away from us. I was embedded for twenty days. I couldn't have access to information one day. I found reporters from, Reuters, AP, and CNN, available at the same location we were at. I heard them talking afterwards about the briefing. They were briefed on future operations which were not supposed to be broadcast until the end of the operations.

Then I asked the duty officer why I wasn't invited to that briefing. The duty officer was a captain. He said, "I have to consult with the commander." He returned and said, "I asked the colonel. He said 'You know, guys, you are a station with a reputation.'" The big thing is: The American government wanted me to be here. Okay? And I think there is a line of policy which should be enforced from top to bottom. Yet with us, if we spoke about the Thuraya phone, we're out. That also meant that information was being leaked to other organizations we did not know about. So it was not equal, nor were we equally treated. We did not have equal access to other sources.

After this ongoing confrontation about lack of access, I was talking to the station and said, "Look, you have to contact the Department of Defense [DOD]. If we don't have access to information, I should leave. I could be on the desk verifying and researching stories." So, after lots of contacts, the

Marines were supposed to take me to Nasiriyah. They said it was never possible because they were nervous about security. I then had two good days. They started water purification at Nasiriyah. The second day, they took us to a medical facility at the same site. Then we were free to move with the crowd.

The Marines said, "Okay. This time, one hour. Tomorrow, you will have two hours." Local civilians were coming to show us what was happening in the city, and the level of damage, for example; their criticism of the U.S.; and of the slowness of resumption of electricity, and food, and water, and other aid; of the slowness of American response. Because it actually was true. They criticized Saddam. They criticized Americans. They criticized Al Jazeera. We reported they were happy to get rid of Saddam Hussein. Yet they have their own reservations about the slowness of getting water. For example, they objected to the searching of women at checkpoints by men. That is very difficult for any Arab. One of the people cried on camera because his wife was touched by American soldiers.

Some of their complaints were things the captain should answer. I said, "We will turn on the cameras, but this will not be an easy ride." I told him, "We are going to put you on camera and these are the things you are going to explain. It will be a cross-examination, to put things in perspective. That is your chance." He told me the colonel was busy. I said, "He can refuse to answer, or he can ask anybody else—his officer or whatever, the media officer or whatever. So come and speak." In the end, I couldn't get the American commander to make any response available, so I asked my station to insert the words "This report was censored by the American military."

In Nasiriyah, a member of Free Iraqi Forces [FIF] came up to me, saying, "We hate Al Jazeera. We hate you. You supported Saddam Hussein. Now we are near to power. When we get to power we will kill you. We are not happy with what you are reporting."

I then went to discuss this threat with the colonel. While the media officer was usually the go-between, I grabbed hold of the colonel when he was walking toward his tent. I asked him what he was going to do about it. He said, "What is this?" He seemed as if he didn't know anything. He said, "I will have to speak with the media officer." I later went into the commander's tent. He said, "I can't jeopardize the life of my Marines. We are not trying to boot you out. I just want you to get this right. We know you need to move. You need to do your work."

I offered to be moved to another unit, the Fourth Brigade, which I didn't want to do. Of course, I had to consult with the station about everything that was going on. They spoke to the guy at DOD, and the guys with the American embassy here, because it is a matter of safety. It was really serious. They wanted me to move with the First Marine Division, which was fighting near Baghdad's airport.

I waited for a whole day. The station wanted me to move forward to the battle front. I said that I have only one concern. It takes time to build the trust, so if I'm going to move, I expect that the station would give the right image of Al Jazeera to whatever unit I am moving to, because I do not expect to spend two more weeks overcoming preconceptions.

After another day of waiting, I was contacted by Camp Commando, which offered me a place with the British press center at Basra. That was something I didn't want, because I already had two colleagues who were reporting from Basra. I had experienced the Brits in northern Kuwait. It wasn't much better. The British briefed the Arab media much worse than the Western media, CNN, ITN, Fox Sky Channel 4, English news. All were briefed on maps in the tent of the commander. We were not. If we got anything, it was a few brief words. They had five minutes for us, one hour for them. So, it wasn't any different actually.

Meanwhile, as I waited for an answer, I had to stay inside after the FIF [Free Iraqi Forces] incident. I wasn't angry because I was not supposed to show up outside. I was not afraid of the civilian people in Nasiriyah, but the Marines were afraid that the FIF guy would talk to someone in the town, and they would shoot at me and any Marines sent to escort me. So that was the story. I talked to my editors. We decided to disembed. We waited for transportation back to Kuwait. Then CNN also decided to become unilaterals. On April 9th, the day Baghdad fell, they decided to make one convoy for both CNN and Al Jazeera. We left Iraq.

Overall, the embedding process was a good thing to try. In the process, you need different teams in different places so you can get an overall view of what is going on. Being a unilateral is better, on the condition of making security available to the reporters who are in the war theater. I saw American television crews using ex-special forces and ex-Marines to provide security. When you come in with the American forces, the Iraqi authorities would say that you were a traitor because you did not have a visa. So, if you had walked into Baghdad, you could have been arrested as a traitor. That was a real danger.

THEY FIGHT. WE REPORT. YOU DECIDE.
Fox News Reporter Rick Levanthal

"It's a helpless feeling to be in a situation where everyone around you is armed and people are shooting at you and you can't shoot back."

The most any of us ever come close to seeing and hearing massive explosions is at Fourth of July fireworks or football halftime celebrations. The pyrotechnics are part of our "bombs-bursting-in-air" mythology, a skyward symbolic display of our democratic heritage. Fox News unapologetically trumpets these patriotic sentiments, and gleefully draped its coverage of Operation Iraqi Freedom in the red-white-and-blue bunting of flag-waving Yankee pride. Not surprisingly, while many media critics believed that Fox News' jingoistic bias went overboard, the troops thought otherwise. They embraced the network as their very own. They loved Fox. Their families and friends back home loved the cable network. By tapping into the heartland's muscular nationalism, Fox's ratings increased dramatically. Yet part of Fox's viewing success was due to the front-line efforts of two embedded reporters, Greg Kelly and Rick Levanthal, who were both singled out by *USA Today* for their exemplary broadcasting work on the battlefield.

We talked to Levanthal in mid-June. The New York City Bureau reporter, who was one of the first journalists on the scene when the World Trade Center was struck, honed his stand-up chops over the years with coverage of TWA Flight 800, the Mississippi floods of '93, and the O.J. Simpson trial. He was en route to La Guardia Airport to fly to Chicago for a national cable television convention where he was a member of panel discussing the merits of embedding. During the war, he had traveled with the Third Light Armored Reconnaissance Battalion out of Twenty-Nine Palms, California and then moved over to the Second Battalion, 23rd Marines, which is a reservist Marine infantry battalion.

■ ■ ■

The war had just started. We were out of the vehicles, outside on the ground in a prone position right on the berm—this big sand wall—with a great view of Safwan Hill, which is not a mountain, but a big landmass probably three to five kilometers away from the Kuwaiti border. We had a great view of U.S. Coalition Forces dropping napalm and 2,000-pounds bombs on an airfield there. It was incredible. We could feel the concussion from the bombs when they went off. Gigantic explosions. Cobra-type helicopters were coming in with these Hellfire missiles. Later that night, we took incoming. The first mortar round went over our heads, and hit quite a distance away from us, and then a short time later—and I was on the satphone doing a live phone at the time—another came and probably hit fifty yards beyond our vehicle. We heard it scream right over our heads. If it had blown up in front of us, we probably would have been sprayed with shrapnel, but it hit past us and the shrapnel went off in that direction. But it freaked everybody out. It was a close call and our driver took off. I was live at the time so people back home were hearing that. It was pretty exciting. That was the first night of real fighting. Earlier that night, we got word that the southern oil fields had been set on fire, and I was apparently the first to report this news. It was exciting because I was getting exclusives. When I first went over, I didn't know if I would be actually going to see or do anything and before I knew it, I was right in the middle of the action.

I've been to a lot of places and seen a lot of things, but this was by far the hardest thing I'd ever done. Take covering the O.J. trial for example. Well, that was just a circus. Any time you have a celebrity or a well-known person on trial, it becomes a media event and the hours can be long and a bit tedious, but you get to go back to your hotel every night. You eat actual meals and you have access to creature comforts. This was a completely different world. We slept either in the back of a cramped vehicle on a hard metal bench, wedged together, or outside on the ground on rocks, or dirt, or sand, or mud. We were woken up constantly by explosions or the turret turning on our vehicle searching for threats on the horizon, artillery firing, incoming, outgoing. We also were on the move in some cases at night, so it was very difficult to sleep. We didn't have a lot of food. I wouldn't say we had a shortage, but we were eating less than some units were. It was just a very exhausting, difficult experience. I lost eighteen pounds in six weeks. When I got home I joked about the Baghdad diet. All you have to do is wear a forty-five-pound bullet-proof vest and eat one-and-a-half MREs a day and try not to sleep more than four hours a night, and I guarantee results. We didn't get any care packages, though I had offers from people back home, especially from viewers. We had tremendous support from people watching. The most amazing part of the experience was how many people we touched and how many people we reached back home.

I had access to e-mail on occasion with my laptop. I could hook it up to our satellite phone, and when we had time, and the ability to do it, we would log on. Toward the end, it was a lot easier than it was early on. I was able to read e-mails from hundreds of people. Every morning when I did the eastern time show with Shepard Smith, he would read the e-mails to me on the air. He would talk to me about how many hundreds of thousands of e-mails they were getting on a daily basis, and would read questions to me the viewers had written in. What soon became clear was that there were thousands of people—family members and friends of the Marines we were with—who were watching religiously to see their loved ones and that gave them great comfort. They were very grateful and it's not often in this business that you get thanks from people. More often than not, they wish we weren't there. In this case, they were just so happy that we were with their guys, so happy they could see them, and know they were okay. That was very rewarding.

I saved a bunch of the e-mails. There are a couple that are really compelling. One woman told me that she heard my voice and it reminded her of her husband who had died a year before. She wrote that my interaction with the Marines reminded her of how her husband would talk to people and draw them out. She began watching every night to see me and, I guess, to remind her of her late husband. I was floored by that.

My youngest daughter, who is seven, wasn't really aware of where I was or what I was doing. My ex-wife was careful in how and what she told her, and she doesn't watch news on TV. My oldest daughter, twelve, was very aware of what was going on and she was worried. She was scared for me and she felt a lot better when I came home. My mom was pretty freaked out by the whole thing. I grew up in Silver Spring, Maryland, and my parents still live in the house that I grew up in. I have a sister and a brother. I didn't hear from my brother, but I talked to my sister more than once and she, too, was very concerned; she and her husband were listening—she has satellite radio in her car—to Fox on the afternoon that I was in a firefight just north of the Iraq/Kuwaiti border. I had called in and I was reporting live during the gunfire. Our unit was probing to see what kind of enemy was out there.

To backtrack for a moment, I was in Alpha Company and we probably had about twenty-five light armored vehicles [LAV] in our unit. An LAV has eight wheels. These vehicles are durable and rugged, and good in all terrain—dirt, sand, on hills, and gulleys. In about five minutes, they can be turned into a boat. It has props on the back and you can actually drive it into a body of water and cruise at slow speeds across a river. We never did that, but they're very versatile; they can drive seventy miles per hour on land. The one I was in was an LAV-25, which has a 25mm Bushmaster Chain Gun that looks like a tank turret on the roof. The Bushmaster rapid-fires a high-explosive round, but usually they would just shoot in groups of three: "Thump, thump, thump." It has good range and could do some serious damage. They tend to kill tanks.

The firefight occurred after we had passed the Rumala oil fields. We were driving north, but sort of along the eastern side. We had gone ahead of all the units to make sure that it would be smooth sailing for the follow-on units. We were trying to make time and it got dark. We kept traveling at night and drove right into an ambush. Apparently, several hundred Iraqis were waiting for us. They lined both sides of the road. They had RPGs, mortars, and AK47s, and as the lead vehicle got close to them, they opened fire. Our convoy came to a halt, with the Iraqis coming down the line—driving and running through the desert on either side of our line of LAVs. They would pop up from behind sand dunes and fire at us and then keep moving. I heard the first shots way ahead of us, and then they started getting closer and closer, and before I knew it, my vehicle saw targets in the desert and started opening up on them. That went on for about an hour. I was in the back of the vehicle the entire time. I waited probably twenty or thirty minutes before calling the story in on the satellite phone. We were getting shot at and we were shooting back and that's what my sister heard. She and her husband were listening to it in the car and she told me that she got so upset, she started crying and had to turn the radio off.

I don't even know if any vehicles got hit. I mean, it was not a fair fight, and the Marines say they don't want a fair fight. They want to kill everyone who tries to kill them. They want to have better guns, and more of them, and in that case, apparently they did. The guys who were attacking them were poorly trained and poor shots, and they just were beaten badly. I was told that some were only thirty yards away. It was dark and you couldn't really see much. The Marines could because they had night vision goggles. But I couldn't see the enemy, which was very disconcerting because I could not see what the Marines were shooting at. What I did see were the tracer rounds flying out from our vehicles across the desert, and then I would see an occasional explosion when one of them hit a target.

It's a helpless feeling to be in a situation where everyone around you is armed and people are shooting at you and you can't shoot back, and there were times when it crossed my mind that, "Hey, it would be nice to have a firearm of some kind." I understand that that's a bad thing in terms of rules of the game. There are reasons why journalists aren't armed and I understand those reasons. If the enemy suspects that journalists are carrying weapons, then journalists are fair game, and if we're captured, they'll consider us spies. If it's someone else who is captured and they know that some journalists are armed, then they may just figure that all journalists are armed. It's just a road that I'm not willing to go down, and I don't think that anyone else should either.

During that firefight, the Marines believe they inflicted dozens of casualties and took none of their own, but I later interviewed a guy who told me that he personally killed nine guys. He said that he saw in his sights when one of the Bushmaster rounds hit a guy in his chest and just basically vaporized him. Blew him to bits. He told me that he kept waking up every morning, seeing what he saw in his sights when that round hit that Iraqi soldier. He felt that he had done the right thing; that he had done what he was supposed to do, but he was weirded out by it. This guy, he's a kid. He was twenty-one years old. He trained for this, but he never had actually shot anyone before and the act of doing it stuck with him.

These were very professional young men. They didn't fit the mold necessarily of that gung-ho image. I was surprised because back in the day when I was growing up in the D.C. area, I had a job as a doorman in a couple of nightclubs. I worked with a lot of military guys. These guys were classic jarheads—big, strong, chiseled, and just ready to pound the crap out of anybody who got out of line. Most of the guys who we were with in the war were not like that. They were more cerebral, they were very polite; they weren't necessarily all pumped up. They were just like normal guys who took a job in the Marine Corps. I was very impressed with their work ethic, their dedication, their attitude. Those guys did not complain. My photographer Christian Baldabini, and I would commiserate about how awful things were, but we didn't hear the Marines doing the same thing. They just pretty much took it in stride. They were used to it. They knew it was going to be like this and they were ready to do it for much longer than we were.

There were several casualties in our unit. One guy went to sleep with his weapon in his sleeping bag, and it discharged, and he killed himself by accident. They liked having their weapons close by, I guess, in case of trouble, but he hadn't stored it properly. There was another guy, before we left the base camp, who committed suicide. He wasn't in our company; he was in the next company. That shook a lot of people up. There were no Marines killed from either of the companies I was with while I was there, but two guys were wounded by a friendly-fire incident. They were in an LAV positioned next to a farm and there were some Cobra helicopters scouring the area, trying to take out Iraqi armored vehicles that were just abandoned all over the place. These vehicles were hidden among the farms and canals. The helicopters would seek out these vehicles and blow them up, but for some reason they mistook this Marine LAV for an Iraqi vehicle and opened fire with their Gatlin gun and tore up the vehicle, and actually hit two Marines with shrapnel. One guy was in the hatch; if he had been popped out of the hatch, he told me later, he would have been killed for sure. But as it was, he took some shrapnel on the neck and the other guy had some pretty bad wounds in his leg and his arm; so both of them were okay, but it was a scene straight out of a movie when we showed up. The medics were patching up their wounds, and they were calling for an airlift medivac to get them out of there. Within minutes, this helicopter showed up to take them away.

I didn't report this live friendly-fire incident for Fox because, due to driving logistics and camera setup, we weren't physically able to, while I was gathering the information at the scene. During the activity, I told the captain that I wanted to go live and he said he needed me to wait until he could talk to his commanding officer to okay the broadcast. That was the rule that we were living under. Before I would go live, I would clear it with the commanding officer or the captain of our company and let him know, "Hey, we want to go live" and based on circumstances, normally the answer would be yes, and in some cases, the answer was, "I need to check with the CO first." And this was one of those cases where he said "Look, we need to check with the CO. We've had this friendly-fire thing, we want to make sure that such and such has been notified."

I was never influenced by Fox News to shape my coverage a certain way. I had more freedom in Iraq than I've ever had on any story in my entire broadcasting career. It was remarkable what I was able to do. There was no pressure and there were no expectations. They told me, "Whatever you can come up with, whatever you can get on the bird, whenever you can go live, just come up and we'll take you. Call us, we'll take you." We had an engineer who followed behind us for most of the time we were there, so when we could, we'd link up with our engineer. He had a satellite dish—a fly-away—that he would set up with a generator, turn it on, and gave you the signal, and we could actually do a real live shot where it didn't have that herky-jerky thing you get with the videophone. But when we couldn't go live with the satellite dish, we would try and go live with the videophone, but that also required power and some setup time. If we couldn't go out with the videophone, then I would go live on the telephone. They would take me just about any time I was able to call in or had anything to report. They would take me in most cases for as long as I could go. I mean, for the 11:00 show with Shepard, I was on some nights for the entire hour or forty-five minutes at a time. I would do these twenty-minute live shots. You just don't get that kind of freedom on normal stories and I had no producer. There was no apparent PAO watching over my shoulder to see what I said. I just talked about what I saw, and what I heard, and what was happening around me. I did a lot of interviews with Marines, and asked them whatever I felt like asking them. It was wonderful to be able to have the freedom to do that daily.

In some cases, I would interview whoever was closest to me because we had a lot of time to fill on some days. I would just grab someone and say, "Hey, how's it going?" "What are you doing?" "What's your story?" "Where are you from?" "Want to say hi to anybody?" "Were you involved in that firefight last night?" There was one Marine, however, who stood out. He was a big, good-looking kid. He was like the guy that you would picture as the classic Marine in the commercial. He was about six foot, three inches, probably weighed about 240; and he played high school football. He told me that at his peak, he was bench pressing 450 pounds and his dream was to play college football. He joined the Marines because he had some problems in high school. He got into some trouble and blew any chance at a scholarship, but he joined the Marines, cleaned himself up, and his goal was—when he got out of the Corps—to go back to school and play college football. He was a real character. One day, I was doing a live shot and Brian Kilmeade was the anchor at the time, and he was talking to someone else in the studio about how the army was playing Simon and Garfunkel's *Homeward Bound* as they were driving into Baghdad. As I was hearing this in my ear, I said, "Hold on a second, Brian. Are you telling me that the army is listening to Simon and Garfunkel?" He goes, "Yeah." I said, "The Marines would never do that! They don't even know who Simon and Garfunkel are!" Marines have got this image to protect. They need tough guys. So I said, "Let me ask this Marine over here," and I turned to him and I said, "Hey, when you go into Baghdad, what music will you listen to? What would be your first choice?" And he said without hesitation, "*Kill 'Em All* by Metallica!" Apparently the entire newsroom broke out in laughter and cheers.

Everyone at home saw more of the war than I did. I saw what we saw with our unit. I saw almost no other coverage of the war, so when people talk about different networks and how they did and all that, I can't really talk about that, and I can't compare the tone of the coverage because I honestly didn't see it. But the families of the Marines were watching and they all were thrilled with the coverage, and so were the Marines we were with. The Marines all seemed to love Fox and they were glad that we were there. They would speak disparagingly about other networks and they just loved us. I'm not going to lie; I'd rather have them like us than dislike us. I mean, if I have a choice of being with a network that they didn't want around versus a network that they did, I think I'd choose being with a network they did want because we're going to get better access. They appreciated the tone of our coverage. Fox was supportive of the troops, supportive of U.S. efforts in the war. Fox News president Roger Ailes has gone on record saying, "Hey, these are our troops. Those of us living in the United States, we're Americans and these are our soldiers and our Marines and they're fighting for our freedom, so there's nothing wrong with supporting them." My own feeling was, "Look, I am going out there and report on what I see." There was no mandate or directive except "Listen, you're going to go embed; just be careful. Don't put your life in danger and when you can, report on what's happening." That's what I did and, honestly, I came away extremely impressed with the attitude and the performance of the men in uniform. I have no hesitation saying how great a job they did. I saw a level of professionalism that left me very impressed.

TRYING NOT TO GO DEAF ON THE GUN LINE

Boston Globe Reporter
Scott Bernard Nelson

"I had my crisis on the first night of the war."

As *The Boston Globe* ramped up its editorial battle plans for the Iraq war, "a hundred people in the newsroom wanted to go overseas," says business reporter Scott Nelson, thirty-one, who was one of fifteen people selected for the mission. Only three were embedded; he won that lottery, too. "The editors sat down and went over the list and whatever alchemy they used, they came up with the names. They were looking for calm people who didn't appear to have strong, prejudicial opinions about the war. They wanted relatively mellow people who wouldn't melt down in a war situation."

Writing about money or banking is fairly sedate stuff; it's not like covering murder cases. Still, Nelson never shied away from high-profile stories and applied his business reporting skills to the post 9/11 rebuilding of the financial district in Lower Manhattan and the Catholic Church's impending money woes caused by the sex abuse scandals.

The inexperienced combat correspondent, however, experienced his first and only near-meltdown during the war's opening phase. These under-fire jitters soon passed, and he remained in control throughout his extended war assignment, even pointing out a sniper to his vehicle's gunner when they ran into an ambush outside Baghdad. He saw plenty of dead Iraqis but "ceased to be bothered by dead bodies anymore."

Yet death did knock on the *The Globe*'s own door when Elizabeth Neuffer, forty-six, the newspaper's United Nations bureau chief and a foreign affairs correspondent, died in a car accident in Iraq on May 9. "Just before the war they had a meeting of what they called the Iraq Pack," recalls Nelson, who has been with *The Globe* for three years. "They had us all together in one room and Elizabeth came in and talked to everybody because she had just been back through Iraq and Iran. She covered the first Gulf war. She had a fairly good sense of what we were about to get ourselves into and what the lay of the land would to be in Iraq. She was very concerned about safety. And so she really wanted to hammer home to everybody the things we could do to keep ourselves safe and what we could expect from the Iraqi people and what we should be careful of and what we should know. She didn't cover the war itself, she was going in to cover the aftermath. And I just missed her in Kuwait by a day when she was going back in.

"While it was called a car accident, I would say it was a car accident under Third World conditions on a highway that had military activity over it with craters and rubber tank treads all over the road. These rubber stops are placed between tank treads so that when tanks do run on hard surfaces they can run really quickly. Whenever they would travel more than fifteen to twenty miles per hour on the highways, the rubber stops all come flying out. Right after the war a lot of the highways were littered with these rubber things from the tanks. In addition you have uniquely Third World mix-up traffic of rented BMWs, cars from the forties and fifties, and horse-drawn carts. So it's a really strange mix up of traffic on a really bad highway. So accidents like that are more prone to happen, and that is what happened to Elizabeth."

■　■　■

I was embedded with the Second Battalion, Eleventh Marines. The Eleventh Marines is not really a regiment in the truest sense, but a regiment made entirely of artillery units, and each battalion within there gets loaned out to other real regiments. Here it got loaned out to the Fifth Marines for the war, so essentially we were the artillery component to the Fifth Marines. They used Howitzers or cannons. The 155mm Howitzers are towed behind seven-ton trucks and weigh about 17,000 pounds a piece. In Vietnam they were using Howitzer 105s; these are Howitzer 155s now. They have about a range of thirty kilometers, give or take. They used a dozen different kinds of shells. When they're shooting at something a long way off, they use rocket-propelled, or what they call RAP, rocket-assisted propulsion. You can tell they were shooting the RAP shells because after the boom when the cannon goes off, ten seconds later you hear the rocket kick in. The rocket gives it extra propulsion as it goes down-range. Each of those guns can probably shoot a round every thirty or forty seconds.

I was in the gun pit for a lot of the shooting. The pit is extremely loud. It depends on a number of factors, such as what kind of powder is being used and the size of powder charge. On the opening night of the war while we were still in Kuwait, I went out to the gun line with one of the Marines. When the first shot went off—the Iraqis were already shooting back at us but were shooting long, to the south of us—I thought we were hit. We were thirty feet behind the gun. I knew it was going to be loud, but it was just pure noise, and white light, and heat, and smoke, and almost a sulphur smell. It just envelops you. I thought for a second, "Wow, they hit us. The Iraqis had just fired and they got us." But it was just the back draft from the guns.

You should probably wear earplugs to prevent yourself from going deaf. What most of the Marines did was that they just tried to plug their ears, and turn, and not stand directly behind the gun. Before I found out I was going to be with an artillery company—I didn't know until I got to Kuwait—I was with a reporter from the AP who had spent time with an artillery company in the first Gulf War. He now wears hearing aids and he blames that at least in part on the Howitzers. He told me to get good earplugs, which I did before I went out to the desert. I had both the rubber kind you stick in your ears and I had those cup ones that you wear over the top.

The Marines in the gun pit were young. They were kids. Most of them on the gun line were the younger enlisted guys because that's the front-line position. Even the guys in charge of a gun were only sergeants. The older guys, the officers, weren't on the gun lines for the most part. They're the ones making decisions, talking to headquarters, deciding where the guns are going to be aimed, but they were not the ones actually implementing it.

Firing a Howitzer uses much more technical skills than I would have guessed before I got there. It's an engineering process, essentially. Every time they got to a new site, they would first survey it. They'd do this twice. The company commander sets up a plumb line and an arc, and then one of his lieutenants also surveys the site to make sure they match. They have to match exactly or they do it again. They want to make sure they know exactly which direction the guns are pointing so that they don't shoot in the wrong direction, because with artillery, unlike infantry, they told me over and over, "We can't make any mistakes. We shoot the wrong thing once and it's an international incident. We have to know exactly where we're shooting or we can't shoot— we can't risk it."

Once everything gets situated, the guns all have a computer-guided aiming system. Everything on the battlefield these days is done through GPS. So once they get the GPS grids, they will double-check to make sure the gun is pointing to where it is supposed to be pointing, and then they will give the okay and they'll fire. But in some cases that doesn't work, like in a sandstorm. So they had to actually do it the old-fashioned way and to try to line up the gun almost like a rifle. There are points along the barrel of the gun for aiming. That took a fair amount of skill. I certainly wouldn't have known how to do it, but these guys, that's what they do for a living. They train at Camp Pendleton in California. They do it over and over again a thousand times so, for them, it seems second nature.

The thing that surprised me most about the Marines was their lack of machismo; their lack of chest-thumping and bravado. I think that if I'd known them when they were in California on base, there would have been a lot more of that kind of nineteen-year-old, twenty-year-old trash talk that is typical. Especially from Marines, I imagine. But it was absent almost entirely here. Once the real shooting started and people were dying, that just went away. Everybody was quiet, and nervous, and more introspective. There were not a bunch of Rambos running around. They were mostly nervous kids who just wanted to get home, they wanted to get back to their girlfriends, they wanted to get back to their moms. They just didn't particularly want to be there.

There were no deaths in my unit. One forward observer, a lieutenant, took shrapnel through the neck but he lived. Two guys fell in a hole and broke their legs. One guy got in a fight and lost several teeth.

I would see the effect of these shells afterwards. I mean, we could see the explosions and we would come up on the aftermath scene when we would be driving through. The closest feeling you could get to understanding their kind of devastation was what I heard on the radio. For most of the war I traveled in the Humvee of the company commander, Captain Matthew Koligh. He was a captain at the time. He's since been promoted to major. I was able to hear the updates that he would get. On one occasion, I especially remember while the Marines were shooting, he got back a report of how they were doing, and the infantry commander up front said, "Hey, you guys are doing a good job. All we're finding here are arms, and legs, and pink mist."

When there were large numbers of Iraqi troops moving, which only happened at the beginning and end of the war, the Marines used these cluster bombs for artillery shells. Each shell had eighty-eight grenades in it. They would shoot rounds, waves of these things, sixteen or eighteen at a time. Whole battalions would be shooting cluster bombs—eighteen bombs going off at a time. You do the math, that's a lot of grenades going off. Imagine them going off all at once, some hitting the ground, some going off in the air, shrapnel going in every direction just slicing people up. They would shoot them all on top of one unit of Iraqis and they would kill everything—animal, vegetable, mineral.

The only way to defend against that is get out of the area—otherwise you die. I have a friend who was with a light armor reconnaissance unit up front, and one of those cluster bomb shells misfired and landed on his unit. They made a mistake on the GPS coordinates, and one of those shells landed over the top of this convoy of light armor vehicles. Everybody was inside the vehicles, nobody was out in the open, and even so, all of their tires were flattened on these light armor reconnaissance vehicles, and through the armor, one guy lost an arm, somebody else took shrapnel in the head and chest. They ended up with several serious wounds. The whole convoy was stopped by one shell.

One of the difficulties of being in an artillery company is that you feel disconnected. In this war—for whatever reason—the Americans chose to not employ a lot of airpower except over Baghdad. Outside of Baghdad the skies largely remained empty. In fact, they remained empty so much that early in the war the Marines were very concerned—you didn't hear any planes or any helicopters for days at a time. Later in the war, you started to see more attack helicopters patrolling a lot more heavily.

At times the Marines felt like they were all alone at the end of the world, and at times they would lose radio contact with even other Marine units. Sometimes they would go twelve hours, fourteen hours without radio contact with anybody, hoping to run into somebody eventually so they could stop, and talk, and figure out how to get their frequency back online because the frequencies were all coded and changed. If you got somehow out of the loop, and your codes weren't matching up with everybody else's codes, you couldn't talk to anybody, and you were all alone. You didn't see anybody in the sky, you didn't see anybody on the horizon, and you really felt all alone out there. The lack of air cover in those times made people feel very isolated.

There were a number of occasions where I felt scared. I had my crisis on the first night of the war. I figured that people were going to die. This was not just another assignment that allowed me to get front-page stories in *The Boston Globe*. We had just pulled up to the Kuwait-Iraqi border at dusk. The fighting was starting and there was a huge oil fire burning at some gas-oil separation plant just across the no-man's land from us on the horizon. It had been blown up by someone, one side or the other. The Iraqi artillery positions saw us and started shooting. The shells were going a little bit long, landing a couple of hundred yards behind us, but these shells triggered what they called "snowstorms." Snowstorm was the code word for indirect fire, and they told us before the war if you ever hear snowstorm that means radar has picked up incoming, either mortar or artillery fire, and we were automatically to assume that any indirect fire could be a chemical attack. We had been briefed on this and, heck the war's not even fifteen minutes old, we're still in Kuwait when we heard the first snowstorm call. Over the radio you heard people yelling, "Snowstorm, gas, gas, gas . . . snowstorm, gas, gas, gas!" Everybody drops everything and puts on gas masks. You're already wearing your MOPP or chem-bio suits. At this point you now have on the rubber boots, the rubber gloves, the gas mask, the hood. You're fully MOPPed up and your heart is racing. You're sweating underneath the gas mask. It's running down your face but you can't get to it because you're under the mask. You're getting increasingly hot and uncomfortable, and everybody is trying to dig a hole to be able to get out of the way of shrapnel or fire. So I'm digging a hole madly, it's dark, the Iraqi artillery is landing a couple of hundred yards away, people are yelling "gas-gas-gas" over the radio, the Marines are scrambling around trying to get their own guns set up so that they can return fire, the huge oil well is burning in the distance. American helicopters are coming in low right over the top of us, and then we hear their Gatlin guns going off as they go across the border. They're shooting. This is something straight out of *Apocalypse Now*, and it felt like a movie to me, but, then I realized that this was the real moment of truth. Once I was able to calm myself down, I said to myself, "All right, this is the deal, this is what you signed up for. You know people die in war, you knew you were going to be out here, so, suck it up and live with it. Cover the stories that are here, stop worrying about it. You can't do anything to change it now." For whatever reason that seemed to help me.

I had several other close calls. There were several times when we were directly shot at, and there were several times that we had indirect fire at night. At one point, a mortar round landed only 200 yards outside our camp while we were sleeping. Again, that triggered a "gas-gas-gas" call and everybody is scrambling out of bed trying to figure out what that was. During the big Biblical sandstorm that everybody talks about early in the war, we were trying to move that night and finally we just had to give up and stay in place. The sky went from a really strange orange color to pitch black by two or three in the afternoon. People basically huddled under a truck or inside a Humvee for ten, twelve, fifteen hours straight without moving. Then, at three or four in the morning, the rain came and the sand turned to mud. The Americans realized the Iraqis had not stopped moving during the sandstorm. They were trying to take advantage of it, because that was the one time when American airpower wouldn't pick them up. So suddenly on the ridge in front of our position, there was a significant Iraqi presence. They were a couple of kilometers away. A column of tanks, five or ten kilometers away to our north, had come on in the dark, and as soon as the sandstorm lifted and the rain started, all hell broke loose. The sky just lit up with rockets, and artillery, and that lasted for maybe a half an hour. I could hear on the radio everybody yelling, "We're surrounded, we need help," calling things in trying to get F14s in the air. Then the sandstorm picked back up, and then nothing. You had no idea what was going on again for another six or eight hours. You don't know who got who, who was doing what. You had to hunker down and wait again. It was a really eerie experience.

Probably the time that I thought I was most at risk was after Baghdad had fallen. We were circling to the north side of the city. We just had two or three days of relatively heavy fighting just before Baghdad. What ended up happening was that we hooked up with the tank battalion that was with the Fifth Regiment, and they led the charge along the east side of the Tigris to the last fifty or sixty miles up into Baghdad. The Republican Guard had stayed in mostly little towns, tanks led the way going through, and picking off the bunkers, and the tanks, and the guns through there. The artillery fired right on their heels. Literally, we were within a kilometer of where they were most of the time. You could see them shooting and fighting. On a couple of occasions we pulled off to the side of the road, and did what they call hip shoots, which just means they didn't even set up a position, they just stopped and shot off the road. That was when we saw a lot of dead bodies. We saw burned-out vehicles, and blown-up personnel carriers, and bunkers that had been destroyed. We started to see Republican Guard clothing and weapons dropped on the side of the road. We started to find weapons caches. That was really only a two- or three-day process, just before we got to Baghdad. Before that it was mostly fedayeen and a few militia guys here and there, and then once we got to Baghdad we felt like, ah, it's over. The Republican Guard walked away, they didn't fight.

The war was over and as we circled around to the north of the city, we were ambushed. It was a perfectly well set-up ambush by some militia guys.

Unfortunately for them they couldn't shoot. They had a textbook ambush set up but they couldn't use their weapons. They probably didn't have the ammo to train with AK47s, so they couldn't shoot worth a damn. We were coming along the right side of the road; fifty or sixty yards away was a series of little buildings, maybe a little industrial complex of some sort. Along the left side, probably 150 yards away, were some trees, but it felt like fairly open country. To my three o'clock, right beside the Humvee I was in, someone started shooting out of a window from one of the buildings. He panicked and shot too soon. The other guys in the ambush hadn't yet started shooting. He shot at our Humvee, and he missed. I assume he was shooting at the gunner on the top because he's a good juicy target sitting up there, but his shots hit the dirt along the side of the road; I have the whole thing on audiotape, oddly enough. I rarely did this in the war but I was actually just recording ambient noise. You hear the AK47s start going off, but everybody started saying "What in the hell was that?" Everybody's looking around, and some of the Marines in different rigs picked up on it, and then other guys in the ambush also open up fire on both sides. The Marines returned the fire. In my Humvee, we had a moment of confusion. Nobody really knew what was going on. For a second, I was the only one who saw where the shooting was coming from. I pointed it out to the gunner and he sent about ninety 50-cal bullets into the building, and took care of that. Afterwards, I've had to do a little hand-wringing about that moment—whether that was the right thing for me to have done. Should I have just strictly been an observer? Did I cross some journalistic line? But at the time, all I knew was that the guy out there was shooting at us.

At some level if you're being honest with yourself, you get much closer to the story than you would normally ever allow yourself to get. For two months, we were in the most important place in the world. Everything we wrote they wanted to put on the front page. Any time I called CNN, they would put me on live TV. You were in the center of everything, and as a journalist that is as good as it gets. I don't feel like I'm going to freak out in a bar in twenty years, and beat somebody up because of repressed rage or something. One good thing about having children, who are absolutely not caught up in those events, is that I came home and they got me right back to the here and now, and to what my priorities really are and should be, so I haven't brooded about it, or dwelled on it nearly as much as I might otherwise. I don't feel like I have any long-term effects from this. I hope not. But like everything else, you never know until you get there.

SEMPER FIDO! ON DUTY TO SNIFF BOMBS
CENTCOM's Jocko

"Jocko never runs out of energy."

Every journalist or visitor entering U.S. Central Command (CENTCOM) media headquarters in Doha, Qatar, must first pass by a gauntlet of security checks, including a long, good sniff administered by one of the bomb-sniffing dogs on duty. Talk about being in the presence of real newshounds, though these CENTCOM canines are highly trained Belgian Shepherds (also known as Belgian Malanois). We wanted to know more about one very noble-looking dog which was on duty during our visit. Jocko's handler was helpful with some information, but due to security issues he refused to reveal his own name or the names of Jocko's three other colleagues. Jocko is a male and regularly eats Science Diet dog food.

■　■　■

Jocko is the best darn explosive-sniffing dog in the world. He would ignore a T-bone steak to get the object he is looking for. He would also ignore the steak to play with the squeaky toy you give him as a reward. Jocko never runs out of energy. Never quits. At the end of a twelve-hour day, he is still yanking on the chain.

He can sniff potassium. C4. Smokeless powder (that is stuff like your bullets). In our training we use the actual stuff. He gets more excited when it is the real thing. He yanks the chain. You read his signals. When it's time to get ready to check someone, his back legs are moving. He's like, "Wheew! I wanna go! I wanna go!"

He is a good dog. Just like I said. His drive is so high. That is his downfall, if anything, because he wears himself out. He won't pace. The other dogs, they pace themselves, especially in this kind of heat. He gets along great with people. Kids could grab him, people could hug him, he would not snarl or bite. But if he sniffed a target substance, look out.

The other thing is that when he senses that there is a possible target, he wants to rush through the usual routine. He is telling me, "C'mon! I know where it is. Let's cut to the chase!"

THE BIRTH OF EMBEDDING AS PENTAGON WAR POLICY

Deputy Assistant Secretary
of Public Affairs Bryan Whitman

> "The United States military has an obligation to control the battle space."

Thank you, William Safire. In his March 9, 2003 column, *The New York Times* op-ed essayist reviewed the etymology of embedding:

> The term been around since the end of the 18th century when a British naturalist observed that "calcareous substances are in general found where flints are embedded." Embedded was later defined by Merriam-Webster as "to enclose closely in or as if in a matrix" and was used by native speakers more loosely to mean "to stick into so deeply that it's hard to get out."

In the 1980s, computer system engineers and software programmers relied on embedding to describe certain technical features. A quick search on Amazon reveals dozens and dozens of computer software and hardware books with embedding in the title.

In the months leading up the war, the word moved from the desktop to the battlefield, and "gained a new metaphoric extension," in Pentagon-speak, to define a brazen approach to media management. Embed also means "to fix in the memory," and given what the word now connotes for war journalists, it's safe to say that embedding has been embedded in the newsroom. Yet one nagging difficulty remains. Tracing its military origin has proved as challenging and elusive—when exactly was the word first used at the Pentagon?—as locating, you know, those weapons of mass destruction.

One of the first media mentions of "embed" occurred on the eve of the Afghanistan war during a segment of CNN's *Reliable Sources*, a talk show hosted by *The Washington Post*'s Howard Kurtz. Guests for the September 29, 2001, program included Mark Thompson, national security correspondent for *Time*, Frank Sesno, CNN's Washington bureau chief, and Barbara Cochran, president of the Radio-Television News Directors Association. It was Cochran who said, "I understand that the military has said that they are going to make efforts to, as they say, embed journalists with small units that are going out, but I don't believe that's begun to happen yet."

While a smattering of journalists were embedded with military missions in Afghanistan towards the war's end, like Operation Anaconda, the policy associated with embedment wasn't articulated until an October 30, 2002, press conference, when Secretary of Defense Donald Rumsfeld briefly explained the military's new media maneuver to the Washington bureau chiefs of the major news outlets.

One of the chief policy architects behind this new weapon of mass communication was Bryan Whitman, forty-four, who grew up in a Pennsylvania military family and received a master's degree in communications from Oklahoma University. When we spoke with Whitman, the Pentagon's deputy assistant secretary of public affairs, in early June, almost all the embeds had either left Iraq or were working independently. The next week, Whitman's boss, Assistant Secretary of Defense for Public Affairs Victoria Clarke, unexpectedly announced her retirement.

■　■　■

I reported to Victoria Clarke, and her boss was Secretary of Defense Donald Rumsfeld. That's the chain of command here. I'm the deputy for media operations. I supervise 100 people in three major directorates—one is the press office here in the Pentagon. One is the media support branch, and they take care of things like arranging the Secretary's interviews, as far as doing all the advance work on the road for when he's traveling, involved having a photographer for the department. The other branch of my organization is called Defense Visual Information Directorate, and they are responsible for Department of Defense [DOD] imagery—which includes the oversight of combat cameramen throughout the services.

My first exposure to the Pentagon was during the first Gulf War. I was in the office of the Chairman of the Joint Chiefs of Staff under General Powell at the time. Before Desert Storm, I worked in the National Military Command Center, and that was my first exposure to public affairs. I started off as an infantry officer and I was later transitioned into Special Operations with the U.S.

Army. I was assigned to the Fifth Special Forces Group. Each Special Forces group is oriented toward a specific geographic area. The Fifth Special Forces Group is the Middle East, and so I spent a lot of time in Somalia, Saudi Arabia, Bahrain, Oman, Jordan.

In Somalia I was the Special Operations commander for the withdrawal of all U.N. forces out of Somalia. That operation was called Operation United Shield. We had no U.S. forces on the ground at that time. There were Pakistanis, Indians, Malaysians, Egyptians, and those from Bangladesh, to name a few. This was after the Mogadishu raid. The U.N. had decided that it was going to withdraw all its forces, and the United States was going to assist in that withdrawal, and so my unit was deployed throughout the country in what we called Coalition Support Teams. For example, we provide AC130 air coverage for the withdrawal as they moved back into the seaport and the Mogadishu Airport. We never experienced anything quite as dramatic as reported in *Black Hawk Down*. It was more of the hit-and-run ambush type of thing. This was a withdrawal under pressure but I wouldn't say it was under any sort of direct fire, though one of our Humvees did come back with a few holes in it. None for the worse, and I didn't have anybody injured or killed during that mission so, by my standards, it was a success.

After Somalia, I was in the military until 1995. Afterward I spent about a year as the director of government and public affairs for the USO here in Washington, D.C., working on various legislative initiatives and public affairs—including coordinating publicity for celebrity entertainers. When the opportunity came around to come back to the Pentagon and to work in the press office, I jumped at that opportunity. I worked as a public affairs officer in the press office for a year or two, and then the opportunity became available to be the deputy director of the press office. I was the deputy director of the press office until last April. That's when Victoria asked me to take on this job as her deputy assistant secretary for media operations.

During the summer of 2002, when it looked like there was a possibility that we would be engaged in combat in Iraq, several factors were developing simultaneously. News organizations were coming to us and saying, "Should we go to combat, this is how we would like to cover it." They hoped to cover it from the front lines, alongside the troops in the field. At the same time, we were looking at what our goals should be. We knew that information warfare would be very much a part of any sort of conflict. We knew that Saddam Hussein was a practiced liar, who used denial and deception to deceive the international community. We looked for ways that could mitigate Saddam's lying, and of course, one of the things that came to mind was exactly what the reporters, editors, and bureau chiefs were asking for, and that was to put independent objective observers throughout the battlefield.

Pools are always the least preferred method of coverage, short of no coverage at all. We used it in Gulf War I and I'll tell you why. In 1991, reporters didn't have the type of technology and capabilities that exist today. They did not have the ability to file from the field like they can today. There was not the option of sending images and video without lugging along tremendous amounts of equipment, and so that's a major factor. A better comparison is Afghanistan because it's much closer in time. One may ask, "Look, you didn't do this in Afghanistan, why do it during Operation Iraqi Freedom?" The technology was the same, obviously. Technology didn't move too much in those intervening months, but what was different was the nature of the mission. At the beginning in Afghanistan, we only had a very small number of forces on the ground. Special Forces had to infiltrate into some difficult situations, in arduous environments and in very small numbers. The opportunity for wide-scale embedding didn't really exist. There were plenty of unilateral, independent journalists roaming Afghanistan. Let's face it, they were in Afghanistan before military forces were. They certainly didn't need our permission to go to Afghanistan, but they were restricted to certain areas. The United States military has an obligation to control the battle space. What I'm trying to say is, every conflict presents itself differently given the mission, access into the war theater, and the technology that the news media has, and so each situation has to be looked at differently.

I think you'll probably find that we got our ground rules about right in Iraq. They were only designed primarily to protect operational security and to ensure that we weren't doing anything that was going to endanger our personnel. Quite frankly, I've never met a reporter who has ever intentionally or willfully compromised one of our U.S. military missions. It's just not in their nature. They don't want to do that. Furthermore, it's inconceivable that they'd want to compromise a mission that they're actually a part of. They'd be endangering their own lives.

Embedding as terminology has been with the military for some time. In fact, embedding had been a term I've been using for years. We didn't sit around a table and say, "Okay, we need to come up with a new term," or, "We're going to create a new type of coverage." Embedded coverage has always been in existence. During World War II we had reporters that were embedded—I am told that on D-Day, between thirty and forty reporters went ashore with U.S. forces and reported on activities. During Desert Storm in 1991, Molly Moore, *Washington Post* Pentagon correspondent, went out with the Marines and stayed out there. She was, for all purposes, an embedded reporter.

I was given the opportunity and privilege to execute this program at the seat of government here for the Defense Department, but I would not want to claim sole credit for anything. Torie Clarke had the vision and energy to make sure that the senior leadership understood the importance of this. Secretary Rumsfeld had the wisdom and the courage, along with Chairman Richard Meyers, to embrace this bold initiative, which in turn—funny how the military works—solicited an awful lot of support from commanders all the way down the chain of command. We discussed many things. We made a whole list of bad things that could happen—everything from journalists being killed, to violations of the ground rules, to reactions of commanders if there was a violation of a ground rule. We talked about ways in which we would try to mitigate some of that and what our actions would be. We did public affairs planning like we would do for any other form of war planning. We war-gamed it. Commanders in the field didn't view the news media as the enemy. We certainly don't here at the Pentagon. In fact, this experience has taught me a couple of things, and one is that we really do have enlightened commanders. We have commanders at all levels in the United States military who understand and respect the role of the press in a free society.

We did acknowledge, up front, that we were going to get reporting of the good, the bad, and the ugly. The good goes back to what I call the inescapable qualities of the U.S. military, and we saw a lot of reporting about just how well they did their job. But bad things are going to happen because soldiers are human, and we did see bad things happen, and they got reported on. One that comes to mind is when a group of troops at a checkpoint fired on a vehicle that looked like it was trying to charge the checkpoint. When the shooting stopped, there were several civilians who had been killed, but there was no military and no explosives. They were just civilians who had, for whatever reason, not yielded to the instructions and the warning shots that were fired. And they all ended up dead. But an embedded reporter was there—*Washington Post* reporter William Branigin—and he maintained his objectivity and reported the event just like it happened. He also reported—again the beauty of embedding—exactly how bad those soldiers felt about what had just happened, and how it was the darkest day in their lives, and how they brought so much to bear on themselves for this tragic accident to happen. So you got the full news package, as opposed to some sterile account from the Pentagon or spokesman saying, "Today, yes, we had an incident and some civilians were killed at a checkpoint when they failed to stop."

I offered a total of 920 embed positions. I got back names, or acceptances, from 775. That number, though, represented some embeds who I wasn't able to get into the country where their units were operating. There were about twelve embeds who were slated to go to Saudi Arabia, and I never got them in there because of visa issues. Our military units were there and prepared to accept them. Turkey is another example. I had some people planning to go to some air bases there but it never happened. Another example was the First Armored Cavalry Regiment. Baghdad had fallen by the time the regiment had started deploying, and so many of the news organizations pulled their embeds from the unit. These reporters had found a way to operate independent of specific units. So, the final number was approximately 600 embeds.

You need to look forward when you look at the embedding program. Every military conflict is going to present a set of unique circumstances, and challenges, and geography, and mission. The news business is dynamic and capabilities will change the way in which we get our news and the way that news is reported. I don't make any hard, fast rules about the past or the future, when it comes to the embedding. I won't be so bold as to say that you're going to be able to take every situation in the future and make it a model after Operation Iraqi Freedom either. By contrast, unilateral reporters had every bad thing that can possibly happen, happen to them. They were killed, wounded, captured, detained, lost on the battlefield, and committed security violations that caused them to be removed from the battle space. Just about everything bad that could happen to a journalist happened to the unilaterals out there. Now, that's not to say that some of those things didn't happen to the embedded journalists, but the United States military has an obligation to control the battle space. So, reporters who are out there will be treated like any other civilian who is found on the battlefield. What embedding allowed for was a framework which commanders and reporters worked under to ensure both could accomplish their mission without compromising the journalists' integrity or the success of the military mission.

THE HEMINGWAY LEGACY
Kansas City Star
Staff Writer Matt Schofield

> "We kill people. According to Marines, they
> believe this more than anyone else. There was
> a very cool, professional way of looking at this.
> It sounds really weird, but that's what I saw."

Ernest Hemingway's association with war and reporting is well, deeply embedded in our literary consciousness. In World War I, he was an ambulance
driver in Italy until he was wounded, and that wartime experience provided
background material for his early novels and short stories. The very first newspaper articles he penned as an eighteen-year-old cub reporter for the *Kansas
City Star* foreshadowed his lifelong preoccupation with men at war. Here's a
passage taken from "Recruit for the Tanks," dated April 18, 1918:

> *A line of men wound from the front room of the third floor of the
> Army recruiting station, Twelfth and Grand Avenue, through the hall
> and halfway downstairs. Some of the men were jostling and laugh-
> ing, others looked sober and looked thoughtfully at the posters on
> the wall. Mechanics in overalls, bookkeepers, stenographers, school
> teachers who would have difficulty with the physical examination,
> and athletic college students, all were in line. The head of the line
> stopped at the door of a room where a freckle-faced young second
> lieutenant sat at a desk. He nodded, a man was admitted, asked a
> few questions, sized up by the lieutenant and then either told he was
> not wanted or given a card to sign.*
>
>   *"It's the spirit of adventure which brings them up here," said
> Lieut. Frank E. Cooter, of the Tank Corps, the latest branch of the
> United States Army. "Every man in line there is a potential crusader.
> They may not have realized it until today. Then they came up to en-
> list. We do not offer anything easy. The tank work is dangerous, of*

course, but men will always apply for clean, dangerous work with a chance for quick advancement."

With the arrival of World War II, Hemingway was at the pinnacle of his career. Not only was he one of the most famous writers in the world, but with an outsized ego to match, he felt compelled to thrust himself into the martial limelight. He futilely hunted for German war subs and spies off Key West aboard his fishing boat. He shared wine and war strategy with officers and enlisted men alike in France as a pistol-packing, jeep-driving correspondent.

Eighty-five years later, another writer with *Kansas City Star* ties found himself covering a different war in a different century under different conditions. Although he's written about such diverse subjects as a sixty-year Holocaust love story to a pro-tobacco law firm, Matt Schofield's connection to Hemingway is palpable in another way. Taped to the wall over his desk is a copy of a bookkeeper's memo from 1917 concerning the new hire, E. Hemingway.

Schofield filed fifty-three stories for the 300,000-circulation, Knight-Ridder-owned *Star*. Throughout the war, other papers in the nation's second-largest newspaper chain published many of his war dispatches. Schofield's reportorial signature is a sharp eye for detail and a Hemingwayesque ability to locate the heart of the story through the gradual accretion of facts. Here's an excerpt from his May 4 story about a makeshift Baghdad cemetery:

> *Ten-year-old Saad Sammir offers a tour of his little cemetery on the grounds of the Al-Aksan Hospital. "Here is a small mound of dirt; this is a for a baby I buried. He was very little. Here is the biggest mound of dirt, a momma and her baby died together. She was holding him very tight, and we could not pry them apart, so we put them in the same hole.*
>
> *Saad is here because many schools are still close in the wake of the war. He guesses that he has helped dig 100 graves. The cemetery is temporary. There are only 150 graves, only 64 of them are still occupied. The graves are no more than two feet deep, and some are simply at ground level, with dirt from a nearby hole piled on top. Hands stick out the sides of some, and feet out of others.*
>
> *Saad smiles. He is paid 1,000 dinars for each body that he buries or reburies. For the first few weeks, that means as much as 7,000 dinars a day, or about $2 at the old rate.*

■ ■ ■

The Hemingway hiring notice over my desk is from the old bookkeeper's ledger book from 1917.

It says: "Miss Power, please put these men on the payroll. E. Hemingway $60.00 a month. Fitzpatrick $110.00 a month. G. K. Wallace $135.00 a month." Then it's signed. I keep the notice as a reminder to never let anyone else tell you what your value is. I'm hoping mine is sixty bucks a month or more. One of the first questions Marines and soldiers in Baghdad would ask me was "How much hazard pay do you guys get?" The answer was, "None. We get not a dime." They were always stunned by that. I went over because I thought it was a hell of a story to cover, and a hell of an experience. I wasn't looking for extra money.

I took along a book by Joseph Galloway, *We Were Soldiers Once . . . and Young*, and two collections of Ernie Pyle's writings. Pyle had this casual approach to a serious topic and he got his point across very plainly and pristinely, but he kept a sense of humor going. This guy went ashore on D-Day and Iraq wasn't that kind of a war. The moments for me were more along the lines of keeping your ears open for the voice of the guys around you; don't get caught up with just a few officers. For example, my column called "The Marine Calendar" was well received. From the moment we arrived, guys would be talking about the week by saying, "Wednesday's coming." I think Wednesday symbolized the day the war would end, and they'd start talking wistfully about Friday and Saturday. They'd be training in the Kuwaiti Desert. It'd be hot, and miserable, and they'd be sweating, it's near 100 degrees in the Kuwaiti Desert, the sand blowing into their eyes, and someone would say, "Hang on, hang on, Wednesday's coming."

It was an incredibly hard life for these Marines. A number of embeds didn't expect the difficulty of day-to-day life. We had no idea how difficult it was to live in those situations. I had no idea. One disadvantage of having not been in the service is that you went in there completely ignorant of how tough it is. Going in, I thought it would be an expanded camping trip, and in a sense it was, but it was like an expanded camping trip from hell. It's unbelievably hot, there's no chance of a shower; you've got twenty days without a shower at one stretch. Water is rationed, the food is ridiculously bad at times, and you're forced to sit and wait in trucks for five, six hours at a stretch. Then you move on convoys that rumble along at twenty miles per hour and you'll be moving for ten, twelve hours at a stretch. One night we were moving up north into Iraq and we came into a sniper zone, so we had to hunker down in the back of a truck. It was incredibly uncomfortable. The Marines were told not to fire back. They were angry about that and they felt really naked. They felt completely exposed because this was a six- or seven-mile sniper zone and it took us two and one-half hours to drive through it, weaving back and forth. In blackout conditions. Later, it turned out to be a mine field, so we had to follow this stupid little two-rut lane. Then we stopped, and everyone was told, "Listen, we're in a mine field. We're not going any further because it's pitch dark. Sleep on the trucks or sleep under the trucks, but don't go outside the tracks of the trucks." So all these guys hop off the trucks immediately—as quickly as they can—because they want to go to the bathroom. They all urinate under the truck and a bunch of guys get down there and they sleep under the truck! You get used to this kind of repulsive way of living.

At times they'd get really angry, just screaming at each other. If you're with anyone for that amount of time, especially if it's twenty-four hours a day for weeks on end, you're going to snap at each other. I didn't see any fistfights. That would have been a breach of discipline that would have been dealt with fairly severely. But I saw people get angry and yell, and then isolate themselves as much as they could in a corner of the truck to calm down. There wouldn't be apologies in the sense of, "Oh, I'm sorry," but there'd be apologies in the sense of they'd make some stupid joke about themselves to come back into their graces.

The Marines I was traveling with belonged to the Seventh Engineering Support Battalion. Their function was the removal of obstacles and to build or blow things up. They were responsible for removing some of the defensive sand berms on the Iraqi-Kuwaiti border with bulldozers, removing the high-powered border fence, and pushing the final sand berm into this deep anti-tank trench that was inside Iraq.

The battalion works like a construction company and builds camps for the Marines, whose fighting forces move like a slinky. These guys would go out in front and remove the obstacles so the fighting forces could go past them and beat back a path, and these guys would then create temporary camps. To make a temporary camp they would mark out an area with a surveying team, and then take the bulldozers and start building berms. They'd scrape off two or three feet of sand and push it together. These walls of sand can reach ten feet high and sometimes will stretch around a camp that is six or eight square kilometers large. Six feet of sand will stop most bullets and so they're defensive berms—for protection. When we got near Diwaniyah, the fighting was going on about two kilometers away, so we were essentially on the front. We were making a camp that was for guys at the front as well as being a stage for the last attack on Baghdad. Within these berms you can store massive amounts of ammunition and fuel that can be camouflaged. Spies won't know what they're looking at from a distance. They can't tell how many people are inside that camp. They can't tell if there's ammunition, or fuel, or food. You set up hospitals in that zone. Eventually they start setting up field showers, so that the guys who are coming back from fighting have twelve hours to get rested or get a quick shower before going back.

In the field it was all pup tents—little camping nylon jobbies that just kind of pop up. Most of the time when we were moving, we didn't use tents, though; we just slept on the ground. The officers also slept frequently on the ground or just in the trucks. They had pup tents as well, but whenever there was time, they'd put big areas of camouflage netting over their area of sleep. As soon as you set up a camp, you set up camouflage netting over any vehicles; that disguises the shapes from the air, so if there's any kind of air attack, they won't know that they can hit a fuel truck, or a Humvee over there. You want to disguise what it looks like from above. Despite there not being an Iraqi air force, I sensed they were thinking of spies looking from a distance. There was quite a long time when there were spies around us. One sniper killed a Marine about 100 meters from camp. The Marine was looking up above the berm and was shot in the head.

We once were camped where there had been a fairly large-scale Iraqi ambush. We were part of a long convoy that was ambushed. We didn't know at the time it was ambushed because the ambush had been eight miles ahead of us. We were camped right where we found the bodies of 150 Iraqi soldiers. It was really odd because it was not what you expected to see. The Iraqi soldiers were so old. I mean they were my age or older, and I'm surrounded by American soldiers and they're all very young. I'm forty-one and the Marines frequently told me, "Boy, I hope when I'm your age I can still walk around!" Or, "Wow, when I'm your age, I hope I still have all my faculties and I don't need to wear diapers!" They're young enough that they have this notion that forty is really, really, really old. Generals and some of the lieutenant colonels would be a little older than I am; the higher-ranking people and master sergeants, were about my age. But generally speaking, these guys were young, and here were these dead Iraqis with balding, graying hair; and the thickness of middle age. They had wrinkled faces. They wore the scarves of the Republican Guard.

What had happened is they jumped over a berm and tried to ambush a group. They had some rather bad intelligence evidently, because the group they tried to ambush was a fighting force of close to 1,000 U.S. Marines, and with some light armored vehicles with 25-mm cannons, which turned on them. From what we heard, the fighting didn't last more than about two minutes. They were blown from the top of the berm back into a little gulley behind. They were almost perfectly lined up along there. I'd see a body and then five feet later, another one; and then ten yards on, another one; and then another ten yards, another one. They were spaced out. They weren't piled on top of each other. I didn't find it overly disturbing. I should have, I suppose, because it looked very military. There was something professional about the way they had attacked, and there was something professional about the way they were killed. It was very sad, but I was more disturbed by their age than the fact that they were dead.

After overpowering them, the Marines in front just kept moving on since their battlefield would be just a little bit ahead. Meanwhile, for the other Marines there was an enormous amount of curiosity in finding out how the Iraqi soldiers were living; how they were setting up their ambushes. So a lot of studying was going on: looking into the holes they dug; these guys were eating—they had the yellow humanitarian aid food bags; looking at the weapons that they were using; trying to get some kind of information because at this point the war was still on and they were thinking, "Okay, we're going to see a lot more." They had AK47s and a few of the bigger machine guns. I was told they had a 50-caliber machine gun. I didn't see that. They had RPGs and cases of ammunition.

The Marines weren't gloating. It didn't seem to bother them that these guys were dead. Their attitude was, "This is the job. This is what we do. We kill people." According to Marines, they believe this more than anyone else. There was a very cool, professional way of looking at this. It sounds really weird, but that's what I saw.

One of these Iraqi soldiers had been bound, gagged, and shot in the back of the head by his own people, so the Marines made a special effort to cover his body immediately. They took out one of those little field blankets—those silver field blankets—and they used that to cover his body as a show of respect, because they assumed he must have been killed either as a spy, or because he refused to attack, or maybe he was executed for wanting to surrender. They left the other bodies out there on the ground—not for a long time, but for a full day and maybe a day and a half—then they started burying them. I didn't see the burial—I heard it going on, but I didn't see it.

I never got close to Iraqi civilians until I was on my own in Baghdad, so I didn't have any military connection at that point. While I was embedded, I saw how dangerous these temporary camps were for Iraqi civilians. You don't just walk into the camp and you don't just walk out. It's secured. If Marines saw Iraqi civilians coming toward them, they were going to have guns trained on them the whole time. Anytime anyone drove a car, there was a gun, and when I say "a gun" it may have been thirty guns. There was this constant belief that anyone could be the enemy. I didn't see this as a great opportunity to talk to civilians. I didn't like these conditions; I don't like talking with people when they're having a gun pointed at their head; it just doesn't seem like a good idea to me.

When I got into Baghdad, I had a chance to sit down with a fedayeen who was refusing to leave his house. He had been terrified of the destructive force Americans could bring to bear. I talked to other Iraqi soldiers as well who were blown away by how quickly this war was brought to them. They had no idea what to expect. "American tanks were so fast; the American weapons were so destructive; the American air support was so overwhelming."

There's no way that the fedayeen would have spoken to me if I had a military escort. Instead I relied on my fixer Amar. He's a college student in Baghdad, but his college was closed. He was a translator, a driver, an advisor, at times a bodyguard. A do-everything guy. A journalist's helper. He'd go out in the streets at night, and talk to people, and find out what the undercurrents were, what people were talking about, what were their greatest concerns; get the rumors of where things were happening that would be of interest; and he was able to find a couple of people who had gone into hiding, including this fedayeen.

The fedayeens' image was really overblown. The Iraqi people were given this picture of them as superheroes. They'd show them on television jumping out of planes and shooting people as they're falling to the earth on parachutes and eating live animals—just these intensely violent superfighters. They wore all black, with this ninja look, and they were deadly, and they never missed. They were ruthless and were there to protect the nation of Iraq. An image was built up around them that they were terrifying and Iraqis needed to be afraid of them, but their training actually wasn't nearly as intense. This guy told me that they didn't serve all day, every day. They were called in occasionally to serve by a patriotic song that would be played on the airwaves, and when this song played, that was the call for the fedayeen to report, but he said there was no superhuman training going on. He wasn't a fearsome-looking guy at all. He looked very afraid; he had the look of fear in his eyes. He wasn't the sort of man who, if you ran into him in the street, you'd be frightened for your life. He had been a theater major at Baghdad University. Every family had to give a son over to serve in the military. He was chosen because they thought he probably looked the part—he doesn't know for what reason he was chosen for fedayeen. He says he never actively sought to be in the fedayeen; he was just drafted. People around Baghdad would say this was pretty much the case—the way it worked. They would take the people they wanted. In college he played Othello. The role, when I met him, was Gilligan playing Othello. I'm trying to think if there's a Shakespearean counterpart—a man whose past is coming back to haunt him. He had been part of a group that weren't nice people. They didn't do nice things, and for a long time, they were completely in control. As long as he played along, he never had to fear anything, and now because of that, he is paralyzed with fear. He's a man afraid to leave his house.

WAR JUNKIE

BBC News Special Correspondent
Ben Brown

> "The BBC policy is not to say *our* troops, it
> was just British troops."

Founded in 1922, the British Broadcasting Company's first broadcasts aired an orchestral concert, regular news bulletin, dance music, and a play written for radio called *The Truth About Father Christmas*. Ten years later, it offered its first UK shortwave service, and in 1937, Wimbledon tennis was broadcast for the first time. The following year, the first BBC foreign-language service began, and it was in Arabic. Over the next several decades, the BBC grew into a recognizable global brand that's heard around the world in English and in forty-two other languages. And say what you might about their perceived anti-American bias, BBC correspondents, with their authoritative-sounding diction, often set the journalistic bar for analytical news reporting.

We talked to Ben Brown, a Special Correspondent for BBC News since 1988. His foreign news reporting has taken him to see the fall of the Berlin Wall, the first Gulf War, Rwanda massacres, Kosovo, the final collapse of communism and ouster of Mikhail Gorbachev, and civil war in Chechnya. His war coverage has netted him several international prizes, including the Bayeux War Correspondent of the Year Award. When the Iraq War began heating up, Brown, forty-three, knew where his next overseas assignment would take him.

■　■　■

I like covering wars because you feel like you're watching history. You're in the front row of history. You want to be involved, no matter how big your role is. Even though conditions are definitely uncomfortable and miserable, somebody once said, "If there's anything worse than being out here, it would be not being out here." That's my motivation.

I embedded with the British. They had rather a hybrid thing. They had individual journalists embedded with frontline units, but they also had a thing called the Forward Transmission Unit, which was attached to their military headquarters of First Armored Division, which was the main British fighting force there. We moved with them across the border from Kuwait into Iraq. The idea of this was that you got a big overview from the British headquarters of how the battle is progressing—the emerging strategy. We were also able to have our big satellite dish so that we didn't have the restrictions that the frontline embeds had. Our TV facility was called Hub and Spokes. We were the Hub and the individual embeds with frontline British units were Spokes, and they were supposed to send their pictures back to our Forward Transmission Unit. We would then relay them back to London, or we would package their pictures up because quite a lot of the time, what was happening was there were too many individual reports or individual bits of footage. London would ask me to package up all the pictures of the day and embrace some of the military strategy that we were getting, and put it together into one piece for our television nightly news. We don't really have anchors in the field. Subsequently, after a couple of weeks, I semi-broke-off from this unit in order to get a bit more frontline footage of my own and worked sort of semi-unilaterally with some other British units.

My view is that in nearly all conflicts you tend to be with one side or the other. For example, with the Chechnyan war you really have to be on one side or the other if you're on the frontline; otherwise you end up mincemeat. This idea that you're embedded or unilateral is a bit artificial. Rwanda was slightly different because there was genocide going on. It was just all-around chaos. We would head in with the United Nations. In Bosnia, most of the journalists tended to be with the Bosnian-Muslim troops, or if you were on the other side, with the Bosnian Serbs. But obviously, in Kuwait and Iraq this was more regulated in the sense that there were rules by which you had to abide. You'd have to do training in Britain before going out; we'd have to do quite a lot of courses on chemical weapons, wearing gas masks, wearing chemical protection suits—we had to do a two-day course on that. We were officially accredited as Ministry of Defense war correspondents, with little passes, and little Union Jack armbands. Because our own BBC had already sent us on a training course on to how to wear a gas mask and all that, we ended up doing exactly the same course for the Ministry of Defense, so that was overkill. But the Ministry of Defense said they have a duty of care and they have to be satisfied that they've looked after you and prepared you for eventualities.

During a day trip to Basra with the Irish Guards, there was one incident when we were in a Warrior armored car and got out. This Iraqi guy who was playing dead suddenly jumps up with a rocket propelled grenade and he's about to shoot it at us. The machine gunner on the other Warrior, which was alongside us, opened fire and killed him. Though my cameraman and I felt bad about this guy being killed, I thought that maybe I should run up and shake hands with the British soldier. Afterwards, back at the headquarters, we congratulated the gunner who had killed him on the basis that he saved our lives. So you could argue that I was getting too close to the military in some ways.

I don't feel that our objectivity was ever suspended, really. I was very aware that this was a very unpopular war and also that a lot of our audience — at least half, maybe a majority of our audience — were against the war in the first place. So there was no way that you could be gung-ho. The BBC policy is not to say *our* troops, it was just British troops.

Once Basra had fallen, we tried to interview a lot of Iraqis. I mean, they were still very nervous even after Baghdad had fallen; they were nervous about talking because they weren't yet convinced Saddam really had gone. The themes of liberation were not as joyous as people had been expecting either in Basra or Baghdad. One guy said to me, "We're not happy, but we're not unhappy." People were relieved Saddam was gone, but at the same time, nobody likes to have their country invaded, and they were angry that there was breakdown of law and order.

I never felt like a target. I've been in Iraq quite a lot over the years and the people are very sympathetic to the British. A lot of them have been educated in Britain, especially doctors. They're very cultured and educated. I always felt very welcome, both before the war and after the war.

During the first Gulf War, I was in Riyadh, Saudi Arabia, where Schwarzkopf had his headquarters. I then drove up to Kuwait when it was liberated. This time around I did feel a déjà vu, actually. I remember the hysteria among journalists in the first Gulf War, when people were genuinely worried about whether chemical weapons were being used and everyone clamored into their chemical protection suits. This time around, it was kind of "Here we go again." I felt a lot more skeptical. I never really believed there were weapons of mass destruction. I didn't believe that Saddam had the capability to probably use them, because he hadn't in the first Gulf War, so to be honest, I never really paid attention in all those training courses on how to put on a gas mask. Instinctively, I just felt that it would never happen.

It was hard for anyone who was embedded to give analysis, but we relied on people in London or Doha to do the big picture stuff. I could do a bigger picture than the individual frontline embeds because I had the British army commanders briefing me, but in terms of analysis of how well or badly the war was going—whether it was on schedule or not—we did do that definitely. Maybe we were overly critical after a few days when it seemed that the war was going slower than had been expected, because first we had been saying it was going to be a rush, then because it was going slow, it had all gone wrong. Maybe we veered too dramatically.

We kept our people in Baghdad. So obviously, we covered the other side of it comprehensively. In terms of showing the victims, I felt we were a bit constrained. I saw a few bodies from a distance, but that was about all I could get away with. The BBC has their own guidelines, which are based on years of audience complaints. We know what the audience will tolerate and what they won't. Whereas other countries like Japan are happy to see close-ups of people blown up, the British audience does not.

One incident in Baghdad stands out for me. We were at the Palestine Hotel and the American Marines there came under fire from a building across the river, and they all ran down to the river and were firing wildly at this building. I thought that that highlighted the difference between the American and the British army, having spent some time with both. The British were far more restrained. I'm not just saying that because I'm British. I thought the Americans were very jumpy and occasionally trigger-happy, frankly, and certainly one of our British TV colleagues was killed by American fire. We as the media felt very nervous approaching American checkpoints all the time.

I was amazed by the scale of the chaos in Baghdad. When we drove into Baghdad there was just so much shrapnel and bullet casings on the road—we had four flat tires in the space of an hour. We saw a thief who'd been caught by shopkeepers and a mob was just stomping him to death in front of us. That was a shocking image. Overall, there was just this surreal feeling of the American troops in Baghdad after years of living there under Saddam—that was weird.

I am going to Afghanistan soon. We want to see the country we invaded earlier. We want to see how nation-building is going there and by all accounts, it's going badly. The U.N. is saying forty percent of the country is a no-go and it's too dangerous. The Taliban are re-emerging and doing some vicious things like executing relief workers. They're trying to terrorize the international community by making it difficult for them to work in Afghanistan. So we have a thing where we don't let stories disappear and we like doing follow-ups.

The prognosis for nation-building in Iraq is possibly easier than Afghanistan, but there's genuine criticism that can be leveled against the Americans and the British for not having thought things through more closely and more properly. If you're going to have a war, they could have prepared much better. But ultimately, Iraq is a fantastic country with a rich heritage, with highly intelligent educated people. With all the natural resources, sooner or later it will be a great country. We have to wait and see.

HIGH-TECH DESERT RATS
Wired Reporter Josh Davis

"The unsung heroes of the war are the geeks
who are wiring the systems that are supporting
the shooters."

Don't bother cramming freelance writer and documentary filmmaker, Joshua
Davis, into some tidy, predictable category. "I aspire to be my generation's
George Plimpton," boasts the twenty-eight-year-old Stanford graduate and San
Francisco resident who has trained as a matador, competed in the world arm-
wrestling championships (144-pound category), traveled to Antwerp, Belgium
to investigate a story about man-made diamonds, and tagged along with the
U.S. Army's Eleventh Signal Brigade as its convoy of trucks rumbled through
Iraq. "The mission: to establish a digital beachhead in central Iraq," he wrote in
Wired magazine. "Without this advance node and a handful like it, the Army's
Third Infantry Division cannot receive the precise targeting information it needs
to fight its way into the capital."

■   ■   ■

I have been writing for *Wired* for about a year and a half. It was my idea to follow the Signal Brigade and basically see how the war was wired. I used to own
a technology company in Los Angeles that did visual effects for motion pictures, so I had basic knowledge of networking and the terminology. I certainly
was not an expert in any way, but I could be conversant on the subject.
Technology is definitely a lot slicker in Hollywood than what I saw in Iraq and
Kuwait, where it was kind of down and dirty in the sense that these guys were
out there in the middle of the desert trying to make servers work. On the other
hand, what I saw in Qatar at Central Command was far more Hollywood-like,
where you would walk into a room and plasma screen monitors displayed the
Global Commanding and Control System.

My focus was not on the munitions or where bombs hit. What I was
paying attention to were the underlying networks that would communicate

military information. It's certainly true that we can see our own troops. It gets a little more complex when you talk about seeing the enemy. If you could have a drone floating above the enemy with infrared capability, then you can get those types of images. But a lot of times the drone can't stay there all the time, and there can't be drones at all places at all times. While you look at the Global Command and Control System (GCCS)—known as "Geeks" to the soldiers in the field—which monitors movements and attack orders of all the units, it's real time only insofar as our troops. There's still this question of intelligence. You can take the intelligence about enemy troop positions and input it into GCCS. But if these troops move and there's no update, then there could still be problems.

The military wants all these great systems. But all of this high-end technology is running on systems that are inherently vulnerable right now. The military sees these systems in the private sector—video conferencing and instant messaging—and they want them because it allows them to be a more effective army. The problem with that though is that if they were to rely on their standard procurement process, it would take them five years to get anything and by the time they got it, it would be completely outdated. What they end up doing instead is to say, "Okay, forget our procurement process, we're just going to buy off-the-shelf systems and we're going to make it work." The end-result is that they have consumer-grade servers and equipment that were not meant to be used in the types of environments that the military is using them. For instance, what I saw on the border with Iraq was a bunch of relay stations that were running HP servers. These servers were sitting in the sand. You and I can go buy this stuff right now if we wanted to. These were sitting in racks, in tents in the desert, and it was very dusty and hot, and when a dust storm would come through, the filters and the fans on these systems would get clogged, and they would overheat. The guys who were assigned to take care of these systems were going out of their minds trying to keep them cool. There was a private first-class whose job was to vacuum the servers twenty-four hours a day. He had to sit there, vacuuming with a Sears & Roebuck vacuum just like the one I have in my closet. He was nervous because the temperature was inching up. We talk about all this high-end technology but what is it running on? It's running on generators, but at a certain heat, the oil that lubricates the parts of a generator will become too viscous, and it won't provide enough lubrication and the generator will blow up. That happens at around 130 degrees Fahrenheit. I was there when it was past 120. If the generators across the desert blow up, the entire system goes black. Then all these soldiers who were trained to use the system would have to rely on their compasses and their maps.

There's any number of environments where this system would not operate in the way it should. That has this kind of amazing ripple effect when you think about it, because all of this high-end technology is great, and it looks fantastic from afar, but what if the system that's running it collapses? The way the system works is that they're using primarily line-of-sight wireless radio on the battlefield to communicate all the data back to the border. Then at the border, because it's more secure, they set up larger dishes that can then take in these line-of-sight communications, and shoot them up into satellites. For the next war, one big step would be going from a land-based line-of-sight system to a complete satellite system. Right now they're heavily dependent on this line-of-sight transmission methodology, because the uplink speeds of satellites are not fast enough to sustain, the encryption is not entirely figured out, and it's very expensive right now to use satellites. There's not enough bandwidth to support an entire military. Moving to satellite would remove a lot of infrastructure.

The information strategy employed in the Iraq War was called swarm tactics. The idea was that technology ensures that forces don't have to be very close to each other anymore. What you can do is spread them out, roll them across the terrain, and then when any individual unit comes under fire, a commander theoretically can call it in, and the information infrastructure is so good now that other forces can respond immediately. The information does not have to go through layers of hierarchy and paperwork. You have commanders who can instantly see that somebody's in trouble, and send air support, and the nearest unit as backup.

Because of swarm tactics, the unsung heroes of the war are the geeks who are wiring the systems that are supporting the shooters. With swarm tactics you don't necessarily need to secure the rear, and so these geeks from the Signal Brigade were definitely out there on the line. The Signal Brigade can be some of the most dangerous jobs because when you're going out to set up a wireless network, your job is to take a giant antenna and go to the highest ground possible and set it up, which is basically like drawing a big old bull's-eye on your face. You're saying, "shoot me." These guys joke that they have some of the highest mortality rates. They were fatalistic because I don't think they thought, "I might get killed." They're more like, "I'm just going to do my job. I'm just going to do what I'm told."

In the army everybody knows how to fire a gun. Everybody knows how to use a compass. Everybody knows how to read a map, particularly if they're trained to use GPS devices. The convoy leaders I saw were using eTrex GPSs and without them, they'd say, "I would have no idea where I was going." One of the guys said to me, " If we run out of batteries, this war is screwed." They are developing the next generation GPS, which is basically a response to the eTrex's of the world. Once again it's going through this long governmental process. The soldiers are like, "Forget it, I'm going to buy my own at Walgreens."

All the troops had GPS systems mounted on the hoods of their trucks that were updated, minute by minute, second by second. A more immediate fear on my part was that you have all these vehicles out in the desert in enemy territory that are running GCCS. What happens if they're ambushed, and what happens if somebody suddenly takes over a truck or a Humvee that hasn't been shut down properly? Imagine if the guy gets shot and the system's running. An Iraqi walks up to it and right there on the screen is a map that shows the position of every U.S. troop. When I asked these questions to the soldiers, they'd say, "There's a number of fail-safes. For instance, if we shut down the vehicles, the system automatically shuts down. If we turn off the engine, it shuts down. If we turn it back on you have to log on." What if you get shot before you could shut it down? "Well, then Plan B is throw a fire grenade into the vehicle." How are you going to throw a grenade if you're already dead? To me that seems to be a major problem. There was no good answer.

We have all these new technology capabilities, and what is surprising to me is the fact that the army is just now using them. A lot of what I saw felt like a field test. This was the first time a lot of these systems, like instant messaging, were being used. One of the great quotes I heard came from a colonel who told me, "I'm sure we'll figure all of this out after the war."

In my story for *Wired*, I described how instant messaging was used. Some soldiers in the field saw a bunch of dead sheep at the side of the road. At the beginning of the war, everybody was completely paranoid about biological and chemical attacks, and so they see a pile of dead sheep and they think they're in the middle of a chemical attack. In previous wars, they would have stopped everything, thrown on their protection suits, and taken a half day or more to deal with this issue. Now somebody typed into their laptop, "This is what we're seeing, can you give us some cultural context?" There was an analyst, I believe in Washington, D.C., who responded, "Hey you know, I've spent a good deal of time in Iraq and I know that this is a very common thing. When animals die in the field they just drag them to the side of the road, pile them up. Don't worry about it, keep rolling."

One of the funny things about this instant messaging is that they were using off-the-shelf programs. They're buying these systems and they're running them on their secret internet, the SIPRNET, so it's not like you or I could send them an instant message; you have to be on that net in order to participate. When you sign up, it assigns you an icon, but a lot of these artillery generals and artillery commanders had no idea how to set it up. They didn't have the time and all they cared about was the functionality. The end result is that they were assigned icons whether they wanted to or not. So you had all these artillery commanders being represented by buxom blondes while they were fighting the war.

Here's another example of how instant messaging worked. This story was told to me by an intelligence officer who said that a group of tanks was rolling into Kabala Gap and the tank commander sent an instant message saying, "We're going to be actually deviating from our previously announced course. We're going to be moving in this new direction. What's the latest intelligence?" An analyst, once again back at the Pentagon, had just received the recent satellite imagery and was studying it when he saw this message because he was participating in the chat room. He just happened to be studying this particular area where this tank battalion was. He saw that there was a group of Iraqi tanks in the direction that these guys were headed and he was able to instant message back saying, "You're headed for an ambush." So this connection flattens the command structure between analysts who are back in the Pentagon and frontline commanders in real time. It allows somebody who would not have been able to participate before to participate.

When Iraqi command posts were overrun, there would obviously be a lot of valuable intelligence, but the intelligence would be in Arabic, and sometimes it would be coded. In previous wars, the evidence or intelligence was boxed up and sent back. Maybe it was deciphered six months or a year later. Now you have a lieutenant whose job it was to go in there and take digital photographs with an off-the-shelf digital camera. He would go back and upload it to the GCCS system, and analysts back in Langley and the Pentagon would have the intelligence translated into English by the next morning. This makes a huge difference. It represents a completely different way of operating in war.

While I was riding in the convoy I always felt in constant fear of an ambush. It was a ninety-seven-vehicle convoy with huge missile launchers and forty-eight wheel trucks. These are the military's largest vehicles. I don't know how much missile launchers weigh, but the Heavy Equipment Transports (HETs) are fifty tons, without the missile launchers on top of them. As we were moving north—for various reasons that have to do with technological breakdown—most of the trucks at the end of the line did not have a radio, though the truck at the very end had a Motorola Talkabout. It had a range of a thousand feet and was the kind people use when they go skiing to keep in touch on the slopes. So, we were rolling along on this freeway, and there's a big berm on the right side of the road, and suddenly there's this pop-pop-pop pop. I didn't know what it was. I never heard AK47 fire before, but the guy who was sitting shotgun flipped off the safety, and started taking a bead on the berm, and said, "Get down!" I dove for the floor, and huddled there while he tried to see where the shots were coming from. I was thinking, "Should I face my butt or my head to the bullets, because they didn't give me a helmet." Since we didn't have a radio, we couldn't call the ambush in. We couldn't call for backup. We were on our own. The convoy's rule was: don't stop, just keep rolling. We drove on for five minutes until there was no more gunfire. None of the bullets had hit our vehicle. Finally when it was clear that there weren't any more gunshots, the sergeant who was sitting shotgun turned back to me and said, "Well, now you're a real war correspondent."

THE CHECKPOINT KILLING
Washington Post Reporter
William Branigin

> "Stop him, Red One, stop him!" He shouted that
> at the top of his voice. . . . Then the Bradley
> opened up with its 25-millimeter cannon."

Two weeks after Baghdad fell, *Washington Post* reporter William Branigin toured its open market for gun sellers in the al Jadidah public plaza. He described the "metal-on-metal sounds of men locking and loading—jamming banana-shaped bullet clips into AK47 assault rifles and working the bolts—then firing bursts into the air." It was like any other Middle Eastern bazaar, except instead of produce, clothing, and trinkets on sale, more than 100 men milled about, buying, selling, examining and test-firing weapons ranging from revolvers to submachine guns. One man was offering an old tommy gun with a cylindrical magazine for the equivalent of forty-six dollars. He said he looted it from a headquarters of Saddam's fedayeen militia. Other weapons for sale included Soviet-designed AK47 assault rifles starting at about twenty-five dollars and at least one U.S. M-16 assault rifle—origin unknown—for eight-four dollars. Abed, the open-air gun dealer, said he had a night-vision device in his shoulder bag and hinted that heavier weapons were available, including the RPG7 rocket-propelled grenade launcher.

Branigin's careful attention to detail came into full worldwide view in April when he wrote about a March 31 civilian shooting outside Karbala. U.S. troops had fired on a Land Rover packed with thirteen Iraqi civilians at an American-held intersection after the driver ignored shouts and warning shots. Despite being an embed with the U.S. Army's Third Infantry Division, his description of the sequence of events that led up to the shooting and the deaths that followed were at odds with the Pentagon's account. But the experienced fifty-year-old foreign correspondent, who served in Bangkok, Manila, and Mexico

City news bureaus, stuck to his journalistic guns, contrary to Pentagon-sourced reports in key U.S. newspapers and wire services around the world. Only Branigin got it right.

■ ■ ■

I covered the first Gulf War. I figured this time around I would try not to repeat the mistakes I made then. In the Gulf War, I started out in what they called a CUCV—basically a Chevy Blazer painted tan, essentially an SUV. I was in that with a public affairs officer (PAO). We were going across the desert trying to keep up with tracked vehicles. It was horrendous for a few reasons. One was trying to go fast over the desert in a vehicle that bounced around like crazy. But the real problem was that we just had no idea what was going on as the cavalry division made its famous left hook. We had no radio communications in that vehicle and we traveled at night. Of course we could not see anything anyway. Later on I transferred to a medical track. It just made a world of difference. Not only was the ride a lot smoother, but I could put on a radio headset and hear what was going on. I could hear commanders giving orders. In those situations, it's much more important what you can hear than what you can see. A lot of time you'd drive all through the night and there was nothing to see anyway. And even in the daytime, all you could see was a huge cloud of dust. That was the main lesson I took from the Gulf War. You had to be on the net—the network of military communications.

This war I spent most of my time in an M88, an armored recovery vehicle. It's a fifty-six-ton monster. The only thing heavier is an Abrams tank. Its purpose is to pull tanks and other armored vehicles out of the mud when they get stuck. It can tow a tank. There are four hatches and three crew members. I sat in back, and could pop up any time out of my own hatch whenever I wanted to and see what was going on. I also had a CVC helmet with a radio headset. I could not only hear what was going on, but could also speak to the three guys on my vehicle, and even to the company commander, as long as it was an appropriate time to break in.

A couple of days were spent pulling tanks and Bradleys out of marshes. One day, we spent nine hours in one marsh, and got stuck three times. It really felt like I was wasting my time. Fortunately, this was during a pause and not much was going on anyway. Still, it was frustrating. The M88 certainly had its advantages. The major tradeoff was having to be with that vehicle when it was doing mundane things.

It was pretty uncomfortable being inside the M88. But I knew from experience it could be worse. There was a box in the back that was like a plastic footlocker that I sat on. When I wanted to see what was going on, I would open the hatch and stand on that. I would try to take precautions but see as much as I could. The important thing was the headset, and I had that on most of the time. A lot of times, I would have to write my stories sitting on that box while we were moving. With an eight-hour time difference, there were many times I was up until 1:00 to 2:00 A.M. filing. I had an Iridium satellite phone with an antenna attachment that consisted of a wire with a magnet on the end. I would open the hatch and stick the antenna magnet outside, usually on top of the 50-caliber machine gun, which was the highest point on the vehicle. That worked pretty well. Sometimes I would plug my computer into an inverter that was hooked up to one of the vehicle's batteries, but I couldn't do this all the time, especially when the engine was not running. So I had to be very aware of the battery power of my computer. Sometimes I would write out my story longhand and then type it on my computer to save power. At the end of some days, I was so tired that I was falling asleep at the keyboard. Having no lights at night was also a problem. I often had to read my notes and type by the light of my computer screen, and even that had to be blocked because we were under blackout conditions. The crew would complain from time to time that they could see light coming up out of the hatch from the computer screen.

The M88's ride was fairly smooth. Not like it is in a vehicle with tires. The M88 has tracks like a tank. The only thing smoother that I rode in was an Abrams. The trouble was that dust covered everything. It would get into the computer, an IBM ThinkPad. I had a shaving brush that I would constantly use to wipe dust off my computer keyboard and screen. I really worried that the dust would cause the computer to conk out on me.

I didn't want to spend the war only watching tanks being pulled out of a ditch. In fact, there was this one occasion where the battalion was moving forward and the M88 I was on was ordered to haul some piece of equipment back to the maintenance point. Which meant that we would be way behind. Earlier, I'd written a story quoting the guy who gave that order, and he was very happy with the story. His relatives saw it and knew he was okay. So, when this was happening, I told him that if the M88 has to go back, I really have to get off it and get on something that is going forward. So he changed his mind and let us go ahead. By then the battalion was pretty well split up. We were scattered.

One day, there was a small group which included the M88, a couple of other tracked vehicles, and an M113 medical track. We were in a position under some trees off the highway southwest of Karbala, near a farmhouse. The area was very rural. I was sitting in the vehicle listening on my CVC to the company commander communicate with his platoon. The company was holding Highway 9 and controlling this intersection of a road that goes to the east at the same level basically as the town of Hilla, but it doesn't lead to Hilla. This one platoon was on the road that comes from the east and then deadends into a T-junction on Highway 9. It was from that direction that this vehicle came. It was a paved road, not dirt, but it was a rural area, and the commander saw this vehicle coming. He started to become very alarmed. Two days before, there had been a suicide car bombing and four soldiers of the First Brigade had been killed. That happened south of where we were, in a place we had come from, but the commanders were still spooked by this. It was the same division. The word had gone out to be wary of suicide bombers. For that reason, my battalion was not going to go anywhere near a vehicle or let any vehicles come near them. So this vehicle was approaching fairly fast, from what I understand. The platoon that was out there was apparently not paying attention, was not ready for it. The commander's voice became louder and louder until he was shouting, "Fire a warning shot!" He ordered them to fire a 7.62 round from the Bradley's machine gun. He yelled, "Fire into the engine block." I was about a mile away in the M88, listening and writing notes. Then he was shouting: "Stop fucking around!" Finally he shouted, "Stop him, Red One, stop him!" Red One was the code name for the platoon leader. He shouted that at the top of his voice. Then the Bradley opened up with its 25-millimeter cannon. It sounded like five or six rounds in rapid succession. That just destroyed the vehicle. Then the commander said what I later reported: "You just fucking killed a family because you didn't fire a warning shot soon enough!"

I had tried to keep up and write it all down as best I could. I was writing by hand in my notebook. The commander was really angry. At about this time, the medical track with us sped off to go to the scene. I regretted that I wasn't aware it would immediately leave, and it didn't occur to me to jump out and say "Wait a minute. Can I go with you?" I just couldn't tell the vehicle I was in, the M88, to go somewhere. It is a big tracked vehicle, and it had orders to stay put. I was probably a mile away. I could see the scene on the highway when I popped up. After a while, a crowd gathered on the highway.

The military commanders all said from day one that they understood embedding was going be for better or for worse. I attended the first media boot camp held in several different places, mostly with the Marines at Quantico. Everybody had said they realized we would have to tell the truth and that there was gonna be stuff they didn't like. Later, I was able to interview the medics and get a clearer picture of what happened. The regret I have was not being able to get to that scene. But my main concern was the conversations back and forth on the radio. A few days afterward, we drove by the scene. The vehicle was still there by the side of the road. It was an old Land Rover and it very unfortunately fit the profile of a suicide bomb vehicle. Apparently these old SUVs were what was being used by suicide bombers.

I later talked to doctors and an Arabic interpreter who had talked to the survivors. They said that they were on their way to Najaf but it was never really clear why. It wasn't clear whether they were fleeing someplace, or just that they were on their way to see relatives in Najaf.

At the time, the officers said the division was going to investigate it. In the end, no disciplinary action was taken. It was judged to be an unfortunate accident. Nothing ever happened to the platoon leader, and he stayed in his position. In fact, the following day, in sort of a bizarre atonement, a family came up to the checkpoint position. It was an Iraqi farmer and his wife and a son who was about ten years old. They had a daughter about three years old who was having a lot of difficulty breathing. They said she was dying and asked if the soldiers could help. This platoon leader's Bradley ended up being the one that took them to the American medical aid station where they saved the girl's life. She had pneumonia.

I talked to the platoon leader the next day briefly. He claimed that he had fired a warning shot. He said the vehicle was coming in at a high speed. He said it had not behaved the way all the others had when they approached and saw the Americans. The other vehicles would then just turn around. But the real dilemma here was that they didn't have any warning signs out or concertina wire across the road. On the one hand, that sort of thing is really necessary to prevent civilians from injury in that exact situation. On the other hand, there was still a war going on, and you do not want to advertise your presence.

Well, I felt sorry for everybody, for the family, for the survivors. It was just a terrible tragedy. One woman had lost her two children who were sitting on her lap. There were fifteen to sixteen people crammed into this vehicle. The adults had children on their laps. Which is why all the children died and some of the adults survived. That was really tragic. I also felt sorry for this platoon and the platoon leader, who was a twenty-three-year-old lieutenant and very earnest. It's also a terrible burden for him to bear.

Personally, I've seen things like this happen before. I'm sure I would have been affected more viscerally if I had seen the bodies. But just listening to it like that, I was a bit removed from it. So it didn't have as strong an impact on me as it might have otherwise.

The Pentagon was giving a much different version than what I reported for the *Washington Post*. So my editors asked me to provide some more details and to basically work it into my story the next day, to report on the aftermath and confirm exactly what happened. The Pentagon was saying there were seven dead, out of thirteen people in the vehicle. I went back and checked again. It was actually ten dead on the spot. Another passenger was evacuated with critical injuries, and he died later at an American field hospital. That brought the toll to eleven. A medic had given the surviving family members ten body bags. Apparently the Pentagon's initial lower figures came from the platoon leader before they removed the bodies from the vehicles. One mistake I made: It was a Land Rover. I initially understood it to be a Land Cruiser, a Toyota. So that was a mistake I had to correct the next day.

The assistant managing editor for foreign news, Phil Bennett, said he thought it was a very important story and was done well. It was some time later in Baghdad that my colleague, Peter Baker, told me he had written a piece for the *American Journalism Review* in which he cited my reporting as an example that being embedded didn't mean "in bed." The only comment I got from the battalion commander was, "I read your story." That was all he said. I said, "Well, you know, it was real unfortunate that the shooting happened." He just left it at that.

WHAT ROMANCE ABOARD THE WAR BOAT?

Jerusalem Post Reporter Janine Zacharia

"If people fall in love on the ship and get married, they're immediately separated after that and sent to different ships or different spots in the navy."

Embedded reporter Janine Zacharia thought she'd have plenty of free time aboard the USS *Theodore Roosevelt* so she brought along a copy of Gabriel Marquez's *Love in the Time of Cholera*. But the Washington bureau chief for the *Jerusalem Post*—Israel's English-language daily newspaper—quickly realized that the supersized aircraft carrier lacked certain cruise liner amenities. "I couldn't bring a drink and chair up on the flight deck, and start reading my book," said the twenty-nine-year-old Melville, New York, native, who spent five years in Israel as a reporter for the *Jerusalem Report* and Reuter's News Agency. As part of her three-week stint with the *TR* (that's what U.S. Navy personnel call the mammoth vessel), she lived and moved freely among the 5,500 residents of this floating city in the eastern Mediterranean Sea.

■　　■　　■

The *Jerusalem Post* got two embed slots—one for maritime and one for ground troops. The paper decided to send me to the maritime slot. The Pentagon told me about a week before I left that I needed to be in Cyprus by a certain day, and from there I would be boarding the *Theodore Roosevelt*. So that was pretty much the way it worked out.

To prepare, I read up on aircraft carriers and ships and satellite-guided bombs. I met with retired Rear Admiral Steven Baker, who had been on the *Theodore Roosevelt* during the first Gulf War. He gave me some good background as well. I had some experience covering Israeli military things— weapons and things like that, but this was my first time actually covering a real full-scale war to any extent.

We were eleven embeds on the ship, including a British photographer who was based in India, an AP photographer, a producer and on-camera guy for German television's VDF, a CNN reporter, a Russian reporter, and a reporter from the NBC affiliate in Norfolk, Virginia, which is the TR's base. In addition, you had embarks—people who would come for one day or two just to do a quick feature and then get off. They didn't really get the access that we had.

There were very few places that were off limits to us. One place we couldn't see was the nuclear reactor, or reactors; I believe there were two. There were definitely, of course, classified rooms, but we could ask to go into those and then they would take down computer screens that were showing classified material. So we had a pretty good run across the ship from talking to pilots, walking through the hangar bay, going up to the bridge.

The bridge is not very exciting. The captain goes up there usually to watch planes returning or taking off. There's a lot of people standing around, looking out, doing all different kinds of things. I didn't really understand initially the science of steering the ship into the wind, and getting a certain speed of wind, except for when the planes are landing. It's really a quite precise science. It's impressive. I was there twenty-four days, and it's just amazing every time you watch a landing. These pilots consider themselves the top. They talked down a lot about how the air force has 10,000 feet to land on and then they go off and have a beer, whereas these guys are on these ships for six to nine months. These pilots land in 400 feet and so they think it's a lot more challenging. There was one squadron as a whole in particular, which is known as "The Hunters," and they were the first U.S. Navy reserve fighter squadron called up in fifteen years. They weren't expected to be called up, and they filled the hole in this air wing.

There's a hierarchy within the air wing itself. The F/A-18 pilots are definitely the top. They are older; they're all reservists; most of them fly for American and United. They were the elite pilots on board. They exhibited real leadership. They competed among themselves in terms of landings. They'd have tail-hook contests. When they're not flying, they serve as landing service officers and they go out and watch their colleagues land. They give them grades for the angle, the speed, the approach on a scale of zero to four. So it's pretty competitive in a friendly kind of way.

You've got 102 pilots on the ship and there's 5,000 people, with 1,900 of them serving these pilots, basically. Each squadron comes with its own maintenance people, who work on their planes; they know the pilots and they all work together as a team. There are tons of people running around working on these planes. It's twenty-year-olds working on engines. It's pretty extraordinary. The pilots were all kings and queens, but the most regal were definitely the F/A-18 pilots. There were three F/A-18 squadrons on board. I never saw more than five or six women pilots. There were 800 women aboard. Women have only been on the aircraft carriers since 1993. They pretty much do everything that the men do. It seems to me they were well integrated. Doing everything the men do—up on the flight deck, in the hanger bay, making sure planes fit into certain spots, directing people on the flight deck to make sure everybody's in the right spot—everything from the menial sort of labor to flying. They do pretty much everything that makes that ship work.

Sex is forbidden on the ship. It's definitely forbidden for the enlisted, and forbidden between officers and enlisted; when you talk to officers, it's a little bit looser. There is a no physical contact rule. One woman said to me, "You know, I can't be making sure that this twenty-million-dollar F-14 fits into its right spot while I'm worried about whether my boyfriend's mad at me or not." So they kind of all get it. It doesn't mean that there's not people hooking up on the ship. They definitely are. In fact, when I was there, I think one couple got caught, and they had to have a meeting with the senior enlisted person. They really look down on any kind of sexual anything.

The activities are very 1950s on board. They had an ice cream social one night with karaoke. An enlisted woman got up to sing *Respect* by Aretha Franklin, and the guys were really getting into it. They were cheering and she started swaying a little bit, but the command master chief, this woman, shook her finger, got up behind her on the stage, and stood there with her arms crossed to make sure that she didn't sway.

When I talked to the command master chief about this "no relationship" thing, she said, "I can't let this deteriorate into the dating game." If people fall in love on the ship and get married, they're immediately separated after that, and sent to different ships, or different spots in the navy. They're not allowed to stay together. The navy wants them to stay focused on their jobs. That's why people work fifteen, sixteen hours a day.

The other thing is that the ship is totally dry. They are allowed two beers after forty-two or fifty-two days at sea, which is a big deal. So they have O'Doul's. During one Saturday night, the executive officer was hanging out with some of the pilots for some pizza, and bought a round for me and some pilots. It was kind of ridiculous! It was O'Doul's nonalcoholic beer!

This culture, where they want to keep everybody focused, is puritanical in many ways. Apart from no touching and no drinking, there's a lot of prayer on the ship. A lot of people told me that they need religion. You had four full-time Christian chaplains on board. Their services were always being advertised on the internal TV networks: "Come to a Methodist prayer service," "Come to a Baptist service," "Church services on Sundays." Every night at 10:00 P.M. One of the chaplains would do an evening prayer on the PA system: "Heavenly Father, thank you for bringing home all of *TR*'s people safely and for protecting us out here." There was another time during the *TR* Madness Basketball Tournament, which mimicked the NCAA's March Madness—they had twenty-four teams—and during the finals, everybody just stopped in their tracks during the prayer. Everyone bent down on one knee—people were really devout, which I thought was very striking. You go on a carrier for six to nine months; you need something to sustain you.

Initially, I did a lot of reporting about the ship's protection systems. It has its antimissile system. I thought about the USS *Cole* in the beginning, but we weren't porting, for one, and being in the Med, I felt very safe in this city. These floating cities cost billions. They give the U.S. a real strategic advantage. You have the perfect example when planes weren't able to take off from Turkey because they weren't able to base there. They just put the carrier right off the shore and then they could do whatever they wanted; they don't need basing rights with these ships. It gives them a real advantage when it comes to combat.

Among the enlisted, there was very little understanding of the politics in the Middle East. These were mostly college-age kids, so they were kind of the equivalent of college kids in America. If you do a poll of college kids in America, they probably don't know much about the difference between Iraq and Iran, or who the prime minister of Israel is either. So I tried to keep that in mind when I was talking to people. One person said to me, "Yeah, we're going to take control of Iraq, and we're going to hand it over to Sharon." When I mentioned Israel, they would say, "Oh, were you scared to live there?" What struck me was that most of them weren't really concerned about ousting Saddam, but about when were they going home. That was really the main question—when were they going home. That's all they wanted to know.

They had been on the ship for ten months. They were turned around on their way home when they were sent back to the Gulf. Ten months on the carrier is an extraordinary amount of time. You've got these young parents. It's extraordinary that these people choose to enlist. When you talk to them, they tell you it's either they want to see the world, or maybe financially to help pay for education, or they always wanted to be in the navy. A lot of people come from families of navy people, but when I saw this young mother—they had a program where they would read children's stories on camera and then they would mail a video home—crying as she's reading the *Three Little Pigs*, I'm like, "What are you doing here? There's no other job for you?"

Once the actual war started, the ship shifted to this night schedule, but life changed very little for the people on board. They were putting real bombs on the planes as opposed to dummies and they were carrying out real missions. You know, if you're a cook, you're a cook, no matter what. If you're a maintenance person, you're going to work on the plane the same way you would no matter what. Even the pilots on their combat missions, this is what they do; this is what they trained for. After a combat mission, they'd come back, take a shower, watch a movie, go to sleep, and they'd start another day. You eat, you sleep, you do your job, and maybe you work out, and that's pretty much what you do.

Toward the end, when the story was becoming a little bit repetitive, I felt like it was time to go. All the embeds pretty much drew the same conclusion about the same time. The war had moved fully to the ground troops, and most of us left around the same time.

The rules were they wanted us to stay the duration. But we could leave whenever we wanted to. We had flexibility that the guys with ground troops really didn't have. I was flown in a helicopter to Cyprus. From there, I flew to Tel Aviv, and spent nearly two weeks in Israel before coming back to D.C.

I think the embed process overall was very good. You had to be skeptical a little bit when the Pentagon praised it, and it was frustrating watching a lot of the coverage from the ship. I felt completely disconnected about being there. I would call contacts of mine in Washington to find out how the war was going. They had a phone line dedicated for use by journalists, so that was kind of nice. It was like a regular phone line that routed calls through Norfolk, Virginia, but I also brought a satellite phone. That was kind of tricky because you'd have to go outside and find the signal, and if the ship turned, sometimes you lost it.

In general, being an embed was an invaluable experience. I learned about a completely different part of our country—the navy. I didn't know a lot about the navy, and now I feel like I've acquired a new understanding of something important that's made me excited about military reporting. I had a very positive experience and I haven't talked to many embeds who had a negative experience. Now that I've done sea, I'll probably choose land next time.

ON THE ROAD WITH UNILATERALS
Los Angeles Times Translator and Driver
Mohammed Fahmy

> "People now used the destroyed Jeep as a
> landmark: "Drive to the Terry Lloyd Jeep, turn
> left and drive five more kilometers to the bridge."

Mohammed Fahmy was born in Egypt and emigrated to Canada where he studied at Concordia University and Vancouver City University. He graduated with a degree in marketing and public relations and went to work as a sales manager in a multimedia studio there. At twenty-nine, he had a good life, but his mother lived in Kuwait and pestered him to come visit her. "Her name is Wafa," explains Fahmy, sitting in the lobby of the Kuwait Sheraton in a U.S.-style collegiate sweatshirt. "It means loyalty. She said 'I am getting old. There is no taxes here.' So I flew to Kuwait for a job interview at Kuwait University. To my bad luck, this war started. I had a friend at CNN. One day, he called me up and said the *Los Angeles Times* needed a driver and translator. Our first story was about the camels being moved around because the army was taking their place." By the war's end, Fahmy was battle-tested and an enthusiastic jack-of-all-trades. *L.A. Times* correspondent Tracy Wilkinson said, "To call him merely a translator and driver is terribly inadequate. Mohammed was more like a colleague, helping us plan the next day's stories."

■　■　■

I now realize that the media is much more honest than people think, because when I was working with this amazing crew, they would not use a quote unless they had the full name, the age, and the occupation of the person they interviewed, or else the quote was not valid. This definitely encouraged me to look at journalism in a totally different way.

There were many tense moments being around journalists. Definitely the most intense moment was getting caught in a crossfire at a Basra bridge about four days before the city fell. Civilians were stopped at the checkpoint by the British. I was with Mark Magnier and Brian Rolski, who were speaking to the captains and the soldiers. All of a sudden, incoming mortars started falling. It came from a technical college at the edge of Basra. The civilians started getting out of control. It was chaos. The British, of course, were defensive, and we got caught in the middle. That was the first time I saw myself dead. The strangest thing about this is that during the actual crossfire, Mark grabbed two of the civilians who were panicking, and he was asking them questions as they ducked behind a tank, "Why are you panicking? Where are you going?" I was amazed he could keep his composure. I remember I have never ducked that fast. I was surprised that I was more afraid than actual civilians who were there. That proves that they are used to that, and I am not.

We traveled throughout southern Iraq in our rented Pajero. We went through Safwan. We went to Umm Qasr, then Basra, then Nasiriyah. That is where my role ended. We had been there for a few weeks. We were pretty tired sleeping in the car and outside. No hot showers.

Mark was a unilateral, and we were all proud to be unilaterals because we got more stories. We had more freedom. We got more humanitarian stories. We were able to go to the families' houses. We were able to deal with ex-prisoners. The embedded journalists were just covering the army and how the war was going on. Mark said that the unilaterals are considered the Special Forces of the journalists, because they go in, they do the job, and then they leave.

Sometimes they don't leave. They die. When Terry Lloyd of ITN was killed, we were a good 300 meters away. We were contemplating whether to follow his two-car convoy. It was a very confusing situation. This was during the first few days of the war when most of the unilaterals barged into Iraq through the back way and not through the normal entry. There were about 200 journalists from many news organizations. We were not clear where to go. What roads were safe, which were not. There had been stories that Umm Qasr was secured when it wasn't. What I know exactly is that Terry Lloyd's car went further down toward Basra, to the Azubehr bridge. That is where it happened. The Iraqis were in a pickup truck. but they used the ITN car as a decoy. The American tank crew shot at the people they were going to shoot at but they got them by mistake. Around midafternoon, we went back to the cloverleaf under the bridge where all the journalists were gathered. They huddled close to the British checkpoint. Then the news came that Lloyd had died. The car was completely burned when I saw it. I know that two people are still missing:

the translator who they picked up from the Kuwait Sheraton and the French cameraman. There are reward signs all over Iraq to find them. People now used the destroyed Jeep as a landmark, "Drive to the Terry Lloyd Jeep, turn left, and drive five more kilometers to the bridge."

There was complete paranoia. Some people were saying, "No, no, no! This is not true. This is not happening." Then I remember somebody from the *Chicago Tribune* came up to me and he said that there were land mines on the road. I asked, "How did they look?" He said, "They are black and are square." But these were pieces of rubber highway treads from tanks. At this point I knew that there was a lot of confusion. The fog of war — too many journalists driving around together.

Mark was being cautious and intelligent. We did not make any moves unless he spoke to the military, took their opinion, asked if there had been any incoming or outgoing shells. He used a lot of common sense. We all took part.

I was impressed by their ability to work at the end of the day. They ran around from early in the morning. Running around interviewing under the hot sun, eating very little food, driving a lot. Then at the end of the night they had to sit down, and write a good story and file it in the middle of these mosquitoes. There was no light sometimes. The battery plugged into the cigarette lighter.

Of course everybody used a satphone — a Thuraya satphone. As a unilateral you can use it. The embedded, no — because it can actually signal and show the enemy where you are. The other thing about having a satphone is you need it to file. It connects to the Internet. You could either do the battery thing with the car, or you could use a generator like we had. You could use the Kuwaiti cell phone up to Umm Qasr and Safwan. As soon as you get further, you had to use a satphone. I was impressed when they had to work under their blankets because the army would say we don't want any lights in the area.

I also did some editing for them, checked the Arabic names, checked the spelling. I made sure the feel of the story was right because I was translating everything that he was putting there. He wanted to make sure he didn't write a wrong word here. This really amazed me — very careful, very honest.

They paid me $400 a day. I saved some of the money and used some of it to visit my girlfriend in Dubai. She is Iraqi. We had a lot of fights about this war. I told her that the war was the best thing that ever happened to her country. We had a big fight. She had mixed emotions. She said, "Oh, civilians are going to die!" I said, "Listen, this Saddam guy has killed a million already. He even forecasts how many people he will execute." In fact, Mark and I had found documents in a police station in Safwan that said 50,000 Iraqis would be executed the next month. We had gone inside the building while it was burning. We even went to some of the prisons where there were files of people who had been executed. I have so much pride uncovering these documents. I felt that I was more than a driver and translator. We were a team.

MISHANDLED BY HIS IRAQI MINDERS

New York Times
Staff Photographer
Tyler Hicks

> "A symbol of the whole regime collapsing was Iraqi civilians running down the street with Uday Hussein's prize racehorses in tow. Some of them were white."

It's late afternoon on the last day of April, 2003, and *New York Times* staff photographer Tyler Hicks, thirty-three, is finally able to relax in his hotel room at the Baghdad Sheraton. The sun in streaming through the window. Down below at street level, you can see the Tigris River. Though Hicks is nursing a minor head cold, he is far removed from the non-stop, hectic, life-and-death conditions he experienced throughout the war. Thin, graceful, and poised, he sits on the couch in a casual T-shirt, surrounded by laptops, satellite transmitters, digital cameras, and satphones. His words come slowly, sometimes abstractly, a reflection of his immersion in symbols and images formed in the midst of chaos.

In 1997, Hicks decided to devote himself to serious photography. He quit a staff job at a small newspaper in the Midwest and started to cover Kosovo as a freelancer, joining mentors in the risky calling of combat photography. By 9/11, Hicks' work earned him a staff position shooting for *The New York Times* in Afghanistan where he distinguished himself covering Operation Anaconda. In Iraq, Hicks' work spectacularly caught the explosions on the first night of shock and awe, and the surreal atmosphere of looting, and the occupation of Saddam's palaces by country boys from the U.S. military.

■ ■ ■

I grew up in Westport, Connecticut, so I spent my weekends in New York City. I would go to a museum or photo book store. I spent hours, and hours, and days, and weeks doing this. There were so many people who inspired me, like those first war photographers such as Matthew Brady, lugging his huge eight-by-ten view cameras—him and his mule. Talk about serious commitment there. Some of the photographers working in the Vietnam War, like Don McCullin and Larry Burrows, were guys doing absolutely amazing work. They really got me excited about getting out there and doing photography in a serious manner. So, after studying photography and journalism at Boston University, my first job was at a small newspaper in rural Ohio. The Troy Daily News is a small, 14,000 circulation daily paper. I was there for about a year. I then moved on to the Wilmington, North Carolina Morning Star which is about a 60,000 circulation daily. I spent nearly four years there. Then I began to really think about what I wanted to do in photography and why I was taking pictures. I came to the conclusion that what I was doing was not satisfying. I didn't feel like my pictures meant anything. That was very important. I needed a new, more serious direction. But that experience at both those newspapers was very good—learning about photography, and light, and different situations. It helped me when I actually did go out into the field. Then I didn't have to worry about a lot of things. I felt a little more grounded.

I decided to visit Kosovo in late 1997 for the first time. The Serbs were in full swing with their ethnic cleansing. The ethnic Albanians had not yet formed the KLA. I didn't know a whole lot about what was going on there. I checked it out, to see what was going on. It had been in the news, but it was not a big story yet. It was something that I just gravitated toward. I got there and was absolutely shocked at what I saw. I saw an entire culture of people being abused by another. Massacred. It was my first exposure to a growing wartime situation. It was very clear to me who were the good guys and who were the bad guys. It made me think about what you can do with photography. It can be used as a tool to get your message across. I wanted to be a part of that effort.

My first trip to Iraq was in the beginning of October. It was followed up by two more trips. This having been the last one, of course.

The heavy bombing started the second night we saw bombs fall. There were a couple of small hits the night before. There was a big concern about having a view. We knew the bombs were coming. We were on the east side of the Tigris, which is a residential area, whereas the west side was where all the palaces, government buildings, all these things, were. We knew that's where the targets were. We knew that these two hotels, the Palestine and the Sheraton, would became the frontline viewing platforms for journalists. Some people had hotel suites with panoramic views. Unfortunately, we weren't allowed to stay in this hotel before. I didn't have one of these rooms. I only had a partial view. That night we went and got onto the roof. We had to push a partially broken door that was the entrance to the roof; we kind of helped it off its hinges the rest of the way. It started out with a small group of us on the roof, but it quickly grew. The word spread that there was a view up there, and so we were taking pictures. We were able to shoot the whole thing. You could actually hear the cruise missiles come straight over the hotel and then smash into these palaces on the other side of the river bank, with Iraqi anti-aircraft fire going up all around the hotel as just one after another cruise missile came over.

I had my camera steadied on the hotel ledge with a jacket, so I was able to photograph the whole thing. It was really quite amazing to watch. We hadn't, in nearly six months of covering Iraq off and on—depending on whether I had a visa or not—been allowed to take pictures of any palace building. Suddenly we found ourselves taking pictures of these palaces bursting into flames. So, it was quite an exhilarating experience. I can only imagine what it was like for the Iraqi civilians to watch this, having lived under this regime for twenty-five years. But it was a good feeling. Something everyone was quite happy to see.

Still, it was a little unsettling to see the cruise missiles coming in quite low over our heads. They sound like a low-flying aircraft, a bit more high pitched. You hear it coming for some time. It becomes quite loud. You can quite literally hear it passing right overhead. I don't know how high it actually was, but it sounded like when you are at an airport, and you hear an airplane landing. When they hit the buildings you can feel the percussion from it. After the big wave of bombing ended, we didn't know if there was more coming. A group of ministry thugs appeared on the top of the roof and told everyone to get off of the roof. We brushed them off. We thought, "They'll go away." They immediately came after photographers. They smashed several video cameras, and threw one photographer's camera, which was still attached to the tripod, off the edge of the roof. This started a mad scramble of people to get off the roof and run down the stairway, to get your pictures out of there. You didn't want your camera taken away with the disk of flashcards.

It was amazing that the ministry of information and the press center functioned up until the very last day. We were forced to work with the Iraqi ministry of information at the press center. It's a Mukhabarat organization, which is designed to watch what you do and extort as much money from you as they can while they are doing that. There were the fees imposed on journalists: satphone fee, one hundred dollars a day; press center fee, additional one hundred dollars a day. The rules were you had to use the satphone only at the ministry of information. You couldn't have a satphone in your room. Of course, a lot of people did so, but it was difficult to work. You couldn't have your dish out on the balcony. You had to close the curtain and try to get a signal through the curtain from inside. You had to make sure the door was locked. In the latter part of the war, when we were at the Palestine Hotel, they actually would have guys come around looking for people using satphones in their rooms. They would come and bang on the door. Next thing you know, they were in the room looking around. You'd have to be ready to stash the phone pretty quickly.

The government-appointed minders made working as a photographer very difficult. It was extremely frustrating, going around the city but not being able to take pictures. No photos of any government buildings. There was a long list of things we were not allowed to photograph. Because of the high profile of *The New York Times*, we had the most strict of any of the minders. Our minder on this last trip was an ex-general in the Iraqi army. He served in the Gulf War and fought Americans. He had been injured by Americans. He would proudly display a scar on his hand, which was achieved by an American bullet. This guy was obviously the real thing, and he presented himself to us as our new minder, and he was the lowest of the low of these guys, a real bad guy. He was extremely strict. He had an attitude, a military demeanor about him. He would have temper tantrums when he felt that we had done something out of his control. These temper tantrums in the form of a drill sergeant yelling at a soldier. He eventually disappeared for a while, which was an enormous relief to us. The next time he resurfaced was at our room in the Palestine Hotel. This was in the last week of the war. He arrived with two strongmen, two big thugs also from the Mukhabarat. I was sharing a room with John Burns, *The New York Times* correspondent. I had gone out to photograph something; I can't remember what it was now. All of our laptop computers were gathered, four computers, as was an $8,000 satellite telephone, one of my digital cameras, the lens and $6,000 in cash. While they were in the room, collecting this equipment, they accused Burns of being in the CIA. They threatened him. The most disturbing part about it was their childlike behavior in rummaging through our box of food, filling their pockets with tins of tuna, and then pouring chocolates down their mouths, and literally fighting over chocolates. These are grown men. To me, really, this is such a clear indication of the desperation of the last days of the regime. Coming, demanding money, stealing equipment, and even taking everything that they could get their hands on. Then they said, "We'll be back in five minutes," and we never saw them again.

I was left with one camera. I had friends with computers who helped me get by. Burns went over to the manager of the Palestine Hotel and said that we had been ripped off by those guys. Because they had been staying at the hotel, the manager opened the room they had been staying in and they had left my own computer there. They had taken everything else. But for some strange reason, they were in a rush and didn't take this one. I was quite relieved to have it back.

The ministry people weren't around any more as American tanks advanced along the western edge of the Tigris River. Iraqi soldiers were running up the river bank, some in their underwear, abandoning the palace grounds. We knew the war was over, but we were reluctant to drive around. We didn't know what was going on. Being here, you had very little information. We didn't know where the Americans were. We didn't know where Iraqis were and what their reaction would be to us driving around. I talked to a few other photographers who had done some probes around and had seen some looting, but they hadn't really gotten, or done much with it yet. Everyone was testing the waters at that point, which was smart. We got two cars of people together, and headed out in the direction of Saddam City. Immediately we saw widespread looting going on. It was as if the people were waiting eagerly. I imagine that people had things scoped out for quite some time, and were just waiting for this day. People were perfectly happy.

The first thing that I saw that was a symbol of the whole regime collapsing was Iraqi civilians running down the street with Uday Hussein's prize racehorses in tow. Some of them were white. He had a large collection of very expensive racehorses, and these guys were running down the street, not riding them, but leading them with a rope tied around their neck and running them down the street. No saddle or anything. Others were pushing his white BMW down the street. Nothing was sacred. Literally the only things that were immune from looting were the mosques. Maybe not all of them, but for the most part.

As we took pictures and proceeded toward Saddam City, we saw the first Americans who we were able to see during this war. Several tanks by the side of the road were securing the road, soldiers on foot, taking up position. We immediately got out of the car and we were taking pictures of them. Started talking to them and thanking them for getting there. We obviously were waiting a long time for them to arrive. There was fear among us that we would be used as collateral and taken hostage. Taken as prisoners. Accused of being spies. This was a real concern. Especially with the amounts of corruption going on, and also, some of our friends and colleagues were taken to Abu Ghraib prison—four or five people. Two from *Newsday* and Mollie Bingham, an American freelance photographer; and two others who disappeared. They were arrested. Taken to Abu Ghraib, which is one of the world's most notorious prisons. It is really a nasty place. I had been out there before.

The first time we went into one of the palaces was a bizarre experience. It felt like you were trespassing in somebody's home. It hadn't yet been stripped by looters. It was one of Uday's palaces. It had ornate, gaudy decoration, but very little sense of taste.

What was dangerous was the looting specifically of banks. The looting of the palaces were done by civilians. They wanted some furniture and some things. It was a large-scale domino effect going on in the city. If everyone else is doing it, I might as well get in on the action, too. Then, over time, a different type of looter came, which were the armed thugs. Real gangs. Real bad guys.

There was one incident where a bank was being looted. I was actually at a gutted and looted library doing a story about it across the street. I didn't know it was a bank. I walked across the street to see what was going on. At that time, gunfire erupted inside the building I was standing next to, which I then realized was a bank. This time I was not interested in being around sporadic gunfire. So I was about to head back across the street to the library where I'd been, when two guys with Iraqi-made AK47s ran out of the bank and grabbed my camera and bag. Two other men intervened to try and help me out of it. A large argument and a crowd formed. There was a lot of tugging and pulling. I wasn't keen on fighting for my equipment. It's never smart to fight for a thing with armed men. You always give it up. Because I was surrounded by a crowd, and these guys were working on getting me out of the situation, I eventually pulled away, and managed to run down the street and get out of there.

At this point, there is not one war image that sums it all up for me. Although our movements were incredibly restricted, it still was a very important part of the story. I felt that I have the understanding of how people were living under that regime. When it unraveled it became very revealing. It was revealing while we were here. Seeing people live the way they were living. I think the pictures of the last days of the regime will have the most lasting value. This was before the looting. Despite the amount of restrictions we had on us, these were images we were still able to take and are not ever going to be repeated. We will never see these things again.

There were different things that offered small glimpses into the Iraqi military regime. one of which was a rumor that circulated very quickly that people had seen a parachute landing in the Tigris River. An enormous crowd gathered. Before we knew it, everyone has seen the parachute. You had soldiers beating the bushes; lighting them on fire; shooting aimlessly into the bushes.

In another incident there was a destroyed American tank on the road toward the airport. The Americans had just secured the airport. The ministry allowed us to photograph this scene where the battle had taken place, and the Iraqis were claiming a big victory.

I saw these old-looking soldiers with bayonets and knives and very aggressive guys looking very victorious. I could only think to myself, "What are these guys thinking? They must be terrified." They were told that they had to come out and jump up and down on a tank, and allow the media to photograph them. It was some kind of last-ditch attempt to rally the troops, but you could see that all of these guys were going to ditch their uniforms in a matter of days, if not hours, and be back at home hiding.

ABSURDITY OF WAR
British Lieutenant Colonel Robert Partridge, Public Affairs Officer

"My speciality is making guns go bang in the film industry."

Lieutenant Colonel Robert Partridge looks like he could easily play one of those world-weary British officers sitting around the luxury hotel in Damascus in *Lawrence of Arabia*, waiting to cut a treaty with a desert sheik. In the Iraq War, he served as the senior British media operations officer in Kuwait City, riding civilized herd on outraged journalists who thought the Brits were too restrictive and constraining. But he belies the stiff-lipped career officer caricature popularized in film. How, you might ask? Partridge's embrace of cinematic absurdity was honed during his civilian career as a special effects technician on feature movies made in Great Britain.

■　■　■

I am the deputy director of the Coalition Press Information Center in Kuwait. I am a reserve. Back home, I am a special effects technician. I own a special effects company making movies. I've been doing this for eight years now. The most recent films I worked on were *I Spy* with Eddie Murphy in Budapest, and *Gosford Park*. My specialty is making guns go bang in the film industry. Special effects, not via computer. These are physical effects on location.

My dual career actually followed a very natural path. I joined light infantry. Served for six years. No battle experience. I have a big yellow streak down my back. I moved into media operations when the army found I did this for a job. They said, "Come help us do what you do," simply because I understand the camera.

Because it is a bit like a busman's holiday in the U.K., I tend not to like war movies. But if you want a few, I think Robert Altman's *M*A*S*H* was fantastic. In fact, I did *Gosford Park* with Robert Altman, which was great if you like a bit of closure. I saw *Apocalypse Now* as a very young man and I enjoyed its action. But as I watched it again and again, I saw the parallels with the *Heart of Darkness* by Joseph Conrad and Marlon Brando's Kurtz, and the kind of way that it showed the further we got up the river, the more we separated from civilization, and the more bizarre becomes the behavior of people in war.

Here at the Hilton we had this Russian harpist playing for us in this air-conditioned luxury with all these shops. When the missiles started flying over nightly, we'd suddenly get into all our protection suits. On the Kuwaiti weekends—Thursday and Friday—giant Disney characters would walk around the hotel lobby and nearby streets. Bugs Bunny came round this one corner and there was a young soldier in his MOPP suit with his gun. He is unsure if Bugs Bunny is a terrorist or not. At that time, the Scud alarm is going off, "Wah Wah." If I had written this in a script, no one would ever believe it. Then I hear a boom as a bomb goes off down the road. We take off our respirators, we unzip our ridiculous protection suits. And we all go and eat smoked salmon while the Russian harpist plays, and then we do it all again. We get into our cars. We put on all body armor, we drive up the road into Iraq while thinking, "Hang on! Somebody actually wants to kill me here." Then you come back to the Hilton again. It was very strange. If I were to write *Public Affairs, Private Lives*, which I might well write, it would be more like M*A*S*H than *Apocalypse Now*.

In our work, we see a lot of the images the media produces about war, but only a few really stay with you. That picture of the armless boy, Ali, in the hospital with those burns—that as a father, must grip anybody. How can it not? It is very difficult to say, "I didn't do that." We all did it. Those who sent us did it. Those who voted for it, and those who did not. There are no innocents in this—except children like him, which is very sad. As a parent, it is very difficult. I was talking to my colleagues here, and at various times we talked about what gets to us, and it is always the children. Grownups want to dress up in combat gear and shoot each other. All right. Fine. But when you bring the women and the children into it, that's wrong. This is my only war story. I was in Kosovo and I'd had a bad day. There'd been a shooting. I rang home and spoke to my son who was five at the time. He said, "Oh, how are you, Daddy?" I said, "I'm fine." He said, "Oh, have you been in a battle today?" I said, "I've been in a bit of a battle." I was puffing myself up a bit. He said, "Did you kill anyone in the battle, Daddy?" I replied, "No, I didn't." I started to deflate. Then he said, "Oooh, did you die in the battle, Daddy?" That was it. I lost it, for the rest of the day. To my son, if you shoot someone, you get up at the end, because it's a game to him. I've always remembered that, and I always want to hang on to that conversation, because that's a good reference point as any to war.

"ALL IS VANITY"
Los Angeles Times
Reporter Geoffrey Mohan

"Look, we're destroying large parts of this country, and the first sergeant is worried about litter."

"I'm a staff writer assigned to the Metro desk. I was actually borrowed by foreign for this war," says *Los Angeles Times* reporter Geoffrey Mohan. "I tell people they looked around the newsroom and tried to figure out who they would miss the least." That kind of self-effacing humor has allowed the forty-one-year-old journalist to weather some dicey assigments. Before making the war-correspondent rounds in Afghanistan with just a driver and translator, he had been the Latin America Bureau Chief for *Newsday* for three years. "I was based out of Mexico City and would travel down to Colombia, usually by myself, so I would obviously go wherever the story took me. While I certainly confronted far more outright combat in Iraq, in terms of just an overall sense of menace and danger, Colombia was worse because it's a very, very unpredictable country."

■ ■ ■

I was with the U.S. Army's Second Brigade of the Third Infantry Division, and within that brigade I was in the Fourth Battalion, Sixty-fourth Armor Regiment, and within that I was placed with the C Company, which was known as Cyclone. Being embedded was like going on some sadistic camping trip—ninety-five percent camping and about five percent of hair-raising fighting. Most of the camping I've previously done in the desert was just a few days at a time in Joshua Tree. I was asked in a survey from the Department of Defense what was the worst part about covering the war, and I wrote back on the survey that it was the same thing that GIs complain about—brutal conditions, sleep deprivation, and horrible food.

We had spent forty-eight hours straight driving through the desert to reach the first objective near the city of Najaf, where we met with a lot of mortar fire, small-arms fire, and harassing fire on the supply lines. Afterward, we wound up spending three days locked down tight in the desert between Najaf and Karbala, because of these unbelievable sandstorms. Actually, it was a three-day sandstorm, where visibility at some points was effectively zero. They're really like sand hurricanes. A guy from one of the tanks actually got lost while walking between tanks and spent the whole night outside.

During the sandstorms, I basically stayed inside a Bradley fighting vehicle with four soldiers. The Bradley's living compartment—if you could call it that—is about the size of a suburban half-bath. There was a private who was in the back compartment with me, two guys in the turret, and then a driver, all of whom had to find a place to sleep during the night when we were locked down. One guy would sleep in the turret, another would sleep in a chair that was in the back part of the Bradley, I would sleep kind of piled on the gear, and the other guy would sleep on the floor. The driver would sleep in his own compartment, which was about the only comfortable place in the Bradley; it was a nice reclined seat. If conditions were safe enough, we'd venture outside and sleep on a cot, or on the sand, or sometimes on the back ramp of the Bradley, which I did for several nights.

During the three-day sandstorm, you pretty much had to get out during the day and deal with the wind the best you could, since you would go stir crazy inside the Bradley. But for the most part, you just had to hunker down inside the vehicle. We read magazines, we talked, we chatted, we took naps. A lot of times you were trying to catch up on forty-eight to seventy-two hours of almost no sleep. I had a history book called *The Peace to End All Peace* about the formation of the modern Middle East. It was an appropriately boring tome that would help me get to sleep at night. I also read the book of Ecclesiastes one night from the official battalion Bible that was handed out. It was interesting to read the constant repetition of "all is vanity." Then I actually started on Job. I kept to the austere Old Testament.

We had a copy of *Hustler* and *Maxim* and *Stuff* magazine—one of the several rules that were violated. I don't think anyone was really paying too much attention to that particular rule, although the first sergeant seemed obsessive about litter. He was always demanding people dig trash holes, or burn the trash, and not leave behind too many signs in the desert. That was exactly what people laughed at. They said that over the horizon, you could watch the rockets fly from one side of the horizon to the other, and explode on whatever city or other objective they had in mind, and people would joke, "Look, we're destroying large parts of this country, and the first sergeant is worried about litter." I don't know, maybe it's something genetic in first sergeants, but they're just made to be tough on people for no reason whatsoever.

Once we got up to the outskirts of Baghdad, we ran into a pretty nasty ambush. It was the Medina Division of the Republican Guard. Things went poorly for the American side for the first fifteen, twenty minutes and then quickly turned around, and the American unit managed to chase them out of there. But for a while, it was pretty nasty. It was an intense barrage of rocket-propelled grenades, small-arms fire from AK47s, 30-mm rounds from their armored personnel carriers and tanks. It was very well-coordinated in the beginning. They were aiming at weak points on these Abrams tanks.

In our company, there were fourteen tanks and one Bradley—and that was the Bradley I was in and called in mortars, and artillery, and air strikes in support of the ground battle. The Bradley is set up with communications gear and the tank is a much more spartan arrangement. On a tank you have a driver, a loader, tank commander—they're all working on direct fire. There's no real room on the vehicle to do anything more. The Bradley has an indication system. They can laser targets, so they're tasked to do that as well as do direct fire, which is what this Bradley wound up doing.

From the back of a Bradley, you really don't see a whole lot. There are two small portholes, each the size of about a car stereo, that you could look out of, so they're very hard to see, and it's very hard to see from the back of the Bradley. So much of the battle is very difficult to see firsthand. You could hear it over the radio; you could hear the voices calling out for support, or calling out for help, or alerting other vehicles to attackers that were coming at their flank. It was just a chaotic mix of all kinds of screaming, and yelling, and orders, and counter-orders. People talking over each other. People shouting that their guns were jammed, that they needed help, for instance, or people yelling that they had forty or fifty dismounts—as they call the infantry—coming at them.

During the ambush, I kept wondering just how thick the Bradley's armor was. I was grateful that I couldn't see more than I actually did see because I thought, maybe in that case, ignorance is bliss. Probably if I had seen a bit more of what was going on outside, I might have been a bit more scared. Once the fight was over and we could get out of the vehicle, it was kind of a creepy feeling to stare off into the distance at the tree line, and at different houses, and wonder whether there was anyone crouched, and waiting to fire a rocket-propelled grenade at us. So it was actually pretty frightening.

There were several dozen casualties on the other side and none on ours. There were some slight cuts and wounds to people who got shrapnel from the RPGs, which left fist-sized dents on a lot of these tanks. A few grenades punched some holes in some of the more lightly armored sides of the tanks, but an Abrams tank is extremely hard to penetrate. There are very few vulnerable points on it, the main one being the engine compartment in the rear.

When we were still in Kuwait, before they actually went across the border, they took me out in the tank just to show me how the systems worked. I operated the turret and the gun, in other words, just spinning the turret and moving the gun. I joked with them that I was aiming the gun at different American camps and different vehicles out there just to see what it was like to aim it and move it, and I said there were a few people that would have regretted meeting me that day! It's always interesting to play with these things, even though they are ultimately weapons of death. It's fascinating from a technological viewpoint to see how they work. The Abrams is an amazing bit of technology.

Going through the desert that first forty-eight hours, there were quite a number of tanks, five or six tanks at least, that had breakdowns. They, in fact, replaced entire engines and transmissions—they call them power packs—on several of these tanks. They bring a tank recovery vehicle that has a derrick on it, and it literally lifts the engine right out, drops it down on the sand; they open a crate, take another one, drop it in there, and then four or five guys work on it with wrenches and other tools, and replace an entire engine and transmission in a tank in the middle of the desert in a little bit over an hour. It was like the wartime equivalent of a NASCAR pit stop! The mechanics were the most unheralded part of this operation. These guys were working like galley slaves. When the brigade would stop, their work would just start. Everyone else could relax. They would have to scurry around and fix every piece of machinery from tanks that threw tracks to tanks that needed new engines to Humvees that had broken down. Some of these mechanics had been in the army for a while. Some of them were in their thirties, which is old for the army, but basically everyone out there was a teenager to mid-twenties. So it was a young man's job.

After that ambush we entered Baghdad a few days later and it was fighting all the way into the city. Once the company took one of the entrances to the

Presidential Palace, it then had to fight off vehicles that were flying across this bridge on what seemed to be suicide missions, coming straight at their positions. It was a lot of people in civilian clothes; they were firing weapons at us, so it was clearly aggressive intent. Inexplicably, they would not respond to warning shots, and just keep accelerating, and coming faster and faster at this tank, which is, if you've ever been near a tank that was firing, there's no way you could keep coming at a tank accidentally. I mean, there's nothing subtle about a firing tank. One of the cars that was hit exploded in a way that led me to believe it had to be packed with explosives or ammunition; it was not the normal way you would see a car erupt into flames. They would fire warning shots either with the 50-caliber, or with what they call their coaxial machine gun, which is different caliber, and then they would fire with the main gun, if they had to, which is 120-mm bore. You could stick your whole arm in that up to your shoulder, that's how thick that gun is. There were some vehicles that came across the bridge that responded to the warning shots and turned around and went away. It wasn't that the gunners fired at everything indiscriminately, but it was just astounding to watch a vehicle continue to come forward after dozens if not hundreds of shots had already hit the engine block and the windshield. You had to wonder what was motivating these folks to do these suicide runs.

Whenever there was a head-to-head direct combat between Americans and Iraqis, it was almost always a brutal slaughter of the Iraqis. Many of the men in this company, contrary to the cliché about these soldiers, were frustrated that they were even fighting back. They just wondered why these people didn't just put their weapons down and surrender, that it wasn't worth giving up one's life for Saddam Hussein.

Earlier, the unit had gone south and east to fight units of the Medina Division, a military objective, and they were blowing up vehicles left and right—ammunition trucks, artillery emplacements, tanks, armored personnel carriers that were all hidden in the tree line. I suspect that many of them were cold; in other words, the engines were not running and had not been running. They were camouflaged in the tree line to keep away from the aircraft that had been bombing in that area for the previous weeks. I suspect a lot of them were not manned. When we arrived the place was absolutely vacant; there wasn't a soul there. A lot of these vehicles had been abandoned. So the soldiers really relished driving down a road, firing all their weapon systems. They watched the mortars successfully blowing up all this equipment; quite a few were getting a charge out of that. In terms of relishing killing, I found most of them felt indifferent to bad about it. They felt like, "Well, this is what we do. These are people who are trying to kill me as well. I don't like it, but I don't necessarily dislike it either. I just have to do it."

There were lots of people who were saying, "I just wish these people would realize that they can't win this and surrender rather than making us kill them." There were definitely people who felt that way. It was a sense of relief when you saw Iraqis surrrendering. A lot of people would say, "They did the right thing. We're going to treat them right. They're going to live to see another day." Even amongst the folks who were talking a tough game before the war started, saying they were eager to go out and kill Iraqis, I don't think—when they were forced to actually do that—they took a great joy in it. That's kind of a cliché that you actually don't really see on the battlefield.

I have no regrets for my coverage. I thought my reporting had the right amount of compassion for everyone who was involved in these battles, both the "enemy" and the soldiers I was embedded with. Maybe I have some regrets on having gone in the first place, and exposing myself to that kind of danger when I have a family at home. I never saw a public affairs officer the entire time I was out there. I joked around with John Koopman of the *San Francisco Chronicle* about that, exactly, saying that maybe the PAOs didn't want to be as far up toward the front as we were. I tried to adhere as much as possible to the letter of the law of the agreement we had signed, and that was not betraying the current position or the future movements of troops I was with. If I had any doubts, I would ask my captain or someone above him about how to identify where we were or where we had been, and never ran afoul of the rules, or never had anyone actively trying to keep anything out of the paper that was crucial to the story. I mean, for me saying you're in the outskirts of Baghdad is close enough for most readers. Why I would have to specify any more than that.

Being an embed was a win/win situation for the military, because it produced a lot of firsthand accounts—and really compassionate accounts—of what it's like to be a soldier or what it's like to be on a battlefield. The military knew that they would get that kind of "positive reporting." There was just as much negative reporting. We wrote about friendly fire; we wrote about civilian casualties; we did not pull punches on those topics and we questioned all those incidents along the way. It was very strange for me personally because no matter how much you guard against it, you start to identify with the people that you're embedded with, particularly when you're being shot at. You start to look at the other side as the enemy; you lose sympathy toward the enemy dead, or those that you classify as the enemy. There were several incidents where I really did feel that way and was shocked at how I adopted that posture. In retrospect, I look at it as perfectly rational under the circumstances, but it wasn't something I expected to see in myself. I would see a body that I knew to be someone who had been firing at the U.S. positions and I would not really feel much sympathy. I adopted the same kind of graveyard gallows humor that anyone who's been a war zone usually adopts. I once made a joke to a photographer about interviewing one of the dead in a bus that I knew to have been full of weapons and soldiers. You say these things to get past the situation, but later you look back and say, "Gee, that was kind of morbid and cold."

MY FIRST WAR

Newsweek Reporter Kevin Peraino

"Soldiers, especially at that level, speak honestly. They just don't care about what they say. They speak the truth."

Kevin Peraino, twenty-six, was *Newsweek*'s youngest war correspondent. He impressed his editors and readers with unflinching, realistic, personal portraits of the men of Charlie Rock Company at the vanguard of the Army's drive to Baghdad. Embedded with four other young U.S. Army soldiers in a Bradley fighting vehicle, Peraino caught his peers at their best and worst with cultural accuracy. Here's Peraino describing the war's launch: "They jumped off on the night of March 20 to the sound of 'Bodies' by the heavy-metal band called Drowning Pool, blasting over a loudspeaker atop a Humvee."

■ ■ ■

I wanted to be embedded. I'm pretty young. I went to Northwestern University. I am from Ridgefield, Connecticut. I asked to cover Afghanistan and they didn't let me go because the editors thought I was too green. So, with Iraq, I felt it was my time. They said, "Go ahead." *Newsweek* had started planning for the war long before we knew embedding was going to be this elaborate. The ground forces were a better place for a less-experienced journalist like myself.

I've worked at *Newsweek* long enough to know that we have some very wise editors and senior writers in Washington who do a good job of taking a cold eye to reports that come in. In some cases, we wrote our own stuff. In other cases, we filed one of many reports to the lead writer. The writers we have in Washington, like Evan Thomas, are very effective in crafting pieces in a way where they're not casting a one-sided light on it. Jon Alter wrote a piece wondering if embedded journalists would end up in bed with the military. There certainly was a risk to that.

I was with the Third Infantry Division. It was Task Force 369. They call it 300th Sixty-nine Battalion. It was Charlie Rock Company. Basically, I spent the war in a Bradley fighting vehicle with one set of guys. I figured you wouldn't get much at a battalion level. I wanted to talk to the privates and the corporals who were on the front lines, and so this would be a good way to do it with a small cast of characters. Most of my war reports focused on these four guys in a Bradley. I got along quite well with them by the time the war was over. In fact, they were over here last night, hanging out in my Baghdad hotel room since they were still in the area. There is no doubt you like the people you cover. The real disadvantage is that you had zero freedom of movement. I was stuck in this Bradley the entire time.

The Bradley commander was a guy named Captain Mike Pecina. The gunner was Corporal Timothy Smith. The driver was specialist Jared Agnetti, and the private in the back was Philip Davis. I was in the back with Private Davis. Usually the Bradley has eight or six people in the back. With just the two of us it was pretty roomy.

Soldiers, especially at that level, speak honestly. They just don't care about what they say. They speak the truth, which is so refreshing. Especially when you cover generals or politicians in Washington—and where there is so much double talk. That is the great thing about being with those guys. They just told it like it is. I knew that they weren't guarded and they forgot that I was taking notes. They'd talk on the radio and not really care to think that I was listening. My stories showed their blunders as well as the good things that they did. For example, when they arrived at the airport they started blowing up commercial airplanes. Their commander comes on the radio and says, "You're really pissing me off!" They later read that and said, "Oh no! I can't believe you're writing this stuff down." But then one of the guys turns to me, "You know, Kevin, you told the truth and the truth is ruthless." That is a quote from Bobby Kennedy. It made me feel good to realize that he appreciated it.

One of the things I wrote about in *Newsweek* was the difficulty in knowing who were the good guys and who were the bad guys in Iraq. That was a struggle all through the country.

Only when we crossed the Euphrates and went to the airport that we started seeing the first steady serious fire. There had been small resistance all the way up from Najaf.

I was in Captain Picena's Bradley when we got to the Euphrates Bridge. We pulled off to the left before the bridge. The battalion first went with the smoke platoon, which blows smoke to obscure the bridge. As they were blowing smoke, the battalion sent Zodiac speedboats across the river to inspect the bridge to see if it was damaged, or if there were explosives planted. It has been partially blown but was still passable. So the Bradley I was in took off to the side. It shot a lot of vehicles, mostly trucks and blew them up. They probably had soldiers in them. Half the time there was no way to tell. That was when we started seeing one or two large caliber artillery shells landing pretty close. Was I frightened? You're in the back of this armored box. You don't feel particularly vulnerable until you step out. It was a thing I wondered about. I had never been in war.

The fear level changes when you step outside and you don't know what's around. That happened at the airport later on. We got to the tarmac. We'd been in the Bradley for twelve consecutive hours. We were sweating. There was a sandy mist inside the back of the Bradley. We hadn't slept. We knew there was fighting still going on, but we just had to get out of the vehicle. So we got out. There were all these soldiers milling around. Then I heard pop, pop, pop. Because you heard that all the time, you don't always react. Most of the time the shooting's not close, so you don't do anything at first. You just kind of stand there and look around. I heard it again. I took my cues from the soldiers. I saw them running. It was time to get back inside the Bradley. Then, one soldier in the back with me said that you could see the rounds land in the dust right behind where we were standing. There were probably a dozen Bradleys on the tarmac, and everybody packed in and drove off to another site on the tarmac. Then it happened one more time. We got out and you could hear rounds coming close, so we had to pack it in again.

The troops I was with were going to secure this control tower, and then something hit the Bradley. It might have been an RPG round. It was a loud bang—shook the vehicle—but the commander said, "Keep driving! Keep driving!" The other guy says, "I can see the smoke. It's right here." Then they pulled off to where they thought it was safe, and looked out and inspected the vehicle. You could see where something had hit it, but it wasn't like what you'd expect an RPG would do. It wasn't like a big black mark. It almost matched the paint. Who knows? It could have been a mortar. It could have been an air burst.

Overall, my war experience in Iraq made me realize how normal everything is. A real sense of normalcy develops when you're out there. It's almost a shock how much time is spent just hanging out, doing nothing, and you're not scared at all. Then something wakes you up. You get shot at, or you know something happens, and you realize it's not really safe, even though it's safe most of the time. Just for my own learning, I'd like to see a war from the generals' perspective. Then try a unilateral kind of coverage.

MAKING THE MEDIA FEEL AT HOME
Sergeant Major Carol Sobel, Public Affairs Officer

"In the first Gulf War we would have liked
to have done more. Our hands were tied."

It's a civilized refuge inside the Kuwait Hilton. The desert flies and heat are gone. The air-conditioning calms frayed nerves. This modern oasis is ideal for journalists to recharge psychologically worn-down batteries or talk to the public affairs officers whose job it is to facilitate safe passage into the war zone. Working out of an office inside the Hilton, Sergeant Major Carol Sobel, a thirtysomething career army public affairs officer based in Fort McPherson, Georgia, was a godsend to many reporters with her quick problem-solving and gracious ways. When we sat down and talked with her, she didn't let the quiet chamber music playing in the Hilton corridors mask the sorrow she experienced watching American POWS on Al Jazeera television.

■   ■   ■

This was the third time I have come to the desert because of Saddam. The first time was the first Gulf War. The second time I had to deploy to Israel with the Patriot missiles for Desert Fox. Now as the senior enlisted adviser, my primary job was to advise and keep an eye on everything. When we were putting the journalists through the embed process as far as the nuclear, biological, and chemical (NBC) gear was concerned—I was doing the training. When we were starting the registration process, and hundreds of media people were coming through here, I helped funnel where they needed to go. I was just helping out, though the soldiers here were actually the ones who made all of that really happen.

The folks on the front desk were in charge of getting them registered. We had soldiers responsible for issuing the equipment. We had folks who were responsible for training them on the equipment. We tried to make it as seamless as possible, though we did have issues with visas, getting in and out of Kuwait.

But that wasn't just for the embeds, that was the unilaterals as well. For those who came in on military air, they had to return on military air. Some had to stay for a while unless we were able to get visas for them.

We were making history and I really wanted to be part of that. In the first Gulf War, that is, folks were under the impression that we really didn't want to have journalists there, but that's not true. The Saudi government did not usually allow journalists in their country. The 160 or so journalists who did end up coming into the country were there on our invitation. We brought them to Riyadh. The problem was not that we were trying to keep people out. The problem was that we weren't allowed to talk about deployment. So the whole time that we were doing that left hook and getting into Kuwait, we weren't allowed to let reporters even talk about what was happening at the time. Therefore, as far as history is concerned, it never happened, because they weren't able to get the stories out right away or with the detail they would have liked. Once the war ended, journalists said, "We weren't able to write about it."

They had wanted to cover the fight but couldn't. The way embedding was done then, you weren't really embedded. You were issued to the public affairs officer (PAO), and the PAOs had to entertain you. PAOs were under the same movement restrictions as anyone else. We weren't able to drive up and down the line of battle looking for a firefight to take these journalists to. We had to stay in the sector that we were in. Because we had to worry about friendly fire, just like everyone else. So the journalists were not out front with the tanks like they were in this current war. They were back with us in public affairs. All we saw was the result of what the tanks did. It was too late. It was old news. In the first Gulf War we would have liked to have done more. Our hands were tied.

Finally, with the second Gulf War, I felt like this was the first time I was able to do what we always talked about doing in public affairs—getting that word out by using the media to tell the story. The first time!

We were fortunate that our office here at the hotel had a pretty good range of American TV. We had CNN International and Fox. At the same time we were also able to watch the Arab stations, usually Al Jazeera or Abu Dhabi. When those America POWs were captured, we watched what Al Jazeera was showing and it was really, really bad. Folks back in the States had absolutely no idea what was really shown. If they had shown this video back in the States, families would have been able to identify their loved ones. I'm glad that it was not shown. It was just so shocking because you were able to see how some of them died. Each one of them looked like they were shot right between the eyes. I thought these kids were just murdered. At first I was angry, and then, about a day later, I cried.

They were turning the dead prisoners' faces to the camera. You couldn't see who was doing the turning. You just saw hands moving the heads. Some of the bodies were half clothed. You could tell that they were forcing the captured prisoners to talk, and at that moment the Geneva Convention was being violated. They seemed so scared. You just knew that just off-screen there was someone with a gun to their head—just by the looks on their faces, you knew—and it haunted me.

Regarding the embedding process, I read the negative articles which argued that it was designed for propaganda, but I found that the majority of those folks were writing them from a nice office safe somewhere. They were just looking from afar and making observations on something they had no real contact with. We had some wonderful unilaterals, and I think that if we continue to use the embed process, we need a better idea of what the unilaterals are going to do, and they need to have a better idea what they are going to do. They assumed they were going to be able to get into Iraq at the same time as embeds and travel and make observations. But folks were calling us, "Please help us. We are stuck in the middle of a firefight." "Well, where are you?" "Well, we don't know." It was frustrating for us because we couldn't provide what the unilaterals were asking us for. They felt that getting a media badge that called them unilaterals would give them shelter, safety, but that was not the instruction we received on what they were supposed to get. In the future, if we are truly going to have unilaterals on the battlefield in the way they want, then they have to make allowances for it, or we just have to tell them, "Look, it's just not going to work. You're on your own."

There were reporters who managed to get into Iraq, and get their stories, and not get killed. We had a few who got killed. In some cases they had some scary stories to tell about just avoiding getting killed. We tried hard to keep people from getting into that position. When folks starting going across the border, we told them, "Don't do that, because you're going to get killed." When the first few were killed and we were very upset, I Googled "killed journalists" and what popped up was that a lot more were killed in Afghanistan. Apparently this is something that happens. Now, how much of it are we going to be able to tolerate? We personally weren't able to do a whole lot about it because public affairs are not really in the operational chain. We don't always have input to tell a commander, "Hey, you gotta stop what you are doing on this mission and go over and save these guys." We just don't have that ability, and it frustrates us because journalists just don't understand that we don't have that ability. They just say, "If I can call you on the phone, obviously you can come get me?" "No, we are not AAA." In a way, we were glad that they called us because otherwise we had no idea where they were. In the future, there has to be some method of protecting unilateral journalists when they are allowed on the battlefield, even though they are not embedded.

GOING LIVE
CNN Correspondent
Martin Savidge

> "There was a constant battle between Martin
> Savidge, who was with the Marines, and Martin
> Savidge, who was the journalist. It was a
> conflict of the soul."

In a satellite-phone interview with The *Cleveland Plain Dealer,* conducted during the first week of the war, CNN embedded reporter Martin Savidge—he had been an anchor and reporter at a local Cleveland television station for twelve years—confessed that whenever "communication blackouts are lifted, I'd like to say the first person I call is CNN at Atlanta, but it's not. I call my home, my children."

This wasn't the first time that the golden-tongued war correspondent was covering a military conflict, and surprisingly, it wasn't the first time that he was an embed. In early 2002, he was in Afghanistan, bored silly while camped out at the army base outside Kandahar. "We were living on base for six weeks," Savidge recalls. "We knew there were missions going on, but never got to go on any of the missions. It was ridiculous; the guys covering the war in Washington had more information than those of us who were right there.

"Finally, when the Anaconda mission was announced by the Pentagon, journalists wanted to know why one of the biggest battles of the war was not going to have any reporters covering it. And Secretary of Defense Donald Rumsfeld said, 'There are six journalists embedded with that operation.' That was the first time I had heard the term 'embedded.' And I happened to be one of the six journalists. The others were from *USA Today,* AP, *Army Times,* and AFP.

"I wrote every day of what was going on with Anaconda and the perspective of being out there. But embed as a term didn't really stick in my mind at that time. It didn't seem to take on the significance that it has in this most recent war."

Savidge made the most of his second embed experience—with the First Battalion Marines. With a crew of four, they outfitted their Hummer, dubbed Warrior One, with a small collapsible satellite dish, videophone with satellite-tracking capabilities, and three cameras. It was show time.

■ ■ ■

I work for a twenty-four-hour news network. The emphasis of our network is LIVE, LIVE, LIVE—as much live as possible. To facilitate that, we weren't doing a lot of packages, which are these videotaped, two-minute reports—to encompass a day, maybe even a couple of days—that are carefully written, with interviews that you have edited, and is a compilation of what you have seen. Initially, we were working under a number of restrictions in Iraq. We could only work in daylight. We couldn't use lights at night and we were doing so much live that there just was very little time to do a package. So what you ended up with was just an of-the-moment what was the unit doing. What I thought was lacking in the coverage was that sort of depth, putting it into perspective, and adding the fabric of the story. There just wasn't time for that because the emphasis was always, "What's happening right now? We want to know where you are, where you're moving, what the unit is doing." It was a trade-off, but the element of good, in-depth, focused reporting was sacrificed somewhat, but there was also the historic first that much of this war was live! I mean, the first Gulf War—other than the Scud missile attacks and the bombing of Baghdad—that was the only live stuff you really saw of that war.

Sometimes you saw battle scenes live, so you had to have the right equipment. We had this tracking satellite and we were almost always plugged in. See, there were a lot of times that we were plugged into CNN—not on the air—and they were just monitoring us. They were just watching and waiting for something interesting to happen. We had a civilian Humvee, which CNN purchased in Kuwait. It was eleven years old. So, obviously, it was a seller's market on Humvees in Kuwait before the war. Everybody, at least television-wise, wanted one. If they were going to go into the desert, that's what they needed. All the media wanted to have vehicles because, well, for many reasons. One, mobility; two, it offered a sort of a workspace; and three, the media needed a means of transmission, which meant you needed electronics, which then meant you needed a source of electricity. So if you had your own vehicle, you could then hook up an inverter or maybe even have a generator; you supply it with power and if you have power, then you have a means of communicating with the outside world.

CNN actually bought two Humvees, and we outfitted them with all the latest technology of a tracking videophone, which was basically—yeah, the old stuttery videophone, but at least this one would work while you're roaring along. Then we also put a standard satellite transmission dish on it, which offers a much clearer, sharper image. However, you've got to be stationary, and you've got to set the whole thing up, and that's problematic. It works well if you're going to be in one place for several hours. Oftentimes, you never knew how long you were going to be stationary. So, I didn't get as much use out of that.

There was a huge debate at the Department of Defense (DOD) and the media regarding vehicles. The DOD had said absolutely no vehicles for anyone out in the battlefield. I understand their reasoning. It was explained to me that it was a safety issue. How could you have civilians driving vehicles as part of military convoys, especially if they come under any sort of attack, and especially at night? Well, the Humvee issue went back and forth, but before we embedded, we contacted the Marine unit we were going to be with and drove the vehicle out to their camp. We met with the commander, showed him the vehicle, showed it to his communications people and said, "This is what we would like to bring. On top of that, we have a driver who is ex-military and he was wearing night vision goggles." After the driver went out and practiced a few times at night with the unit, he said okay. So essentially, even though the unit commander said it was fine, the DOD was still saying no. So we had to sneak it in. The colonel said, "Make sure the vehicle is at such and such a place so that we will bring it into our camp."

There were four of us. The driver was a former British SAS whose nickname was Smudge. SAS are a unique breed, much like, I guess, the Navy SEALs or any Special Forces guy. There's the guy behind the camera, or what we call the photographer, Scott McWhinnie; there was the engineer, Gerard Kane; and myself. That was the minimum. The engineer's job was to repair, to point at the right satellites, and do all the sophisticated electronics that satellite technology required.

The soldiers were excited to have CNN. Every day they would come by and say, "What do you know? What's the latest? What are you hearing from home?" That was commonplace. I think they were excited because of CNN's reputation. Most were excited because they knew that their families would be able to watch them. We were greeted with the utmost respect and welcomed. We were told it was cool, it was great, it was terrific to have us there, and I'm talking the average Marine. Their attitude was, "Look, we're not asking you to make us out as choirboys or to make us out like Arnold Schwarzenegger, that we're one lean, mean killing machine. We want you to just show us as we are and what we do."

As someone who covers war, I believe you should show every single aspect of it, because otherwise you give people the misimpression that war is a very sanitary, very clean, relatively painless type of campaign, and it's not. I mean, you see the smart bombs in the Pentagon video. What you never see is what happens after the nose camera goes to hash. What was the explosion like afterwards? What was the suffering of the people on the ground? Did they linger for hours, maybe days? You don't know any of that.

We didn't allow human suffering to be seen in America. There is a tendency on the part of domestic networks not to show that, because they know that the American public is revolted by it, and they don't want to make the American public uncomfortable. It's censorship, and I've seen it many times before, so I'm not surprised by it.

Let me give you an example. We were on the outskirts of Baghdad, I can't remember the exact date, and we were going through an industrial complex. The complex was thought to have potential weapons of mass destruction and was home to bad guys. Our photographer was riding with this Marine unit in their Humvees with the 50-cals and machine guns. They came across two Iraqis running with weapons—AK47s and sidearms. They shouted at the men, "Stop!" and the men didn't stop, so they opened fire. The first guy dropped before Scott could even get his camera out. Right in the chest. The second man gets hit, and the camera's rolling, and from the perspective of the camera, you're seeing the bullet going around in by his feet. He goes down. Knocked down, flat on the ground, and then he begins to roll around a bit, and then you see him start to get up on all fours and it's clear he's out of the fight—or he looks to be out of the fight and I don't see a weapon in his hand. At that point, four or five Marines, including one on a 50-cal, open fire on him again. He's obviously dead. That footage we fed into CNN. We had warned CNN as we always did any time there was anything really graphic because, any time new footage came in from the field, CNN would take it right to air. I called them ahead of time and said, "Look, at the end of this feed, there's some pretty graphic stuff, an Iraqi being killed, and you have to make a determination." I've heard talk that it will air someday, but it has not yet.

You have to realize that people die in war. I'm not saying all wars are bad—
I am saying all wars are awful. There is no such thing as a pleasant war. I've
been in enough of them to know that. War can be justified. There could be
reasons why, as a last resort, you go to war. You must know that once it starts,
it's a horrible, terrible thing. People die gruesome, terrible deaths. But in
America we'll edit that down. Especially anything that deals with U.S. service
personnel. I can think of a case in point before the war began: the shooting of
the two American civilian contractors in Kuwait. I got there right after it happened. Well, the guy who had been wounded was already transported, but the
man who had been killed, he was still there, and as a photographer, you shoot
everything and let Atlanta decide what it's going to run on the air. The locals,
meaning *Kuwait Press*, ran the shot of the dead man on the front page—up
close, right in the face. To do this is common in many other parts of the world.
In the U.S., what they showed was a bullet-riddled vehicle: Sanitized.

Here's another case in point. It's not war related. You may remember the
Pennsylvania state treasurer who shot himself on air? It was at a press conference. I was there. The huge debate at the local levels for the station I was
working with was, "What do you show? When do you stop it?" They said, "We
will freeze it at the moment that he puts the gun in his mouth and we will
continue the audio." I didn't agree with that decision, but that's what they did.
The audio, though, is almost worse, because now that you no longer have an
image showing what's happening, you become much more attuned to the
audio, and the audio is awful—the screaming, the retching, people vomiting,
the calamity—and your own mind begins to paint an image that is even worse.

In this war, there was a constant battle between Martin Savidge, who was
with the Marines, and Martin Savidge, who was the journalist. It was a conflict of the soul. The reason is because if you are in a fight as a noncombatant, and that your life and your fate are in the hands of the unit, there will
form a bond with the soldiers. I know I did. No one who has not been in combat can really understand this, and it's very true, because your lives depend on
the person next to you. The hard part for the journalist is that you've got to
somehow rise above it, and try to look on it thoroughly and with honesty. It's
like you're having an out-of-body experience.

There were three different occasions when I felt things were getting dangerous—when you get that free-fall sensation in your stomach. It's that feeling of dread or nonspecific fear, and I've had it several times in covering
conflicts. The first time was when we were going out with a Marine explosive

and ordnance demolition (EOD) team, to go blow up some Iraqi hardware, specifically tanks and armored personnel carriers that they had found abandoned behind a village. I said, "Let's go out and watch them blow up some stuff." We'd been trying all morning to get on with the videophone, but couldn't due to all the satellite congestion. Then we drove our Hummer, while Scott, the photographer, was walking in front of our Hummer with another Marine on foot. We were following in our vehicle, moving about three miles an hour through this village when out of an alley, an RPG was fired. You heard the hiss and then you heard the explosion and the shattering of glass and the concussive force. Initially, we were like, "What the hell was that?" Then it quickly dawned on us that that was an RPG, and we're now under attack and, of course, we thought, "Are there more? And where are they going to come from?" Because it wasn't initially obvious where it had been fired from, and I was fearful that there were more, and that this was going to be some sort of concentrated effort to pick us off. It didn't happen. The Marines certainly fired a lot back. Right after the first RPG hit, in the confusion, Gerard, the engineer, who had been continually redialing on the videophone, shouts out, "We're in!" meaning we were now connected with CNN. So all this was playing out on television for forty minutes. You had friendlies firing the 50-caliber machine guns and M-60s at targets that I couldn't see; at the same time the demolition team is going about planting the charges. You've got huge explosions going off in the background, and tanks exploding, and fire, and secondary explosions. It looks like a Hollywood movie back lot.

The second occasion was after the terrible sandstorm. It was just after sunset. A frag order came up. A frag order stands for fragmented order, which is not a full-blown order; this is much different. It's like, "This is what we need you to do right now." The frag order was that there was a fuel convoy coming in — twenty-five fuel trucks, quarter of a million gallons of fuel that was essential to keep the Marines driving forward toward Baghdad. The route that they were going to take needed to be patrolled, and safeguarded, and this convoy needed to be met. So we drove off after the storm into the night. We had been warned there was going to be trouble along the way, that there had already been reports of RPGs along the route. What made it worse was the fact that there was cloud cover. It was really pitch dark with dust still hanging in the air, which meant that night vision goggles were worthless. So you're driving in near total-blackout conditions. I don't even know how the amphibious assault vehicle (AAV) operators knew how to see. I guess they had some sort of infrared equipment they could rely on, but it's very dicey and was the reason the AAV I was in ran into a Humvee and then got run into by another AAV. We drove right through a house—an Iraqi house! Fortunately, there was nobody in it. At that time, in the chaos, in the total dark, I had another fear that we were going to get picked off. I never liked the Amtraks because I know that as ponderous, bulky, and secure as they looked, they're not. They're made of aluminum. A 50-caliber machine gun would turn it into Swiss cheese, and even a 7.32mm fired within a range of 100 yards will go through it. A medium machine gun and an RPG would turn it into a flaming coffin, because it had fuel cells on the side, and an RPG would just devastate you. You're inside, it's very crowded, and it's very hard to get out of, so I did not like the vehicle. The next morning, there were just eight of these Amtraks upended in marshes and nosed into canals.

The last incident was in Baghdad. The Marine scout teams had already been in this sector. They reported lots of people on the streets, indications of looting, but no signs of Iraqi opposition military, or any bad guys. Having heard that, and believing it was going to be an historic day, I went to the colonel and said, "I would like to go into Baghdad with the same unit we began with— Bravo Company—because the reports are saying that it's going to be a triumphant entry into the city. This looks like it's going to be the last hurrah." The Colonel said, "Fine. No problem." We got no farther than ten feet into the start of the drive into Baghdad when our Humvee conked. Some Marines quickly got out a tow bar and hooked us up to one of the lead Hummers and off we went again. Being towed through the streets of Baghdad and greeted by the crowds, and the cheering, and the waving, and the smiling, and everything, was terrific. I don't think the U.S. military had ever seen such a reception in fifty, sixty years. You could even see it in the faces of the young Marines. As the lead element of the convoy began crashing over the bridge that was to link them with the army on the other side of the Tigris, they came under heavy machine gun fire. My photographer, Scott, was in the lead Hummer. They were getting hit, but couldn't figure out where it was coming from. Finally, it dawned on them that it was coming from below where there was an Iraqi gunboat underneath the bridge firing at them. Once they ascertained that, well, they quickly pointed all their weapons down on the boat and it was a fairly one-sided battle.

After the initial gunfight on the bridge, RPGs and machine guns started firing toward our convoy. I was about five or six vehicles back from the lead. The Marines just opened fire with everything they had and it became a battle.

We'd already been on a wild ride, because once the convoy was attacked, they started driving erratically and defensively. We were dragged over medians and bouncing over curbs. I began to wonder if the driver of the Hummer up front remembered we were still back there being towed, and we were live on the air at that time, and so it was chaotic. You just hear us getting thrown around our own vehicle and the camera can't stay steady on anything. There was one point where he finally stopped. We jumped out quickly to try and get a better view of the fighting, but the lead vehicle towing us takes off again. The engineer, Gerard, who's running the camera, and myself managed to claw our way back into the Humvee and get going again. An Amtrak had punched a hole through a brick wall of a building, and the driver of the Humvee shouted out that we're going in—which is fine, you've got a nice hole in the wall, but you've also got a huge pile of bricks. He went over and dragged us right over. I thought the whole bottom of the Humvee had been ripped off. Then we got bogged down in the field. The wheels sank into the mud. Because we're dead weight, the lead Humvee just couldn't drag us any more in a field and he kept reversing and forwarding, reversing, but what he was effectively doing was turning the towing bar into a battering ram that was now smashing into us. We're finally shouting, "Just get rid of it, just disconnect the tow bar, leave us here!" because he was trying to get out of the line of fire. We realized that we're not going anywhere. They finally rode out to try to continue the attack, but in the meantime, we were dumped in the middle of the battlefield, and the engine won't start and it won't move, and the engineer went to work trying to fix the fuel pump, and get it started, and the driver went to work trying to change the tire, and I kept asking if I could help. Smudge says, "There's nothing you can do." So, I said, "Fine. I'm going to go make coffee." I went and got out the little campfire stove we had, and sat in the battlefield, and made coffee.

As the afternoon waned, and it seemed we were safe, CNN's international desk called and said, "We want you to think about disembedding." CNN had no one in Baghdad at that moment. Nic Robertson and the Baghdad coverage crew had been kicked out by the Iraqi government, so the facilities and the workspace were still there, but there were no correspondents. They wanted a correspondent in Baghdad. I told them, "The problem is, it's getting dark and I'm not going to risk our crew. We just had one hell of a day. The city is not safe. Trying to drive to wherever the Palestine Hotel is after dark is not a good idea." They concurred with that, and I said that we would try in the morning, after I discussed disembedding with the colonel. I later told the colonel, "I would like to disembed." I explained the reason why. He was fine with that. He said, "It was great having you. Hate to see you go. I understand why you've got to go. Tomorrow we have to do a patrol which will take you right by the Palestine Hotel, so we'll make sure you get there safely." That's how I ended up there on a Thursday. I left Baghdad the following Monday. I'd been at this for three and one-half months. I was burned out. I was exhausted and tired. I had enough. It wasn't that I was afraid. It was just that I realized that I wasn't focusing well. I was still digesting a lot of what I'd seen and been through personally. I realized it was time to go.

THE ARAB PERSPECTIVE
Abu Dhabi TV Correspondent Amir Al-Mounaiery

"His body was still warm. There was a slight smile on his face. It seemed to me he was smiling because he knew he was going to heaven."

On the same day Saddam's statue was yanked to the ground on April 9, 2003, television stations worldwide also aired footage of a smiling, glad-handing Saddam Hussein strolling the streets of an upscale Baghdad neighborhood. Clad in a black beret and an olive military uniform and greeted by throngs of well-wishers, the week-old original feed was from Abu Dhabi TV, a United Arab Emirates–based station that dropped its Arabic-language programming of sitcoms, game shows, and documentaries for around-the-clock news during the war. Who knows if that videotaped image was a Saddam imposter or the real McCoy?

In fierce competition with Al Jazeera and Al Arabiya for the growing Arab market, Abu Dhabi Television (ADTV), which launched its satellite channel in 2000, emerged as a major player in providing critical war coverage to over 100 international media organizations that included CNN and Reuters. The station spent a year readying itself for the war. Three correspondents worked out of its Baghdad studio and offices, with other reporters scattered throughout the country's hot spots.

"We decided from the beginning that we were not simply going to take the feed or be dependent on a big network like CNN or the BBC and broadcast the signals," said the head of Abu Dhabi TV, Ali Al Ahmed, in an interview with Middle East Business Information. "We are addressing Arab viewers. Yes, people in the Arab world are more sympathetic to the Iraqi people. That also puts more responsibility on us. We're not going to show horrific pictures just for the sake of attraction. Some people would say that the West is watching a different war on TV than the Arabs. I think they are watching a different war because there is a different perspective. We try to maintain that balance. It's like standing on top of a basketball."

On the evening of April 30, we talked with one of Abu Dhabi TV's Baghdad correspondents. Our interview took place in front of the Palestine Hotel. Amir Al-Mounaiery, thirty-seven, had spent a tense day filming the local reaction to American military shooting civilians in Fallujah. Al-Mounaiery, who worked for five years for the BBC in the Middle East, is typical of many Arab correspondents and their cameramen, bravely inserting themselves into raw, emotional situations where civilians are mourning their dead. But Abu Dhabi TV reporters gained further notoriety for standing on the roof of their offices when U.S. missiles were whizzing overhead so they could pan and tilt and zoom in their cameras on the latest, biggest explosions while others relied on static cameras operating remotely. On the morning of April 8, Amir found himself being part of a larger story.

■   ■   ■

I worked twelve hours the previous day, doing a lot of live shots on the roof. I had arrived in Baghdad just three days before. I'd finished my work at 4:00 A.M. At 6:30, I woke up because there was a lot of shooting outside, and I went up to the roof. About 300 meters away, I saw a U.S. tank firing. I called the station and said, "We have firing everywhere!" Then I went down and woke up my cameraman and told our engineer that we're going live. I started to offer commentary on what was going on. About 8:00 A.M., I felt that it became very dangerous. We saw aircraft coming in, buzzing. They were flying so close that if I wrote my name on my hand they could read it, you know? All of a sudden I saw a firefight on our station monitor. I knew its location because I could see the bridge. I couldn't believe it was this close to our building. It said "CNN exclusive" with the feed. I thought the correspondent was embedded with one of the tanks nearby. The American tank started to fire on one of the buildings, the Planning Ministry. I said, "Maybe something is wrong?"

I was at the monitor, using the mixer, shifting between three cameras. The others in the office got down on the floor because they were scared. The people from Al Jazeera were up there on the roof with us as well; Tareq Ayoub was moving the camera just a little bit.

Then I saw three aircraft maneuvering. Flipping around, like in an air show. They were firing big flares to light up the area, even though it is light already and they didn't need it. But anyway, we have a huge sign on the roof saying this is Abu Dhabi TV. They can see it from above. I saw above my head one of those A-10s. I could see the plane clearly. I didn't realize there was another one behind my back. Suddenly, I heard the buzz of a rocket or some-thing. I have two cameramen with me. One of them said, "Get down! This is a rocket!" I got down and then I saw the rocket hitting the wall in front of me. I saw that black thing hit and explode. If I hadn't gone down, that rocket would have hit me.

The shrapnel hit Tareq Ayoub. It went straight to his heart. He was an ex-cellent man. I carried his body to the car below. He needed to be taken to the hospital for immediate medical help. I couldn't see any blood. His body was still warm. There was a slight smile on his face. I cannot really describe it. It seemed to me like he was smiling because he knew he was going to heaven. I then saw his eyes flicker open. He was looking at me with great intensity. This happened just a moment before he died. I wanted to tell him, "I'm sorry. This shrapnel was meant for me, not for you."

There was no one with a weapon in our building. Not at all. First of all, if there were snipers, the U.S. military snipers with their telescopes can see us clearly. We look like civilians. I was just standing there with bare hands. Any sniper could see us clearly.

Some critics say the Pentagon was using the media as a tool, and I believe them. With full respect for BBC and full respect for CNN, they didn't do a good job in this war. I really respect them. They are my ideal, but not this time, definitely not. As for Al Jazeera, they are professional, definitely, without a doubt. But the propaganda they show weakens their case.

After this war, I realized we in the media are the soldiers of politics. Not the military soldiers. We are the soldiers. I am proud that Abu Dhabi TV showed all sides, everything. You can see CNN showed only part of the war—their favorite part. They didn't show any of those anti-American rallies, or the civilian casualties. They just showed crowds welcoming American soldiers and clapping hands. It is selective journalism—like Saddam did. This was the Arabic way. We used to do this with the government stations. Now, we are switching roads and we wonder: Where is America? Where is the American dream? Where are the British? Freedom of expression, where is that? Now I don't know.

I lived in Britain for ten years. I worked with the NBC Middle East Broadcasting Center and then I moved to Abu Dhabi TV. I learned a lot from them and now I wonder. Peter Arnett, what happened to him? His getting fired by NBC was crazy, definitely. I wonder, why? This was like an Arab ruler getting mad at a journalist for having an opinion. When it happened, I didn't believe it. I saw Peter about three days ago. He was working with the *Daily Mirror* and Al Arabiya. I am sad for him, definitely. I am sad for any journalist who is trying to do his job. Yet in the end, he is fired and is taking peanuts to keep doing his work. He is a great, and dedicated man, and is just thrown out like this? C'mon! This is such disrespect.

They say the Arabs must modernize their society, like our TV station, but it depends on how you describe the modernization. I am Egyptian. Our civilization has been around for thousands of years. America's has been around for 250 years. First of all, whatever Americans call a democracy, it doesn't mean they have to export it to other countries. Just leave them alone. I have been to the United States several times. The people are very easygoing and friendly. They say good morning. But in the end, they don't know what's going on outside the United States. This is the whole problem.

MARRIAGE UNDER FIRE

Washington Post's Moscow Bureau Chiefs
Susan Glasser and Peter Baker

"Peter and I are very concerned about one
another's safety. It's always more horrible to
be the one who's left behind."

She graduated from Harvard and was managing editor of the *Harvard Crimson*.
He flunked out of Oberlin. A love of politics drew them to Washington, D.C.
They were two Beltway wonks, hardly distinguishable from so many others
who converge on the nation's capital while still in their twenties. She became
editor of *Roll Call*, an insider's tip sheet for Capitol Hill. He earned his press
chops as reporter for *The Washington Post*. She migrated over to the *Post* as
deputy national editor in charge of investigative reporting. They met for the first
time in 1998. He fast-tracked his way to becoming the White House correspondent during the Clinton years. She moved over to the national desk as political reporter. They married in September 2000, and four months later moved
to Moscow where they became co-bureau chiefs for the *Post*. The Afghanistan
war drew them in; he covered action in the north while she pursued stories in
the south and in Pakistan. In Iraq, he was an embed; she was not. He observed
war from the cocooned safety of the Marines' command staff headquarters.
She roamed a volatile southern Iraq in a Pajero SUV, dodging ambushes and
angry mobs. They stayed in touch virtually every night by satellite phone. Meet
Susan Glasser, 34, and Peter Baker, 36, one of *The Washington Post*'s most talented couples in the tradition of legendary executive editor Ben Bradlee and
Style writer Sally Quinn. We sat down with Baker at the Kuwait Hilton in late
April, and because she was busy in her hotel room packing for their flight back
to Moscow, we interviewed Glasser by phone in mid-June.

■   ■   ■

Susan Glasser

Peter and I came to Russia as our first foreign assignment. I was interested in the idea of covering the former Soviet Union and the new emerging Russian society, with the Russian history, culture, and politics. It's a big, complicated story with fifteen different countries, and there are certainly wars in the post-Soviet space, as they call it here. On September 11th, I was at the Russian embassy at the time, listening to a press conference with U.S. Undersecretary of Defense Doug Feith and his Russian counterpart. They were talking about the missile defense system, which became a kind of antiquated Cold War–type dispute between the U.S. and Russia, when his pager started going off. We just finished the press conference, and we were on our way to another press conference at the Marriott, when the first plane hit, and all the Pentagon guys started to hop on their phones. We were so far away that there was nothing we could do in Moscow.

Within two days, Peter left for Central Asia, and was the first American newspaper reporter into northern Afghanistan after September 11. I ended up in Uzbekistan for more than a month. I reported on Central Asia and the new U.S. military presence there. That was very much a part of Russia's sphere of influence. It presented a whole complicated new presence for U.S. policy-makers in an area where human rights are dismal, where economic reforms have not been successful, and where the U.S. now has a huge incentive to essentially woo dictators like Karimov in Uzbekistan. The U.S. desperately needed his assistance. It went back to backing questionable leaders for strategic reasons. Human rights groups estimate there are as many as 7,000 political prisoners in Uzbekistan, many of them religion-oriented who were arrested for doing nothing more than wearing a beard in public or going to the mosque on Fridays for prayers. It was extremely difficult to report from there. It wasn't even so much a question of pressure from the regime as an absolute inability to interview anyone in a position of authority, and to get any real information about the situation.

I was back in Uzbekistan when Kabul fell, and then to Pakistan for a couple of weeks. I traveled to Afghanistan when they started the campaign in Tora Bora. There was virtually no ability to contact the American military then. It's funny, in the Iraq war there was such a sharp distinction between embedded and unilateral reporters. In Afghanistan, everybody was unilateral. The American military was sort of a shadow presence in the country. I never even spoke to a military official until March of 2002 during Operation Anaconda.

During the entire Tora Bora campaign, not only did I never speak to an American or British military official but there were a few times coming up the mountains when the Afghans or the fighters who were fighting with them would force us off the road with their guns. At one point, I was forced into a ditch with Geraldo Rivera while they cleared the road so that the American Special Forces could go up. They didn't want us to see them, and they were threatening us with their guns, and wouldn't say why.

Some women journalists faced resistance because they wore Western clothing. I never wore a burqa. I refused to even try one on. But yeah, I wore a *shalwar kameez* and a black head scarf in Tora Bora every day, which was absurd to me. Like going off to a war in a dress. In many ways it didn't hinder my ability to work in Afghanistan; it just made it easier. Not surprisingly, the Afghans were very interested to talk to a woman reporter. There's not really a category for professional women except for professional prostitutes. So I felt a certain amount of unwanted attention from the Afghan warlords. They were very attentive.

Peter and I think of ourselves as careful. In Afghanistan, the problem is that you want to be cautious. I wasn't a cowboy. But you never really have good information. Many times in Tora Bora, we found ourselves in situations that were very dangerous, where we were being shot at or within range of mortars, or too close to the American bombs. It was not because we were trying to imitate the war photographers and be the farthest forward. Very often, you think you're going somewhere that's safe—and it's not. You would be stopped every five minutes and told that you're far away from any hot spots. Then you ended up at the very front of the battle line. We always traveled pretty much in convoys each morning.

After the war, too, I went back to Tora Bora to try to find out what had really happened there. I was the first Western reporter to go back, along with my colleagues at the *Boston Globe*. I feel that my piece really tried to shed light on what the nature of the fight really had been. Especially because the Americans and the Pentagon were bragging about this great victory, which it wasn't. They had paid huge amounts of money to corrupt local fighters, who were engaging in side deals to let some of bin Laden's men pay their way out into Pakistan.

Peter Baker

I was in Afghanistan for six months covering the war without meeting an American soldier. Only after the real fighting was over did I spend any time with Americans. In the Iraq war, I was embedded with the First Marine

Expeditionary Force, specifically with the command element, which means Lieutenant General James Conway and his staff, who ran the Marines during the war. They were also in charge of the Brits who fell under the Marine command. This group was commanding 85,000 men. It was a good experience. It was interesting. It was different than a lot of the embed stories you will hear, because it wasn't so much filled with sights and sounds as a matter of seeing the battlefield from a higher altitude. Every day, we were able to get into the combat operations center, which was the classified location they actually run the war from. There were display screens with reconnaissance videos, troop maps, and satellite imagery. You had live streaming video from, say, Predator or Hunter reconnaissance vehicles, and you could watch them as they were bombing. There was a list of all the orders that went out, and e-mails and reports coming back, and so forth. We signed an additional agreement beyond what normal embeds did. We agreed to have our stories reviewed for security because we were getting access to things that normal embeds weren't. It went very smoothly. They never took anything out of the stories that was truly objectionable. It was no trouble ninety-eight percent of the time. The other two percent usually involved something like location—a specific location we would give away. We would almost never put any future operations in our stories to begin with.

Most days, my reporting was a long memo or file that I would send in to the *Post* and they would use as part of the broader overall story of the day's action. We had access to information that was not coming from the Pentagon or Central Command in Doha, and so a lot of the meat of the day's events on the battlefield was coming out of that headquarters. You could see what they were seeing in terms of their assessment of the territory. One memorable night for me was watching them bomb the crap out of a convoy of eighty vehicles with artillery pieces and ammo trucks that were coming out of Baghdad toward the American position, strangely enough. Either the Iraqis thought they were going to try to set up a counterattack, or they were fleeing the city and didn't realize they were heading right into the jaws of the enemy. On the black and white video screen, you can clearly make out artillery pieces being towed, and the other vehicles. You could make out the guys jumping out of vehicles and running for the woods. They clearly were hearing planes coming over them. They clearly knew what was about to happen, or had seen what happened to the guys in front of them. Then the command center called in grid coordinates. They were looking at the screen and saying: "Grid six five eight," or whatever. Somebody else on the phone was calling into somewhere else, and about three or five minutes later, suddenly the screen would go all white with a flash of a weapon. Then it would come back and you would see smoking, smoldering vehicles. The ammo trucks were particularly striking because there would be secondary explosions one right after the other. It was all silent.

It was an odd disconnect. It's hard to sit there and watch a video like that and really process what it meant. It's easy to be detached about it as they were and had to be. It's their job. They had to think about what they were doing in a strategic sense, and I don't fault them for that. But there is also obviously a humanity to the situation. Men are dying at that moment and you are watching it happen live in front of you. That is the problem with a high-tech war. In some ways it may seem more bloodless than it really is. In the end what we saw was a flash on the screen. We didn't see a broken body or the incinerated corpse.

While the convoy was being struck, the command center was excited. They cheered. They applauded. It was definitely a boisterous environment. I don't want to exaggerate. Most of the time they were working on laptops. They were laptop warriors. They were monitoring and evaluating reports that came from the field, taking notes that they needed to respond to, and doing things like that. If they had a firefight in one particular sector, they would scramble Cobras or provide close air support with Harrier jets or F-18s. They were working constantly to make sure that troops stayed within their boundaries to minimize friendly fire.

Susan Glasser

I got to Kuwait in early January. All along my assignment was pretty clear, which was go into Iraq as a unilateral and to start writing the story of what happened to people in southern Iraq under Saddam. In the end, we were unprepared and the military was unprepared for the scenario because we believed the optimistic things we had been hearing from the military in Kuwait: "In Basra, they'll be throwing flowers, there'll be parades." We thought we could go in and start doing independent reporting right away. We rented four-wheel drives and bought walkie-talkies. I traveled with a small number of Americans from print publications. We did not have drivers, and most of us did not have translators, because we didn't want to bring in someone from Kuwait. We wanted to go in and hire somebody in Iraq who would be able to show us around the local scene. We didn't want to be stuck there with a Kuwaiti. Iraqis hate Kuwaitis. We also thought that it was going to be much easier to work in

Iraq. We had images of going to the English department at Basra University. We did have one translator who was Lebanese, and he worked for *Newsweek*. Then we hired a local doctor, Dr. Rafid, to be a translator, and later a fixer who we found in the hospital at Basra. He didn't really speak English, but he was unbelievable and he worked as a nurse. He used to work as a human smuggler, helping people escape Iraq and go to Iran and Kuwait. He knew everyone and we just felt totally safe going anywhere with him. He was great with crowds and knew when we should leave. When we went into Iraq the first time, our convoy was seven cars, and when we went back in to stay, it was three cars. The main people with me the whole time were Ed Gargan from *Newsday*, Rod Nordland from *Newsweek*, and then Terry McCarthy from *Time* magazine.

The idea of an independent journalist covering the conflict was anathema to the military. I think the Public Affairs Officer, Colonel Shields, was never able to work it out, though there was general goodwill on his part. But he was never able to get anything from his superiors, any policy, and his hands were tied. The military was never prepared adequately to address the question of independent reporters working in a war zone. They wanted to channel everything to its own embed program, which was controlled. I wish that hadn't been the case. Well, look, the official policy was never to let us across from Kuwait in the first place. Instead you have to go through, first of all, the demeaning and stressful ritual of trying to sneak through the border. On the second day of the war, obviously everybody decided that they just had to be in Iraq. We left the Hilton Hotel in a convoy of seven cars. It was Saturday. We made it up to the border where there were a lot more cars parked already waiting overnight. A nice Marine there was telling people for hours and hours, "Oh yes, well, as soon as the convoy is done, then you guys can come in behind." But, of course, that never happened. We were hopeless. We waited for a couple of hours until one of our colleagues said, "Let me try to go check out the berm and if I can find a way across." She was able to get across in five minutes. She called and told us how to go, and so those of us in our group—we all had walkie-talkies connected to each other—we just all went, "Okay, let's go now!" Our line of cars pulled out from this parking lot full of twenty or so Pajeros and GMCs.

The sand berms at the border were maybe fifteen feet high, but the military had cut holes through them. They had also put temporary bridges over the trenches. We get to the final trench and there is a temporary bridge over it. A very nice British soldier, rather than stopping us, guided us across, as it was kind of rickety. I was very excited to be in Iraq at last, jubilant that we had found our way across the border. Of course, we had to decide where to go. They kept saying on television that the Coalition Forces had seized Umm Qasr, so we decided to go to Umm Qasr, but things were not, in fact, stable. While we were still on the main road from Safwan to Umm Qasr, U.S. Marines were freaking out that we were in their way. We were trying to figure out from them what was going on, and it turned out they were still firing even while on the main road. Everyone started putting on their flak jackets and the whole atmosphere of glee had turned. We saw some French journalists who had just been in Umm Qasr, and they left saying, "It's not safe, it's not safe." We figured, well, if they don't think it's safe, we don't. A case of being the canaries in the coal mine. So this increasingly long convoy of journalists turned around, and we headed for the main traffic intersection on Highway 8, regrouped, and hung out there for a while. We saw cars coming from the direction of Basra with dead or injured bodies in them. They were local Iraqis. It was not a secure situation and the town of Safwan itself was very unfriendly. Cars were getting stoned; a very bad vibe was coming from the place. It was feared that the Ba'aths still seemed to be in charge of the main town on the border, and there wasn't any U.S. military presence. It was clear we couldn't really work there.

At the end of the day, we decided that we could not remain in Iraq, and several of us decided with our editors that we should leave, and return later to report among the Iraqi population. That first day-trip resulted in a front page story in the *Post* saying that this was a very different picture on the ground from what was being portrayed in the military briefings: American and British troops were still under heavy fire and that the south was not rising up in a great welcome. It took weeks for the situation in the south to change. The ITN crew had been in the same place as us that day, and they'd gone on the road toward Basra, which we had chosen not to go down, and these British television journalists were killed because they had somehow gotten in between the Marines and the Iraqis. The whole day had been an exercise in coming to understand that there was just nowhere safe to operate in southern Iraq. We went back to the Kuwait Hilton. Through all this, Peter and I were always able to communicate by satphone, and in fact, he was still in Kuwait, ready to move forward with the Marines' command center.

Peter Baker

We interviewed all the Marine officers in the days before the war, and as the war began, their biggest fears clearly were possible chemical attack and a really terrible urban battle along the lines of Mogadishu or Beirut. It definitely weighed on them. Baghdad was their worst nightmare. They didn't know what would happen in Baghdad. They talked a good game, but the fact is they would have to adjust. They hoped to get to the gates of Baghdad, and hoped it sorted out. That is ultimately what happened. They may have said that they had a plan for going in, but I don't think they really knew what they would do. All the military guys would say over and over again that the plan goes out the window the minute they cross the line of departure, the minute they start their attack. We watched it happen a million times in small ways. But broadly speaking, the plan went pretty much the way they anticipated. We had a classified briefing of the war plan before it started. I haven't gone back to study my notes from that day but what they had mapped out was pretty close to what happened in broad strokes.

They were constantly reacting to the battlefield and how it was changing. One constant subplot was the hunt for this fellow nicknamed Chemical Ali — Ali Hassan al-Majid, Saddam's cousin and southern military commander. They took a shot at Chemical Ali the very first night of the war. Everybody talked about the cruise missiles they shot at Saddam that first night. But they were also attacking what they thought was the house that Chemical Ali was in. They didn't get him. Two nights later, they thought they had him again in Kut-el-Amara. They didn't get him that time either. Then they thought they found him in Nasiriyah. They sent in a raid. They didn't get him there either. Then there was Basra where they struck his house for sure, and either they did or they didn't get him. I was shown satellite imagery. You would see what the place looked like before they bombed it. It was called BDA, or bomb damage assessment. As far as I know, they still haven't confirmed his death. They think it was him, but even as they were saying it was him, they were chasing another rumor that he was someplace else.

Susan Glasser

We made several other day trips between that initial foray and when we went back in for good. We went to the oil fields of Rumaila. We went to the town of Zubair — a major suburb of Basra. When we heard Basra fell, we decided immediately to go there the next morning. The whole time we were in Basra we stayed at the Basra Teaching Hospital. It's the tallest building in Basra. It was also the only unlooted facility of any significance in the entire city. The British had initially been protecting it. They had soldiers on the grounds and on the roof. Doctors were also guarding the building. Then a few days into the occupation, the British were ordered to pull out and their replacements never showed. A large crowd of looters gathered outside the hospital gates, and the doctors and their assistants were trying to fend them off with guns. I was inside the hospital writing a story, while my other colleagues were on the roof making calls, trying to get the Pentagon to get the British to return. We had already been in a riot earlier that morning at the home of this tribal leader who worked with the British. We had gone there looking for him. It was just total chaos. People were throwing stones at the windows and we were trapped inside. They brought us up on the roof at one point. We called the British, and they came and in about half an hour they broke it up. Sometimes these things happen so quickly you don't even know what trouble you were in. Now it was happening again at the hospital.

I called the British military spokeman and asked him to come help the journalists and that this was the most significant military facility in the area. Their leaving had been a mistake. He basically said in very nicely accented words, "Fuck you." We were unilateral journalists, staying right down the road from the presidential palace in Basra that was occupied by the British as their regional command headquarters, and they wouldn't let us in there because we were unilateral journalists and not embedded. We all had our accreditations from the U.S. military as legitimate journalists, but there was a standing order not to admit any unilateral journalists. The former palace was the only safe place to stay in the city. This would have been Thursday, April 10, the day after the statue fell in Baghdad. Peter was already talking to the *Post* and trying to get help through the Marine commanders because the entire British force reported to that general. Eventually, the mob dispersed. The British soldiers? We never saw them again until 9:30 the next morning, much to the great relief of the entire hospital community.

Peter Baker

It is not our job as journalists to help the military, but it is also not our job to hurt them either. It is our job to tell what happens. They understood they lost a chance to tell a good story in Afghanistan. Most stories that came out after Afghanistan were about Afghans because those were the only people we could talk to. What we saw was the Afghanistan point of view, but you also need the point of view of the military to understand both sides, and we didn't understand both sides. So when there was a bombing in a village in Afghanistan and then twenty-eight civilians died, we didn't see it from the American point of view, and really weren't able to talk to Americans about it in any level of detail. We only talked to the Afghans who lost their loved ones. So the stories only reflected their point of view and didn't have as much balance as everybody would like.

The U.S. military came to a realization that their policy in Afghanistan didn't work. I imagine that Washington came to the understanding that the pressure in Iraq would be overwhelming from media organizations which would leap upon any negative scrap. We would be baying like hounds for any scrap of information. Military guys don't need that. They were also cognizant that the Persian Gulf War system didn't work.

Look, reporters are always more sympathetic to people who talk to them. I was a White House reporter. Obviously I got to know the people I was covering and you develop relationships with them. I covered a school board: same thing. That is true from the state house to every other beat. It's basically the same thing here. You are developing a source relationship with these people, and you have to be able to divorce whatever feelings of friendship you may develop from your objective responsibilities as a journalist. That is true no matter what you do, so the idea that somehow embedding is bad because we get to know these people better is crazy to me. We beg, and beg, and beg for years to get access. Then we finally get it and we go, "Oh, this is a bad thing!" How is it bad? There's nothing bad about it. All it means is that we have to take our responsibilities more seriously.

Susan Glasser

It was clear that Iraqis had been suffering under enormous psychological barriers. On our first day in Basra, we went to a prison which was filled with dozens of Iraqi men. Many of them had been prisoners in that place and had been released the day before. They had come back and were recounting how they had been tortured. They showed us places in the prison where they had been electrocuted or hung on hooks. There were prisoner photographs lying around, which they were showing us. This person was killed, and this person was tortured, this is what they did to him. It was a very powerful and emotional crowd. It was the first place that we visited in Basra. Everyone we met had some relative who had been tortured. We were just stunned at its scope. Everybody spoke in the sense that they couldn't speak freely until they really knew that Saddam was gone. People were haunted by that fear. One former prisoner picked up Saddam's picture off the ground, cut the head off and started eating it, to show me how much he hated Saddam. They were acting out how they'd been tortured, and slowly but surely you peeled back the layers of disbelief that you start with as a reporter. It is important to be skeptical, not cynical, looking for the proof to make it real. One of my colleagues didn't believe this guy, who was a leader of this group of prisoners. Then this guy pulled up his shirt, and his back was crisscrossed with these small knife marks, and the front of his chest was also scarred. We hadn't even noticed his hand, which was totally crippled; three of the fingers were broken. My colleague started to reevaluate the process of how to enter into this new context.

On some level there was a great relief on my part to finally be in Iraq after three and a half months of waiting to be finally be doing something, and it was the most pure form of journalism I'd ever been able to do. These people who had been so oppressed were telling their stories for the first time, and it was a very raw and unmitigated way of experiencing something, a society in the first shock of transition. We were all very conscious of a feeling of overwhelming numbness. Yes, it was horrible what had happened to these people, but it felt like a wonderful thing that they were finally able to tell their stories. Maybe that mitigated the impact of how horrible the stories themselves were. We were the first people they ever met who they could tell this to without thinking that they would be killed for saying it.

Peter Baker

The embedding process was a great, huge step forward. What we had in the past was terrible. The critics have a point about some of the things they say about it. But the choice is not between embedding and free, complete access. Susan made discreet trips in and out of Iraq. She is smart about finding the story, the most compelling story that can be done—and about how to do it safely. The problem with the war was that some of the unilaterals were cowboys and they made it dangerous for everybody. They did crazy shit. They went in front of the front lines, and they got in between battles. That stuff is nuts. It's bad enough they take chances, but they also create an atmosphere that is dangerous for all reporters because people in the country start thinking the reporters are combatants.

Even our command center came under attack. We were fired on a number of times. The first Iraqi shot of the war was a missile at our camp in Kuwait that landed a couple hundred yards away. The explosion felt horribly huge.

You heard the sound. Boom. My heart went through the roof. We had no clue, because the war had just started. I grabbed my gas mask and ran for the bunkers. Then we would do it again twenty or thirty times over the next day or so. But I certainly felt more secure than most other embedded reporters. While nothing is absolute, you sort of assumed that they don't let Marine generals die.

Susan Glasser

It's incredibly important to have independent reporting from a war zone. We didn't want to talk to more American soldiers, who were being wonderfully covered by a lot of our colleagues. We wanted to talk to Iraqis. The overall sense I got from the embeds was you could tell modern technology is now up to the task of covering a war on the ground and showing you things as they unfold in real time, perhaps misleadingly. The main thing it caused journalists to see is the utter uselessness of the set-piece Pentagon briefings.

Peter and I are very concerned about one another's safety. It's always more horrible to be the one who's left behind and it's much more stressful to worry about the other person than about yourself. So, the times when Peter was in scary places in Afghanistan, it was very difficult for me. I'm sure he would say the same about me in Tora Bora or in Basra. We talked about these dangers many times and among ourselves and with our friends and colleagues. We all take risks in doing this. Peter and I have had a wonderful relationship. We really are partners in this business. We share and understand our experiences in a way that others couldn't.

MEASURING THE TRUE COST OF WAR

Peace Activist Marla Ruzicka

"I said to the captain, 'Dammit! I have a couple of hours to get this little girl the help she needs. Please tell me what to do!'"

At an April 6th press conference at Central Command Headquarters in Doha, Qatar, with the American army poised to make its final push into Baghdad, a reporter asked Brigadier General Vincent Brooks about civilian casualties being inflicted. His reply: "It just is not worth trying to characterize by numbers. If we are going to be honorable about our warfare, we are not out there to count up bodies. This is not the appropriate way to go." Another Pentagon spokesman spun this calculated dereliction of accountability by saying, "Our efforts are focused on military tasks."

The Pentagon's reluctance to release numbers seemed to suggest the notion that body counts are so Vietnam. One would have assumed that the American and international media might have aggressively pursued this story. Instead they dragged their collective feet, though a team of reporters from Knight-Ridder did, in fact, research Baghdad deaths in early May. But it wasn't until June 10 that aggregate numbers surfaced. After a five-week investigation, the Associated Press reported that, "at least 3,240 civilians died across Iraq during a month of war, including 1,896 in Baghdad." These numbers were calculated by examining handwritten, blood-splattered hospital logs and death entombed in rubble.

Working alone, Marla Ruzicka, twenty-six, from San Francisco, also pursued her own head count of Iraqi injured and dead. She had formed her own nonprofit organization called the Campaign for Innocent Victims in Conflicts (CIVIC), and organized 150 surveyors to fan out across Iraq, literally going door to door, visiting clinics and families in the smallest villages. Ruzicka is not affiliated with relief agencies, the United Nations, or media organizations. She is a self-supported peace activist who conducted a similar one-on-one interviewing campaign with victims' families in Afghanistan, and it was her results that grabbed the attention of U.S. Senator Patrick Leahy who introduced legislation to create an Afghan victims fund. Six weeks after the fall of Baghdad, *ABC Nightline* devoted an entire segment to Ruzicka, who defies stereotyping as a placard-wielding, anti-war idealist. Precisely because of her insistence on accuracy, she has earned credibility with both journalists and the military.

■   ■   ■

In November of 2001, I was part of a human rights delegation that went to Afghanistan to look at the situation of women, and also to document civilian casualties. I was in Jalalabad in the Tora Bora area during that operation. I was in hospital wards where several civilians who had never heard of Osama bin Laden, or never had anything to do with the Taliban, were hurt from stray U.S. bombs. One woman had both of her eyes torn out. Both arms and legs were broken. I saw children and their bandaged heads. I watched journalists in that Tora Bora hospital room who had covered everything from Rwanda to Vietnam just break down and fall to the ground crying. It's not something that goes away for a lot of them either. I talked to some of these reporters, and I noticed that at a young age they left to go cover injustices, and to put a face to injustices. I was really impressed and said to myself, "Well, that is what I have to do. I want to create a victims fund."

It seemed that calling for the U.S. government to set up a fund was the right thing to do. I returned to the U.S., then two weeks later, I went back to Afghanistan to start advocating for the people who were harmed in that operation. Afghanistan is like my child. Alice Walker said that when you have a baby, your heart is walking outside your body. I met a little girl, Amina, eight years old. She just had this warmth. She held my hand. She cuddled up to me. She sat on my lap. She lost sixteen people in her family, and only survived because it was Ramadan, and she was out in the kitchen making tea. Her father survived, but all the other people in the house were crushed by the bombs. She now takes care of her father because he is emotionally unwell.

In Afghanistan, we used surveyors who had monitored U.N. sanctions of the UN under the Taliban. They knew the country well. They had nothing to prove. They weren't trying to exaggerate, because accuracy is the number one thing. You can't do body counts from media clippings, especially when towns are spelled three or four different ways. You have to be on the ground. You have to have people going door-to-door.

In the July 2002 supplemental bill for Afghanistan, Senator Patrick Leahy from Vermont inserted language that money should be made available to reconstruct housing. When it was clear that war was starting in Iraq, I did the same thing. I worked with Leahy's office to get language inserted in the Reconstruction and Relief for Iraq that said, "We will assist families who were harmed in the operations."

What does this work do to me? I don't sleep. I'm a human being. It drives me. It motivates me. I had an identity change this year. I was one of the most radical people on the planet. I have interrupted President Bush and Secretary of State Colin Powell at their speeches, because I was pissed off that the U.S. doesn't give money for AIDS. I was pissed off that Bush helped screw up California with the energy crisis. These were all things that made me very angry. From a very early age I was an activist. My first political action was a walk-out against the Gulf War when I was school president in eighth grade at Perris Middle School in Lakeport, California. I just don't want innocent people to suffer. I grew up with a twin brother. My mom always said, "You've got to love everyone as much as you love your brother. You have to live your life like that."

I did human rights work with Global Exchange for seven or eight years. I've been all over Central America with them. I'd seen violence. Here were people in Guatemala taking bullets in their back by doing things like voting and organizing their food. Americans had no idea about it. I wanted to learn why it was going on to educate others. I found people in the leftist circles do care, and that is great, but really it has to go beyond that percentage.

In Iraq, probably the hardest thing for me was working with some journalists who told me about a little girl who had about two days left to live. She had ninety percent burns over her body. She was injured as her car was hit as her parents were fleeing Baghdad. Her mother threw her and her three-month-old sister out the window, and she and her sister survived. Little Zahar was three and a half. She was taken to a hospital but with all the looting they were afraid she was going to get septicemia. This was right around the same time of the famous case of Ali when he was airlifted out. The Marines said they would do that for others. I had found out about Zahar on Friday night, but Saturday morning the Marines were leaving Baghdad and the army was coming in. My point person was now gone. I didn't know who to see so we could get this little girl air-evacuated out. I was up all night calling CENTCOM. I had journalists calling CENTCOM. I was doing everything I possibly could. One journalist from England told me to go talk to the captain. This was outside the Palestine Hotel. A ton of journalists were trying to get into the Palestine Hotel. It was impossible. I pushed everyone out of my way. Pushed whoever was trying to get to him and I said to the captain, "Dammit! I have a couple of hours to get this little girl the help she needs. Please tell me what to do!" He said, "Look, we don't have a real formal policy. The best thing to do is to find the captain who is in charge of the area of the hospital." I then drove to the hospital in a taxi and I went up to a tank outside. I climbed up the tank and I said to the private, "Listen! The situation is that we have a few hours or this little girl is going to die. I'm going to go in and check on her. You need to get on the phone to whoever I need to talk to, to get her air-evacuated out." Within three hours we had a chopper there that took Zahar, and a thirty-six-year-old woman and her eighteen-month old baby out, just like that. That private did his job, and I was just so proud of him. He said, "Ma'am. That's my job!" He added, "When I looked at her, I thought of my two little girls at home." He wouldn't even tell me his name. He was the Nameless Hero.

When we later inquired about Zahar, we didn't know if she would live. They said that there was a fifty percent chance. We found out a week later that she had survived. That she had made it back to her family, but then, a few days afterwards, she died of pneumonia. Her little body was overcome by the burns, and her respiratory system was shot. So I went and visited her grandmother to tell her the bad news. She asked, "When is she coming home?" when I walked through the door. She had lost eight people already.

For my mental health, I swim a couple miles a day in Baghdad. I pound the hell out of the water. Some photographer once asked me, "Do you do anything but swim?" I wanted to say to him, "Do you really want to come with me on my day job?"

What I see doesn't leave you. You don't file it. You don't go away from it. If it weren't for these journalists, I wouldn't have been inspired to do what I'm doing. They let me sleep on their floor, and I watched them cry, and I learned from them. My role is not to be a journalist. Look, I have no money. I don't need all the attention in the world. I just need enough. I need to always remember what Che Guevara said about love, and caring about others, and being able just to feel both the hardest and worst things in the world. I can't tell you that Zahar was the most awesome and horrible experience of my life. It was awesome to say, "Let's believe that we had saved her," and then it was the most horrible reality when she was gone. I am not some altruist because I get lonely, I get depressed. I completely feel inadequate. I couldn't save her.

We have to see what happens to victims. That is what CENTCOM needs to do. Now there is no reason why the Pentagon can't do that. They know where the bombs are dropped. They have intelligence on the ground. It's an absolute no-brainer from a strategic point of view. From an American patriotic point of view, Americans do not want innocent people to suffer. I feel like what I'm doing is the most patriotic thing in the world.

GOING FROM GROUND ZERO
TO THE GROUND WAR

Newsday Reporter Graham Rayman

> "I was covered in dust for two weeks.
> Baby wipes were more important than
> the M-16."

"Covering the war was a lot like an extreme camping trip," wrote *Newsday*'s
Graham Rayman in one of his dispatches as an embedded reporter with the
eighth Marine Corps Engineers, based out of Camp Lejeune in North Carolina.
"Until, that is, Iraqi missiles started cutting worm trails in the sky to the north
and west of us. I dove into a skirmish trench with the other 150 Marines in the
company and watched the missiles climb in the sky like red-and-yellow fire-
flies. Looking to my left and right along the trench, I saw some Marines praying and bug-eyed, but I also saw others cracking jokes and even napping. After
watching the first two volleys, I opted during the next five volleys over ten
hours to fall back on my personal motto (Ignorance is bliss) and commune with
the sand."

Ah, the ubiquitous sand. He did more than seek communion with the grit.
He slept in it, he ate it with his MREs, he breathed it. It was Rayman's primary
nemesis for the duration of the war, even inside the Humvee—a real bummer.
"One ride took twenty-six hours," he recalls. "I swear it's designed to take in
dust and expel oxygen. One of eleven Long Island, New York–based *Newsday*
reporters and photographers sent overseas to cover the war, Rayman was the
first to come home. (Two of his *Newsday* colleagues had been briefly abducted
and detained by the Iraqi secret police for several days.) He flew out of
Baghdad into Kuwait City on an U.S. Army helicopter. "The trip was heaven, "
he said.

■　■　■

I've been with Newsday for about ten years. I've covered police, city hall, and spent a year and a half covering September 11 local news before I got the war zone assignment. The idea was that I would look at the momentum created after the September 11 attacks and its effect on U.S. foreign policy in Kuwait and Iraq, but the conclusion I found was that there was no relationship to September 11. The Marines I was with didn't talk about September 11. Unlike in Afghanistan, where there was some urgency, in this conflict there was no urgency. There was no need to go in. Our country made a choice to go—the President made a choice to go into Iraq, but he could have waited a year, or two years, or five years, and it wouldn't have made a difference. In general, the Marines were mostly interested in getting home because a lot of what they do day-to-day is difficult, hard labor.

You couldn't help but get close to them. They took me in and treated me as if I was a member of the company. It was such an intense, intimate setting. For example, I was in the back of a Humvee for hours on end with these guys, and covered with dust, thirsty, and it's unclear whether you're going to be ambushed. You have no idea what's going on around you, because one of the things is that the individual units were given minimal amounts of information about what was going on around them, so they have no context. They don't know if they're going into an area that is dangerous. I was never really able to get a decent answer to that. Their commanders wanted them to treat every situation as potentially a major threat, so they wouldn't be relaxed, or maybe it was just easier to handle them if they weren't sure what was going to happen in the next few hours. But that was one of the most difficult parts—not having the big-picture sense of what was going on around. Let's say that there was another military unit a quarter mile away. They didn't even know who that was. It wasn't an automatic that they would go over and check. I even had better communication gear. I had a satellite phone and they had their old radios. These old radios were one of their main headaches. They were cranky and unpredictable. One minute they might work fine; the next minute not. I'm not an expert on radio gear, but I got the sense that it was pretty old stuff that pre-dated the Gulf War and could have been twenty, thirty years old. The Humvees were at least fifteen years old; some of their trucks dated back to Vietnam.

That first week, we were in a completely isolated part of Kuwait, where if you make a bad decision with your water, or with your gas, or with your compass, you would just get lost. That's what the desert was like. There were no geographic features. It was just this flat expanse stretching out to the horizon in every direction, and there were mirages in the afternoon. The Marines had set up their tents, which were these nice two-person tents. One day, one of the Marines found a scorpion and banged it around with his knife. That was the big moment in the day. On St. Patrick's Day, they played golf because they were following a tradition. They took out their golf clubs and took some swings in the desert. They were just sitting around waiting for their assignment. They had no idea when it was going to come.

The main task of this engineers' unit was to build temporary bridges over dry gaps or rivers. It was expected that Saddam's army would blow bridges to slow the advance.

They built at least three while I was with them. They boasted that they could build a a thirty-meter bridge in two-and-one-half hours. When they finally got the assignment, it was late in the afternoon, so they had to start work at night and it ended up taking them eighteen hours. They kept working all the way through the night, and eventually they got it done, then they passed out.

To the west of Nasiriyah, there was another bridge that the Marines used very heavily. We were right next to that bridge for a couple of days when the battle was still going on in Nasiriyah. It was quiet, but they expected to be ambushed at any moment, so they dug some trenches around the edge of the camp. They put twenty-hour patrols and twenty-four-hour sentry posts. There were a couple of moments where it appeared that someone was trying to approach their position, so the company laid down some serious firepower. They had M-16s and five or six 50-calibers, and some fired grenade launchers, but they never had to get in a firefight. Some mortars were once fired at the column, and then one day while they were working on a road there was some rifle fire, but it didn't hit anyone.

One of the things about the advance was that, rather than there being one steady column of trucks, and tanks, and troops, and helicopters, units would leapfrog each other. You had a whole bunch of self-contained units jumping over each other constantly. There were situations when the engineers would be completely isolated—up to a mile behind a tank column. These convoys weren't tied in together. They weren't even talking to each other. Just to give you an example, the engineer convoy was a mile long, right? It had ninety vehicles, but only the Humvees had radios. So the first day when it was a twenty-four-hour convoy into Iraq, the individual drivers had no one telling them where to go. The individual drivers had to just watch the truck in front, but what happened was, they got so tired that they started falling asleep at the wheel, and so these enormous gaps would develop in the convoy.

Two weeks in, when we were in yet another convoy and I was choking on the dust, I got frustrated with the whole situation. There was really no way to keep the dust out. I was covered in dust for two weeks. It was impossible. I used baby wipes to get it off. Those baby wipes were more important than the M-16, which, actually, some of the Pfc's offered to let me shoot, but I turned them down. They couldn't believe that someone would be sent into a war zone without any weapon. They would usually ask, "Are you sure you don't want a gun? We'll just give you one. You can have a sidearm."

Two other questions they liked to ask were: "Did you volunteer for this?" They were amazed that anyone would volunteer for it. And, "Are you having fun yet?" I got those questions over and over again. They just couldn't believe that someone would agree to be here. Many of them joined the Marines for reasons that had nothing to do with the fact that they were going to shoot their weapons in any battles. These were engineers. Their motivations are different than the grunts who obsessively train for combat constantly. These guys train also for combat, but not quite so much. I mean, they'll be sent on special exercises, and they'll be attached to these mobile task forces that spend six months at a time on the ocean, just going from port to port, and they'll step off and do exercises there, but the engineers won't train quite so obsessively.

When they joined their butt to be a Marine, it was really more for other reasons—like a college degree or to get away from a bad situation at home, or to get out of the country and see the world. There were those three layers. There were the Pfc's, and then the officers, and then the noncoms. I never got a chance to write the story, but I wanted to write about the interplay between the officers and the noncommissioned officers, because the officers were all young—their captain was twenty-six, the lieutenants were all between twenty-four and twenty-six. The people who had the experience in these areas were the noncommissioned officers, and yet they couldn't—as much as they might have wanted to—just come out and order the lieutenants and the captains to do what they knew was the right thing to do. A couple of the noncommissioned officers have their construction companies that they run on the weekends, and they're listening to some guy just out of college! But I was impressed. They had a lot of respect for the chain of command. That was the bottom line. Many of the Marines were kids from the city, and very small towns, who at first glance might come off maybe as a little bit innocent, but once you get to know them a little bit, they would turn out to have this wonderful quality or skill. There was this one kid, maybe twenty-four, from this small town in Alabama who, could fix just about anything. He was just a genius at mechanical stuff.

Interestingly, a lot of them just wanted to get through the war without seeing any real action, but I think they were excited to be close to a small battle at a canal near the Tigris. The Iraqis were dug in on the opposite bank, and they had mortars, heavy machine guns, and some AK47 positions, but that's just not going to cut it against armor. They had no armor; they had no artillery; they had no air support. The Americans just sat there with a column of twenty tanks and armored vehicles right across the bridge, and the fight was over in ten minutes.

I felt that the Iraqis had been totally overrated. I looked in the foxholes and they had brought their own bags to carry their food, mattresses, and blankets. The Marines were quick about cleaning up the corpses. I saw one body. It was lying next to a truck. I had no idea what had happened there. We just drove by. I wish we could just stop for a minute, and I could ask around, but that was one of the bad things about the embedding process because you couldn't do that. You were forced to be swept along with the unit. A lot of times it is better, as a reporter, to come in a little bit afterwards.

With the embedding, you're only going to get a very narrow picture of what happened; only what that unit sees, and that can really vary. Second, you're not going to be able to follow up very well. It's difficult to follow up without leaving the unit in very uncertain territory and then basically, without any resources. Third, just the fact that you're putting your life in the hands of the Marines is by itself not conducive to objective journalism, right? So it's limiting. But on the other hand, if your aim is to write about what Marines do every day—what their relations are like, what goes through their minds—then it was an excellent idea. Looking at the embedding process, at least from the journalistic side, it's best to have it balanced with people who are also on their own, doing typical foreign reporting assignments. When I covered September 11, the struggle was always trying to pry information out of the city, or the state, or the federal government. They were trying desperately to control the story. They wanted the issue to be the heroism of the firefighters, and the inconsolable grief of the families who lost loved ones, and they wanted that to be the story by itself; not to what extent the construction had anything to do with the buildings' collapse or to what extent political considerations have wormed their way into the issues of the redevelopment. My assignment in Iraq was a much more narrow assignment, which was just to get to know this group of soldiers, this group of Marines, so I didn't have to worry about those big things that I had to worry about with September 11. As far as in a journalistic experience, I felt the stories that I wrote about the Marines, even though it was a very limited subject and I didn't try to answer the broader questions of U.S. policy or the war, was more satisfying than covering September 11 because I had more access. That made it more possible to get some of the different perspectives.

VIEW FROM ACROSS THE POND

BBC News Special
Correspondent Gavin Hewitt

In Britain, Clinton is far more popular than George W.

This high-profile BBC special correspondent has been immersed in American political culture for quite some time. Apart from spending several months a year as the Washington D.C correspondent, Gavin Hewitt, who joined the BBC in 1984, has made three films about President Clinton, including *All the President's Women*, and *The Shaming of the President*. He conducted the first British television interview with Oliver North after the Iran Contra scandal, and later wrote a book about the hostage crisis in Lebanon. For Britain's *Ten O' Clock News* he reported on the September 11 and Bali terrorist attacks, and he later wrote and presented the BBC documentary *Clear the Skies*, which chronicled the hours of September 11 when America was under attack. Now, that Iraq was under imminent attack, he decided to view this war as an embed with the U.S. Army Third Infantry Division.

■   ■   ■

Rightly or wrongly, George W. Bush doesn't travel well. He has a folksy, direct style, very much drawing upon his roots from Midland, Texas, which plays well particularly in Middle America. His use of language, especially when he talks about evildoers, is a Manichaean view of the world. That the world divides easily between good and bad, doesn't play so well outside America. It doesn't play that well within the U.K. I think his directness, his sense of certainty is not what people expect from politicians. I think with Bill Clinton, despite all the scandals that came into him, people liked him in the U.K.; they still do. He was recently here and electrified the restaurant. He has a kind of rock-star element about him that people seem to like, even though if they pause for a moment, they are completely aware of his record in terms of telling the truth. In Britain, Clinton is far more popular than George W.

Blair and Clinton were very close. They were soul mates. They came up with this idea that there was a third way. You didn't have to define yourself as to whether you were right, or liberal, or left, that somehow there was a different way of going about politics. They, in a sense, embarked on the same project. We felt that when Clinton left, Blair would have a hard time having that same kind of relationship in Washington. I mean, clearly George Bush was not a political soul mate. But very early on, Blair established a relationship with Bush, and Bush's view was, "Well, let's see what this man's made of," and, of course, much as 9/11 transformed Bush's presidency, so I think he transformed the relationship with Blair. The one thing that Blair saw early on and without any prompting from Washington, is that he understood how 9/11 had changed the world, and that there was now a threat that had been there before, but now had revealed itself; where there were people who would use any means that they could lay their hands on to destroy our way of life—the American way of life, Britain's way of life, other similar countries. It was that certainty and willingness to stand shoulder-to-shoulder with Bush that began to change that relationship into one where Bush and Blair—they didn't become soul mates, they would disagree substantially on many political areas—but in terms of understanding the threat that was now posed to the free world, they became very close allies.

In the run-up to the war with Iraq, they only needed each other. If it was to be a Coalition, there couldn't be one for Bush without Blair. There was no way that if Bush got cold feet about the war, that somehow Blair and the British could go it alone, so they both needed each other, and they needed to support each other in trying to get as much backing around the world as they could. With the political storms brewing both in the States and in the U.K. concerning weapons of mass destruction, the longer that they are not found, the more unhappiness will be expressed both in Washington and in London about how the various evidence was put together. As they stand together, they fall together. Both were very clear about the threat.

There was, however, a great sense of relief and a certain pride in the way the military operation was run, but American and British troops are going to be in Iraq for a long time. As each day goes by, and the attacks continue on troops, and casualties continue—they're pretty small at the moment, but on a fairly regular basis—then the political temperature can change. As we approach the election in the United States, people could begin to question the whole project in Iraq: "If the threat wasn't there, why are our boys still there? Why are we still taking casualties?"

I must admit that U.S. troops were delighted that 45,000 British troops were coming alongside. Just a few days before the war started, there was an erroneous story that somehow the British troops might not actually join in. There was quite a lot of disappointment because they felt these were soldiers the U.S. can rely on and will do a good job; it's one less thing to have to worry about.

There are differences between British and American soldiers in terms of interacting with Iraqi civilians. The British view is that you get out of your Kevlar, you carry your weapons in a more defensive mode as quickly as you can. You go out of your way to meet ordinary people. You stop off at the cafe that might still be serving coffee, and you start talking and getting a sense of people. In winning the peace, of course, holding those relationships is central to the Iraqi's understanding of what this war was all about. The U.K. troops might have a slightly greater knowledge of the world beyond their borders, they might have traveled a little bit more, but essentially they are drawn from the same economic pool as the U.S. If they hadn't joined the military, their job prospects weren't that good. American troops have much better equipment, better communications, and the computer systems that back up the American forces are superior to the U.K. forces. The British forces seemed very disciplined but are under-equipped. I didn't detect any rivalry between them.

My view of the war was as an embed with the U.S. Army Third Infantry Division, Task Force 130. I joined them in the desert for about a week before the war started, then spent about five weeks with them as they fought their way all the way up to Nasiriyah, Karbala, through the edge of the airport, up into Baghdad itself. For a brief period we had our own vehicle and driver with us. Our driver had been with the British SAS, so he had intimate knowledge about American Special Forces. Because I was with the BBC, they were cautious to start with, but fairly soon they accepted us, and I think they would say we got on well. They felt we would not burn them without due cause. I made it clear early on that I was not going to work with a microphone in their face twenty-four hours a day. There are moments when people would relax, shoot the breeze together, say things which are undoubtedly off the record. I would cut them a little bit of slack. Yet at the same time, I was also clear that if something happened and didn't reflect well on them, I would have to report it, and they regarded that as a fair deal.

On April 6, as we were coming into Baghdad, there were several firefights. I saw quite a lot of civilians lying spread-eagled on the ground, having been shot up in their cars. I did express in my report that if the Coalition would be regarded as liberators in the future, this war had to end soon. There were too many civilians dying. I also raised the concern that whether too much force was being used in some of these firefights. But I put that carefully because, as someone who was inside in vehicles which were being shot at, it is very difficult to reply proportionately. So I raised concerns, which I know that some of the soldiers had themselves, but I raised it in a way which I felt was fair to them, and also fair to the troops.

There were attacks taking place on convoys. This was—whatever anybody might say—unexpected. When we were traveling up that main highway—the only highway where all the supplies were coming up—there was a suicide attack at a checkpoint. I heard this coming over the radio, and it just changed the way soldiers looked at it. From then on, the Iraqis were not people to be talked to, they were people who had to be kept outside the camp perimeter. Anybody who approached or didn't slow down, there was a very real danger they would get shot. The mood that nobody could be trusted went all the way up into Baghdad. Who was friend, who was foe? That was very difficult on the streets of Baghdad. So one way of dealing with that was that if somebody opened fire, they would reply with very considerable force. Given those circumstances, sometimes innocent civilians got caught up into it. I know amongst the troops, they felt, "Look, we dropped leaflets prior to the war; we made it clear when the war starts, stay at home, and you won't get hurt." But people didn't stay at home. Their approach brought the war to an end quicker, but my concern was how much harder would it make the peace?

A great sense of liberation hit west Baghdad the day after Saddam's statue came down. The streets were filled with people running alongside the tanks and saying, "Thank you, Mr. Bush, thank you, Mr. Blair." There was one man who kept running along saying, "Saddam killed my family," and the troops who I was with loved it. They felt a sense of great justification. But everywhere we went we saw solemn, uncertain faces, who didn't like the idea that although they may be being liberated, it was coming at the hands of the Americans and British. The preparations for what was to follow were not sophisticated enough. For instance, there was no television station to let people know what the Americans were trying to do. There was a vacuum.

I haven't seen an economic analysis about what it would take to ensure peace, but if you look at the kind of figures that were involved in rebuilding Europe after World War II or Japan, I just do not think that enough energy went into making sure that within days you would see food coming in, that there were sufficient troops on the ground to provide security. All the emphasis was just get rid of Saddam, and essentially the people will be happy, and the future will take care of itself. This was a failure and has made winning the peace that much harder. We will have to see how long it is before American troops begin pulling out of Iraq. I see them there for the foreseeable future.

I'm not haunted by what I saw in Iraq. I don't have any kind of nightmares. But I do feel a sense of responsibility that we should find out whether the grounds for the war were right. There are important questions that remain to be resolved. In the end, the arguments about war always should be intense, even if war is clear-cut, because the greatest value to civilization is that war always remains the last resort and not something that is entered into lightly. Therefore, the more it is discussed and seen, the more engaged people are in it, I think that is a real service. Some of the new technology enables the battlefield to come into the front room, but all material needs interpreting. It requires correspondents who are prepared to report independently and to report what they see. Technology does a lot but ultimately you've got to have people who are faithful to what they see out there.

THE DISEMBED

Harrisburg's *Patriot-News*
Washington Reporter Brett Lieberman

"I had no idea what it was about, but I felt like
I was being called to the principal's office."

He wrote about health and hygiene issues affecting Marines—the dirt, con-
taminated water, dysentery, the ever-present flies. He wrote about a young
Iraqi schoolgirl who cried at the sight of armed Marines standing in her school's
courtyard. He wrote about reservists forced to put their careers on hold. He
wrote about the litter-strewn, three-story courthouse in Nasiriyah covered in
foot-high piles of ashes, charred records, an opened safe, and broken concrete
and glass. He wrote about the Marines receiving mail from home, marking a
joyous interlude from war's daily grind. He had filed three dozen stories from
Kuwait and Iraq. The final story of Brett Lieberman, the Washington, D.C., bureau reporter with the Harrisburg *Patriot-News,* however, summarized his own
disembedment with Echo Company from the Second Battalion, Twenty-fifth
Marines in Iraq. Echo Company's hometown is also Harrisburg, Pennsylvania.

■ ■ ■

An acquaintance had told me about a Marine reserve unit that was acti-
vated and was about to be deployed. This battalion was made up of Marines
mostly from New York, Pennsylvania, and New Jersey. It was a local story
for the *Patriot-News.* They were lawyers, police, firefighters, cooks, stock-
brokers, and students. Most of the officers were in their thirties, fairly successful. Some people were earning hundreds of thousands of dollars in
their jobs. About ten percent of the battalion were either firefighters or police who worked on 9/11 and were called to serve that day. A police officer
from New York City carried with him two small vials: one was ashes from
Ground Zero, the other was dirt from Ground Zero. He had a huge sense
of pride, and like a lot of those guys, they were doing their part for the war

on terrorism because they knew a lot of fellow firefighters and police officers who were killed at the World Trade Center. One fallen firefighter was
actually a member of the battalion.

I didn't know about my embed assignment until the day before I flew
down from Washington, D.C., to North Carolina and met my unit. I then flew
with them on a military aircraft to Kuwait. For three weeks prior, my assignment kept changing between being approved and not being approved. The
battalion commander wasn't sure he wanted me there because he had some
bad experiences with the press in the first Gulf War. This guy was old-school
and regardless of what the Pentagon was saying, he didn't want a reporter. It
was an extra burden and a distraction. What good could come of it? Everyone
else was very supportive.

I was provided with what is known as NBC gear—for nuclear, biological,
and chemical attacks. On the flight over to Kuwait, I kept practicing putting
on the gas mask. Surprisingly, it is tough. You've got to do it in nine seconds.
You've got to get an airtight seal. It's dark if you're doing it in the middle of the
night. The first time we had a Scud alarm in Kuwait, I probably would have
been dead if it had been real. It easily took me a good thirty seconds.

In the past I have covered military matters, especially the National Guard.
I've covered briefings at Pentagon and military base closures. Never anything
combat-wise. Ninety-nine percent of the Marines I'd met were amazing. Right
from the get-go. Everybody was helpful. I didn't want them to carry my gear,
but they were always offering. People were always asking, "Did you get an
MRE for food?" "You got water?" You know, that sort of thing. People were
very friendly.

I sometimes went out on patrols in Iraq with these guys. In the beginning,
it was nerve-wracking. I was scared because sometimes it didn't really matter
where you were because we were out in the open. Somebody told me that no
matter where you go, just always keep an eye out and think about worst-case
scenarios: If something happens, where are you going to go? A lot of times,
there just wasn't any place to go. In these open areas, there's no natural barriers. Perhaps a few ditches, shrubs. If we had to dive down on my first patrol, it
would have been really disgusting because we were walking by these streams
of sewage, so that would have been the place we would have had to dive into
if something happened.

There were pockets of fighting here and there in Nasiriyah after the initial
large firefight, so it still wasn't a very secure place. The battalion was regularly

confiscating a lot of weapons and bringing in people for questioning. I went on some of these search missions. Most times they would knock first and ask if they could come in. They were trying to be invited in rather than storming through. There were cases though when people weren't home and they had suspicions about something. They would either scale a fence to get in there or they'd knock down a door. I saw that happen a couple of times. They were looking for weapons, and they would ask people to open drawers in case they were booby-trapped. There was one Marine who was actually born in Egypt and he did translation. He became sort of a celebrity; the Iraqis in town were always asking for him. People would give him gifts, food, flatbread. He was invited to people's homes for dinner. But this came with mixed blessings because through intelligence he knew the fedayeen were asking about him. There was a concern that he would become a target at the same time the Iraqis were very welcoming and friendly toward him.

Mostly, they'd find weapons or people would lie to them and say, "Oh, I've got a weapon—the fedayeen forced me." They were AK47s usually, RPGs, bigger guns. You never knew how many were actually hidden underground. At one point, they found a huge cache of AK47 ammunition, mortars, RPGs. You dealt with mostly the men. Some of the women were tending to the family. Young women weren't out in the streets. The young girls in the house were very friendly, but typically, you didn't see young women outside. You'd see little girls, then at twelve, thirteen years old, they seemed to disappear and then come back later when they're older.

On the day before our first patrol through town, there had been a big shootout which killed some people in the village. That night we came under attack at the compound. On the patrol the next day, we saw kids out on the street playing, groups of people just talking near a mosque, but when we got close, everybody would stop. You got cold stares. You knew it wasn't a good welcoming, warm feeling, but you didn't know why they were so unfriendly. You didn't know whether it was because of the shooting the day before. You didn't know whether they were hating Americans, or if they were afraid. Over the next few weeks, you saw some of that change. There was one area of the town, particularly the slums, where people were much friendlier. They were also trying to sell the Americans cigarettes, alcohol, and sodas.

I had written a story that the Marine reservists weren't thrilled with the new aspects of the humanitarian mission. They felt that Marines were trained to be in combat and not trained for humanitarian missions, which the army has traditionally handled the last few years. They either wanted to be in a combat scenario or go home. They weren't saying they wouldn't do whatever they were told to do. The commander of the Fifteenth MEU, Marine Expeditionary Unit—it was the senior unit there and our battalion was attached to them—saw the story, then brought in the battalion commander, and chewed him out. The commander called in the company commander who was with Echo Company, and chewed him out. I happened to be down at battalion headquarters that day and he also chewed me out. His logic was: "We're Marines. We don't complain. We do as we're told." Nobody was saying they weren't doing what they were told, but they had spent a lot of the last year training for urban combat, so they'd rather be doing that.

Other officers told me the story's fine. The average Marine told me the story's fine, "It's actually accurate. What's the deal?" The next morning the commander came over to me to apologize. I don't think he was apologizing because he thought the story was okay. I got the sense that he was apologizing only after other officers had said that his yelling at me was inappropriate. I had felt sort of awkward when he was yelling at me because I was not in the chain of command—I'm not a Marine!

A couple of weeks later, I found out that the Fifteenth MEU knew they were leaving soon, but they didn't know which day, and that other units were coming in to relieve them. There was a concern that these new units were only going to be there for a couple of weeks and not for the long-term. They lacked a lot of the resources that the more senior units had. They didn't have the communications capabilities, level of armor, and vehicles. If there were a bigger plan to relieve these other units on a more permanent basis, nobody told them. The Second Battalion was feeling they were screwed, to some degree. They were worried, not panicked, because they figured things would work out, and they knew that they could handle what they were going to be given, which was to have 900 guys patrol a city of 350,000. They thought, "Well, we could do our basic job, but we're going to have to pull back on a lot of other thing we're doing." They were trying to restart the local police force, and the court system, and basic city services, but now they just weren't going to have the resources and the manpower to do all that. They would just maintain the city, keep order, that sort of thing. They were having an informal meeting to figure this out, "Okay, what do we need to do? What questions do we need answered?" In talking to the executive officer of the battalion, I decided to hold off writing the story that night, partly because, for my purposes, it wasn't urgent, but also there were just so many questions they didn't have the answers to. They were planning on having a regularly-scheduled staff meeting the next morning and they said, "If you could hold off until then, we're going to get some answers in the morning, which we hope will answer some questions." But it turned out by the next morning, things weren't changed, and there was a general sense they were going to be stretched very thin. They didn't have the resources and capabilities of these other units that were leaving. So I go and do the story. I didn't really think twice about it. Actually some of the details that were in that story had been in previous stories, like the fact that the Fifteenth MEU was going to be leaving, and how the city was being divided by sector.

The story ran in Saturday's paper. Around Saturday morning about 6:00 A.M. when we got up, I found that I had an appointment at the Public Affairs Office at the Fifteenth MEU. I had no idea what it was about, but I felt like I was being called to the principal's office. I knew it wasn't good, but you don't know what you did. The lieutenant colonel told me that they didn't want me there, saying that I was endangering the Marines' lives by telling the enemy exactly what's going on, and where they'll be. Then I ended up yelling at the Public Affairs people who echoed the same thing because they were abusive, yelling at me. They brought up the rules and I argued that everything was on the record. Secondly, a lot of these details had been in my previous stories. They were saying that I had written about "future operations," which is against the rules, but in all those cases I'd asked the battalion officers, "Can I say this, can I say that?" and everything was fine. There were no problems at all in the past stories. I wasn't able to argue with anyone over a captain there at the Public Affairs Unit. My case was then sent up the chain of command to the First Marine Expeditionary Force. I tried bringing up how the rules state how disputes are supposed to be resolved, and they didn't want to hear it. Throughout the day I was in limbo.

Later that day, they told me to get my gear and leave Echo Company. The next morning they dumped me at this airfield south of Nasiriyah and put me on a plane out of Iraq. They weren't MPs. They were Marines just doing their job. I flew to Kuwait City. I was there when Geraldo Rivera was disembedded from 101st Airborne. I was told by the Marines I was with that he was escorted back to the Hilton for a debriefing; which I didn't get.

In conversations I had with average Marines before I even left, they were upset about what happened to me. They kept saying things about freedom of the press. They thought it was bogus. They said, "You can quote me. Do you want me to write a letter?" These are average Marines for the most part. Even officers were telling my stories were fine, but I told them, "You don't need to get dragged into this."

I spent my time in Kuwait at the airport. I was there for twenty hours, then flew home. My story about being disembedded began to leak because family members of the Marines received phone calls. I was also discussed in chat rooms. The Marines' family members, girlfriends, parents were upset. My being forced to leave was a disservice to everybody because the Marines themselves really liked the connection. I was able to provide with my satphone group e-mails to learn what was going on at home—like one Marine whose wife was due to have a baby. It was a disservice to the families back home because now they didn't know where their loved ones were, what they were going through anymore. There was uncertainty. They may get a letter or not; they may get a phone call or e-mail, but the logistics were difficult in Iraq. The mail had never been good. The whole time I was there, the Marines got mail maybe three times. So they really lost the connection. To this day, I still don't think I did anything wrong. I was just disappointed at how it ended.

THE SOUND WAR
National Public Radio
Correspondent Eric Westervelt

> "If I'm going to die covering this war, at least
> I want to get some good tape."

You compliment a photographer by telling him he has a great eye. But what do you say to a radio correspondent? Honestly, it is an equal compliment to say he or she has a great ear, because the magic of editing sound and painting word-pictures often ignites the imagination. In the modern era of television, the radio correspondent may not carry the clout or influence that yesterday's greats like Edward R. Murrow displayed during World War II, but that hardly means that these knights of the microphone come up short as reporters. Founded in 1970 with ninety public radio stations as charter members, National Public Radio maintains this country's aural tradition of newsgathering (wasn't America's first celebrity war correspondent Paul Revere, who rode through the streets of Boston crying, "The British are coming"?). Now serving an audience of twenty-one million Americans each week, NPR sent several reporters to cover the Iraq war. We interviewed one of its correspondents, Eric Westervelt, thirty-four, who was embedded with the Third Infantry Division and the Battalion Task Force 164. Westervelt has been with NPR for seven years and has reported on a diverse range of topics, including the massacre at Columbine High School, the Florida presidential recount, and blues artists.

■　■　■

The power of the radio medium came through during coverage of the Iraq war. Radio has an intimacy and immediacy, like hearing directly from the grunts on the ground, the sounds of their Bradley fighting vehicles, or Abrams tanks, or the artillery going off. Radio brings the listener into the story sometimes in a way that print and TV can't. That is not to knock my brothers in print and TV. They do what they do extremely well. But I got e-mails from listeners who said, "I watched the war on TV and I listened to NPR. I often felt I was more at the scene with your reports when you described what's going on, and we'd hear the sounds of the soldiers, and some of the fighting."

There were some reactions from listeners I didn't get a chance to read until I got back to the United States. One was almost funny. One guy wrote: "God damn! Motherfucker! Yeah! Bring it on! That's what I'm talking about." Others said, "I've been waiting for that kind of war coverage." Others wrote, "Thanks for bringing us the immediacy of the war, and for letting the soldiers speak freely." We let some of the profanity stay. I told my editor early on, "This is combat. They are young soldiers. They swear. Bleeping out all their language is counterproductive. Let it go." The senior editors said, "Yeah, we agree. This is not a feature on line dancing or gardening." Several listeners wrote saying, "Thank you for treating us like adults and letting the language go, because this is combat. One listener, though, wrote, "Well, I'm really ashamed NPR has given in to the sensationalist war coverage. Your story today by Eric Westervelt, with sounds of battle, and explosions, and tanks, and God forbid!" Sensationalist? What would they like instead? A story about war with people drinking tea?

I tried to paint a picture with words and sound that drew the listener in to what was chaotic, scary, frightening—and also occasionally heroic with tense situations on the ground. I can remember being interviewed while sitting in the back of a Bradley fighting vehicle with the satellite phone just sticking out of the back turret area, where they used to load the TOW missiles. Because it was night time, we had light discipline going on. I couldn't go out and find a nice comfortable patch of dirt and set up. I'd have to stick my satphone out the rear end of the Bradley, and point it toward the right satellite, and fire it up. I'd be talking live on the radio either to *Morning Edition* or *All Things Considered*. I'd be describing what was going on, what we did that previous day, or afternoon. Sometimes the sounds of the battle or of that night's activity would creep in and the host would say, "What's that sound we're hearing?" I'd say, "That's the turret of the Bradley fighting vehicle traversing as the commander and his gunner are looking through their heat sensors and night vision for Iraqi fedayeen. They are making sure no more fedayeen are attacking tonight. They will be switching on and off all night, protecting this company."

During a morning interview with *Morning Edition*, the host, Alex Chadwick, was talking to me and I was describing a battle that had taken place earlier, but now it was a bit of a lull. An Abrams tank literally drove by two feet away. A guy I knew was in the Abrams, and he was sticking out the turret, and he waved to me as he drove by. I felt safe. He wasn't going to run me down. But it had this enormous sound over the radio that was just like a jet plane taking off.

I'd call up and do live two-way interviews, as we called them. Or I would send in produced pieces that would be a combination of the sounds of the day mixed with my writing, and quotes from commanders, and grunts on the ground. I carried an Audio-Technica shotgun microphone. It has a big wind-protector around it. It was handheld with a pistol grip. I had two Sony Mini-Discs strapped around my neck. If one went down, I'd switch to the other one. A producer of *The Evening Show* naively asked me, "Well, why did the sound go dead there?" "Well, you try diving into a ditch." If I'm going to die covering this war, at least I want to get some good tape.

I actually had several brushes with death. The first time was the last Friday in March when I went with a group from Alpha Company in their Bradleys and tanks down to a small bridge on the outskirts of Najaf. They were going to broadcast a surrender message to this small group of fedayeen still there. We had been fighting for several days. The intelligence and Special Ops thought that these guys were done and broke, and they might be ready to give up the ghost. I was out of the Bradley walking in bright sunshine. It was a beautiful day. I approached the edge of this bridge. Alpha Company started broadcasting this surrender message in Arabic. "Attention! Attention! Elite American troops are surrounding you. Surrender and you will be treated humanely under the Geneva Convention. You'll be given food, and water, and treated with respect. But give yourselves up." They responded to the message with RPGs and mortars.

At first, people were confused about where the firing was coming from exactly. One of the guys from the civil affairs team that was broadcasting the surrender message said, "It's coming from over there!" He pointed to a palm tree grove right near a hospital and a factory over a small bridge that led into this suburb of An Najaf. Another commander, Major Mike Donovan, came up and said, "What the hell are you doing on that side of the Humvee? This firing is coming from there!" He pointed to the buildings. "Holy shit! I guess we should get over to the other side," I thought. You can hear the RPG in the story I did when I hit the deck under the Humvee; it's sort of a szzeeeuungh sound. Then the tape goes blank. While I was ducking under the Humvee, I realized some situations were not only good moments for journalism, but that I might also be recording my own death.

Another time I was reporting from an abandoned Iraqi military police station. They had left behind food, shoes, and blankets after hearing U.S. tanks rumbling, and so they fled across this little footbridge. I was describing this scene for the radio audience, when this soldier who was two feet away from me opened fire with his machine gun. I thought, "That's good tape, but I hope I can get out to file it."

Because I was with a front-line unit, I was able to get a pretty complete view of the war's progress. While it wasn't the complete picture, I did the best I could to put what they were doing in context. I had access to intelligence reports, to the artillery, to the commander's briefings. I received a lot of cooperation from the company commander. I had earned their trust. I was careful to say this is what I'm seeing, such as when I would describe our location, I would say, "I'm one of the furthest north in Iraq near An Najaf." If some host would say, "Well, we're hearing there is rationing at the front." I could say, "Well, I'm at the front and at least with my company and my battalion; water, fuel, and food are doing okay. There is no rationing here. It may be happening with other units of the Third Infantry Division." Then I'd broaden it into the larger picture and say, "These are long supply lines coming from Kuwait. They are vulnerable. The Iraqis are vowing to attack them. They certainly are vulnerable and U.S. forces are concerned about that." I never tried to paint the whole picture because I couldn't. There were other NPR reporters. It was the job of our other embedded reporter with the Marines or our unilateral with the Kurds in the north, as well as our guy in Qatar, and our guy at the Pentagon to broaden the view and, of course, our person in Baghdad, Anne Garrels. Sometimes it was frustrating because I knew more about the big picture than I could necessarily say right there on the radio. I would have liked to have told my audience more about the overall strategy, but obviously I couldn't always do that.

In this age of reality TV, and instant news, and hyper-saturation of media events, we need more than ever an unsanitized, real-as-we-can view of combat and war. However clichéd it may sound, war still is hell. To be able to bring a snapshot of that to listeners is a valuable public service. Because we do sometimes forget, with the debates on Capitol Hill and the Pentagon briefings amidst the rush of media and Internet, the fact is there are still eighteen and nineteen-year old American kids with guns using sophisticated equipment to kill people to achieve specifically-stated foreign policy aims. We must be able to tell their story and bring people closer to the reality of combat. Not in a way that was done during some of the reporting of Desert Storm and other conflicts where the media were kept in a cage. This was a chance to get our hands dirty, and by extension get our listeners' hands dirtier by telling them this is combat. It's hard work. It's dangerous.

I don't have war nightmares, but there were some eerie moments from the war I still replay in my mind. About a day and a half after the firefight on the outskirts of An Najaf, the situation was still tense. The local people—mothers, fathers, brothers—began to show up and retrieve their dead from the battlefield. Some of the bodies were disfigured. They were mangled and clearly stiff after almost two days. The Iraqis were literally piling them in the backseats or trunks of their Toyota-type cars. These big, stiff, sometimes bloody bodies, would be sticking out of the back of cars. It was a really poignant, sad moment when you realized, "Yeah, they may have been the enemy, but they were also brothers, sisters, husbands—fully human—and were for whatever reasons, were conscripted, or otherwise fighting for a cause, or forced to fight."

The U.S. soldiers respected their coming to get their dead. They said, "Let them do that." But it got tense when some of the relatives began wailing. Some were crying. Some women became hysterical. Some were throwing stones at U.S. soldiers. They weren't a security threat. It was more like a "damn you," gesture. Then the commanders said, "Well, we might have to cut this off. This is getting kinda tense." I remember talking to one of the soldiers and trying to get his reaction. I asked him, "What do you think of this?" I wasn't trying to rub his face in it. But this was the outcome of the battle the other night. He said, "Well, I can't get emotionally wrapped up in this. I need to maintain my focus." In some ways the look on his face revealed he was moved by the retrieval of dead fighters, but his words were from his training: "I'm keeping my hand on the trigger and making sure none of the guys in the cars that go by me are going to ambush me."

Another eerie scene was on the Thunder Run into Baghdad on April 4, where I witnessed heavy fighting. Cars were careening toward the convoy, and getting whacked, getting destroyed. I saw all this up close. Then I saw two parents and two kids trying to flee the other way in a car when they were attacked. There was a secondary explosion. It might have been a case where they just got caught in the crossfire between the Iraqis and Americans. Whether a secondary explosion blew them up, I don't know. But when we passed them, the car was completely on fire. The mother was dead. The father was falling out of the burning car—crawling slowly and completely on fire. Two little kids, five to seven years old, were on the median next to the car. They had gotten out of the car in time. They were standing there crying, looking dazed, watching their parents die while an armored column rolls by. Personally, that was the darkest image I saw of the horror of combat. It haunts me today. Part of me wanted to jump out of the back of the Bradley and grab the kids, but we were moving fast. Bullets were flying. You hoped that medics saw the children and did something for them. I hope those kids survived.

OUR WARRIOR YOUTH
Rolling Stone Reporter Evan Wright

"Marines will make fun of everything: The
Pledge of Allegiance, George Bush. The Marines
are not brainwashed to worship the President.
They are brainwashed to worship the Marine
Corps. That's all they believe in."

Rolling Stone magazine devoted a whopping 28,000 words, spread over three
consecutive issues, to the Iraq war. This mammoth allotment of publishing real
estate allowed its correspondent, Evan Wright, thirty-eight, to follow a single
Marine platoon and craft the kind of combat memoir that functions as literature,
evoking the haunting narrative intensity of Michael Herr's *Dispatches*—one of
the most savagely honest books to emerge from Vietnam.

The twenty-three-member Bravo Company platoon that Wright was embedded with was part of the toughest, most badass, elite First Recon Marines, of the
First Marine Expeditionary Force, attached to the First Marine Division—"cocky,
arrogant bastards" according to General James Mattis, commander of the Marine
ground forces in Iraq. As these commandos furiously pushed across the desert
plains and fertile valleys of Iraq, crammed into Humvees, "eating candy, dipping
tobacco and singing songs," Wright recorded their changing moods, their sleep-
deprived observations, their scatological insights, their amazing killing ability, their
uncensored views of war. Little escaped Wright's reportorial net—as one machine-
gunner told Wright, "One universal fact of being in the Marine Corps is that no
matter where we go in the world, we always end up in some random shitty place."

Another Marine, swimming in a gin haze, "brings up a subject so taboo
and almost pornographic in its own way, I doubt he'd ever broach it sober
among his buddies. 'You know,' he says, 'I've fired 203-grenade rounds into
windows, through a door once. But the thing I wish I'd seen—I wish I could
have seen a grenade go into someone's body and blow it up. You know what
I'm saying?' The other Marines just listen silently in the darkness."

How did Wright manage to pry loose personal secrets from the Marines? What journalistic front did he present to allow this insular band of brothers to lower their guard? Why did they trust this civilian outsider? Or did these Marines walk unsuspectingly into a media ambush? And what truth-telling tactics were employed by this talented writer who has penned magazine profiles on tree-living radical environmentalists, skateboarders, porn stars, and Ohio State sorority girls. "These girls were the toughest subculture I'd ever gotten into," recalls Wright. "They were such mean and nasty people."

■ ■ ■

It sounds corny, but these Marines were such a great group of people. I can imagine a million interest groups who would hate these guys for their foul mouths and blasé attitude toward killing. I was lucky about *Rolling Stone*. I once did an article on a young skateboarder for *ESPN the Magazine*. It's owned by Disney. The story was about black skateboarders. Kind of a weird phenomenon in America since it's primarily a white suburban pastime. There is this phenomenal skateboarder called Stevie Williams who has all these fans, and he is from Philadelphia. I went with him to his home, which is basically the ghetto. I am with him and all of his friends and I am getting it down. When I handed in the article, I had to excise the language and clean it up. It was amazing how differently the story read once they had bleeped out everything. I don't swear a lot in my personal life. But corny as it sounds, it was part of the poetry of both the skateboarder's and Marine's language.

I studied medieval and renaissance languages and history at Vassar College, and it was a very language-oriented major. I studied Italian, Latin, and Old English. I lived in Italy and spent a lot of time in Europe. It is only funny in retrospect because I ended up working for Larry Flynt at *Hustler* magazine. It was actually a desperation move, because I had come out to Los Angeles to write screenplays and it wasn't going very well, and the only paychecks I was able to get were from the telemarketing industry. So, I started working at *Hustler* and the first journalism I ever did was at the magazine. I had no training, though history was a good background for journalism. I was trying to overcome the stigma I felt about writing pornography, which is really what I did most of the time. I was immersed in the world of porn and wrote about it. I was the news guy of porn. I really liked its subculture, which was misunderstood by people. After I left *Hustler* I became a freelancer for *Rolling Stone*. My first story for them was about the old Aryan Nation headquarters near Coeur d'Alene, Idaho. I always try to find something likeable in my subjects, but I could find nothing in those Aryan people to like. Really nothing.

I did another story called "Mad Dogs and Lawyers." It was about the San Francisco couple who were attorneys who owned the dogs that killed the woman. That article was just picked up in an anthology called *Best American Crime Reporting*. I dunno if it is a big deal or anything. I only got $250 for it. There was another story I did about a skateboarding gang. They weren't really a gang but they fancied themselves one. They were called the Piss Drunks. I went to interview one of the guys at 9:00 A.M. Saturday. I walked in the house and he puked in the sink because he was so drunk. He then smoked crack for the rest of the interview. That was a good one. I realized if you're doing a story on a group of teenagers and young guys who call themselves the Piss Drunks, there is a high likelihood that a lot of them will be drunk as you're doing it.

I then covered the Afghanistan war for *Rolling Stone*. I did two pieces. In fact, the whole embedding process actually started in Afghanistan. The problem from the military's standpoint was that it didn't start when the war did. So all the combat heroics weren't covered by reporters. I had arrived after Operation Anaconda. Everything was pretty much over. I guess, having covered war once, I wanted to try to again. Actually, I was in contract negotiations with *Rolling Stone* about a month before the Iraq war started, so I thought it would boost my standing if I volunteered to go to Iraq, hoping that we wouldn't have the war, and that it would just spike my pay for that contract. That is the honest truth.

What *Rolling Stone* learned in Afghanistan was that you needed to get there early. Once I got embedded with the First Recon Battalion, they were going to put me with this support unit in the rear. The people who are not even engineers. The guys who stack MRE boxes. I talked to the battalion commander and he made a decision which apparently he now regrets, which is he let me go with the front-line companies, but I had to turn in my Thuraya satellite phone even before the ban.

I liked the idea that no one—especially my editor—could find me once I got with the front-line company, because I do better when I spend a lot of time with the material. My equipment turned out to be just paper and pens. I had a tape recorder, but I didn't use the tape recorder that much because I had a finite supply of microcassettes. I was saving them, because if I had to interview some general I would tape record him. I don't like reporter's notebooks because I can't tuck them in my back pocket. I use these $12 Molskenai notebooks that my sister bought me. They are the latte of notebooks. They are made in Italy or France. Hemingway used them supposedly. It is a marketing ploy: They are bound with stitching. They are made with high-quality paper; it's thin but it's strong and there are a lot of pages in it. So I had a bunch of those. The reason I emphasize that is because I think it is really important to always have your notebook with you. I find it is better to write a lot in front of people if you're going to be around them. They get used to it. The other thing is my writing is so illegible. It protects me from people being able to read very easily what I'm writing.

Yes, the old papyrus technology. I went back to its home in Iraq. I have observed other reporters in combat areas. They have so much equipment. Even wire service guys who are beaming up stories from their laptops. They have to get in line of sight with the satellite. That takes time. Even if you have solar panels, they never work. So you have to worry about recharging your battery. It becomes this big technical problem. You're tethered to it. So in my situation, I would not have been allowed to go with the actual front-line troops had I carried equipment. I don't know if this happened to other reporters. I know some print guys who did have satphones and who did go close to the front. But most of the people covering the war were not magazine people. So it's a technical advantage being low tech.

How did I get these Marines to open up with me? I seem to do a good job with all sorts of subjects, whether it's people in the military or people in prison. I use some specific techniques, like I will spend hours talking about trivial things which some people take as a sign that I like them. I am extremely curious about people, so it is genuine, and it usually goes from there. Sometimes if they are starting to shut down, I will just start blabbing. It drives them crazy. Just to shut me up, they will start telling me something. The other thing is something I learned in the porn industry. I would often tell people something revealing or supposedly vulnerable about myself, because if you reveal something uncomfortable about yourself, it creates a sense of intimacy. I'm not consciously trying to con somebody into opening up to me. It's more natural. Having worked in the porn industry, I was around people who let it all hang out. I was already comfortable about having conversations about things that you just normally don't bring up with people.

There was this time when the platoon was paranoid that their commander was trying to kill them. The Marines would talk about it: "Oh, he will be sitting around with his high officers and someone will ask, 'What happened to you in the war?' Someone will say 'Well, I lost ten men.' Then he will say, 'I didn't lose any,' and they will be like, 'Man, you didn't see shit!' " They were going on about this—and death was no laughing matter out there—but I said to them, "I hope you realize as a reporter I am in the same situation. If anybody gets killed out here, I have a much better story." It's the truth, right? I often will tell people things like that, and that breaks down the barrier. Although I have to question at the end of the day whether everything I am doing is just one big fraud.

The embedding process is such a passive experience. With most stories, you have to kick in doors and stuff. But I found that once you are in the military culture, people will start talking to you. So you don't have to worry about that. By the way, I should point out something that a guy named Iceberg Slim said. He wrote a book called *Pimp: The Story of My Life*. He wrote these books in the fifties and sixties, which were about ghetto life in the thirties and forties. All the lingo in hip hop that kids think is new? It's all from him. The books are filthy and perverted. He said that when you move onto the mark, always tell him something revealing about yourself. Like, "Oh my wife cheats on me," or, "I have a drinking problem." Something really embarrassing. When you do that, it ages the friendship, he wrote. As soon as you do that, you can move in for the kill. I guess that's what I do, too. Iceberg was the master of con. He was in prison half of his life, so I guess he wasn't the total master con.

In the beginning, I didn't like the platoon leader, Brad Colbert. He was twenty-eight years old and an Afghan war veteran. But as a reporter, it is important to check yourself and evaluate how you are really reacting to this person. Forget that you are a reporter for a while. It also helps when they are shooting people or getting shot at. Colbert rubbed me the wrong way when I first met him. I also didn't have a lot of confidence in him. Physically he didn't look like the big, giant Marine that was going to spit bullets at people. So when we were rolling into combat together in the same vehicle, I was thinking, "I hope this guy doesn't freak out." He was a great surprise, because he helped keep everyone alive in the vehicle, and because he was really cool. He has a code of conduct he does his best to adhere to. The first time that made him seem like a bad guy was when they were throwing out humanitarian rations to these Iraqi kids, and he said, "Vote Republican!" I am pretty apolitical. I am a member of the libertarian party. I don't care if he is a Republican, but I thought, "What a snotty remark!" These kids are starving and he is mocking them. Then it kind of sickened me because, well, he's right. This was brought to them by Bush and the Republican Party.

When I first met him, he was obsessed with technical problems like operating the radios. Before the war started, Colbert was always sitting by his computer. Lecturing people about this thing called the Nine Line and how to call in an air strike. He made me go through it. I thought that he was one of those geeks who is obsessed with computers, and dungeons and dragons and this is all a fantasy for him—and that he was going to snap the moment somebody shoots a gun at him. When he confessed he listens to Barry Manilow, I said, "Oh, God!" I mean I listen to some pretty bad music, too. But Barry Manilow? It's just a personal thing. Right before the first ambush, he turned to the guys in the vehicle and he said, "Gentlemen, you're gonna have to earn your stories." I heard that and I thought, "Man, that's pretty corny. This guy doesn't even think he is in a war. He thinks he is in, like, some Marine training commercial. Now we are all going to die!"

One of the strongest memories I have of him is of the first ambush at a town called al-Gharraf, when everyone's weapons jammed constantly. My first memory is of looking around, looking at Colbert. There are all these muzzle flashes and fire coming into the vehicle even. He is calm. I saw his gun jam. He didn't panic. He used another piece of his weapon called a 203. It is a grenade launcher. He was just calmly firing into things and I remember looking at him and thinking, "He's got things under control." It's funny how a small thing like that really stuck out in my mind.

Colbert's vehicle took something like twenty-two rounds. Colbert actually had pieces of bullet fragments in his ear. On the very next day, there was this horrific sandstorm. They didn't have much sleep. There was a lot of periodic shooting as they were moving north. Lot of gore and dead bodies. Then they were ordered at the last minute to move to this airfield deep behind enemy lines. Then the orders kept changing. They were told that British paratroopers were going to invade this airfield, or drop on to it, and the Marines were supposed to observe it, and make sure there was nothing there. Then at the last minute, at dawn, the Marines who hadn't slept much in forty-eight hours, were woken up and told, "You have five minutes to get on to the airfield. We're seizing it!" Everyone got in the vehicles, and they were forming up this line, and they started speeding down this road. Colbert's vehicle, which had three Marines in it, gets this message over the radio that there are four Iraqi T-72 tanks on the airfield. There were Republican Guard. There were also these anti-aircraft guns, which actually can be devastating. Then, the new order was given: Any people you see on the air field are declared hostile, which means shoot anybody you see. Doesn't matter if they are holding a weapon. Doesn't matter if it is a woman running away from you with a baby in her arms. They are declared hostile.

Colbert was dealing with all these different problems. He was getting this information but so far had so little understanding of where the airfield actually was. Colbert sat in the passenger seat. Corporal Joshua Person, who grew up poor in a small town in Missouri, was the driver. They were saying, "Our map shows a fence on this airfield. We have bolt cutters. We're gonna have to cut through it." They don't even know what they are driving into. They just think there are tanks there. Meanwhile, I was in the seat directly behind Colbert. Another Marine was sitting directly behind the driver, Corporal Trombley, nineteen years old and a newlywed from Michigan. He had already developed this peculiar relationship with his weapon, a SAW (Squad Automatic Weapon). It is a medium-caliber machine gun that fires 762mm rounds. He had already displayed a lot of interesting behavior. He talked to his gun. He said, "Gee, I wonder if she killed anyone yet?" The other Marines in the Humvee were going, "Would you cut out that cheesy, B-movie dialogue from bad World War II movies?" This is going on and Trombley, who was sitting next to me, said, "There's men with guns," or something like that. He identified them as Iraqis. Now under the rules of engagement at the time, he can shoot anybody he wants to, because any person is declared a hostile.

We were inside what amounted to a free-fire zone, but that's a Vietnam term they don't use any more because it sounds bad. They would rather say, "Everyone is declared hostile." That is the new politically correct way of saying, "Shoot anything that moves." But despite the fact that this was a free-fire zone, the Marines in vehicles ahead of us did not fire on these young men. Trombley opened up on them with his SAW. Really it was two short bursts of bullets. Like two three-to-five shot bursts. As he was doing it, he said, "Shooting motherfuckers like it's cool," a phrase he had heard other Marines use. Trombley was one of the youngest Marines in the unit, and he hadn't proven himself.

They went to the airfield and nothing was there. It was a big joke. They raced around. A couple hours later they set up camp. They were triumphant because they beat the British paratroopers to the airfield. They have gone through these ambushes. Everybody was really excited. They sat down and were told, "Hey, guys, you get to rest for a while." This was the first time they really rested in a week. Right at this moment, some Bedouin women came to the edge of the camp. They were dragging this heavy bundle across dirt fields.

The medical corpsman, Timothy Robert Bryan, went out there and asked, "What's going on?" The women opened up this blanket and this boy about twelve years old, rolled out. He's got four entry wounds in his ribs and his stomach, and no exit wounds, which means the rounds zipped around inside of him. His older bother, about fourteen, was hobbling around, shot in the leg.

Again, being a reporter, I'm thinking in the back of my mind, "This is gruesome. This is awesome. This is perfect. I've got everything now. This is the honest truth. I was there when the shooting happened, and everyone knew that Trombley was the one who shot them."

The boy's mother was gesticulating, gesturing, like she was talking to God. She was opening her mouth and no sounds were coming out. She was so distraught carrying this bundle that her robes had fallen open and her breasts spilled out. It was like some Biblical scene of grieving.

Then these other Bedouins came. They were nice to the Marines. They knew what happened. Our interpreter translated, "Oh yeah, you guys were the ones that shot our boys." They were gentle about everything with the Marines that the whole thing was just a shock. The medic didn't think the boy was going to make it. When a medevac was requested, the commander denied it at first. What happened now is the medical corpsman and a couple other Marines came up with this plan. They put the boy on a stretcher and they carried him down to this tent where their commander was. This was a really big deal in the Marine Corps. Though the commander said, "We can't do anything," the boy was now technically in the care of the battalion physician who said, "Hey, I actually live near the headquarters tent. Technically, we can carry him down there and I will render him aid there."

On this technicality, they carried him down to the tent and were not committing an insurrection. They were merely assisting the physician. They also brought the grieving mother and grandmother. The sergeant major, the senior enlisted adviser of the battalion, came up and said, "Get the fuck out of here!" But the commander then reversed himself, and ordered the two shot kids and their families to be taken to a shock trauma team. There was kind of a happy ending in that the kid allegedly survived, according to the Marine Corps. At least I was told he did, but I would have preferred to see this for myself.

Colbert emerges here as the hero of the story. He had arrived on the scene a little bit later and said, "I am responsible for this." Several Marines were angry at Trombley. Colbert was kneeling close to the woman, and started crying, but he didn't make a big show of it. The mother had covered herself by then. The thing that impressed me is that he was involved in the scheme to get the kid medical help. I thought, well, if he is really this careerist, which he supposedly is, would he say, "I am responsible?" Would he shed a few tears? No, he would say, "Well, I am not signing off on this." But he was right there. He carried the stretcher down right past Trombley. The Marines were saying things like "Trombley, look at what you did." Colbert told them to stop. So that scene is where I really changed my mind about Colbert, who by the way, graduated from Mountain Warfare School. He once climbed Mount Shasta on a broken ankle.

The whole mantra of a Recon Marine is to be swift, silent, and deadly. They are supposed to sneak in. They are never supposed to be seen. A Recon Marine is a failure if the enemy finds him. These Recon Marines were constantly at the front of their own battalion and their battalion is often thirty miles behind enemy lines. They were often sent in as a lightning rod for action in this conflict. They were thrown into Humvees, and they didn't even have Humvee military operating licenses. They were given these old machine guns they weren't trained specifically on, and were thrown into spots to get attention. If there was a known ambush point, they would drive right into it. I was extremely terrified throughout these situations. We once wandered into an ambush in a town called Muwafikiyah. We were surrounded on three sides. It's called the kill zone, the kill box. The enemy had put an obstacle in the road in front of us. The Marines were trying to turn around. All the Marines knew we were in a classic kill zone. They knew this was an ambush once they saw the obstacle. Everybody in the vehicle knew this except me. That's one of the things of being blissfully ignorant. I knew it was getting bad, but I didn't know how bad it was. Your body shows signs of fear that are, in normal circumstances, embarrassing. I wasn't aware of how badly my body was trembling all over until we rolled out of the kill zone. I noticed this because my feet were banging on the floor, and I felt very cold, like I was freezing. The medical corpsman, Bryan, said it was normal. With the adrenaline pumping, it sends all the blood to your interior and restricts the flow to your extremities.

It got bad again at this cigarette factory in Baghdad. It was pretty late in the game, around April 10. Five of us, including the platoon commander, decided to walk around its perimeter. We get out in the open grassy area where we started taking sniper fire. All I could think of was that comedy, *The In Laws*, starring Alan Arkin and Peter Falk. They both start taking this enemy fire. Alan Arkin is a dentist. He says, "What should I do?" Peter Falk is yelling. "Serpentine! Serpentine! Do a serpentine walk." When you are taking a single round at a time, you don't hear the bang of a gunpowder explosion. You hear a crack. It's a much sharper sound. It is the sonic boom of a bullet crossing the sound barrier. Then you hear the zing. I learned if you hear the crack and the zing, it's very bad. Afterwards, this Marine sniper said to me, "You know what? Serpentine only works if you're being shot at by a really good sniper. If he's bad shot, it doesn't help you anyway. You want to go in a straight line and just get the hell outta there."

When I look back on it, I was in a lot of nasty situations. I saw things that were remarkably violent, such as the body on the road that looked like a smashed tomato crate. But I was not really disturbed by it, which was an interesting thing. I think it's partially because I grew up around a lot of gruesome talk. My mother was a defense attorney, so there was a lot of murder talk around the table, and she dated the county coroner for a while. But also, movies like *Black Hawk Down*, which is so graphic and very realistic. With *Black Hawk Down* in particular, the Marines watched it over and over again. I think that the author, Anthony Swofford, who wrote *Jarhead*, refers to these movies as Marine pornography or war pornography. I probably panicked less in combat situations because I'd seen it all in the movies. It shows how powerful movies are. Along that same line, I've played a lot of violent video games and see a lot of gruesome, violent movies. Like a lot of other people in our culture, I am your average desensitized American. I have not had any nightmares, but there hasn't been enough time yet. I've been working steadily since I got back, but when I have a vacation, that will be a good time to start losing my mind.

Ultimately, the sum of everything you have experienced as a person informs what you write. So, in addition to classical literature, there are a few things in my background that put me in synch with these Marines. Before working for *Rolling Stone*, in the three years I spent working for Larry Flynt and writing about some people who murdered, I learned that people who make pornography for a living and people who kill have a lot in common. They both do things that are taboo and excite equal measures of interest and revulsion in the general public. Both groups are occasionally lavished with frenzied media interest yet they remain pretty much equally misunderstood by everyone.

When I first got to the Middle East and wasn't yet embedded, I floated around and met random, infantry soldiers. The Recon is the elite of the Corps. There was a paradox where the U.S. Army is supposedly less brainwashed than people in the Marine Corps. But people in the U.S. Army are much more controlled personally. They won't say things that sound unpatriotic. Marines will make fun of everything: The Pledge of Allegiance, George Bush. The Marines are not brainwashed to worship the President. They are brainwashed to worship the Marine Corps. That's all they believe in. So you can talk bad about anything, but not the Marine Corps. You can say anybody in the Marine Corps is an a-hole. You can say everything he is doing is wrong. As long as you always say, "But I still love the Corps." I saw this right away.

After my *Rolling Stone* article appeared, the Marines who were in it have been actually very supportive of me. The commander was a little bit mad, but not the Marines in the platoon. Marines throughout the Corps and officers throughout the Corps have gone out of their way to contact me and say, "This was really a great article. You showed the bad side of the Marine Corps." I have come to believe that they really do take this idea seriously that they try to be honest. There is this rawness about how they talk and they seem to be totally fine with it. Their wives seem fine with it. Whereas before, I was getting letters from army wives after my Afghanistan war coverage saying that I was unpatriotic. The Marine wives who e-mailed thought it was funny. For example, I wrote about these Marines who were discussing John Wayne Bobbitt: "He had sex with a midget." The Marine gunnery sergeant said, "Yeah, a Marine will fuck anything." He was married to a nice, funny woman who wrote me. She said, "Yeah, that sounds like him."

So why did I cover this war? You know that old dictum: Know thyself? A life unexamined is not worth living. I sort of feel that way about the media. For some philosophical reason a society should try to know itself. That is how I view my role in it. I also found out that no matter how great the story is, when you get home, if you pay your rent late, you get a three-day notice on your door here in L.A. They are pretty hard about that.

SHARP SHOOTERS

Combat Cameraman Staff Sergeant Ronald Mitchell

"I'm completely against embedded journalists because it takes soldiers away from their jobs to protect somebody who volunteered to come over here."

Those nocturnal green-hued television images of Private First Class Jessica Lynch being carried on a stretcher by Special Ops commandos into a waiting helicopter were taken by a relatively unknown and unheralded division of the U.S. Army. Combat Camera's task is to document the Army's permanent official visual history, often transmitting images to the Joint Chiefs of Staff, the President, and various military officials. Combat Camera team members like saying, "The brave ones were shooting the enemy; the crazy ones were shooting the pictures." Originally known as Signal Corps photographers, these dual shooters (Combat Camera soldiers are required to carry sidearms) were on hand to record famous WWII events such as landings in North Africa. *Life* magazine used the Signal Corps' library in its first venture in book publishing—*Life's Picture History of World War II*.

During U.S. troop buildup in Vietnam, Combat Camera soldiers continuously documented the longest and most visually recorded war in U.S. history, covering Medevac operations, counterinsurgency, Psyops pacification, and the turning point of the war—the Tet Offensive. Over forty million feet of motion picture footage was shot. The broadcasting media selected portions of this footage to bring the war into our living rooms. Iraq, of course, took place in a much different media environment. Network and cable television now fielded their own armies of cameramen, but this development didn't preclude shooters with the Fort Meade, Maryland–based Fifty-fifth Signal Command from netting the video exclusive of the war.

We talked to one member of the Combat Camera Team, Staff Sergeant Ronald Mitchell, twenty-five, from Newark, Ohio. Though he didn't personally participate in the Lynch rescue mission, he earned his valor in other ways. At a firefight in a small town south of Baghdad, he was wounded by shrapnel yet continued shooting with his camera—and with a rifle. He later received a Purple Heart medal, one of several awarded to Combat Camera in Iraq.

■   ■   ■

We had air-assaulted into Karbala on a Chinook helicopter. When we landed, there was some enemy fire going on, so we had to land farther away from the town than we expected. It was the hottest day of the year, maybe 105 degrees Fahrenheit. We had already drained our water before we even hit the town. It was that hot. Once we did hit the town we started receiving more fire, and we were stuck in a position for about two hours. We were not able to move. It was pretty difficult.

My fellow combat cameraman Luis Azzara was with First Battalion and I was with the Third Battalion. He was on the far right flank and I was on the far left flank attacking the city of Karbala. Once we were finally able to move, we starting receiving more fire. The Bradleys and tank that were with us provided great cover. A lot of 105 Howitzer artillery was coming in. As combat cameramen, we had pistols, but with so many infantry guys around us, this didn't come into play.

Some of the enemy were in mosques. Most of them were shooting from rooftops. Because the houses are built close together like row houses, the fedayeen could jump from roof to roof. By the time we were able to shoot back, they were on to another rooftop. The enemy was so far away it was hard to focus in on them with my small Sony PD150 mini-DV camera. I didn't have long enough of a lens for that.

We took over a house and then we started receiving fire there. Actually one of the Bradley guys who got killed was right outside our house. He was brought inside and received medical aid. My photographer had a picture of him. I was there shooting video. But as a Combat Cameraman, you are a soldier first and you always want to make sure your unit is getting taken care of. You want to make sure that the medics are there to take care of the infantry when they're hurt.

We didn't know at that time how badly he was hurt. They evac'd him real quick. We found out the next day that he had died.

I've been deployed and done this so many times that when I'm filming, I don't really think about it. I just shoot because that's my job. But when I get back in the office and start looking at what I shot, that's when I stop and think, "Man, I could have died today!" Or, "This soldier here is hurt and I'm not. How did that happen?" I know a couple of times when there were guys right next to me that got hit and I didn't. So it makes you say an extra prayer at night.

Our level of work—compared to the old days—has changed a lot because our equipment has improved and because there are many more photographers in war zones. During World War II, it was only Combat Camera and you had to take what you got. Now because there is so much embedded media, it makes us step up our video standards. There's competition. Your lighting's got to be correct, you've got to get the right angle, because you're competing with the civilian media. If they don't get the shot they'll get fired. We can't get fired, but we get yelled at pretty badly if we miss a shot. We can get "counseled" and that's pretty bad.

While filming a firefight in Mamyudia, just south of Baghdad and near the Republican Guard barracks, we were hit by a fragmentation grenade from the enemy. My partner was taking still photos. He put his camera down to perform first aid because there were so many people injured. Myself, I picked up a rifle from one of the downed soldiers and, in between firing back at the enemy, I was also taking video of the enemy.

What had happened was that we were on a patrol. We had gotten a late afternoon mission to follow this platoon that was going to go clear this town. Mamyudia was a small town, only four kilometers long. We had moved through three kilometers of the town and everybody was getting happy because it was Palm Sunday and they had a barbeque lined up for us that day at camp. The Iraqis had been nice and friendly. We only had one more kilometer to go when we found some weapons caches. Then we came up to this Ba'ath Party house, and we found several RPGs. It was nothing really big, nothing to get excited about. We just wanted to keep on moving and complete our mission, but the crowd outside the building had started to gather. Pretty soon, we had at least 500 people outside. We then heard some AK47 fire, and as soon as everyone turned to see where the fire was coming from, a grenade exploded. I got hit. I had some shrapnel in my eye, my leg. My partner received pieces in his leg and in his ankle.

We took twenty-two casualties that day. Two people had been shot. I was thinking, "What's going on now? What are we going to do?" Then everything from training kicks in. It becomes your instinct and you just move with the flow. You're not even thinking about what's going on, you're just reacting to the situation. There was only about thirty to forty people in the platoon with us, but luckily, on the other side of town, there was another platoon. When they heard the firefight, they rushed over and they doubled our size. Later in the day, we were receiving fire from a mosque, and we had to go clear the mosque, and everybody saw me with a rifle out there. They were like, "Wow! Just look at this guy! A Combat Cameraman with a rifle. What's going on?" We earned a lot of respect that day from the others because they knew "we can count on these soldiers."

We are always encouraged to get some film of the enemy. In this operation, you could not see their faces because they were either hidden or they weren't even shooting at you. They would just hold their rifle up and just pull the trigger. They wouldn't even know where they were shooting at, but you could see some of their muzzle flash. They were just shooting pretty much to keep our heads down.

Our job is important because we're recording actual soldiers out there. People who see our released combat footage, whether it's military analysts or network audiences, are not hearing just a news story and maybe a clip or two. They're actually seeing the faces of soldiers going through the action. It provides that home touch, that intimate feeling of, "Why, this could be my next door neighbor, my brother, my cousin." It's not just some guys in tan uniforms wearing an American flag. It gives you that up-close stuff.

I'm completely against embedded journalists because it takes soldiers away from their jobs to protect somebody who volunteered to come over here. We're actual soldiers who were sent over here. We don't get protection. We carry a 9-mm pistol, but that's pretty much it unless things get hot. Another thing I hate about the embedded media is that nobody is checking their imagery. Like they're just pretty much renegades out there. They can shoot anything, and put out any kind of story, and a lot of times they'll put out a bad story depending on how they feel about the military. They have a little agreement that they can't be kicked out of the country, or they can't be kicked out of the unit unless they do something extremely dangerous, put soldiers in harm's way.

We were actually there the day Geraldo wrote our position in the sand. If you look at the video, I'm in the crowd. Everybody was just looking in amazement how he was drawing a map in the sand on TV and telling our whole plan. Everybody was in such a state of shock that nobody said anything. We couldn't believe he was actually doing that. I think he was just trying to be a journalist. He was just trying to put out the information. But that's another thing about embedded journalists. We're trained, we sit in on briefings, we know what not to say, we know what's classified. Sometimes we go out on missions and stuff happens but we can't release it. But if you sent out a load of journalists and you're not checking what they're sending, they could be sending anything.

The way Geraldo walked around the camp seemed kind of funny. He walked around like he was a superstar and he should have everything taken care of. It's the same thing with the CNN guys. They have a whole ton of equipment. A lot of times it makes us angry because we'll get kicked off a Chinook flight so that network crews can get on it. It's like they'll take care of the civilian media before they'll take care of the soldiers, because the civilian media does have a bigger audience than us. I understand why they do it, but you get a little angry at it sometimes.

I heard about Brent Sadler and his CNN crew being armed and firing back at the Iraqis in Tikrit, theoretically, if I were a civilian journalist, I would have an armed guard with me. You are in war and bullets don't care who they hit. But I can see why the other journalists would probably be mad because the enemy might try and target you. Just by being there with the infantry, you could be a target regardless.

We don't get much feedback until we are back home. Not instantly. But over time we do. Once they finally get a chance to look at the footage and they use it for briefings, they don't really give us individual praise. They just say, "Combat camera did this great work and that's why we have them." It is pretty much because half the time they don't know who shot it. A lot of these times, our footage or imagery will simply say Department of the Army or Department of Defense.

MAINTAINING A FAMILY LEGACY

Fox News Producer and Reporter
Maya Zumwalt

"I felt like I inherited a battalion of brothers."

She went off to war with the expectation of working solely as a Fox News producer, but by the time she disembedded from the 82nd Airborne Division, she
had spent quality time in front of the camera, airing over thirty live reports,
assembling several news packages, experiencing a fierce firefight, and much to
her dismay, going a yuck-filled month and five days without a shower. "I didn't
use perfume because Lord knows that would have attracted those flies," joked
Maya Zumwalt. To those who follow naval history, the name Zumwalt is legendary. Her grandfather, Elmo Russell Zumwalt, Jr., was an admiral in the U.S.
Navy during the Vietnam War and later became Chief of Naval Operations. Her
father, Elmo Russell Zumwalt, III, was a lieutenant, junior grade in the U.S.
Navy during the Vietnam War.

■　　■　　■

I was incredibly close to my grandfather. He just passed away about three years
ago. He was seventy-nine. I was twenty-five when he died; I'm twenty-eight
now. I lost my father at a young age to cancer—due to his exposure to Agent
Orange in Vietnam—and I was thirteen when he passed away, so my grandfather definitely became not only a grandfather, but obviously a father figure
as I was growing up. It's been proved that Agent Orange has been linked to a
number of cancers, two of which my father had—Non-Hodgkin's and
Hodgkin's lymphoma. My brother also had a severe learning disability that our
family believes is linked to Agent Orange. My dad was sick for a number of
years—from when I was seven until about thirteen. It was a difficult time period in my life. It was a constant roller coaster ride—him going into remission
and then getting the cancer back—but it made me definitely stronger as a person and made me appreciate the value of life.

I grew up in Pinehurst, North Carolina. It's about an hour-and-a-half south of the Raleigh-Durham area. I was actually born in Fayetteville. Post-Vietnam, my father was an attorney there, and we used to vacation in Pinehurst, so when he passed away, we ended up just moving there.

I was drawn to cover this war as an embed because I grew up on their stories from Vietnam. I have always been curious about what war is like and what combat must have been like for them. Those are the main reasons I jumped into doing this. I was on the TR—USS *Theodore Roosevelt*—for the Afghanistan war. Being on the aircraft carrier was fun. The ship's older brass, like the rear admiral, all knew my grandfather. They were very respectful and spoke very highly of him and what he did to change the navy. It was great to hear that his legend still carries on even after he's passed away. He definitely had an effect on minorities and women. Many people come up to me, especially African-American males, saying, "Your grandfather made it so I could get in the navy and I could move up in the ranks." That was good to hear. He really shook up the chain of command so the little guy could talk to the big guy.

I wanted a different experience for Iraq and it's also what *Fox News* assigned me. Originally, I was supposed to be with the Fourth Infantry but at the time it was still up in the air whether they were going to Turkey or not. So I covered the 82nd Airborne Division—an infantry combat unit. The 82nd is out of Fort Bragg, North Carolina, which was great for me because I grew up watching them on the local news.

Ever since September 11, I've been traveling as part of Fox News's international team which is based out of Washington, D.C. As a producer, I actually do everything an on-air person would do: asking questions, writing, coordinating the logistical end of it. They tell you where you need to go, wherever it is—Baghdad or Kuwait—and you're the one getting on the ground first, and setting up logistics, and then you're working with a correspondent to turn out the story that day. You divide up the story; you'll go hammer out three interviews, and that person will hammer out some interviews and then you get together at the end, and you put it together.

I was in Israel for about three months and I've been in Kuwait. I was in Baghdad in December, and part of January, and then Qatar and Jordan. I've been in that part of the world for the past two years now. I was in Ramallah, Bethlehem, and Gaza for thirty days during the turbulent period. I was there when the Palestinian militants took siege of the main church in Bethlehem. I couldn't believe this was where Christ was born. I couldn't believe what was taking place inside the church. I remember going inside it right after all the militants had come out of the church. It had been looted. It just reeked of urine and stale food. There was clothing everywhere. There were scorch marks from gunfire on the Virgin Mary's face on a statue in the courtyard. I always try to keep my objectivity in these types of situations. I'm just trying to gather the facts since we're doing live shots every hour on the hour. I try not to think beyond the surface strokes until afterward. I keep a journal so I try to digest it all then.

We started out in Kuwait during the Iraqi War, basically waiting for the 82nd Airborne to parachute into and seize Baghdad International Airport. All their equipment had been loaded on these C-130s when the bombing campaign started. As we wait, there's a lot of nervous energy. You just didn't know what to expect. We're watching the war on TV, and all these Scud alerts were happening. I remember the first Scud alert and you're running to the bunker. You're trying to make sure you have a good seal on your gas mask. You're jammed inside the bunker with all these soldiers. A couple of people are praying. Everybody is reacting differently and I thought, "What am I getting myself into?"

The 82nd's airport mission was soon scrapped. They were no longer going to parachute in because when the Third Infantry Division had gone past the southern towns, kicking up the dust, the fedayeen and paramilitary forces were holding these small towns hostage. The 82nd then got sent by ground convoy to these southern towns where we were based outside a small town called As Samawah. These guys had spent probably twenty-four hours de-rigging all their equipment off these planes and then driving about twenty-two hours by ground convoy, and as soon as they land on the ground outside of As Samawah, they started in a firefight. So it was quite an experience just keeping pace with these guys. They didn't sleep. I wasn't fighting or anything, I was just observing on the sidelines with my cameraman Grigory Khananayev.

The 82nd said there was no need for us to bring a vehicle and that proved to be really hard for us. So Grigory and I would ask to get onto different supply vehicles. We had a ton of equipment with us in big cases. We'd ask, "Hi, can you take this for a pack of cigarettes?" You don't beg, but I mean it certainly helps. They were a good group of guys, but the last thing they were concerned about was us traveling with them since there was usually sixteen to twenty men jammed in the back of a truck.

Sleeping accommodations were rough. There were no tents. We slept out in the dirt in an open field where we were parked in a staging area outside As

Samawah. One of my biggest fears at night was getting run over by a Humvee or a Bradley vehicle. Soldiers slept in their vehicles but we didn't have a vehicle. Since there was always a medical tent somewhere, what I would try to do is put my sleeping bag in between the ropes of the medical tent. Throughout the night I would hear the wounded coming in with their gunshot wounds. It was amazing to hear these army doctors and medics working on the U.S. soldiers. I remember one guy coming in. He must have been nineteen years old. He was shot in the face and he was apologizing to his commander because he got shot. He says, "Get me back out there. I'm sorry."

It was always hard to sleep because you're also hearing the gunfire and the artillery rounds going off in the distance. You're sleep deprived but it's adrenaline that keeps you going. You go through these waves of being completely exhausted, then you're in the middle of a firefight, and that gets your adrenaline going, and you want to get the soldiers' stories out. You want to tell viewers about the situation because you know that families back home are watching and the American people are very interested in how the U.S. soldiers are doing. So when I would get the story on-air, it's that extra boost of energy I would get to keep going.

After we left the staging area in the open field, we ran into a tough situation. We had taken over a military building inside As Samawah. They had sent a Special Ops team in first to clear it. We drove in on these convoys. It was hot, I've got the bulletproof vest on, the chemical suit on. It was unbearable, so I took off my helmet and vest as I was unloading our Fox equipment into this building when I saw a tracer fire. I looked at my cameraman and I said, "I saw this tracer fire." He said, "I think you're seeing things." Right as that happened, you could hear bullets flying and it was a firefight. A bus was in front of us, and a truck behind it, and there were enemy fighters inside with their AK47s. The bullets were close enough for me to hear and see them strike. I immediately got flat on the ground and crawled over to get my vest back on. As that's happening, a little bit farther down the road, there was another enemy ambush. Obviously, the ambushes had been timed perfectly. My cameraman grabbed his camera and yells over at me, "This is your time to do a phoner!" I crawled over to get the satellite phone, and luckily I got a signal, and was able to do a live phoner while this was all happening. As I'm doing all this, a soldier comes over to me and he says, "You have got to move. You are in a horrible, horrible position!" My first reaction was to get the story out instead of thinking about safety. He then gave me a quick lesson of where to stand and where not to stand during a firefight. I'm doing these phoners hourly at this point and it's all light control, which means you can't use lights at night. I had this poncho over my head so I could use my little flashlight and a soldier comes over to me and says, "Ma'am, you're probably going to want to move from where you are." I said, "Well, this is the only place I can signal live." And he goes, "Well, there's three enemy in the perimeter." I went, "What? There's three men roaming around here with guns—the enemy?" He goes, "That's correct, ma'am." I was like, "What are you guys doing?" He says, "We're working on that now!"

They called me ma'am! I'm twenty-eight. I don't think I ever felt old, but these guys were all eighteen, nineteen years old, early twenties. Since the 82nd is an infantry combat unit, there were no women with them. I was the only woman with the battalion. Soldiers kept asking me, "Why are you doing this? Why are you with us? You don't have a gun. You're not trained for this." I think they were in awe of why I was doing this. They were also like my brothers. They really looked out for me and I developed a number of friendships. I felt like I inherited a battalion of brothers, honestly. A soldier would come up to me, holding a letter from his mom and say, "Oh, my mom got to see me because you interviewed me. She thanks you." Or sometimes I would let somebody use my satphone. Before I would interview somebody live, I'd say, "Hey, why don't you make a quick phone call to your parents, girlfriend, or wife?"

I'm quite comfortable with being a producer, so I have never wanted to go on-air. Luckily, once I got into it, I wanted to get the soldiers' story out there. Though the first time I was on-air, I was in Kuwait and my God, I was so nervous! I didn't get into this business wanting to go on-air. I had sent my résumé to Fox, and it was very important for me that my grandfather not be involved in my first job process. He wanted to help me so badly, and I was grateful for that, and I appreciated his support, but it was important for me to do it on my own. He wanted to call everybody he knew. I didn't want that. So he was respectful of that and was always very supportive through the years with me. I wonder though—I talk to my mom about this—what my dad and grandfather would have thought of my being in Iraq. I think they would have been supportive, but they would have fought it, particularly my grandfather. There's no way he would have wanted me out there because it was a combat infantry unit. I'm just speculating. He didn't want my father going to Vietnam and fought my dad, who wanted to serve his country. After my father's first tour, my mom told me that they were in Subic Bay in the Philippines and having dinner—my parents were engaged at that point—and he told the family that he was going to go back for another tour. Everybody was really upset. My grandfather shook his head. My father said, "Those guys on my swift boat on the rivers are still out there fighting. I come home when they all come home."

I remember my grandfather saying that every morning he would get the casualty list delivered on his desk, and he felt guilty as he flipped to the back to the Zs to see if my dad's name was there. My uncle—he's my dad's brother—was a Marine in the Gulf War and Vietnam, and he said, "I never thought we would have to worry about a female Zumwalt going to war!"

THE FALLUJAH INCIDENT

London *Daily Mirror* Reporter Chris Hughes
and Freelance Photographer Julian Andrews

> "As a photographer, I think I made some small
> difference. Perhaps in six months' time or a year's
> time, a military academy in America will say: 'This
> is what went wrong in one town in Iraq.' "

Two non-embeds, Chris Hughes, forty, a London *Daily Mirror* reporter, and
Julian Andrews, thirty-five, a freelance photographer hired by the two-million-
circulation paper, traveled west of Baghdad to the Sunni stronghold of Fallujah
on April 30, where they soon encountered escalating local unrest. This city of
100,000 was seething and on edge. And it did. An earlier anti-U.S. demonstration had turned ugly, and violent, and deadly. But as the intrepid *Daily Mirror*
team reported, what triggered all this violence was somewhat at odds with the
official U.S. military explanation. Today, with its viper's nest of Saddam loyalists
and Syrian, Jordanian, and Saudi terrorists, Fallujah remains both a symbol of
Iraqi resistance and continual flashpoint for guerrilla attacks on American soldiers in postwar Iraq.

■　　■　　■

Chris Hughes

The *Daily Mirror* carried a double-page spread describing the fact that the
photographer, Julian Andrews, and I saw U.S troops open fire on a 1,000-
strong demonstration of Iraqis, which I believe to have been totally unarmed.
We had been standing at the school where the first shooting happened.
Fifteen civilians had been shot and killed by U.S. troops during a demonstration that got out of hand two days before. We had thought something else might
happen on the next day and we wanted to be there to see it. We arrived early in
the morning. The school was called The Leader or something. Which might

be a reference to Saddam Hussein. Locals were claiming lots of things. One of the claims they made was that one of the houses had been entered by U.S. troops and was looted. So I asked the guy, "Would you swear on the Koran that this is true? And in front of the photographer?" Then there was intense negotiation between the translator who is a Shia and this guy. He then started backtracking a lot—as you can imagine. He did say that things were removed from his house—like a chicken—but I didn't know whether that was true or not.

About a thousand people were gathered there. They were four deep, one hundred meters long. They were very angry, very agitated, whipped up into a frenzy by religious leaders, but they weren't armed. I've seen more violent demonstrations in London. Anyway, they walked to the U.S base, which was about 400 yards around the corner from the school. The troops retreated but their guns were aiming at the crowd. So then a couple of kids ran forward and they were throwing their sandals at the troops. None of this was violent. None of this to me was a threat. I was in between the sandals and the troops. It was intense because the soldiers were quite clearly on edge and appeared scared, even though I couldn't see their eyes because they had goggles on. They were all camo'd up. Then by a bit of a coincidence a three-vehicle army convoy went past to the Ba'ath Party former headquarters, which was now occupied by U.S. troops at Fallujah. The last of these vehicles was a Bradley fighting vehicle. Then something happened. Somebody threw something at the Bradley, and the guy in the back of the Bradley opened fire. He put his thumb on the machine gun. We ran a picture of that in *The Mirror*. People were screaming, shouting. People ducking for cover. We ran to the wall to get away from it. We were between the Bradley and the wall. By which time, the Bradley was gone. The twenty-second burst of automatic fire was over.

I later learned two died. I only saw one dead. His head was blown off. You don't need to know the details. Basically the soldier opened fire, but the army claimed afterward that they were shot at by an AK47. But I was in that crowd minutes earlier and I didn't see one gun, which is unusual for Iraqis. I didn't see a gun, or a knife, or a stick. Just those sandals and banners, lots of banners.

Some of the townspeople piled all the injured and the dead into the back of a white pickup truck, and then took them off to the local hospital. After we got to the hospital, feelings were running high, so we left because people were swearing at us and abusing our Iraqi translator for bringing us there. We were told in no uncertain terms to leave. So we did.

The *Mirror* ran a headline: U.S. TROOPS OPEN FIRE ON CIVILIANS FOR THE SECOND TIME IN TWO DAYS. Then our story appeared. The photo showed the soldier's thumb on the trigger, which as a photo, was pretty damning. I think it proved at the very least they fired without looking—with an automatic. But I wanted to make sure I wasn't filing a picture that was misleading, and whilst we know in our minds what we saw, it's one thing, especially when you're working and you're trying to think of your safety. Everything seems to be going so slowly, but because of the digital technology, the camera actually timed the whole shooting incident. It was eighteen seconds, but eighteen seconds of automatic weapons fire is a helluva lot of rounds.

Julian Andrews

I heard shooting starting, and to me it sounded like it was coming from the rear. So I swung my camera lens around and began taking pictures. The whole top of this one poor guy's head was blown away. When I got over to him, since I am not a medical person, I don't know whether it was just his muscles and nerves reacting. He was still moving around, which was not a particularly pleasant thing to see.

I took my pictures to one of the ex-Special Forces guys who was working as a security advisor over here. I went through the whole scenario and then he described how the Bradley machine gun worked. There's a butterfly switch on the back of the gun, which you flick down to fire the machine gun. When I took the picture it's up. In one of the frames, the lever is horizontal, and in one of the other frames the soldier has his thumb pressed down on it and the lever is right down. So he is definitely firing the machine gun, and we are talking large rounds at virtually point-blank range. It was absolutely appalling.

As a photographer, I think I made some small difference. Perhaps, in six month's or a year's time, a military academy in America will say: "This is what went wrong in one town in Iraq. This is how not to do it." They will be able to say that because we were there.

CROSSING THE JOURNALISTIC DIVIDE
Atlanta Journal-Constitution
Military Affairs Reporter Ron Martz

> "Do you realize it's been twenty-four hours
> since we've been shot at?"

The donkey had been there all day as troops rolled south of Baghdad on Highway 8, blowing up Iraqi artillery, anti-aircraft weapons and trucks loaded with ammunition to prevent reinforcements from reaching the capital. Tethered in the middle of a field next to a crate of ammunition, the donkey was surrounded by exploding weapons and ammunition. Bullets and pieces of metal whined through the air and explosions rocked the ground.

For more than two hours, as Charlie Company tank crews tried to replace the tread on one of their tanks, we watched the donkey graze, seemingly unaware and unconcerned about what was going on around it. After a while, the soldiers began pulling for the donkey, willing it to survive in the midst of the chaos. And when it came time to leave, one of the soldiers asked First Sgt. Jose Mercado, forty, of Quebradillas, Puerto Rico: "Shouldn't we blow up those crates of ammo by the donkey?" "I don't want to kill that donkey. He didn't do anything to anybody," Mercado said.

This excerpt from one of Ron Martz's "War Diaries" for the *Atlanta Journal-Constitution* demonstrates why that newspaper's military affairs correspondent is no stranger to the odd ironies of the battlefield. He understands combat all too well. The thirty-year veteran of foreign news reporting has previously covered the arrival of U.S. troops in Croatia and Bosnia, the first Gulf War, the Contra-Sandinista war in Nicaragua, Soviet withdrawal from Afghanistan, and incarceration of Taliban and Al-Qaeda prisoners at Guantanamo Bay, Cuba. While embedded with Charlie Company of the U.S. Army's Third Infantry Division

(Mechanized), Martz, fifty-six, often wrote about war's quiet, haunting details like "the woman in red stockings dying in the middle of the street," or "the night the dogs dug up the dead," or "the young Muslim wife so fearful of someone seeing her naked foot she would not allow a medic to treat her wound," or "the suicide bombers fused in death by fire." Despite his complete mastery of war reportage, the former Marine ended up drawing critical fire from media hardliners on two separate occasions when he helped a medic treat two wounded U.S. soldiers and an Iraqi civilian by holding up a medical intravenous drip bag.

"I felt like it was my duty at this point to help this [Iraqi] out however I could," admitted Martz in his column. "I asked him about his family several times. He said he had three babies and he spoke a little broken English. He kept saying, 'My three babies, my three babies.' I don't know if I helped keep that guy alive, but I helped free a soldier to do what he's supposed to do and I helped that particular civilian make it through that particular traumatic time. My conscience is clear about that. I would rather have done what I did than not do anything and sit there and observe and say, 'Sorry, I can't get involved because I'm a journalist' and have to live with that for the rest of my life."

Martz's actions bring to mind Heisenberg's Uncertainty Principle, a famous axiom of scientific experimentation that states that the presence of the observer affects the results, however subtly. Purists argue that journalists should strive for a godlike impartiality. A classic example of how difficult it is to remain a neutral observer can be seen in David Halberstam's description of watching an anti-war Buddhist monk burning himself to death in Vietnam. "I had never felt such conflicting emotions," wrote Halberstam in his 1964 classic, *The Making of a Quagmire*. "One part of me wanted to extinguish the fire, another warned that I had no right to interfere, another told me it was too late, another asked if I was a reporter or a human being."

By crossing that journalistic divide between objectivity and involvement, Martz had made a simple, irrevocable, and compassionate choice. War reporting could wait.

■   ■   ■

In Iraq, I got a request from my bosses at the *Journal-Constitution* to call our public relations department because the drip bag story was getting national and local attention. They wanted to know the details and what my thought processes were at the time. When I later went through my e-mails, I found that there were a lot of readers who responded to that particular story and who had heard it on NPR. That was the first indication that I had struck some sort of chord with people. My fiancé had sent me some stuff from those on-line blogs. I noticed that there seemed to be quite a bit of conversation not only about that incident but also about the incident involving the two soldiers who were wounded next to me.

When it comes to helping the wounded, whether it's soldiers or civilians, I'm sure there have been other incidents like mine, but I don't recall any off the top of my head. In Vietnam, Joe Galloway, who wrote *We Were Soldiers Once . . . and Young*, talks about helping the wounded, and he actually got involved in the battle. Joe carried a weapon during Vietnam, as a lot of correspondents did over there, and in many instances for them, it may have been just a macho thing of being able to carry a weapon, but for him it was a matter of self-preservation. If I had felt that my life was in imminent danger or a soldier's life was in imminent danger, I may have picked up a weapon in Iraq and done something, but as it was, we had enough firepower around us that my little contribution would have been rather superfluous.

We faced danger, but it wasn't all day long, every day. It was the kind of thing where you'd be in contact on a regular basis. About twenty-four hours into the ground war, we made the big sweep through the south and then up toward Baghdad. Our first contact came a little over twenty-four hours after we crossed the border. At that time, we were about two miles away from the first battle. The *Journal's* photographer, Brant Sanderlin, and myself were riding in soft-sided Humvees, so they didn't want us near the fight. But after that first firefight, we got into an area where there were a number of opposition forces—Ba'ath Party, fedayeen, or actual government troops.

The task force I was with—Task Force 164—basically led the charge into Baghdad and I was the only print journalist there. Of the eighty-five embeds in the Third Infantry with us, I honestly don't know how many experienced as much combat contact as we did. Every day we were taking fire in some form or fashion. Some days it was heavier than others. When you least expected it, guys would pull up in a car 200 yards away and fire rocket-propelled grenades or small arms and then run off. I remember once we got to Baghdad and things started settling down a little bit, Brant came to me and said, "Do you realize it's been twenty-four hours since we've been shot at?" We both sort of sat there and looked at each other. "Hey, yeah, that's right!" It became commonplace to hear weapons going off or RPGs whizzing overhead. I hate to say it, but there were times when you became blasé about it, like "Well, how close was it?"

The day the two soldiers, Private First Class Don Schafer and Private First Class Chris Shipley were shot, we were riding on Highway 8 and headed into Baghdad. Our job was to go near the center of the city and then continue on Highway 8 west to the airport. I was in the back of the armored personnel carrier (APC). It has a hatch on the top that opens up and if you've got enough room, you could probably put six people back there who can stand up and look or shoot out. That particular time in the APC, there was the driver and then the first sergeant who was sitting in the vehicle commander's little hole with a 50-caliber machine gun. In the back there was the assistant medic, Specialist Shawn Sullivan, and myself. Riding in the back of the APC, it was difficult to see anything that was going on outside. So on that particular day, I told the first sergeant, "I really need to see what's going on to be able to describe what you guys are doing." He was reluctant but said, "Go ahead and open up the hatch."

We had picked up Shipley and Schafer after their tank caught fire. Shipley had been the driver of that tank and Schafer came from another vehicle. They both got into our vehicle along with several hundred pounds of gear and two dozen five-gallon plastic water containers that they'd used to try to put out the fire on the tank. They got in with their rifles and, as the convoy moved into Baghdad, they were firing and I was standing in the back, looking directly to the rear. I was leaning over because we had stuff piled up on both sides that I thought would provide some measure of protection. Plus we had vehicles to our front and back that I also thought would provide some protection. Schafer was standing immediately to my left. I was at his elbow as he was firing to the rear. Shipley was standing directly behind me, firing out to the left front and to the left rear as the vehicle moved forward.

It was loud, as usual. I had my ear plugs in. We all wore them. You pretty much had to. As we were riding along and they're firing and reloading, Schafer says, "Ow, my arm!" and he holds it up. I lifted up his arm and saw blood coming out. I saw a hole in his armpit. He says, "I've been hit!" and I start yelling, "He's been hit!" I grabbed him as he collapsed into my arms and we fell back down into the corner of the APC. As I am falling, I see Shipley, who has already been hit. He is face down on the tan-colored steel deck of the personnel carrier. There is blood everywhere as Schafer falls back. His blood is not squirting in the air; it's just flowing out of his head. Sullivan, who was firing off to the right front, sees us fall back and then he sees Shipley. He grabs Shipley and pulls him down. Then Sullivan goes to work on the two of them. I'm in the corner, kind of trapped by Schafer, who's laying on top of me and my legs are caught up underneath some of the equipment. About the only thing I can do is to hold onto Schafer. I could reach over just far enough to grab Shipley's hand as he's being tended to. I grabbed his left hand while he kept saying, "Ow, that hurts!" Then I discovered that he had also been wounded in the left arm. I tried grabbing his right arm and alternated talking to both wounded men.

There are both instinctive and sound medical reasons why you should talk to people who are badly wounded. I did the same thing with the Iraqi who was hit at the intersection. It's like, "Grab my hand, squeeze my hand, and let me know you're okay. Let me know you're listening to me, and that you can hear me." That way, it's harder for them to go into shock if you keep them talking and alert. It keeps their mind off the pain.

My first thought when I helped the medic take care of the wounded soldiers was not about losing my journalistic objectivity. Instead, I wished that I had taken a combat lifesaver's course before I had gone to Iraq so that I could actually have been of some help to the medic who was treating these guys. He was trying to treat both of them at the same time, so he'd go back and forth. I was trying to help him as much as possible, but at the same time, not do anything that's going to further hurt the two wounded guys. The medic was telling me, "Just encourage and talk to them, make them squeeze your hand." I'm not really thinking about writing; I'm thinking, "I hope these two guys don't die. I hope that we get them to the airport, get them some additional medical help." I'm hoping that the Medevac helicopters will be there. It wasn't until after we had gotten out of the vehicles, gotten another medic there, and the medical evacuation helicopters arrived, that I finally had time to think. My first thought was, "I have to write about this," but it took me a long time. I had to have a long talk with myself about what I was going to write that day, because it was very emotional for me to see those two young kids hurt as badly as they were. I wondered, "Why did Schafer and Shipley get hit and not me?" We were all in the line of fire.

E-mail reader reaction to my stories about helping the two soldiers ran about fifty-fifty, negative and positive. The positives thanked me for helping these soldiers. There was a wide variety of negative e-mails. A number of people objected to my inserting the word "God" in there, when I wrote that "God had some hand in this." Just the mention of God or religion is anathema to many people. Then there were people who said that I was taking up the space of a soldier and that I shouldn't have been there in the first place. Others thought that I should have been shot rather than those two. Many wrote, "How can you be so egotistical to think that God spared you and injured those two soldiers? That He likes you better than He liked those two soldiers?"

Before going into this war many thought it would be a cakewalk. But once we started taking the amount of fire that we did on that first run into Baghdad, and then those two kids got hurt, our attitude in the task force changed. The next day, we found out we had to return to Baghdad, this time to stay. I thought that it was going to be a bad day and that there were going to be a number of casualties. I wasn't thinking it was going to be like street fighting in Somalia, because I had done some research into Somalia and what happened there. I didn't get the sense from the Iraqis and from what I read that they were going to, as a people, fight to the death. They didn't seem to have that same sort of loyalty to Saddam that the Somalis had to Adid. Only the Syrians and the fedayeen had that same sort of willingness, and they were not in large numbers.

The fedayeen apparently never did understand the overwhelming odds against them. The soldiers and I would sit around and talk about that. That stunned them, too. Why do individuals with a rifle or guys in a pickup try to take on a tank? Some of the prisoners they captured indicated that they thought that they could disable tanks with an RPG. I don't know if it was religious indoctrination making them believe that they were fighting for a higher cause and therefore that they were going to be victorious. What motivates fanatical resistance against an overwhelming force?

The task force I was with had been convinced by intelligence that the Medina Division, which was their primary target, was going to capitulate and that the whole unit was going to surrender, but there was never any mention in the intelligence briefings that I sat in on about guerrilla tactics of the fedayeen or Syrians or Ba'ath Party members or anything like that. I honestly don't know where the failure in the intelligence community came in on that. I've seen a couple of things that indicate that there were some assessments mentioning Syrians and some very fanatical fedayeen who were going to fight. But I don't know if it was discounted by the military or whether it was just ignored, or whether it didn't get passed on—or just what the deal was.

When you were as far forward as I was with the tank company—there were seventy-nine people in it—all I knew for the most part was what I could see and what I could hear on that particular day. Occasionally, I'd go back to battalion headquarters, and they were getting these same intelligence summaries. That was the broadest scope that I had, back at the battalion level. I never got back to brigade level where you got a wider view. What I was trying to do with my writing was tell the story from the soldiers' perspective of that particular unit—their frustrations, their fears, their anxieties, the lack of intelligence, whatever the case may be. One of the complaints that some people e-mailed me was that I did not take into account the broader perspective. One woman suggested that I watch more Fox News to get a good view of what's going on in the war. I resisted the impulse of writing her back and saying, "I'm sorry, but the TV reception in the back of my APC is a little bad right now," but she wouldn't have gotten the joke. She would have thought that I had a TV back there.

We heard about the supply lines getting stretched thin, but from where we were, it wasn't so bad. By the time we got to Baghdad, we were told to get out of our chemical protection suits because we were drinking too much water and they could not keep us supplied with enough water. That was right about the time we got into what soldiers refer to as "the slime zone,'" near Baghdad. They figured that once they got into that area it was the most likely place that would be hit with biological or chemical weapons. It started right around Karbala, which is about 100 kilometers south of Baghdad. They were not so much concerned about nuclear weapons, but by that time, everybody was wearing the chemical protection suits, and the rubber boots, and everybody was sweating like crazy, and drinking too much water. Still, we never ran out of water; food was never a problem with the unit I was with. They had told the soldiers to pack for five days. "When you get to Baghdad in five days, you'll get re-supplied then." Most of the first sergeants, the old senior enlisted guys, said, "They say five days, we're going to take ten." So we never suffered a shortage of food. By the way, the MRE enchiladas were pretty good, as far as MREs go. The new MREs were a significant improvement over what they had during the first Gulf War. Those ones had this strange preservative smell whenever you opened them, but the new ones don't have that smell, and they actually have a pretty wide variety of entrees. The only problem I had with them is they have no breakfast entrée. You ate a cheese enchilada or Thai chicken for breakfast. They had vegetarian MREs so some of them were actually pretty good. They have a lot of things that go with them. Some had pretty good oatmeal cookies.

Most of the time I slept in the APC. There were occasional nights when we were able to take a cot from the vehicle and stretch out. Sleeping in the back of the APC was cramped and uncomfortable; it was hot back there and we wore the chemical protection suits. Usually the hatch was closed just to prevent anything stray from being thrown in or being shot in there. We'd open it just to get some air on occasion, but most of the time it'd be shut.

There were many days when it got so crowded in the back of the APC with all of the gear they've got, even though there's normally only four or five people riding in it, it was very claustrophobic. Often I'd be sitting back there trying to write, things are bouncing along and the only thing I can liken it to is like being on an airline flight when you're in the middle seat next to two very large people, there's no air conditioning, and somebody's throwing sand in your face the whole time. Every ten seconds you had to wipe your screen off because it got covered with sand. But the writing wasn't as bad as trying to file. There was one occasion when we were under fire and I needed to get to the photographer Brant [Sanderlin], who rode in another APC. I ran out of my APC over to his APC, and I saw him. He's standing there inside the vehicle, he's got his laptop in his left hand and he's holding his Thuraya satellite phone up through the commander's hatch to get a direct line to the satellite sending his photos as we're under fire.

I gave people a picture of modern warfare from the perspective of the soldiers for the first time since Vietnam. There were a number of people who didn't like that picture, based on a number of e-mails that I got. They did not want to hear that the war did not go as it apparently came across on TV. Rumsfeld apparently said that it was meticulously planned and flawlessly executed—but it wasn't that way at all. The unit that I was with had specific missions all mapped and planned out, but one of the axioms of warfare is that plans and strategies don't survive the first contact, and that was very much the case here. Once they got that first contact about twenty-four hours into the war, everything changed. The unit did a lot of things that it was not supposed to do. They were changing things on the fly and many people didn't want to hear it. The public didn't want to hear that there was chaos, that civilians were killed. They wanted to hear that it was going according to plan and that apparently is what people wanted to see on TV.

My intent was to be as close as possible to the front because I felt like this was an unprecedented opportunity to give the American public a real true picture of what goes on during war. In the first Gulf War, I was with this same division. It was then known as the Twenty-fourth Infantry Division. It was re-named after the war, but it was basically the same mechanized infantry division out of Fort Stewart, Georgia. The difference between that war and this war was that the duration was considerably shorter. It was only a 100-hour ground war and it was a much more of a long distance, classic tank warfare campaign. It was tank-on-tank, tank-on-armored-vehicle kind of thing over very long distances. Some of the contact was from a mile or even up to two miles. At that range Abrams tanks can effectively take out other armored vehicles. We'd be riding along in the desert and all of sudden, we'd see a Bradley or an Abrams roll off into the desert. There'd be a little shooting, and then way out in the distance you'd see a plume of smoke, and you'd see Iraqis surrendering. That war just didn't have the feel of close combat.

I was part of the press pool system they had back then. They had established a very intricate pool system, and there was a lot of jockeying back and forth before the start of the war about who would be with which unit. The way the pools worked out, there were a lot of reporters who did not get placed with units that were of interest to their particular readers. I went with the Twenty-fourth Infantry Division because I got along well with the commander of the division—General Barry McCaffrey—who went on to become the drug czar under President Clinton. There was a mutual understanding between us. He wanted publicity for his unit and he wanted the people back home to be able to read in the *Atlanta Journal-Constitution* what the division was doing. McCaffrey was ahead of his time in terms of the army and how it dealt with the media. It was his opinion that you tell the story and be up front with people about what you do. If you make mistakes, you admit them. Don't try to hide them and let the press know what you're doing because they're going to tell the story to the American people and that's the story they want to tell. So I got out somewhat independent of the pool, as did Joe Galloway, who at the time was working with *U.S. News and World Report*. He went with the Twenty-fourth because he knew Schwarzkopf from Vietnam. Joe went to Schwarzkopf and said, "Who's going to see a lot of action? I want to go with that unit." Schwarzkopf told him, "Go with the Twenty-fourth." We were somewhat independent of the pool system, although anything that we filed still had to go through their censors. The problem I had with that system was that I had to give them hard copies of my stories. I had to type it out on a typewriter and hand it to somebody and then the story had to make its way all the way back to the Joint Information Bureau. That would sometimes take two or three days. I didn't notice that much censorship, but there was no way of getting something in the paper the next day after a battle. Since the war was of such short duration I filed one dispatch from the battlefield, actually.

During the first Gulf War, I used a handy little computer on which I would write the initial story. Then I would re-type it on a little portable manual typewriter and hand in that copy. It just had its own little carrying case. I did it the old-fashioned way. In one battle out in the middle of the desert, I'm typing a story on a manual typewriter on the hood of a Humvee. I thought it was a pretty bizarre kind of thing. Satellite phones were very expensive at the time and very bulky to carry around so they were not in common use.

Well, this time around, I had a laptop and a satellite phone. I had an Apple G3 PowerBook, which is the standard laptop for the *Journal-Constitution*. Then I had a Thrane & Thrane MR Sat satellite phone. It's much heavier and bulkier than the Thuraya and it's much slower and much more expensive to send on, too. I had argued with my bosses for a couple of months that we needed to buy a Thuraya or an Iridium, because the MR Sat was just too bulky, and too slow, and you had to actually stop to acquire the satellite and send. So when my photographer Brant came over about a month before the war started, he brought over a PC and he bought a Thuraya. We then had two satellite phones and two laptops that we could send on. Which was good because there were occasions when I could not send through the MR Sat satellite because that's used by the military quite a bit, and the channels were so full that I couldn't send anything. So I would put my story on a disk and email it back through the photographer's PC, because we had very good success with the Thuraya.

We had gotten word about a week into the war that certain commands were banning Thurayas because they felt the enemy could use them to pinpoint artillery attacks. But the company commander, Captain Jason Conroy, said to us, "You know, they're really trying to crack down on the use of Thurayas and they're taking them away from some reporters. The only thing I ask of you guys is that you don't use them while we're under an artillery attack and don't use them to tell anybody where we are or where we're going. If you follow those ground rules, you guys can continue to use it as far as I'm concerned."

Conroy never tried to review our material. He said, "Yeah, I'm supposed to be looking at every story you do and every picture you guys file. But I'm too busy to do that. You guys are professionals and I trust you. You guys do your job and I'll do my job." He never asked to look at any of my stories until before we left for Baghdad. He said, "I'd like to see some of the stuff that you did." So I gave him a disk with the stories that I had already filed. I didn't get any complaints from him. There was absolutely no effort to censor anything.

Witnessing life and death situations while covering war does have a purpose. It de-glamorizes war. When you see it up close, when you see people around you get shot and get horribly wounded, it convinces you that war should be the absolute last option. Political negotiations and diplomacy should take precedence over warfare every time because war does horrible things to people. Some journalists thought that the stated reasons for the war were just a pretext, but that it was worth it overall because Saddam Hussein has killed so many of his own people. I think there's some merit to that argument. But I'm not entirely convinced that he couldn't have been gotten rid of in another form or fashion. Exactly what that is, I don't know. But the situation that you run into now is that even dictators, and tyrants, and despots provide people a certain security level. For the most part, the majority of the Iraqis had learned how to survive within that very despotic regime. Now you've got total chaos and people do not know how to manage their affairs. It's going to be very difficult for us—or anyone else—to help Iraqis adjust to this chaotic post-Saddam period.

■　■　■

Private First Class Don Schafer Relives his Battlefield Encounter with Ron Martz

Contacted in early May at his Baltimore residence where he was recuperating, twenty-three-year-old Private First Class Don Schafer said, "I read one of Ron Martz's articles. My dad read the others. The one I did read he wrote exactly what happened that day." Before he was a ROTC and enlisted in the army, Schafer worked in a Taco Bell. He retells what happened that day.

We heard a few bullets whizz by. I looked left and right, then it felt like someone had punched me in the back. I could see a bright flash. I felt pressure. You betcha you can hear the sound of bullet and pop when it goes in. I said basically "Ow! My arm! What the hell?" All I worried about was: Would I lose my arm? I felt like I would make it. I was not in excruciating pain. I did not even feel any pain whatsoever. Just that first "Ow! My arm!" after that immediate shock. I could not move. It hurt so badly. My fingers and hand still had movement in them. As I lay in back of PC [Personal Carrier], Ron Martz made sure that my partner was not fatally shot in the head. I'm not sure what had happened, but possibly another round hit the side of PC and pieces went into his eye. His eye was bleeding badly. The medic put a bandage on it and kept pressure on, so all I knew, he took a hit to the head and I got three in my back.

Ron was to my immediate right, elbow to elbow. He was right there. Later he said he was glad we were there, because maybe that bullet was meant for him, but I don't look at it that way.

At first my breathing was nearly normal, but when you get a sucking chest wound, slowly the air deflates, and it is really hard to keep breathing, and keep your lungs filled with air. It collapses on itself. So to stop this, the medic puts plastic over it [the puncture] to inflate the lungs. The problem was the medic found it hard to get at his equipment underneath all that stuff in the back of the PC, so he started fashioning bandages out of packages the dressing came from. He used duct tape to hold the bandages on. We called it 100 miles per hour tape. It's the best stuff in an emergency. Regular military duct tape.

Ron tried to do whatever the medic asked him. He helped him get to the gear. He kept holding my hand, and talking to me, and not letting me go to sleep, because even if I were to go unconscious, if I can squeeze his hand I am still alive. My breathing was too shallow for me to speak.

Ron helped me out of the PC and onto a stretcher when we got to the evac site. The commander's tank followed him. With the helicopter blowing sand and dirt everywhere, Ron stood over me to protect my eyes and to keep my wounds clean. He kept telling me that I'd be okay, because I kept telling him how tired I was. After I got in the helicopter, I felt pretty safe, safe enough to go to sleep. I knew they had all the medical equipment to keep me alive. Ten days later, I woke up in a hospital in Spain.

Ron had given my parents his telephone number and e-mail address. I was happy to hear from him and thanked him for what he did. I told Ron that Shipley and I signed on for the risks. That I'm a soldier and that is what I am there for. He is simply there to write a story and not there to get shot. I know that can happen, but that is not why he is there.

Well, he was also able to tell my mom that I was being cared for by the doctors. Not like the army, which didn't tell her much, and it was a little misleading. They told her that I had multiple wounds under my arm. Thanks to Ron she got the whole story and it helped it was reported. It was a real help to my mom.

I am at home. I've been contacted quite a bit by the news and got quite a bit of publicity. I watch movies, hang out with my friends. It is awkward since I have this robotic-looking arm. My humerus was shattered, so to make it heal properly, it has two pins and a bar holding everything together. The first thing I would like to do when it's healed is to sleep on my chest or arm.

LENDING ASSISTANCE TO A DANGEROUS PROFESSION

Committee to Protect Journalists'
Michael Massing

> "The plan was to relay a message to the journalists inside [the hotel] and ask them to hang bed sheets out the window to make the building more easily identifiable to U.S. forces."

Just before noon on April 8, 2003, journalists covering the battle of Baghdad from the balconies of the Palestine Hotel looked on as the turret of a U.S. M1A1 Abrams tank positioned about three quarters of a mile away on the Al-Jumhuriya Bridge turned toward them and unleashed a single round. The shell struck a fifteenth-floor balcony of the hotel, fatally wounding veteran Reuters cameraman Taras Protsyuk and Spanish cameraman José Couso of Tele Cinco. Three other journalists were wounded in the attack.

About 100 international journalists were staying in the Palestine Hotel at the time of the strike. A Committee to Protect Journalists (CPJ) investigation into the incident—based on interviews with about a dozen reporters who were at the scene, including two embedded journalists who monitored the military radio traffic before and after the shelling occurred—suggests that attack on the journalists, while not deliberate, was avoidable. CPJ has learned that Pentagon officials, as well as commanders on the ground in Baghdad, knew that the Palestine Hotel was full of international journalists and were intent on not hitting it. However, these senior officers apparently failed to convey their concern to the tank commander who fired on the hotel.

Chris Tomlinson, an Associated Press (AP) reporter embedded with an infantry company assigned to the third Infantry Division's fourth Battalion, sixty-fourth Armor Regiment, spent the day inside an impromptu U.S. command center established in Saddam Hussein's presidential palace on the west side of the Tigris River. By toggling a switch on a military radio, Tomlinson could listen to communication within the company unit, and also to the battalion tactical operations frequency, which allowed him to hear conversation between the tank company commander, Captain Philip Wolford, and his superiors.

At around dawn on April 8, intense fighting resumed on the west side of the Tigris in the vicinity of the Al-Jumhuriya Bridge. Reporters, who had clustered on the balconies of the Palestine Hotel, located on the eastern bank of the Tigris, observed a significant counterattack by Iraqi forces armed with light arms, rocket-propelled grenades (RPGs), and mortars. The attack continued for several hours, and, according to AP reporter Tomlinson, snipers on tall buildings aimed at the hatches of the tanks, eventually wounding two members of Wolford's battalion.

Fighting grew so intense that senior U.S. military officers called in air strikes on an intersection and various buildings on the west bank to weaken the Iraqi positions. According to press reports, dozens of Iraqis were killed. An Arabic-speaking U.S. intelligence officer was able to determine that an Iraqi forward observer, or spotter, was directing Iraqi fighters who were skirmishing with U.S. troops.

Tomlinson, who has himself served seven years in the army, noted that, "The first thing they teach you when you're a tanker or an infantry man is to kill the forward observer. . . . That's the highest priority target." He continued, "If you can kill the forward observer, you have no one to direct the ground forces [or artillery fire]. And therefore you completely take away their value."

At some point before the shelling of the hotel, while the tanks were on the bridge looking for the observer, brigade commander Colonel David Perkins approached Tomlinson and reporter Greg Kelly from Fox News.

In some desperation, Perkins explained that U.S. forces were under fire from Iraqis in buildings on the east side of the Tigris, and that they were considering calling in an air strike. Perkins was aware that the Palestine Hotel was on the east side of the river in the general vicinity of where the fire was coming from. He was also aware that the hotel was full of Western journalists. Tomlinson frantically called the AP office in Doha, Qatar, in an effort to get a description of the hotel and to reach people staying at the Palestine. His plan was to relay a message to the journalists inside and ask them to hang bed sheets out the window to make the building more easily identifiable to U.S. forces.

At about the time that Tomlinson was trying to locate the Palestine Hotel, in the late morning, one of the tank officers on the Al-Jumhuriya Bridge who was looking for the spotter radioed that he had located a person with binoculars in a building on the east side of the river. Exactly how much time lapsed between the tank officer identifying this target and the actual firing of the tank shell is not clear from Tomlinson's monitoring of the radio traffic.

In an interview with the French weekly Le Nouvel Observateur, Captain Wolford hinted that he gave an immediate order to fire.

The immediate reaction from U.S. commanders to the attack on the Palestine Hotel was anger and consternation. Lieutenant Colonel Philip DeCamp, Captain Wolford's commanding officer, began screaming over the radio, "Who just shot the Palestinian [sic] Hotel?" according to Tomlinson. Tomlinson listened as DeCamp confronted Wolford. "Did you just fucking shoot the Palestinian [sic] Hotel?" he demanded of Wolford.

The above account is excerpted from the full Palestine Hotel shelling investigative report conducted by the Committee to Protect Journalists (CPJ), which appears on its web site, www.cpj.org. It was written by Joel Campagna, CPJ's senior program coordinator responsible for the Middle East and North Africa, and research consultant Rhonda Roumani. By coincidence, on the same day the CPJ report was made public on May 27, 2003, we interviewed New York City resident Michael Massing, who had traveled to Doha, Qatar, in the official capacity as CPJ's media troubleshooter. A frequent contributor to New York Review of Books and Columbia Journalism Review, and recipient of the prestigious MacArthur Foundation Genius Award, Massing is also the author of The Fix, which explores the failed efforts of the U.S. government to halt the flow of illegal drugs into this country.

■　■　■

My main reason for going to Doha was on behalf of the Committee to Protect Journalists, a group on whose board I sit and which I actually helped to found back in 1980–81. At the time, I was working at the *Columbia Journalism Review* and there were a lot of cases, particularly in Latin America, where journalists were getting jailed, threatened, and even murdered by repressive governments. There was no organization in the United States set up to work on their behalf to publicize these acts and to bring pressure to bear against them, so I and another person who was then working at CBS decided that the American press should try to use its clout and influence to help colleagues in other countries, and so we went ahead and set up our organization.

Over the years, the committee has used various tools, including publicity, the press, pressuring the U.S. government, pressuring foreign governments, sending missions to dozens of countries trying to intercede on behalf of both individual journalists as well as news organizations. We've compiled a very good track record of getting journalists out of prison, helping to keep news organizations from being shut down, giving haven to journalists who have been threatened to such an extent that their lives are in danger if they remain in their countries. Going to Doha was in line with that type of work. We knew that the war was going to be a dangerous enterprise for the press and we wanted to have somebody in the region to be able both to gather information and to be a point of pressure in cases where journalists were in danger.

In Iraq, you had a very strong separation between journalists who were embedded with the military and those who were not—the so-called unilaterals. From the security standpoint—and that's very different from a reporting standpoint—the embedding process worked well. The two main cases where journalists died were Michael Kelly and David Bloom, and while Kelly's death indirectly involved combat, most of the other journalists who died were unilaterals. They were there trying to fill an important function, which was reporting independently of the military, trying to get information in an independent way and, of course, they did not have the type of protection that the embedded reporters had—and they paid for it. They went out to areas that were not always safe; in some cases, they were in areas that they thought should have been safe, such as the Palestine Hotel, and yet there, tragically, two journalists died. Others stepped on land mines, got caught in crossfire, and other accidents also occurred on the battlefield like Elizabeth Neuffer of *The Boston Globe*. By the time you hear of a casualty, it's usually too late.

We were very active in that case when four journalists in Baghdad, including two from Newsday, disappeared because the Iraqi government thought they were spies. We worked closely with Newsday and used our contacts in the field, particularly in Baghdad, to gather information about them. There were many levers in a case like that to work—working with the newspaper or working through the U.S. government—but in a case like that, there's a limit to really what the U.S. government can do. We also worked with Arab governments and news organizations that had contacts with the Iraqi government. One of CPJ's board members, Ann Garrels of NPR, was at the Palestine Hotel trying to get information to see what could be done. The case became highly publicized. They were eventually released.

As for the shelling of the Palestine Hotel, the U.S. government continues to maintain that the U.S. troops were fired on from the hotel. Nobody can corroborate that—and none of the journalists saw any evidence of that. So we felt it was important both to get at the bottom of this incident by having a full investigation, and figure out how it can be prevented in the future. While it was a black eye for the military, certain sectors of the military probably don't care, but they don't like something like this happening. It's possible that if we keep at it long enough, they will adopt procedures to try to prevent something like this from happening again. For instance, one thing that we would like to see is for the U.S. to acknowledge that sites like the Palestine Hotel, where international journalists are staying during a conflict and that are easily identifiable, be regarded as sensitive sites, similar to schools, hospitals, and religious sites, which the U.S. does regard as special cases that are to be avoided, and are to be attacked only in extreme circumstances.

If you look at the incidents involved, the case could be made that journalists were roaming around in areas where they should not have been and maybe should have exercised more caution. The U.S. military argued, "Well, they shouldn't even be there at the Palestine Hotel." But I don't think journalists feel that way. Having reporters in that hotel able to report on what was going on in Baghdad was very important. It's important to have unilaterals or independent journalists because with the embed process, journalists found it hard to report on what was going on beyond the narrow aperture of their particular unit. There was a lot of expected identification with the military people who were protecting them and in that situation, the unilaterals could have a lot to offer in terms of independent reporting. But I wouldn't want to see the embed process be done away with; it could be an invaluable eye on the battlefield. Since this war happened to be very short, and from the U.S. standpoint fairly effective, there was a limit to what the embeds saw that went wrong, but if things had gone wildly wrong, we would have heard a lot about it. You need to perfect the embed process, not do away with it.

When I was in Doha, the mantra was, "Well, we have the embeds to give us the on-the-ground view and then we're going to have reporters and editors outside of Iraq, around the region, in Washington, to provide the perspective and the broader picture." That was where there was a real falling down. I mean, it's just extraordinary the extent to which the American media remained largely ignorant of the Arab world, just as the FBI and the CIA have come into a lot of criticism for lacking Arabic speakers and people with on-the-ground knowledge of the region. The press is even worse off and that badly showed in the coverage. It's also important to keep in mind the gap between television and print media. As difficult a time as newspapers had, TV was miles further behind. The number of people these TV networks sent into the field compared to the amount of expertise they could bring to bear, it's really appalling.

The U.S. television media and the Arabic TV media certainly seemed to mirror one another. Al Jazeera has many seasoned correspondents, and its original staff was trained by the BBC and so there's still a lot of those news values in there, but that group is getting squeezed out by people who have more of an agenda that reflects the politics of the region. These news organizations are sensitive to political trends, and as that region becomes more militant, the TV networks will reflect that. If you look at the Arab world, the opening for political action is so narrow. Press freedom is usually a second or third-tier freedom that develops after some more basic rights come such as freedom to read what you want and freedom of assembly. Like in Africa, for instance, you get newspapers that are highly critical of the government. In the Arab world, you don't really have opposition parties in most places, so you don't even have that level of freedom of the press. There's going to be the need for more general political reform in the Arab world, before press freedom starts to flourish, although Al Jazeera itself has been the vehicle for a sort of earthquake in the region because it is criticizing governments. But in terms of indigenous newspapers in each country, for instance—or other types of news organizations— that might be able to report freely, unfortunately, that seems to be way off. Even in Afghanistan now, people who are trying to do decent journalism are getting threatened and the climate there has become very dangerous for the press.

I spent time with the Al Jazeera correspondent at the Doha press center and then I also met with one of their anchors separately. On the night of April 7, I talked to them in my capacity with Committee to Protect Journalists, because they were worried about the security of their correspondents due to the number of incidents that had occurred, and sure enough, the next morning when I woke up, their office in Baghdad had been bombed and their correspondent there killed. So they asked me to come back and I actually went on Al Jazeera to talk about the attacks on the press and particularly on Al Jazeera and how the Committee was hoping their would be an investigation. That event remains much less investigated than the Palestine Hotel attack. The U.S. government has insisted strongly it was not deliberate. Their newsroom was just traumatized. Most of them knew the correspondent who was killed and they were just in a state of shock. It was a difficult situation for me because I didn't yet know any of the facts of what had occurred, but they said that they just wanted me to go on air as the Committee to Protect Journalists representative to express solidarity with the journalists from a news organization that's come under attack.

The Iraq story is the biggest story of the year, but I get disturbed by the ballooning of media coverage, which then falls off with the next crisis. We're bouncing from crisis to crisis. This is linked to the lack of expertise by our news organizations. The press really should have regular coverage out of Afghanistan at this point. The New York Times used a "flooding the zone strategy" and ran many times more pages of Iraq war news than anybody can really absorb. Meanwhile, the rest of the world gets squeezed out and then when the crises pass, they lapse back into much more routine news coverage. The New York Times deserves tremendous credit for the way that they have maintained their investment in the news side and they still remain by far the best paper in the country, if not the world. But the flood zone approach is not a good one in terms of serving its readers and giving them a view of things, paying attention to things that are not necessarily the crisis of the day. Those special war supplement sections really drove me crazy, too. I tried to read them all and couldn't possibly do it.

I was a supporter of the war in Afghanistan, as were many of my fellow liberals. We were attacked and their country was run by a horrible government that was harboring this highly destructive force and we needed to do something about. Al-Qaeda is a real threat and we need to go after them in a law enforcement way. But many of us feel that the war in Iraq was a big distraction from that effort. We also need to address the broader problems. Just look at the continued misery in countries from Egypt to Saudi Arabia to Syria. The Iraq War showed that while we won that battle, there's a tremendous amount of anger and a sense of humiliation in the Arab world that is going to just compound the problems we face down the road. After the fall of the Soviet Union and traditional left-of-center parties, you have this militant Islam taking its place in this region. How to arrest that and how to provide other outlets for protest and for improvement in people's lives, that clearly is part of the long-term challenge the United States faces.

As for those specific challenges facing journalists, the world's worst places to be a journalist are: Iraq; Cuba, which recently jailed a number of journalists, the worst crackdown in recent memory; Vietnam; Afghanistan; the occupied territories in Israel; Chechnya; Eritrea; Togo; Belarus; Turkey; Colombia, which remains the most dangerous country in Latin America; and China, which I believe, has more journalists in prison than any other county.

My advice to aspiring young journalists is don't be a war reporter, necessarily. Instead be a reporter who goes to difficult areas that maybe are not always immediately in the news. For instance, the Congo is a terrible place and not getting the attention it deserves. Indonesia suppresses rebels in the Aceh province. There are so many places that need good journalistic exposure away from the pack. To me, what is most satisfying and useful with journalism, is going where others are not and bringing to public view situations that do not have the exposure they need, or going to places that have gotten exposure but really need more in-depth long-term analysis to help us make sense of it.

CHOOSING THE RIGHT TARGET
CBS News Cameraman
Mario DeCarvalho

> "I'd love to make three times the money but
> that's just the way it goes. . . . No overtime
> when we go overseas. I wish I could get
> overtime—one billion dollars. I do it for history.
> It's not just a job, it's a calling."

Seemingly time-machined from the 60s, he speaks in hipster lingo, using "man" and "wows" as all-purpose conversational explanation points. So, it's easy to conjure up his cinematic counterpart—the Vietnam combat photographer played by Dennis Hopper in *Apocalypse Now*. But before veteran CBS cameraman Mario DeCarvalho worked in television, his point-and-shoot lifestyle involved a different kind of vocation. Born in the Azores, where his father worked for the U.S. Air Force as a contractor in World War II, Mario later moved to Portugal. At the age of twenty, he was drafted into the Portuguese Army. Portugal was fighting a colonial war in Africa from 1963 to 1974 in Angola and Guinea Bissau, and he served nearly five years in Portuguese Special Forces. Then how did this Portugese Rambo end up as an cameraman for CBS News, where he's worked for nearly three decades? In the words of CBS correspondent Jim Axelrod, who teamed up with him in Kuwait and Iraq as embeds with the Third Infantry, "Mario is one of the all-time great combat cameramen." We talked to Mario from his home in Atlanta, but his story begins in the jungles of Central Africa.

■　■　■

It was pretty rough in Angola and Guinea Bissau. I was twenty-one years old. I was a sergeant with the Special Forces. I was a sniper. We lived for two years in the jungle and never left. Fought guerrillas. The terrain was about the same as Vietnam—rice paddies, palm trees, and bad guys trying to kill you, or good guys trying to kill us, whom they considered bad guys. As far as they were concerned we were the bad guys. I had volunteered for Special Forces because I thought if I had to go to war, I might as well be as prepared as I could instead of being a regular soldier, even though the danger is much higher when you join a Special Forces outfit. In my own interest, to be a well-prepared Special Forces guy, made me know my limits both psychologically and physically. Surgeons operate. Lawyers prosecute and defend people. Journalists report. And soldiers kill people. That is the business they are in. Kill whatever threatens them. That is a thing you have to understand when going in, absolutely. Killing another man is one of the worst things that you can go through. It doesn't hit you the moment you have to do it. This is not homicide, it is self defense. Defense in the heat of battle. Your senses are working at 100 percent. Your training kicks in, and you know what to do, and the most important mission is to protect the people around you. The soldiers try to make it out of there alive. You must come to grips with the fact that it's either you or the other guy. I am not a fanatic, but I am a religious man. It is very hard especially being twenty-two years old. You look in your sights and take this guy out. I understand and feel war in a different way than most people—people who have never been in combat—look at war.

On one mission in Guinea Bissau we had to walk all night. The terrain was rice paddies. We stopped and camouflaged ourselves in the bushes. The operation was not far out of the town of Mansoa. Our operation was to observe the movement of five guys we were fighting against. We saw this guy walk toward us. We heard him shoot birds. Our job was not to engage at that particular time. Just to observe. He kept walking straight toward us and I started thinking, "Please turn. Do not come this way!" He kept looking at palm trees, and he would see something, and try to shoot, and came closer, and closer. I said to myself, "Come this way and I'm gonna have to kill you." He kept coming and kept coming. He was probably ten yards away. All of a sudden he saw us, and he tried to turn his weapon toward us. I had a Heckler & Koch G3 7.62 and I eliminated him. I shot, and ran to him and took his weapon and his little purse because it might have had documents and information we needed. We knew that they would start to shoot mortars at us right away, so we had to hightail it out of there to reposition ourselves. I had a hard time sleeping that night. It's thirty years later and I can still see that guy in 1972. I can see the guy's face and the way he was dressed. It marks you. It gets you. When I returned to the base all I wanted to do was drink all the beer I could. Good thing it wasn't available.

We also made helicopter assaults. That was just the most terrible thing to do. I give all my respect to the 101st Airborne. When you do a helicopter assault, you announce to the entire world you are coming in. It is terrifying. Many times I have jumped out of a helicopter already under fire, with my mission to run toward the enemy and get them before you get killed. In my company of 160 men, twelve were killed and eighty-six wounded in two years. We were pretty involved.

In 1974 there was a revolution in Portugal. They threw out the government of Salazar. When the war was over, they gave independence to the countries where we were fighting. I came back on June 30, 1974 to an entirely different country. The country had been a dictatorship. I returned to a country covered in the communist hammer and sickle. This was new to me. What the hell is this? There was graffiti everywhere. Like wow, man! No jobs. So I tried to take some time off. I finally got a job at the airport renting cars. It was a great job. It put me in contact with people. It was a lot of fun. However, I decided to become a flight attendant. So I quit Avis. Two weeks into my flight attendant course, there was a counterrevolution. They nationalized the airlines. The course was suspended and suddenly I was in the streets and had no job. I was not about to go and ask my parents for money. I was twenty-five years old. Sonofabitch, man. I went back to Avis. They said, "We cannot take you back." However, they had cars which you can rent in Lisbon and drive to other European cities, and leave it there. Guys like me are paid by Avis to take a train to those cities and then would pay me an amount per kilometer to drive the car back to Lisbon.

One time a guy from Avis called me, "Hey, some American television newsman needs a translator. Want to do it?" "How much they pay?" "Twenty-five dollars a day." "What time? Where do they want me!" Twenty-five bucks a day in 1975! Damn! For a guy with no job. Absolutely! The rest is history! Bob McNamara—he is now based in Dallas and still with CBS as a correspondent, he and the crew were covering the counterrevolution. I knew the country real well and took them around. Hey, this was a fun profession. I was right in the middle of history. Then one day at this big demonstration, I said, "Hey! I think I can do sound, man." Then we did a few more demonstrations. This guy who used to be the Paris bureau chief, Van Gordon Sauter, who later became president of CBS News, was in Portugal. They'd always leave after a month. Van Gordon Sauter wanted me to work as a staff sound man in Germany. I really wanted to be a cameraman, but my boss said, "Shut up and learn. Do audio and learn camera over time. I did that. I spent lot of time in Lebanon and the Middle East in 1976 and 1977. I spent a lot of time covering the war in Lebanon and the invasion by the Syrians in November '76. We went to Rhodesia, and we covered the Iron Curtain, and Soviet Union. The next year, they offered me a job as a cameraman in Cairo, so I went. I learned Arabic in trips to the Middle East. I was there for two and a half years—the whole Sadat-Menachem Begin thing. I went to Iran for the revolution. After that I got tired of the Middle East. I said, "Thank you! I want to get out. Goodbye." So they asked me, "How about Tel Aviv?" Hmm, that sounds interesting. So I went there for four years where I learned Hebrew. I covered the 1982 invasion of south Lebanon, and later went to El Salvador and Nicaragua before the Iran-Iraq war started.

I stayed in Israel for four years. In 1984 I got really tired of the region and I wanted to leave but because I spoke Arabic and Hebrew, why would they let me leave? CBS offered me Miami to cover Central and South America, and I said yes because I loved Salvador, and Nicaragua, and Guatemala, and I came to Miami, and spent time in Central America. I covered the drug war. I started to spend a lot of time in Colombia, and Bolivia, and Haiti, and then the Middle East blew up again. Desert Storm was getting underway. In October, I went to Saudi Arabia, and was one of the very few "embedded guys" with the military when the air war started—January 1991, fifteenth or sixteenth, and they put us in a pool. It was absolute bullshit. All the censorship, man, was ridiculous! Terrible! We could do nothing but what they wanted us to do. "Look at how great we are!" We had a Kentucky National Guard PAO [Public Affairs Officer] team taking us around. They were our minders but I didn't want a guy from Kentucky—not that I have anything against Kentucky—telling me to shoot on the right when there is stuff blowing up on the left. That is wrong! I do not want that. The hell with that. Am I with the Soviet Army?

I tell you, combat doesn't bother me much, man. I have seen so much carnage. You have to disassociate and concentrate on your job. A gunner or tank driver has to totally concentrate on gunning and I have to concentrate on the pictures. What can I do? My weapon is the camera. Of the stories I shoot, it's all a matter of organization. People don't understand that behind the reporter there has to be some schmuck taking the damn pictures and it's not a machine. Some of my best friends in the journalistic world are "still" photographers. I know them and have the highest respect for them. You see a picture by James

Nachtwey, you say, "Oh wow!" When you see Jim Axelrod on TV, "Oh, a great report!" My name is not there. We are considered just technicians, but we are artists, too.

Before Iraq, I had vowed that I would cover no more wars. Then why was it worthwhile to come back to cover a war again? Let me explain. When I heard they were going to embed the media, I said, "Okay, I am going. I want to see this." I went to Kuwait and took the NBC [Nuclear Biological Chemical] course for embeds. To me, that was an eye opener. In Desert Storm, they never taught us how to use this shit. David Bloom was in my group. I took a few pics of him with his mask on. I thought, "Maybe this guy's serious."

Our first concern was: "Can we take a vehicle?" They did not tell us if we could take a vehicle. No? Yes? There were three different ways to film. One way was to get your tape to a military helicopter, as they did it in the Gulf War. The second was to do it with small cameras, slimmed-down computers, and satellite phones. The third way was to use the Humvee and our heavy equipment. We had a month to get ready and we prepared for every contingency.

Our Humvee was about eight years old. We certainly did not have the most advanced Hummer. We had an old piece of crap, but it was our piece of crap, you know? What our satellite technician Geof Thorpe-Willett and I did was turn it into the most efficient, reliable broadcast-platform Humvee in Iraq. We worked on the Hummer in a warehouse in Kuwait City. We did everything we could to turn that Hummer into a piece of junk. It was all Geof's idea. We took the damn thing with all our satellite phones, satellite dishes, and went to the desert, and drove like maniacs. We jumped sand dunes and tried to break anything we could. We broke a lot of shit. After we broke it, we came back and not only did we fix it, we reinforced it a lot. Because we then knew what were the weak points of the Hummer; we could fix and re-solder them. We didn't simply replace parts, we re-welded them to make it all a lot stronger. Man, we took care of it, and kept cleaning out the dust and sand, and we just kept going. We were able to rig up a huge five-kilowatt generator in the back of the Humvee, which we converted to JP8 diesel so we could refuel with the military convoys. We took the attitude: "This is my Humvee, my crappy Humvee." So we ripped the air conditioner off the car. We didn't need that in the desert. Instead of a compressor for the AC, we installed a dynamo, a 2,500-watt generator, which runs with the engine when you need it. This would work as a power backup should our main generator crap out.

Conditions were tough in the sandstorms, but I pride myself on my ability to adapt to any conditions. In addition to my regular Sony SX digital camera, for the desert I also took some very useful mini-DV backups—a $2,800 Sony PD 150 and a smaller Sony PC 110. Of course, the big camera was my favorite, and I used it a lot for live shots during the day. It's got a beautiful lens, which alone costs $17,000. That is the big difference right there. The audience may not know when they see it, but subconsciously the big camera does everything smoother and it looks great.

The day before the war started our nightscope camera was stolen. We had carefully prepared for night shooting with this new equipment, but now we were dead in the water. Axelrod was about to commit suicide. He said, "I am screwed! Done! Finished!" With all the action at night, we were toast with no night scope. So I sat in the Humvee and thought, "Assess the situation." This is when my old military training comes in, when you face adverse situations. Our engineer Geof spent twelve years serving in the British SAS. I asked him, "What do you think about this? I have a PC 110, a little camera, like a Baptism or Bar Mitzvah camera. I had it in a Ziploc bag. I'd thought: If all else fails, this camera will be clean from sand. Maybe the night vision goggles could sit directly on the lens. So we tied it parallel to the lens and fastened it with tie wraps, and duct tape, and a piece of cardboard from one of our MREs to make it fit right, and we did it! I said, "Man, we are in business!" Geof said, "We will kill everybody, eh mate?" Whoa! That's right! God is good! And we didn't tell anyone how we did it.

Before heading out to the battlefield, we got on the media bus. Only after we were on the bus, did they tell us where we were going. The next day, we got a very pleasant surprise. The commanding officer told us we could bring the Humvee along. The only rules the military put on us were that we would not broadcast our actual position at the time or take pictures of dead or wounded Americans. That was pretty understandable. I would look at the battle scene and see that I could find a way to shoot it where you could see all the tanks and Apache helicopters without giving up my position.

The criticism I heard when I came back to the United States was that television viewers did not see a lot of close combat. Well, first of all, this was not Vietnam. This was a tank-artillery-air force war. Sometimes, we didn't see anything. If you really wanted to see close combat, ask Saddam Hussein to be embedded with the Republican Guard. Then you have both. I covered my side of the war. I did all I was offered. I did not see artillery destroy Iraqi forces when it happened. Critics say, "No close-up action." I say, "I got what the American military showed us. What do you want me to do? Run after a 155 howitzer shell and take pictures of it falling twenty kilometers away?" My job was to record what happened to the American soldiers. The U.S. Army had a story to tell and it was my responsibility to tell the story through pictures.

The military commanders took it upon themselves to open their doors and did it in a way that is just incredible. We had access to everything. I could walk into the major's military intelligence tent, and ask him questions, and he'd answer—this is what will happen then. He said, "My job is to think like an Iraqi. I think they will do this and this." We knew where a battle was going to be and when they would be fought. I came back with incredible appreciation for people like Lieutenant Colonel Rock Marcone. He's a guy who's what, forty years old or so? The soldiers would follow him to the end of the world if necessary. He went all the way to the Euphrates and his unit sustained no major battle casualties. He was speaking Italian to me, and Axelrod said, "What is this in the middle of Iraq? Guys speaking Italian?"

Of course there were little problems here and there. Miscommunications? Sure there were some. The soldiers were not comfortable with having us around until they realized that we knew what we were doing. Also, it is a point of pride with me that I will not put in danger anyone or myself. It was important to me to be in good shape so no one was put at risk to babysit me. When they move, they move fast.

Some TV crews complained about not being allowed by their editors to show the horrors of war—dead Iraqis and dead Americans. I thought the choice to avoid that was excellent. I was happy with CBS's decision not to show dead Americans or dead Iraqis—provided we can tell the American people that Americans are getting killed and wounded.

As a cameraman, you need a lot more than technical skills, and you make all these artistic decisions in a split second. Like what happened in the little town of Kifl one night. We had made an incredible advance during a sandstorm and we surprised the Iraqis. When we got there, U.S. troops were under fire. So we followed the troops, and the commander says, "Be careful! There are snipers." All of a sudden, we see this barber shop and on the back wall is a poster of the World Trade Center Twin Towers This is eighteen months past 9/11, and here is this incredible view of Manhattan seen from New Jersey with sailboats and a beautiful beach and no destruction. Right in this barber shop in the town of Kifl next to the Euphrates River! I go, "Wow man!" Axelrod says, "It is unbelievable!" I took a bunch of pictures, but something was missing. In my mind, shooting through the broken glass of the front window, and showing the painting in the back was good, but it needed some movement. I need something more than a still picture that would draw in the viewer and link this incredible mural to this war. Then, out of the corner of my eye, I see this M113 armored personnel carrier [APC] coming up the road, but I didn't have time to cross the road to have the APC pass in front of me with the barber shop in the background. I did not have the lens or the time to zoom in to the poster after the APC. It was too far away, and too long a shot, and without some transition, they would never use it. I made a split-second decision. The shot I got, which was used to open the news report, was the reflection of the tank passing by on a piece of broken glass from the front window, then I zoomed in to the Twin Towers poster on the wall. It worked great. It is one of the images I see amidst a tremendous amount of chaos and carnage—this idyllic view of the Twin Towers. It was so good, I commented on it when I talked with Ted Koppel. The next day, he went and looked for it and they put it on ABC Nightline.

My proudest moment was April 2 in Baghdad. We were under small-arms and artillery fire from the Iraqis. A twenty-year old medic in the U.S. Army is taking care of an Iraqi soldier. I do not think in terms of politics. What I saw is this twenty-year-old kid, who was eight years old when I was in Desert Storm, and he is taking care of our enemy, and telling him how we are all brothers. Somebody took a picture of me on my knees taking pictures of this scene with my little Sony PD-150. I am not a reporter who can just go back and weave that scene into his narration. I can't go back to things and restage them. I can just show you the pictures. They don't lie.

Now here is when I get a little bit philosophical. I saw a black guy from Florida, a white guy from Alabama, and a Puerto Rican all living and fighting together in a Bradley—and there is no racism. Just army guys working together, doing an incredible job. Why not figure a way to transpose that to our country in peace time? Why do those same guys, when they leave the military, go back to a white or a black or a Puerto Rican ghetto and lose that togetherness? Why, man? Why? Here is the thing. We depend on those people to risk their lives for our national security. So why can't we tap into this incredible resource?

I was the oldest guy in the entire brigade. I turned fifty-three in the middle of the desert with twenty-three-year olds. They all sang Happy Birthday to me and threw MREs at me so I could choose the one I wanted. When I finally left Iraq I was beat up. I was so darned tired once the adrenaline went away. I have had enough of war. I have done enough. I'm remarried and have children. I saw the embed process and I know it works. Thank you very much, goodbye. Now I will shoot cooking segments or nail classes or whatever they want me to do. I'd love to make three times the money but that is just the way it goes. Just do your job, man. Not for the money believe me, since we make $68,000 a year. No overtime when we go overseas. I wish I could get overtime—one billion dollars. We do it for history. It's not just a job, it's a calling.

I have been involved in wars and revolutions since 1972. Carol Guzzi is a photographer who won a Pulitzer covering Colombia mudslides in 1986. She took a picture of this little girl who later died. Carol spoke about me in her Pulitzer acceptance speech. She said she would never forget me because I dropped my camera and helped another child who was about to die. That is another story, man. My dream when I retire is to be a fisherman in the Azores.

THE PING, PING, PING OF BULLETS HITTING MY CAR

Newsweek Reporter Scott Johnson

> "As I passed the man with the gun, I could see his face and I sensed a weird mixture of joy and anger because he was anticipating a kill."

They weren't embeds and they weren't patient. Newsweek reporter Scott Johnson, twenty-nine, and contract photographer Luc Delahaye, forty, traveled as unilaterals in separate Mitsubishi Pajeros, taking calculated risks during the first days of the war as they pushed far forward on back roads and desert tracks, often leapfrogging slow-moving U.S. Army convoys. Then outside An Nasiriyah, along a wide, six-lane highway choked with tanks and Humvees, they made a fateful decision when they chose to outrace the military's mobile wall of steel. As Johnson later wrote in Newsweek, "The photographer and I got to the head of the convoy and accelerated past. I saw a post with a soldier standing on an island in the middle of the road. I saw he had a gun—but I thought he was American. I was wrong."

Johnson has an amazing story to tell of what happens next. Close to certain death, he experienced an altered sense of time and a heightened yet fragmented consciousness; it's the kind of transformation that is seldom described in the pages of a weekly news magazine. While listening to Johnson relive those events via satphone from Baghdad, we thought of this passage from Stephen Crane's Civil War classic The Red Badge of Courage:

> The song of the bullets was in the air and shells snarled among the treetops. It seemed to the youth that he saw everything. Each blade of the green grass was bold and clear. He thought that he was aware of every change in the thin, transparent vapor that floated idly in sheets. The brown or gray trunks of the trees showed each roughness of their surfaces. And the men of the regiment,

*with their staring eyes and sweating faces, running madly, or falling,
as if thrown headlong, to queer, heaped-up corpses—all were com-
prehended. His mind took a mechanical but firm impression, so that
afterward everything was pictured and explained to him, save why
he himself was there.*

Newsweek ended up paying the Kuwaiti car rental agency $60,000 for total losses on both SUVs. Adding insult to injury, by the time Delahaye, a France-based award-winning photographer, who uses a panoramic film camera and not a digital camera, reached safety and was able to ship his film to *Newsweek's* New York office, the pictures were too late to be used by the publication.

In retrospect, when outsiders consider the results, Johnson and Delahaye's expedition to the front might seem foolhardy—at best. But viewed step by step, each decision was based upon a solid rationale, a careful weighing of costs and benefits. After all, Delahaye had already covered several wars, and Johnson's decision to remain close to him apparently made sense for these two unilaterals whose initiative proved exemplary. Until they ventured one step too many and went past a point of no return.

■   ■   ■

I'm American though I was born in India and moved around basically every couple of years because my dad was in the Foreign Service. I lived overseas since I was ten. I went to college at the University of Washington in Seattle, where I studied comparative literature. I then taught English for a while in Morocco, where I also did some post-graduate work and studied Arabic, before winding up in France. I then got an internship at *Newsweek's* Paris office. It was a very steep learning curve. I started out opening the mail, reading the papers, filing, and doing research. I had a great mentor, Christopher Dickey, who's in Baghdad right now. I started writing small stories and moved on to bigger stories, and then I started traveling, around France and to Belgium, North Africa, and little by little I just sort of hung on and it developed into a good job. Right after September 11, I went to Algeria looking for its links to Al-Qaeda. Algeria has this long, ongoing history of insurgency and revolution. Ironically, Algeria stood to benefit in the September 11 aftermath. Because there were terrorist groups that had operated, both independently and in conjunction with Al-Qaeda, many anticipated that the Algerian government would now get money from the United States to crack down on these terrorists.

September 11 completely changed the arc of my journalistic career. This was my second trip to Algeria and the start of a new chapter in my life. In late October 2001, I traveled to Afghanistan and I covered the war through May 2002. In Afghanistan, I became very good friends with Peter Baker of *The Washington Post* and several others. I became part of this traveling band of foreign correspondents.

Working here in Iraq is strikingly different from Afghanistan. If you're embedded or even if you're not embedded, you have good access to the U.S. military. In Afghanistan, that was just not the case. We tried so many times to meet the Special Forces, but they were very squirrelly. They never wanted to see or talk to us. Every once in a while we ran into them by chance and we might sit down and have a chat. But in most cases they never revealed much. They certainly didn't want to show us what was going on or talk about what they were doing or which Afghans they were working with. The difference between Afghanistan and Iraq is just black and white. It's stunning, really. Right after Operation Anaconda in March, Peter and I ended up getting caught in this very ugly situation in which a Canadian journalist named Kathleen Kenna from the *Toronto Star* was severely wounded. She had been attacked by some guys who threw a grenade at her car. We never figured out who it was but we suspected that it was either the Taliban or an Al-Qaeda or maybe just a very angry Afghan who had his village bombed. She was severely wounded. Peter and I had been to the base earlier that day and we had seen Special Forces there, so we went back for help. They agreed to bring her into the base and ended up helicoptering her out.

Later on, Peter and I started wondering that if we had been able to speak to the Special Forces and to know what was going on and where to go and where not to go and what the situation was, maybe Kathleen would never have gone into that village and been attacked. The non-cooperation of the Special Forces was so intense that it ended up compromising the safety of the journalists working there. It was a complete blackout. We felt that if we had had access it might have helped us. And it might eventually help their cause. So I guess the point of the embed project in Iraq was to show what the military was doing and to make sure that their message was getting out. Because there were so many fewer troops in Afghanistan and because the war was sort of a secret war, the American military mission ended up not being much of a story, whereas in Iraq, the American presence was overwhelming and the war was spectacular. But on a personal level, Afghanistan is such an incredible place—a gorgeous country. It was amazing to be driving around the hills during the war—it was a total adventure. I wrote a lot there, not just for Newsweek, but for myself because it was inspiring and filled with many stories. Afghans were incredibly hospitable. Even those who were anti-American or former Taliban would welcome you to their homes, make you tea. To a young journalist covering his first war, I couldn't have picked a better one. Afghans are visceral and colorful and interesting. I was endlessly fascinated.

A few days before the Iraq war started, all the journalists were trying to get as close to the border as possible. On the Kuwaiti side, there were a series of farms. To get there you had to cross two or three checkpoints. It was very difficult. You'd maybe pass one and get to the second and then they'd make you turn back. Several journalists were trying go through the desert and around the checkpoints to get to the farms. My photographer, Luc Delahaye, managed to get to a farm fairly close to the border, so I joined him. Luc knew the guy who owned the farm, and we stayed there two days. Then the owner got nervous and kicked us out. So we moved to another farm where some other journalists were staying. On the third night, you could hear Apache helicopters firing Hellfire rockets from Kuwait into Iraq. So, the next day we tried to follow a military police convoy but they told us to turn around. We tried again at another place and the same thing happened. At noon, we decided to head toward the western edge of the Kuwaiti desert. Nobody was going out there and it took several hours to get to the border. But we knew that many U.S. Army Third Infantry Division convoys were headed out that way. So with a guide, we got to the berm and crossed into Iraq. As we got through, Luc almost drove his Pajero SUV into the mine field and stopped his car. We decided to take a road that ran parallel to the border, heading southwest. That road would lead us to other breaks in the berm and then to paved roads that the American convoys were going to be traveling. I was terrified, because we were the only journalists around. We were far from any towns, and there were no people. The psychological shift was very intense, knowing that we were in Iraq and that we were now on our own in the war zone. While many of the journalists traveled with a translator and driver, I was driving alone, following Luc in another Pajero.

We found one convoy, but we decided not to take the road that were traveling on. Farther on, we jumped right into a Marine convoy; I tried to follow it but my Pajero SUV got stuck trying to go up this hill. I was sitting there spinning its wheels while a Marine in a Humvee in back of me started cursing. They were really pissed off because they were trying to keep the convoy intact, and suddenly this Pajero rammed its way in and got stuck. Eventually the whole convoy stopped because the commander wanted to find out who these guys were who came along without their permission. We worked it out that we could follow them, which we did for several hours. Everything seemed to be going all right until late that night when we finally stopped in the middle of the desert. It was pitch black, it was cold. We were definitely deep into the country and it was not possible to go back to Kuwait. Then the commanding officer comes over and says, "You can't stay with our convoy. You have to leave at first light. If you try to follow us, then we'll . . . ." He just trailed off. He didn't say what would happen, but it was clear that we were back on our own.

They told us to park our cars in another area separate from their unit. In the morning we woke up early and headed off to the north and west and drove all day. We had a map, and we knew generally where we wanted to go. Obviously we didn't want to get ahead of the U.S. forces and get caught in the middle of the fighting. We kept running across formations of tanks. When we drove up, they would swing around and point their turrets at us. We got questioned a lot. A couple of times we had to stop and guys in a truck would come zooming over, hit the ground and point their guns at us. We had to get out of our cars with our hands up and walk over and say who we were.

It was a surreal environment. It was kind of overcast, and you'd see helicopters and planes, and in the distance you'd hear the rumbling of bombs. There we were, two SUVs in the middle of the desert trying to weave through these military formations to get closer to the front. We were constantly trying to read the situation. Is this a front line? Can we drive this way? Or would it be better to drive forty-five degrees to the south? Since there were no landmarks, we were trying to read the desert landscape, which was unsettling. Eventually we made it to a road where there were a lot of U.S. troops. That was reassuring. By then, we were far north of Umm Qasr. We were just south of Halifa, which has an airfield, just south of Route 8. We were told not to go into that town, so we skirted west and raced through the desert and eventually we made it up to Route 1, the four-lane highway which runs into Route 8.

When we got to Route 8, we stumbled on this really amazing sight. It was a modern paved super highway, four lanes, the first pavement we'd seen in two or three days. I had been awake almost the whole time. I hadn't eaten anything, it was stressful and I was tense. That giant highway was filled with military vehicles as far as the eye could see. Tanks and Humvees and supply trucks and Bradley fighting vehicles—everything. They were rumbling north on the highway towards Nasiriyah. The landscape had changed. It was no longer flat dunes and desert. It began to transform into a lush, green environment in a river basin. I remember when I saw it the first time, it kind of looked like what I thought Vietnam looked like—fields with high grass, muddy, with people walking around the grass stalks.

The locals were staring at the military convoy with complete abomination. There was a huge discrepancy between the mud and the poverty of the villages and the giant snake of the U.S. Army with all its high-tech power. When we got there, I thought, "What have we stumbled onto? Maybe this isn't where we should be?" Luc and I hung out for awhile, then the convoy started to move forward and we followed. Sometimes we'd drive a little faster and we'd catch vehicles in front of us and then we'd slow down and join the next forward convoy, where we encountered the first village. At that point we were the farthest west and farthest north of any of the unilateral journalists. When we came to this village, the tanks had stopped. American troops had fanned out and they were standing around. There were scores of children out in the street jumping up and down and waving and running alongside the tanks. I wouldn't say they were joyful or ecstatic. They were just sort of frenetic. Their movement and activity were strangely counterbalanced by large groups of adult men who were standing like clumps of grass. One group here, one group there, with their arms crossed. It was extremely hard to read this scene. I didn't know whether they were happy to see us or really angry—a combination of the two—or whether the whole situation would erupt into battle. We stopped our cars, Luc got out and stood on the roof of his car and started snapping pictures. I was nervous because I couldn't tell what was going to happen. Every time I saw a group of children or somebody giving me a thumbs-up sign or waving, it reassured me. But then I'd look around and there'd be these guys scowling. It was weird. I was sitting in my car and a guy came up and I rolled down the window. He spoke English. He said, "Are you a soldier?" I said, "No, I'm a journalist." I remember watching his mouth, because it was twitching and trembling. And he was obviously very emotional but I could not tell if he were angry or happy. I added, "What do they think about these Americans, these soldiers?" I had no translator, so the communication was sketchy. He looked at me and said, "I can't talk to you because some people would be very angry." I asked, "Who? Who would be angry?" And he said, "I still can't tell you, but some people will be very angry."

I was following Luc. There was no way I was going to separate myself from him. At this point we were both committed together. But Luc was frustrated because he wasn't getting the kind of pictures he wanted. Every time he'd got out of his car, children swarmed around him and it was impossible to do realistic work in those conditions.

We were stopped somewhere between Nasiriyah and Samara. The previous day when we had stopped by a military encampment, a military intelligence officer there had told us that Route 8 was secure all the way to the town of Samara. We were pretty far up. At that moment, the convoy we were in was the most forward U.S. military unit of the war. We were told we would be fine if we stayed on the road because of constant military traffic. But under no circumstances should we go into these towns because they weren't secured.

As we drove along, we could leapfrog ahead and move to one part of the convoy and drive a little bit ahead and then move back in. Finally we got to the head of that convoy and the question became, "Do we go ahead of this convoy? Or do we stay?" Up until that point, the convoys had been five minutes apart. Suddenly we were in open space. We thought there was another convoy ahead of us, but it was a big gap. We didn't know how far the gap was, but we thought we might as well go ahead. And so, I radioed to Luc and I said maybe we should stop for the convoy. But we decided to just go ahead. We drove for about five minutes. It was open road and we were going pretty fast. At that point another journalists' car had joined Luc and I. They were two photographers, Chris Hunter and Kim Sadak. They drove in the middle, and I was at the rear. I saw Kim and Chris's car pull over to the side right in front of this gas station. But Luc had gone through the gas station. There was a small shack in the middle of the road with several soldiers. It looked sort of like a checkpoint sentry post. So I followed a few hundred meters behind Luc. But as I went through, I glimpsed a guy standing in the median with a gun. A big gun. A large caliber machine gun, the kind of gun where it has two handles sticking out of the bottom that you hold with both hands.

To be honest, I don't think it fully registered that I was no longer in U.S.-controlled territory. We had crossed an invisible border and things were completely different. I was still processing the change but the processing went too slow. As I passed the man with the gun, I could see his face and I sensed a weird mixture of joy and anger because he was anticipating a kill.

Until then, the real threat was not coming from the Iraqis, but from the Americans—getting shot at by helicopters or tanks. So we had marked a horizontal "V" on our vehicles. The "V" was a symbol enabling the military to identify you. If you had a "V" on your car, it meant that the military would see it and say, "Oh, they're friendly so don't shoot them." It was not a press marking. All of the unilateral journalists who went into Iraq had "V"s on their cars. Nobody had "TV." It was *Newsweek* correspondent Rod Nordland's idea, actually.

I don't know if the Iraqis at the checkpoint knew what the hell I was doing. Probably they simply thought that here's a target. Everything happened simultaneously. The instant I saw them. I heard the radio crackle and Luc said, "Weapons, weapons, have weapons!" A millisecond later, I heard bullets popping as they hit my car. The bullets sounded as if you took a small hammer and started hitting metal. Little metallic pops, dull whacks. There must have been at least 15 bullets that hit the body of the car, not the windows. I was thinking, "Are those bullets?"

My thought processes immediately changed radically. Some thoughts were very slow. And others were extremely fast. It was almost as if I were operating at several different levels without fully being able to grasp any of them. It was all very fragmented and disjointed. I was having trouble just comprehending that people were shooting my car and that they were hitting it. It was a terribly difficult to accept this new knowledge. But suddenly I had to. I needed to understand it and deal with it. So when I did, a second or so later, I kept my hands on the wheel but I ducked down. Obviously, I lost my bearings and I couldn't see the road. I started to swerve, but I kept my foot on the gas. A few seconds later, I popped my head up and saw that I was fishtailing all over the road. I tried to correct it, but I immediately overcorrected and lost control of the car and swerved left. Then I put on the brakes, which of course locked up and I slammed into the median and flipped onto the right side. Then the car slid along the median and slammed into a light post, and there the car stopped.

I was thrown out of my seat and just fell down on the passenger door, looking out at the windshield. I don't know if I had temporarily blacked out, but there were a couple of seconds when I can't recall what happened. I just remember slamming the brakes, falling, and all of a sudden sitting there, looking at the window, and hearing men still shooting at me. I could hear the bullets pinging, pinging off the bottom of the car, which was facing them. Just going ping, ping, ping. I thought it was over. At that moment, I didn't see any possible way I would get out alive. My mind was racing and I immediately started formulating several different possibilities, hoping for survival, but they all seemed like dead ends. I concluded, "Okay, I'm going to die here. In the next five minutes, I'm going to die."

I started kicking the windshield to break it so I could get out of the car. While I was kicking the glass, I thought maybe it would be better to climb out of the passenger window, stand up and put my hands up and be taken prisoner so they wouldn't kill me. Then I heard this really loud crack. A bullet had hit the car and exploded out the other side. It was clear they were still trying to shoot me and blow up the car. I could hear them yelling and shouting and shooting—and then I thought, "Well, they'll just run over as I'm sitting here and shoot me through the window." So while I was kicking the windshield, I kept looking for them. "When is the body that is going to shoot me going to appear from the shadows?"

I entertained all these absurd thoughts like, "Wait a minute, I'm supposed to get out." I started to feel overwhelmed with euphoria and despair, racing through all the different possibilities, even of escape. Finally I managed to kick a hole in the windshield and I crawled out. I just sort of glanced around. Fortunately, the way I got out, the car was between me and the shooters. I crawled away and down toward the median. Then I just lay in this hollowed base between the two sides of the median, which was about six feet wide and six inches deep. If I laid down flat on my back or on my stomach with my head on my side and my arm flat, then I was maybe eighty percent hidden. Every once in a while I could hear the bullets pop right over my head. I don't know if they saw me or they were just sort of shooting randomly. I could hear them yelling a little, but the shooting wasn't quite as intense.

At that moment, I felt extremely, overwhelmingly alone. I thought, "Holy shit, what am I going to do? Nobody is here. Luc is gone." It was the most terrifying, horrifying experience I've ever had. I felt completely vulnerable, with no recourse. I was cut off. All of those connections to civilization we take for granted, the backing of a major media organization, all of my friends, family, were gone. All the technology was sitting in a destroyed car, completely useless. All I had was a little curb and a hollowed out space in the dirt. I tried to dig myself further down into the dirt. It was kind of a red-brown color. It was cool and very soft. I was very comfortable. I was so glad to be in the dirt rather than on the concrete or in the car.

I crawled along in the dirt and started muttering to myself, "Fuck, fuck, fuck, this is really bad!" I looked at my watch, and it was completely covered in mud from when I dove in the dirt. I was startled by that. It's weird when you start to notice all these little tiny things. And then I stared at a black bug crawling in the mud. I kept crawling farther and farther away from the car, so that if it did blow up I wouldn't be anywhere near it. Eventually the shooting stopped and I just lay there in the dirt. My sense of time was muddled. Maybe ten minutes later, I heard a low sort of rumble along the road, getting increasingly louder. The closer it got, the louder it got, the more confident I started to feel. It was the convoy. I didn't get up. Instead, I just thought, "Please get here, please get here." Finally the first vehicles started to roll by. I put my arm up a little bit and I waved. Some of them waved back at me, and I thought, "Waving isn't doing the trick. Should I wave a flag?" Then I started yelling, "Hey, look at me, I'm an American! Hey! Help me, help me!" But the vehicles were very loud and either they didn't hear me or they did hear me and didn't care. As they rolled by, I started to worry. "Holy cow, they're just rolling by and they're going to leave me and the entire convoy's going to go by and I'll be here alone again!" After five minutes of this, I just stood up. Which was a huge, extremely difficult thing to do. I felt vulnerable and I didn't want to get up from my little dirt hideaway. Once I got up, I started running as fast as I could alongside the convoy. I was shouting and waving and running alongside the tanks, but the soldiers just looked at me. It was like a nightmare.

You know in nightmares when you sometimes try to run and you can't? Or you are running and then you just can't run anymore? After running for a while, I was so terrified and so shocked by the whole thing—plus I am a smoker—I couldn't run anymore. I had to stop. Then I was walking on the road, waving at them, pleading, and they're driving away. Finally, a Humvee stopped. I ran up and the guy asked, "What do you want?" I said, "I'm an American, I was attacked." They stopped the vehicle. The guy in the passenger seat looked at me and said, "Okay, get in." I jumped in the back. I was elated because I was confident that once I started talking to them, everything would be a little bit better. I was surrounded once again by Americans and comfort. It felt good. I didn't have any wounds at all, except for an abrasion on my back. But that was it. Very minor. Incredible. Then I started trembling—not screaming, but yelling, hyperventilating and wheezing. I said, "You know, they're over there, they attacked me! That was my car, they hit the car." The guy said, "Where are you from?" I said, "I'm a reporter for *Newsweek* magazine." He said, "Oh, cool." The guy in the back seat was just looking at me like I was some sort of alien. I was confused, staggered. Plus I was muddy and terrified. The guy in the front passenger later told me that he was ready to pull out his pistol and shoot me if I wasn't who I said I was.

Much later, I realized that Luc went through his own nightmare with Chris and Kim, which was far worse in some ways than what I went through. They had to abandon their cars and were chased by Iraqis for several hours as they took off in the night on foot through the desert.

Ours were not the only vehicles attacked. The whole convoy was attacked at several different places. It was very clear that the ambush had been set in advance, and that they were going to attack that convoy no matter what. It was very clear they were soldiers and that they had prepared for this. That attack was the first of its kind of the whole war. And subsequent to that night, there were a string of ambushes along Route 8. Initially, the army had planned to take Route 8 and drive all the way up to Baghdad, not going into any other town but using that road as a supply road because it was paved. It seemed easy. They would just blow all the way through Karbala and Najaf, through the airport, and into Baghdad. After that night, they completely changed their strategy. They moved back into the desert and paralleled Route 8 through the desert all the way to Baghdad. The ambushes on the road turned out to be much too costly. It was too cumbersome to clear out every little village and deal with ambushes for 400 kilometers all the way to Baghdad.

Because the guys who picked me up were medics, they started receiving wounded. So all in one day, I got attacked, the ambushes started, there was a battle farther up the road, and then this wounded Marine gets rolled in and I observed the doctors fighting to save his life. He'd been shot in the leg and vehicles pulled into a wagon circle with the medical unit in the middle. It's dark, so they got the green lights out and it was intense. It was a very surreal ambience, an eerie green medical light bouncing off the tanks and the sand and the swirling dust.

The scene brought up a memory of that great moment in *Catch 22* when the pilot is dying and he keeps saying over and over, "I'm cold, I'm cold." The Marine was lying there and they were giving him IV injections and he kept saying, "Can I put my arm under the blanket? I'm cold, I'm really cold." They were hovering over him and the chaplain was kneeling by him and holding his hand and talking to him, asking questions and the green light was swirling everywhere. And meanwhile the tanks were still firing. All of a sudden, the reality of the war and the precariousness of every situation and the extreme delicacy of the situation hit me very hard. It became very clear that this was not a game. This is not something to be taken lightly. It was very serious. I'd just come through a shootout and almost gotten killed. Now here was a guy who'd gotten shot. I am wondering why am I here looking at this guy who got shot? It was the first time I'd thought, "This is completely real, this is war."

I couldn't go to sleep that night in the back of the Humvee because every time I shut my eyes, I started to hallucinate these vivid images, probably because of all the natural chemicals flooding my brain. One of the things I'd kept seeing over and over were images of sand and dunes. And then this bug. It was the bug I'd seen when I was laying in the dirt in the ditch. I kept seeing this bug over and over and over. I also kept seeing very disturbing things—the face of some guy, then the face would transform into this horrible image of death. Then the face would start to melt and all sorts of weird, gross things would happen to the face. The hair turned into snakes. Every time I closed my eyes for a few minutes, the visions would become larger and more intense.

I am much more conflicted now about war. There's something very profound and disturbing about being in an environment where matters of life and death are an issue, not just for the people you're writing about, but for yourself. I really think that changes the way you think about it, the way you write about it, the way you think about life in general, the way you think about war, the way you think about how it's covered. When you're writing and thinking about people who are struggling with life and death in a very direct way, and you yourself are struggling with these issues, it makes your job as a journalist much better. But it's a much heavier burden.

APPENDIX

101900Z FEB 03
FM SECDEF WASHINGTON DC//OASD-PA//
TO SECDEF WASHINGTON DC//CHAIRS//
AIG 8777
HQ USEUCOM VAIHINGEN GE//PA//
USCINCEUR VAIHINGEN GE//ECPA//
JOINT STAFF WASHINGTON DC//PA//
SECSTATE WASHINGTON DC//PA//
CJCS WASHINGTON DC//PA//
NSC WASHINGTON DC
WHITE HOUSE SITUATION ROOM
INFO SECDEF WASHINGTON DC//OASD-PA/DPO//

UNCLAS

SUBJECT: PUBLIC AFFAIRS GUIDANCE (PAG) ON EMBEDDING
MEDIA DURING POSSIBLE FUTURE OPERATIONS/DEPLOY-
MENTS IN THE U.S. CENTRAL COMMANDS (CENTCOM) AREA OF
RESPONSIBILITY (AOR).

REFERENCES: REF. A. SECDEF MSG, DTG 172200Z JAN 03, SUBJ:
PUBLIC AFFAIRS GUIDANCE (PAG) FOR MOVEMENT OF FORCES
INTO THE CENTCOM AOR FOR POSSIBLE FUTURE OPERATIONS.

1. PURPOSE. THIS MESSAGE PROVIDES GUIDANCE, POLICIES,
AND PROCEDURES ON EMBEDDING NEWS MEDIA DURING POS-
SIBLE FUTURE OPERATIONS/DEPLOYMENTS IN THE CENTCOM
AOR. IT CAN BE ADAPTED FOR USE IN OTHER UNIFIED COM-
MAND AORS AS NECESSARY.

2. POLICY.

2.A. THE DEPARTMENT OF DEFENSE (DOD) POLICY ON MEDIA COVERAGE OF FUTURE MILITARY OPERATIONS IS THAT MEDIA WILL HAVE LONG TERM, MINIMALLY RESTRICTIVE ACCESS TO U.S. AIR, GROUND, AND NAVAL FORCES THROUGH EMBEDDING. MEDIA COVERAGE OF ANY FUTURE OPERATION WILL, TO A LARGE EXTENT, SHAPE PUBLIC PERCEPTION OF THE NATIONAL SECURITY ENVIRONMENT NOW AND IN THE YEARS AHEAD. THIS HOLDS TRUE FOR THE U.S. PUBLIC; THE PUBLIC IN ALLIED COUNTRIES WHOSE OPINION CAN AFFECT THE DURABILITY OF OUR COALITION; AND PUBLICS IN COUNTRIES WHERE WE CONDUCT OPERATIONS, WHOSE PERCEPTIONS OF US CAN AFFECT THE COST AND DURATION OF OUR INVOLVEMENT. OUR ULTIMATE STRATEGIC SUCCESS IN BRINGING PEACE AND SECURITY TO THIS REGION WILL COME IN OUR LONG-TERM COMMITMENT TO SUPPORTING OUR DEMOCRATIC IDEALS. WE NEED TO TELL THE FACTUAL STORY–GOOD OR BAD–BEFORE OTHERS SEED THE MEDIA WITH DISINFORMATION AND DISTORTIONS, AS THEY MOST CERTAINLY WILL CONTINUE TO DO. OUR PEOPLE IN THE FIELD NEED TO TELL OUR STORY–ONLY COMMANDERS CAN ENSURE THE MEDIA GET TO THE STORY ALONGSIDE THE TROOPS. WE MUST ORGANIZE FOR AND FACILITATE ACCESS OF NATIONAL AND INTERNATIONAL MEDIA TO OUR FORCES, INCLUDING THOSE FORCES ENGAGED IN GROUND OPERATIONS, WITH THE GOAL OF DOING SO RIGHT FROM THE START. TO ACCOMPLISH THIS, WE WILL EMBED MEDIA WITH OUR UNITS. THESE EMBEDDED MEDIA WILL LIVE, WORK, AND TRAVEL AS PART OF THE UNITS WITH WHICH THEY ARE EMBEDDED TO FACILITATE MAXIMUM, IN-DEPTH COVERAGE OF U.S. FORCES IN COMBAT AND RELATED OPERATIONS. COMMANDERS AND PUBLIC AFFAIRS OFFICERS MUST WORK TOGETHER TO BALANCE THE NEED FOR MEDIA ACCESS WITH THE NEED FOR OPERATIONAL SECURITY.

2.B. MEDIA WILL BE EMBEDDED WITH UNIT PERSONNEL AT AIR AND GROUND FORCES BASES AND AFLOAT TO ENSURE A FULL

UNDERSTANDING OF ALL OPERATIONS. MEDIA WILL BE GIVEN ACCESS TO OPERATIONAL COMBAT MISSIONS, INCLUDING MISSION PREPARATION AND DEBRIEFING, WHENEVER POSSIBLE.

2.C. A MEDIA EMBED IS DEFINED AS A MEDIA REPRESENTATIVE REMAINING WITH A UNIT ON AN EXTENDED BASIS–PERHAPS A PERIOD OF WEEKS OR EVEN MONTHS. COMMANDERS WILL PROVIDE BILLETING, RATIONS, AND MEDICAL ATTENTION, IF NEEDED, TO THE EMBEDDED MEDIA COMMENSURATE WITH THAT PROVIDED TO MEMBERS OF THE UNIT, AS WELL AS ACCESS TO MILITARY TRANSPORTATION AND ASSISTANCE WITH COMMUNICATIONS FILING/TRANSMITTING MEDIA PRODUCTS, IF REQUIRED.

2.C.1. EMBEDDED MEDIA ARE NOT AUTHORIZED USE OF THEIR OWN VEHICLES WHILE TRAVELING IN AN EMBEDDED STATUS.

2.C.2. TO THE EXTENT POSSIBLE, SPACE ON MILITARY TRANSPORTATION WILL BE MADE AVAILABLE FOR MEDIA EQUIPMENT NECESSARY TO COVER A PARTICULAR OPERATION. THE MEDIA IS RESPONSIBLE FOR LOADING AND CARRYING THEIR OWN EQUIPMENT AT ALL TIMES. USE OF PRIORITY INTER-THEATER AIRLIFT FOR EMBEDDED MEDIA TO COVER STORIES, AS WELL AS TO FILE STORIES, IS HIGHLY ENCOURAGED. SEATS ABOARD VEHICLES, AIRCRAFT, AND NAVAL SHIPS WILL BE MADE AVAILABLE TO ALLOW MAXIMUM COVERAGE OF U.S. TROOPS IN THE FIELD.

2.C.3. UNITS SHOULD PLAN LIFT AND LOGISTICAL SUPPORT TO ASSIST IN MOVING MEDIA PRODUCTS TO AND FROM THE BATTLEFIELD SO AS TO TELL OUR STORY IN A TIMELY MANNER. IN THE EVENT OF COMMERCIAL COMMUNICATIONS DIFFICULTIES, MEDIA ARE AUTHORIZED TO FILE STORIES VIA EXPEDITIOUS MILITARY SIGNAL/COMMUNICATIONS CAPABILITIES.

2.C.4. NO COMMUNICATIONS EQUIPMENT FOR USE BY MEDIA IN THE CONDUCT OF THEIR DUTIES WILL BE SPECIFICALLY PROHIBITED. HOWEVER, UNIT COMMANDERS MAY IMPOSE

TEMPORARY RESTRICTIONS ON ELECTRONIC TRANSMISSIONS FOR OPERATIONAL SECURITY REASONS. MEDIA WILL SEEK APPROVAL TO USE ELECTRONIC DEVICES IN A COMBAT/HOSTILE ENVIRONMENT, UNLESS OTHERWISE DIRECTED BY THE UNIT COMMANDER OR HIS/HER DESIGNATED REPRESENTATIVE. THE USE OF COMMUNICATIONS EQUIPMENT WILL BE DISCUSSED IN FULL WHEN THE MEDIA ARRIVE AT THEIR ASSIGNED UNIT.

3. PROCEDURES.

3.A. THE OFFICE OF THE ASSISTANT SECRETARY OF DEFENSE FOR PUBLIC AFFAIRS (OASD(PA)) IS THE CENTRAL AGENCY FOR MANAGING AND VETTING MEDIA EMBEDS TO INCLUDE ALLOCATING EMBED SLOTS TO MEDIA ORGANIZATIONS. EMBED AUTHORITY MAY BE DELEGATED TO SUBORDINATE ELEMENTS AFTER THE COMMENCEMENT OF HOSTILITIES AND AT THE DISCRETION OF OASD(PA). EMBED OPPORTUNITIES WILL BE ASSIGNED TO MEDIA ORGANIZATIONS, NOT TO INDIVIDUAL REPORTERS. THE DECISION AS TO WHICH MEDIA REPRESENTATIVE WILL FILL ASSIGNED EMBED SLOTS WILL BE MADE BY THE DESIGNATED POC FOR EACH NEWS ORGANIZATION.

3.A.1. IAW REF. A, COMMANDERS OF UNITS IN RECEIPT OF A DEPLOYMENT ORDER MAY EMBED REGIONAL/LOCAL MEDIA DURING PREPARATIONS FOR DEPLOYMENT, DEPLOYMENT, AND ARRIVAL IN THEATER UPON RECEIPT OF THEATER CLEARANCE FROM CENTCOM AND APPROVAL OF THE COMPONENT COMMAND. COMMANDERS WILL INFORM THESE MEDIA, PRIOR TO THE DEPLOYING EMBED, THAT OASD(PA) IS THE APPROVAL AUTHORITY FOR ALL COMBAT EMBEDS AND THAT THEIR PARTICULAR EMBED MAY END AFTER THE UNIT'S ARRIVAL IN THEATER. THE MEDIA ORGANIZATION MAY APPLY TO OASD(PA) FOR CONTINUED EMBEDDING, BUT THERE IS NO GUARANTEE AND THE MEDIA ORGANIZATION WILL HAVE TO MAKE ARRANGEMENTS FOR AND PAY FOR THE JOURNALISTS' RETURN TRIP.

3.B. WITHOUT MAKING COMMITMENTS TO MEDIA ORGANIZA-TIONS, DEPLOYING UNITS WILL IDENTIFY LOCAL MEDIA FOR PO-TENTIAL EMBEDS AND NOMINATE THEM THROUGH PA CHANNELS TO OASD(PA) (POC: MAJ TIM BLAIR, DSN 227-1253; COMM. 703-697-1253; EMAIL TIMOTHY.BLAIR@OSD.MIL). INFORMA-TION REQUIRED TO BE FORWARDED INCLUDES MEDIA ORGANI-ZATION, TYPE OF MEDIA AND CONTACT INFORMATION INCLUDING BUREAU CHIEF/MANAGING EDITOR/NEWS DIREC-TOR'S NAME; OFFICE, HOME AND CELL PHONE NUMBERS; PAGER NUMBERS AND EMAIL ADDRESSES. SUBMISSIONS FOR EMBEDS WITH SPECIFIC UNITS SHOULD INCLUDE A UNIT'S RECOMMEN-DATION AS TO WHETHER THE REQUEST SHOULD BE HONORED.

3.C. UNIT COMMANDERS SHOULD ALSO EXPRESS, THROUGH THEIR CHAIN OF COMMAND AND PA CHANNELS TO OASD(PA), THEIR DESIRE AND CAPABILITY TO SUPPORT ADDITIONAL MEDIA EMBEDS BEYOND THOSE ASSIGNED.

3.D. FREELANCE MEDIA WILL BE AUTHORIZED TO EMBED IF THEY ARE SELECTED BY A NEWS ORGANIZATION AS THEIR EMBED REPRESENTATIVE.

3.E. UNITS WILL BE AUTHORIZED DIRECT COORDINATION WITH MEDIA AFTER ASSIGNMENT AND APPROVAL BY OASD(PA).

3.E.1.UNITS ARE RESPONSIBLE FOR ENSURING THAT ALL EMBED-DED MEDIA AND THEIR NEWS ORGANIZATIONS HAVE SIGNED THE "RELEASE, INDEMNIFICATION, AND HOLD HARMLESS AGREEMENT AND AGREEMENT NOT TO SUE", FOUND AT HTTP://WWW.DEFENSELINK.MIL/NEWS/FEB2003/D20030210EMBED.PDF. UNITS MUST MAINTAIN A COPY OF THIS AGREEMENT FOR ALL MEDIA EMBEDDED WITH THEIR UNIT.

3.F. EMBEDDED MEDIA OPERATE AS PART OF THEIR ASSIGNED UNIT. AN ESCORT MAY BE ASSIGNED AT THE DISCRETION OF THE UNIT COMMANDER. THE ABSENCE OF A PA ESCORT IS NOT A REASON TO PRECLUDE MEDIA ACCESS TO OPERATIONS.

3.G. COMMANDERS WILL ENSURE THE MEDIA ARE PROVIDED WITH EVERY OPPORTUNITY TO OBSERVE ACTUAL COMBAT OPERATIONS. THE PERSONAL SAFETY OF CORRESPONDENTS IS NOT A REASON TO EXCLUDE THEM FROM COMBAT AREAS.

3.H. IF, IN THE OPINION OF THE UNIT COMMANDER, A MEDIA REPRESENTATIVE IS UNABLE TO WITHSTAND THE RIGOROUS CONDITIONS REQUIRED TO OPERATE WITH THE FORWARD DEPLOYED FORCES, THE COMMANDER OR HIS/HER REPRESENTATIVE MAY LIMIT THE REPRESENTATIVE'S PARTICIPATION WITH OPERATIONAL FORCES TO ENSURE UNIT SAFETY AND INFORM OASD(PA) THROUGH PA CHANNELS AS SOON AS POSSIBLE. GENDER WILL NOT BE AN EXCLUDING FACTOR UNDER ANY CIRCUMSTANCE.

3.I. IF FOR ANY REASON A MEDIA REPRESENTATIVE CANNOT PARTICIPATE IN AN OPERATION, THEY WILL BE TRANSPORTED TO THE NEXT HIGHER HEADQUARTERS FOR THE DURATION OF THE OPERATION.

3.J. COMMANDERS WILL OBTAIN THEATER CLEARANCE FROM CENTCOM/PA FOR MEDIA EMBARKING ON MILITARY CONVEYANCE FOR PURPOSES OF EMBEDDING.

3.K. UNITS HOSTING EMBEDDED MEDIA WILL ISSUE INVITATIONAL TRAVEL ORDERS, AND NUCLEAR, BIOLOGICAL, AND CHEMICAL (NBC) GEAR. SEE PARA. 5. FOR DETAILS ON WHICH ITEMS ARE ISSUED AND WHICH ITEMS THE MEDIA ARE RESPONSIBLE TO PROVIDE FOR THEMSELVES.

3.L. MEDIA ARE RESPONSIBLE FOR OBTAINING THEIR OWN PASSPORTS AND VISAS.

3.M. MEDIA WILL AGREE TO ABIDE BY THE CENTCOM/OASD(PA) GROUND RULES STATED IN PARA. 4 OF THIS MESSAGE IN EXCHANGE FOR COMMAND/UNIT-PROVIDED SUPPORT AND ACCESS TO SERVICE MEMBERS, INFORMATION, AND OTHER PREVIOUSLY-STATED PRIVILEGES. ANY VIOLATION OF THE

GROUND RULES COULD RESULT IN TERMINATION OF THAT MEDIA'S EMBED OPPORTUNITY.

3.N. DISPUTES/DIFFICULTIES. ISSUES, QUESTIONS, DIFFICULTIES OR DISPUTES ASSOCIATED WITH GROUND RULES OR OTHER ASPECTS OF EMBEDDING MEDIA THAT CANNOT BE RESOLVED AT THE UNIT LEVEL, OR THROUGH THE CHAIN OF COMMAND, WILL BE FORWARDED THROUGH PA CHANNELS FOR RESOLUTION. COMMANDERS WHO WISH TO TERMINATE AN EMBED FOR CAUSE MUST NOTIFY CENTCOM/PA PRIOR TO TERMINATION. IF A DISPUTE CANNOT BE RESOLVED AT A LOWER LEVEL, OASD(PA) WILL BE THE FINAL RESOLUTION AUTHORITY. IN ALL CASES, THIS SHOULD BE DONE AS EXPEDITIOUSLY AS POSSIBLE TO PRESERVE THE NEWS VALUE OF THE SITUATION.

3.O. MEDIA WILL PAY THEIR OWN BILLETING EXPENSES IF BILLETED IN COMMERCIAL FACILITY.

3.P. MEDIA WILL DEPLOY WITH THE NECESSARY EQUIPMENT TO COLLECT AND TRANSMIT THEIR STORIES.

3.Q. THE STANDARD FOR RELEASE OF INFORMATION SHOULD BE TO ASK "WHY NOT RELEASE" VICE "WHY RELEASE." DECISIONS SHOULD BE MADE ASAP, PREFERABLY IN MINUTES, NOT HOURS.

3.R. THERE IS NO GENERAL REVIEW PROCESS FOR MEDIA PRODUCTS. SEE PARA 6.A. FOR FURTHER DETAIL CONCERNING SECURITY AT THE SOURCE.

3.S. MEDIA WILL ONLY BE GRANTED ACCESS TO DETAINEES OR EPWS WITHIN THE PROVISIONS OF THE GENEVA CONVENTIONS OF 1949. SEE PARA. 4.G.17. FOR THE GROUND RULE.

3.T. HAVING EMBEDDED MEDIA DOES NOT PRECLUDE CONTACT WITH OTHER MEDIA. EMBEDDED MEDIA, AS A RESULT OF TIME INVESTED WITH THE UNIT AND GROUND RULES AGREEMENT, MAY HAVE A DIFFERENT LEVEL OF ACCESS.

3.U. CENTCOM/PA WILL ACCOUNT FOR EMBEDDED MEDIA DURING THE TIME THE MEDIA IS EMBEDDED IN THEATER. CENTCOM/PA WILL REPORT CHANGES IN EMBED STATUS TO OASD(PA) AS THEY OCCUR.

3.V. IF A MEDIA REPRESENTATIVE IS KILLED OR INJURED IN THE COURSE OF MILITARY OPERATIONS, THE UNIT WILL IMMEDI-ATELY NOTIFY OASD(PA), THROUGH PA CHANNELS. OASD(PA) WILL CONTACT THE RESPECTIVE MEDIA ORGANIZATION(S), WHICH WILL MAKE NEXT OF KIN NOTIFICATION IN ACCOR-DANCE WITH THE INDIVIDUAL'S WISHES.

3.W. MEDIA MAY TERMINATE THEIR EMBED OPPORTUNITY AT ANY TIME. UNIT COMMANDERS WILL PROVIDE, AS THE TACTI-CAL SITUATION PERMITS AND BASED ON THE AVAILABILITY OF TRANSPORTATION, MOVEMENT BACK TO THE NEAREST LOCA-TION WITH COMMERCIAL TRANSPORTATION.

3.W.1. DEPARTING MEDIA WILL BE DEBRIEFED ON OPERA-TIONAL SECURITY CONSIDERATIONS AS APPLICABLE TO ONGO-ING AND FUTURE OPERATIONS WHICH THEY MAY NOW HAVE INFORMATION CONCERNING.

4. GROUND RULES. FOR THE SAFETY AND SECURITY OF U.S. FORCES AND EMBEDDED MEDIA, MEDIA WILL ADHERE TO ES-TABLISHED GROUND RULES. GROUND RULES WILL BE AGREED TO IN ADVANCE AND SIGNED BY MEDIA PRIOR TO EM-BEDDING. VIOLATION OF THE GROUND RULES MAY RESULT IN THE IMMEDIATE TERMINATION OF THE EMBED AND RE-MOVAL FROM THE AOR. THESE GROUND RULES RECOGNIZE THE RIGHT OF THE MEDIA TO COVER MILITARY OPERATIONS AND ARE IN NO WAY INTENDED TO PREVENT RELEASE OF DEROGATORY, EMBARRASSING, NEGATIVE, OR UNCOMPLI-MENTARY INFORMATION. ANY MODIFICATION TO THE STAN-DARD GROUND RULES WILL BE FORWARDED THROUGH THE PA CHANNELS TO CENTCOM/PA FOR APPROVAL. STANDARD GROUND RULES ARE:

4.A. ALL INTERVIEWS WITH SERVICE MEMBERS WILL BE ON THE RECORD. SECURITY AT THE SOURCE IS THE POLICY. INTERVIEWS WITH PILOTS AND AIRCREW MEMBERS ARE AUTHORIZED UPON COMPLETION OF MISSIONS; HOWEVER, RELEASE OF INFORMATION MUST CONFORM TO THESE MEDIA GROUND RULES.

4.B. PRINT OR BROADCAST STORIES WILL BE DATELINED ACCORDING TO LOCAL GROUND RULES. LOCAL GROUND RULES WILL BE COORDINATED THROUGH COMMAND CHANNELS WITH CENTCOM.

4.C. MEDIA EMBEDDED WITH U.S. FORCES ARE NOT PERMITTED TO CARRY PERSONAL FIREARMS.

4.D. LIGHT DISCIPLINE RESTRICTIONS WILL BE FOLLOWED. VISIBLE LIGHT SOURCES, INCLUDING FLASH OR TELEVISION LIGHTS, FLASH CAMERAS WILL NOT BE USED WHEN OPERATING WITH FORCES AT NIGHT UNLESS SPECIFICALLY APPROVED IN ADVANCE BY THE ON-SCENE COMMANDER.

4.E. EMBARGOES MAY BE IMPOSED TO PROTECT OPERATIONAL SECURITY. EMBARGOES WILL ONLY BE USED FOR OPERATIONAL SECURITY AND WILL BE LIFTED AS SOON AS THE OPERATIONAL SECURITY ISSUE HAS PASSED.

4.F. THE FOLLOWING CATEGORIES OF INFORMATION ARE RELEASABLE.

4.F.1. APPROXIMATE FRIENDLY FORCE STRENGTH FIGURES.

4.F.2. APPROXIMATE FRIENDLY CASUALTY FIGURES BY SERVICE. EMBEDDED MEDIA MAY, WITHIN OPSEC LIMITS, CONFIRM UNIT CASUALTIES THEY HAVE WITNESSED.

4.F.3. CONFIRMED FIGURES OF ENEMY PERSONNEL DETAINED OR CAPTURED.

4.F.4. SIZE OF FRIENDLY FORCE PARTICIPATING IN AN ACTION OR OPERATION CAN BE DISCLOSED USING APPROXIMATE TERMS. SPECIFIC FORCE OR UNIT IDENTIFICATION MAY BE RELEASED WHEN IT NO LONGER WARRANTS SECURITY PROTECTION.

4.F.5. INFORMATION AND LOCATION OF MILITARY TARGETS AND OBJECTIVES PREVIOUSLY UNDER ATTACK.

4.F.6. GENERIC DESCRIPTION OF ORIGIN OF AIR OPERATIONS, SUCH AS "LAND-BASED."

4.F.7. DATE, TIME, OR LOCATION OF PREVIOUS CONVENTIONAL MILITARY MISSIONS AND ACTIONS, AS WELL AS MISSION RESULTS ARE RELEASABLE ONLY IF DESCRIBED IN GENERAL TERMS.

4.F.8. TYPES OF ORDNANCE EXPENDED IN GENERAL TERMS.

4.F.9. NUMBER OF AERIAL COMBAT OR RECONNAISSANCE MISSIONS OR SORTIES FLOWN IN CENTCOM'S AREA OF OPERATION.

4.F.10. TYPE OF FORCES INVOLVED (E.G., AIR DEFENSE, INFANTRY, ARMOR, MARINES).

4.F.11. ALLIED PARTICIPATION BY TYPE OF OPERATION (SHIPS, AIRCRAFT, GROUND UNITS, ETC.) AFTER APPROVAL OF THE ALLIED UNIT COMMANDER.

4.F.12. OPERATION CODE NAMES.

4.F.13. NAMES AND HOMETOWNS OF U.S. MILITARY UNITS.

4.F.14. SERVICE MEMBERS' NAMES AND HOME TOWNS WITH THE INDIVIDUALS' CONSENT.

4.G. THE FOLLOWING CATEGORIES OF INFORMATION ARE NOT RELEASABLE SINCE THEIR PUBLICATION OR BROADCAST COULD JEOPARDIZE OPERATIONS AND ENDANGER LIVES.

4.G.1. SPECIFIC NUMBER OF TROOPS IN UNITS BELOW CORPS/MEF LEVEL.

4.G.2. SPECIFIC NUMBER OF AIRCRAFT IN UNITS AT OR BELOW THE AIR EXPEDITIONARY WING LEVEL.

4.G.3. SPECIFIC NUMBERS REGARDING OTHER EQUIPMENT OR CRITICAL SUPPLIES (E.G. ARTILLERY, TANKS, LANDING CRAFT, RADARS, TRUCKS, WATER, ETC.).

4.G.4. SPECIFIC NUMBERS OF SHIPS IN UNITS BELOW THE CARRIER BATTLE GROUP LEVEL.

4.G.5. NAMES OF MILITARY INSTALLATIONS OR SPECIFIC GEOGRAPHIC LOCATIONS OF MILITARY UNITS IN THE CENTCOM AREA OF RESPONSIBILITY, UNLESS SPECIFICALLY RELEASED BY THE DEPARTMENT OF DEFENSE OR AUTHORIZED BY THE CENTCOM COMMANDER. NEWS AND IMAGERY PRODUCTS THAT IDENTIFY OR INCLUDE IDENTIFIABLE FEATURES OF THESE LOCATIONS ARE NOT AUTHORIZED FOR RELEASE.

4.G.6. INFORMATION REGARDING FUTURE OPERATIONS.

4.G.7. INFORMATION REGARDING FORCE PROTECTION MEASURES AT MILITARY INSTALLATIONS OR ENCAMPMENTS (EXCEPT THOSE WHICH ARE VISIBLE OR READILY APPARENT).

4.G.8. PHOTOGRAPHY SHOWING LEVEL OF SECURITY AT MILITARY INSTALLATIONS OR ENCAMPMENTS.

4.G.9. RULES OF ENGAGEMENT.

4.G.10. INFORMATION ON INTELLIGENCE COLLECTION ACTIVITIES COMPROMISING TACTICS, TECHNIQUES, OR PROCEDURES.

4.G.11. EXTRA PRECAUTIONS IN REPORTING WILL BE REQUIRED AT THE COMMENCEMENT OF HOSTILITIES TO MAXIMIZE

OPERATIONAL SURPRISE. LIVE BROADCASTS FROM AIRFIELDS, ON THE GROUND OR AFLOAT, BY EMBEDDED MEDIA ARE PROHIBITED UNTIL THE SAFE RETURN OF THE INITIAL STRIKE PACKAGE OR UNTIL AUTHORIZED BY THE UNIT COMMANDER.

4.G.12. DURING AN OPERATION, SPECIFIC INFORMATION ON FRIENDLY FORCE TROOP MOVEMENTS, TACTICAL DEPLOYMENTS, AND DISPOSITIONS THAT WOULD JEOPARDIZE OPERATIONAL SECURITY OR LIVES. INFORMATION ON ON-GOING ENGAGEMENTS WILL NOT BE RELEASED UNLESS AUTHORIZED FOR RELEASE BY ON-SCENE COMMANDER.

4.G.13. INFORMATION ON SPECIAL OPERATIONS UNITS, UNIQUE OPERATIONS METHODOLOGY OR TACTICS, FOR EXAMPLE, AIR OPERATIONS, ANGLES OF ATTACK, AND SPEEDS; NAVAL TACTICAL OR EVASIVE MANEUVERS, ETC. GENERAL TERMS SUCH AS "LOW" OR "FAST" MAY BE USED.

4.G.14. INFORMATION ON EFFECTIVENESS OF ENEMY ELECTRONIC WARFARE.

4.G.15. INFORMATION IDENTIFYING POSTPONED OR CANCELED OPERATIONS.

4.G.16. INFORMATION ON MISSING OR DOWNED AIRCRAFT OR MISSING VESSELS WHILE SEARCH AND RESCUE AND RECOVERY OPERATIONS ARE BEING PLANNED OR UNDERWAY.

4.G.17. INFORMATION ON EFFECTIVENESS OF ENEMY CAMOUFLAGE, COVER, DECEPTION, TARGETING, DIRECT AND INDIRECT FIRE, INTELLIGENCE COLLECTION, OR SECURITY MEASURES.

4.G.18. NO PHOTOGRAPHS OR OTHER VISUAL MEDIA SHOWING AN ENEMY PRISONER OF WAR OR DETAINEE'S RECOGNIZABLE FACE, NAMETAG, OR OTHER IDENTIFYING FEATURE OR ITEM MAY BE TAKEN.

4.G.19. STILL OR VIDEO IMAGERY OF CUSTODY OPERATIONS OR INTERVIEWS WITH PERSONS UNDER CUSTODY.

4.H. THE FOLLOWING PROCEDURES AND POLICIES APPLY TO COVERAGE OF WOUNDED, INJURED, AND ILL PERSONNEL:

4.H.1. MEDIA REPRESENTATIVES WILL BE REMINDED OF THE SENSITIVITY OF USING NAMES OF INDIVIDUAL CASUALTIES OR PHOTOGRAPHS THEY MAY HAVE TAKEN WHICH CLEARLY IDENTIFY CASUALTIES UNTIL AFTER NOTIFICATION OF THE NOK AND RELEASE BY OASD(PA).

4.H.2. BATTLEFIELD CASUALTIES MAY BE COVERED BY EMBEDDED MEDIA AS LONG AS THE SERVICE MEMBER'S IDENTITY IS PROTECTED FROM DISCLOSURE FOR 72 HOURS OR UPON VERIFICATION OF NOK NOTIFICATION, WHICHEVER IS FIRST.

4.H.3. MEDIA VISITS TO MEDICAL FACILITIES WILL BE IN ACCORDANCE WITH APPLICABLE REGULATIONS, STANDARD OPERATING PROCEDURES, OPERATIONS ORDERS AND INSTRUCTIONS BY ATTENDING PHYSICIANS. IF APPROVED, SERVICE OR MEDICAL FACILITY PERSONNEL MUST ESCORT MEDIA AT ALL TIMES.

4.H.4. PATIENT WELFARE, PATIENT PRIVACY, AND NEXT OF KIN/FAMILY CONSIDERATIONS ARE THE GOVERNING CONCERNS ABOUT NEWS MEDIA COVERAGE OF WOUNDED, INJURED, AND ILL PERSONNEL IN MEDICAL TREATMENT FACILITIES OR OTHER CASUALTY COLLECTION AND TREATMENT LOCATIONS.

4.H.5. MEDIA VISITS ARE AUTHORIZED TO MEDICAL CARE FACILITIES, BUT MUST BE APPROVED BY THE MEDICAL FACILITY COMMANDER AND ATTENDING PHYSICIAN AND MUST NOT INTERFERE WITH MEDICAL TREATMENT. REQUESTS TO VISIT MEDICAL CARE FACILITIES OUTSIDE THE CONTINENTAL UNITED STATES WILL BE COORDINATED BY THE UNIFIED COMMAND PA.

4.H.6. REPORTERS MAY VISIT THOSE AREAS DESIGNATED BY THE FACILITY COMMANDER, BUT WILL NOT BE ALLOWED IN OPERATING ROOMS DURING OPERATING PROCEDURES.

4.H.7. PERMISSION TO INTERVIEW OR PHOTOGRAPH A PATIENT WILL BE GRANTED ONLY WITH THE CONSENT OF THE ATTENDING PHYSICIAN OR FACILITY COMMANDER AND WITH THE PATIENT'S INFORMED CONSENT, WITNESSED BY THE ESCORT.

4.H.8. "INFORMED CONSENT" MEANS THE PATIENT UNDERSTANDS HIS OR HER PICTURE AND COMMENTS ARE BEING COLLECTED FOR NEWS MEDIA PURPOSES AND THEY MAY APPEAR NATIONWIDE IN NEWS MEDIA REPORTS.

4.H.9. THE ATTENDING PHYSICIAN OR ESCORT SHOULD ADVISE THE SERVICE MEMBER IF NOK HAVE BEEN NOTIFIED.

5. IMMUNIZATIONS AND PERSONAL PROTECTIVE GEAR.

5.A. MEDIA ORGANIZATIONS SHOULD ENSURE THAT MEDIA ARE PROPERLY IMMUNIZED BEFORE EMBEDDING WITH UNITS. THE CENTERS FOR DISEASE CONTROL (CDC)-RECOMMENDED IMMUNIZATIONS FOR DEPLOYMENT TO THE MIDDLE EAST INCLUDE HEPATITIS A; HEPATITIS B; RABIES; TETANUS, DIPHTHERIA; AND TYPHOID. THE CDC RECOMMENDS MENINGOCOCCAL IMMUNIZATIONS FOR VISITORS TO MECCA. IF TRAVELING TO CERTAIN AREAS IN THE CENTCOM AOR, THE CDC RECOMMENDS TAKING PRESCRIPTION ANTIMALARIAL DRUGS. ANTHRAX AND SMALLPOX VACCINES WILL BE PROVIDED TO THE MEDIA AT NO EXPENSE TO THE GOVERNMENT (THE MEDIA OUTLET WILL BEAR THE EXPENSE). FOR MORE HEALTH INFORMATION FOR TRAVELERS TO THE MIDDLE EAST, GO TO THE CDC WEB SITE AT HTTP://WWW.CDC.GOV/TRAVEL/MIDEAST.HTM.

5.B. BECAUSE THE USE OF PERSONAL PROTECTIVE GEAR, SUCH AS HELMETS OR FLAK VESTS, IS BOTH A PERSONAL AND PROFESSIONAL CHOICE, MEDIA WILL BE RESPONSIBLE FOR

PROCURING/USING SUCH EQUIPMENT. PERSONAL PROTEC-
TIVE GEAR, AS WELL AS CLOTHING, WILL BE SUBDUED IN
COLOR AND APPEARANCE.

5.C. EMBEDDED MEDIA ARE AUTHORIZED AND REQUIRED TO
BE PROVIDED WITH, ON A TEMPORARY LOAN BASIS, NUCLEAR,
BIOLOGICAL, CHEMICAL (NBC) PROTECTIVE EQUIPMENT BY
THE UNIT WITH WHICH THEY ARE EMBEDDED. UNIT PERSON-
NEL WILL PROVIDE BASIC INSTRUCTION IN THE PROPER WEAR,
USE, AND MAINTENANCE OF THE EQUIPMENT. UPON TERMI-
NATION OF THE EMBED, INITIATED BY EITHER PARTY, THE NBC
EQUIPMENT SHALL BE RETURNED TO THE EMBEDDING UNIT.
IF SUFFICIENT NBC PROTECTIVE EQUIPMENT IS NOT AVAIL-
ABLE FOR EMBEDDED MEDIA, COMMANDERS MAY PURCHASE
ADDITIONAL EQUIPMENT, WITH FUNDS NORMALLY AVAILABLE
FOR THAT PURPOSE, AND LOAN IT TO EMBEDDED MEDIA IN AC-
CORDANCE WITH THIS PARAGRAPH.

6. SECURITY

6.A. MEDIA PRODUCTS WILL NOT BE SUBJECT TO SECURITY RE-
VIEW OR CENSORSHIP EXCEPT AS INDICATED IN PARA. 6.A.1. SE-
CURITY AT THE SOURCE WILL BE THE RULE. U.S. MILITARY
PERSONNEL SHALL PROTECT CLASSIFIED INFORMATION FROM
UNAUTHORIZED OR INADVERTENT DISCLOSURE. MEDIA PRO-
VIDED ACCESS TO SENSITIVE INFORMATION, INFORMATION
WHICH IS NOT CLASSIFIED BUT WHICH MAY BE OF OPERA-
TIONAL VALUE TO AN ADVERSARY OR WHEN COMBINED WITH
OTHER UNCLASSIFIED INFORMATION MAY REVEAL CLASSIFIED
INFORMATION, WILL BE INFORMED IN ADVANCE BY THE UNIT
COMMANDER OR HIS/HER DESIGNATED REPRESENTATIVE OF
THE RESTRICTIONS ON THE USE OR DISCLOSURE OF SUCH IN-
FORMATION. WHEN IN DOUBT, MEDIA WILL CONSULT WITH THE
UNIT COMMANDER OR HIS/HER DESIGNATED REPRESENTATIVE.

6.A.1. THE NATURE OF THE EMBEDDING PROCESS MAY INVOLVE
OBSERVATION OF SENSITIVE INFORMATION, INCLUDING

TROOP MOVEMENTS, BATTLE PREPARATIONS, MATERIEL CAPA-BILITIES AND VULNERABILITIES, AND OTHER INFORMATION AS LISTED IN PARA. 4.G. WHEN A COMMANDER OR HIS/HER DESIG-NATED REPRESENTATIVE HAS REASON TO BELIEVE THAT A MEDIA MEMBER WILL HAVE ACCESS TO THIS TYPE OF SENSI-TIVE INFORMATION, PRIOR TO ALLOWING SUCH ACCESS, HE/SHE WILL TAKE PRUDENT PRECAUTIONS TO ENSURE THE SECURITY OF THAT INFORMATION. THE PRIMARY SAFEGUARD WILL BE TO BRIEF MEDIA IN ADVANCE ABOUT WHAT INFOR-MATION IS SENSITIVE AND WHAT THE PARAMETERS ARE FOR COVERING THIS TYPE OF INFORMATION. IF MEDIA ARE INAD-VERTENTLY EXPOSED TO SENSITIVE INFORMATION THEY SHOULD BE BRIEFED AFTER EXPOSURE ON WHAT INFORMA-TION THEY SHOULD AVOID COVERING. IN INSTANCES WHERE A UNIT COMMANDER OR THE DESIGNATED REPRESENTATIVE DETERMINES THAT COVERAGE OF A STORY WILL INVOLVE EX-POSURE TO SENSITIVE INFORMATION BEYOND THE SCOPE OF WHAT MAY BE PROTECTED BY PREBRIEFING OR DEBRIEFING, BUT COVERAGE OF WHICH IS IN THE BEST INTERESTS OF THE DOD, THE COMMANDER MAY OFFER ACCESS IF THE REPORTER AGREES TO A SECURITY REVIEW OF THEIR COVERAGE. AGREE-MENT TO SECURITY REVIEW IN EXCHANGE FOR THIS TYPE OF ACCESS MUST BE STRICTLY VOLUNTARY AND IF THE RE-PORTER DOES NOT AGREE, THEN ACCESS MAY NOT BE GRANTED. IF A SECURITY REVIEW IS AGREED TO, IT WILL NOT INVOLVE ANY EDITORIAL CHANGES; IT WILL BE CONDUCTED SOLELY TO ENSURE THAT NO SENSITIVE OR CLASSIFIED IN-FORMATION IS INCLUDED IN THE PRODUCT. IF SUCH INFOR-MATION IS FOUND, THE MEDIA WILL BE ASKED TO REMOVE THAT INFORMATION FROM THE PRODUCT AND/OR EMBARGO THE PRODUCT UNTIL SUCH INFORMATION IS NO LONGER CLASSIFIED OR SENSITIVE. REVIEWS ARE TO BE DONE AS SOON AS PRACTICAL SO AS NOT TO INTERRUPT COMBAT OPERA-TIONS NOR DELAY REPORTING. IF THERE ARE DISPUTES RE-SULTING FROM THE SECURITY REVIEW PROCESS THEY MAY BE APPEALED THROUGH THE CHAIN OF COMMAND, OR THROUGH PA CHANNELS TO OASD/PA. THIS PARAGRAPH DOES NOT AU-

THORIZE COMMANDERS TO ALLOW MEDIA ACCESS TO CLAS-SIFIED INFORMATION.

6.A.2. MEDIA PRODUCTS WILL NOT BE CONFISCATED OR OTH-ERWISE IMPOUNDED. IF IT IS BELIEVED THAT CLASSIFIED IN-FORMATION HAS BEEN COMPROMISED AND THE MEDIA REPRESENTATIVE REFUSES TO REMOVE THAT INFORMATION NOTIFY THE CPIC AND/OR OASD(PA) AS SOON AS POSSIBLE SO THE ISSUE MAY BE ADDRESSED WITH THE MEDIA ORGANIZA-TION'S MANAGEMENT.

7. MISCELLANEOUS/COORDINATING INSTRUCTIONS

7.A. OASD(PA) IS THE INITIAL EMBED AUTHORITY. EMBEDDING PROCEDURES AND ASSIGNMENT AUTHORITY MAY BE TRANS-FERRED TO CENTCOM/PA AT A LATER DATE. THIS AUTHORITY MAY BE FURTHER DELEGATED AT CENTCOM'S DISCRETION.

7.B. THIS GUIDANCE AUTHORIZES BLANKET APPROVAL FOR NON-LOCAL AND LOCAL MEDIA TRAVEL ABOARD DOD AIRLIFT FOR ALL EMBEDDED MEDIA ON A NO-COST, SPACE AVAILABLE BASIS. NO ADDITIONAL COSTS SHALL BE INCURRED BY THE GOVERN-MENT TO PROVIDE ASSISTANCE IAW DODI 5410.15, PARA 3.4.

7.C. USE OF LIPSTICK AND HELMET-MOUNTED CAMERAS ON COMBAT SORTIES IS APPROVED AND ENCOURAGED TO THE GREATEST EXTENT POSSIBLE.

8. OASD(PA) POC FOR EMBEDDING MEDIA IS MAJ TIM BLAIR, DSN 227- 1253, CMCL 703-697-1253, EMAIL TIMOTHY.BLAIR@OSD.MIL.

NOTES AND ACKNOWLEDGMENTS

These interviews are the personal stories behind the media's own war stories. They were conducted in Qatar, Kuwait, and Iraq, and by phone from San Francisco and Boulder. The interviews occurred over a single eight-week period, from late April through late June. The average length of these interviews was 45 minutes, though a handful went 90 minutes. It would be impossible, however, to synthesize all their disparate oral histories into a single, overarching view of the war. Their personal narratives are as varied as their experiences on the battlefield.

On the acknowledgment front, brevity should be the order of the day since these remarks are usually best appreciated by those who've directly extended a helping hand or provided inspiration and gentle encouragement. Here's my acceptance speech recognizing the people who are embedded in my life: Lifelong pal, David Farber, whose keen insights illuminate the many different ways of peeling back the layers of artifice to arrive at hard-fought truths, lessons first voiced more than a quarter-century ago when we both attended the University of Michigan; Kat Guevara, who has a special gift of seeing and sensing the future and who never stopped believing in me; my family, who tolerates my circuitous path through life; the energetic Kristi Connell, who keeps me up on my toes; the sensible Mike Sitrin, who keeps my feet planted firmly on the ground; Minhoi, because "in dreams begin responsibility;" the huggable Martin and Laura Higgins; my energetic band of brothers, including but not limited to: Ian Adamson, Roman Urbina, Scot Combs, Mitch Thrower, John d'Arbeloff, Roy Wallack, Scott Zagarino, and a rascal named Scott Tinley. A heaping dose of gratitude is extended to Lyons Press senior editor Tom McCarthy, who carried this book project, from inception to completion, through the publishing scrum like the highly accomplished rugby player he once was. For superb interview transcription, thank you, Diane Micheli (lasergirl@bizland.com), and your tired fingers can now rest. Praise goes to Ya'aqoub A.A. Abdullah, of the Kuwaiti Ministry of Information, for getting Timothy Carlson into Iraq and an honorary NASCAR membership to driver and translator Musthtaq Khan for getting him out of Iraq by outwitting roadside bandits. Finally, a quick citizen's salute to Major Russell Goemaere of Fort Carson, Colorado, the helpful Public Affairs Officer who opened those early military doors.

—Bill Katovsky

IN MEMORIAM

Paul Moran, thirty-nine, freelance cameraman for Australian Broadcasting Corporation, suicide bombing at northern Iraq checkpoint, March 22.

Terry Lloyd, fifty, ITN TV, Britain, caught in crossfire near Basra, March 23.

Gaby Rado, forty-eight, Channel 4 News, Britain, presumably fell off hotel in northern Iraq, March 30.

Michael Kelly, forty-six, *The Atlantic* and *Washington Post* correspondent, Humvee crash, April 3.

Kaveh Golestan, fifty-two, BBC freelance cameraman, northern Iraq land mine, April 3.

David Bloom, thirty-nine, NBC correspondent, pulmonary embolism, April 6.

Kamaran Muhammed, twenty-five, BBC, Kurdish translator, U.S. friendly fire incident, April 6.

Julio Parrado, thirty-two, *El Mundo*, Spain, Iraqi missile attack, April 7.

Christian Liebig, thirty-five, *Focus* magazine, Germany, Iraqi missile attack, April 7.

Taras Protsyuk, thirty-five, Reuters cameraman, hit by U.S. tank shell fired at Palestine Hotel, April 8.

Jose Couso, thirty-seven, Telecinco cameraman, Spain, also died in Palestine Hotel incident, April 8.

Tareq Ayoub, thirty-five, Al Jazeera journalist, by U.S. missile striking the station's Baghdad headquarters, April 8.

Mario Podesta, fifty-two, Argentine TV correspondent, car accident between Baghdad and Amman, April 14. Veronica Cabrera, thirty-eight, accompanying Podesta, died April 15.

Elizabeth Neuffer, forty-six, *Boston Globe* foreign correspondent, car accident near Samarrah, May 9.

Richard Wild, twenty-four, British freelance cameraman, gunned down by unknown assailant in central Baghdad, July 5.

Jeremy Little, twenty-seven, NBC soundman, Australia, injured in June 29 terrorist grenade attack in Fallujah, died July 6.

Missing:

Fred Nerac, ITN TV cameraman, France, lost in crossfire near Basra which killed Terry Lloyd.

Hussein Osman, ITN TV translator, lost in crossfire which killed Lloyd.

(March 22–July 6, 2003)